Money and Financial Markets

Money and Financial Markets

Edited by Mark P. Taylor

BLACKWELL
Cambridge MA & Oxford UK

First published 1991

Basil Blackwell Ltd
108 Cowley Road, Oxford, OX4 1JF, UK

Basil Blackwell, Inc.
3 Cambridge Center
Cambridge, Massachusetts 02142, USA

British Library Cataloguing in Publication Data
A CIP catalogue record for this book is available from the British Library.

Library of Congress Cataloging in Publication Data
Money and financial markets / edited by Mark P. Taylor.
p. cm.
Includes bibliographical references and index.
ISBN 0-631-17982-8
1. Money. 2. Demand for money—Case studes. 3. Finance.
I. Taylor, Mark P., 1958-
HG220.A2M58 1991
332.4—dc20 90-48374
CIP

Typeset in 10 on 12 pt Times
by Colset Private Limited, Singapore
Printed in the USA

Contents

List of Contributors

Michael J. Artis University of Manchester and Centre for Economic Policy Research
David Barlow University of Newcastle upon Tyne
Tamim Bayoumi International Monetary Fund
Jane Black University of Exeter
James M. Boughton International Monetary Fund
Martin Brookes Birkbeck College, University of London
Keith Cuthbertson University of Newcastle upon Tyne and Bank of England
Laurence S. Copeland University of Stirling
E. P. Davis Bank of England
James Foreman-Peck University of Hull
Patricia Fraser University of Dundee and Bank of England
Stephen Hall London Business School and Bank of England
S. G. Brian Henry Bank of England
Glenn Hoggarth Bank of England
Andrew Hughes Hallett University of Strathclyde and Centre for Economic Policy Research
Alan Kirman European University Institute
Ronald MacDonald University of Dundee
David Miles Birkbeck College, University of London
Paul Ormerod Henley Centre for Economic Forecasting
Kate Phylaktis City University Business School
David Power University of Dundee
Jonathan Slow University of Strathclyde
Richard C. Stapleton University of Lancaster
John C. Taylor University College London
Mark P. Taylor City University Business School, International Monetary Fund and Centre for Economic Policy Research
Ian Tonks London School of Economics and University of Exeter
Ted Walker Henley Centre for Economic Forecasting and Expert Systems Ltd, Oxford
David Walton Goldman Sachs
Peter Westaway National Institute of Economic and Social Research

Preface

The Money Study Group (MSG) was formed in 1969. Its main aim is to provide a forum for research for economists interested in monetary and financial economics through its regular meetings at the London School of Economics and its annual conferences, and an avenue for research dissemination through its publications. From the outset, the MSG has aimed to bring together economists from a wide range of institutions - from universities, the financial sector, research institutions such as the National Institute of Economic and Social Research, and the Bank of England and the Treasury - and has always fostered interest in theoretical, applied and policy-oriented research. It has also regularly invited overseas speakers to its meetings from universities and from institutions such as the International Monetary Fund and the Institute for International Economics. The MSG has always aimed to be pluralist and non-partisan; its committee membership represents a broad spectrum of views.

The present volume represents papers presented at MSG meetings during the present editor's tenure of the post of Secretary of the MSG during the academic year 1989–90. The notable omissions are papers presented at special meetings in December 1989 on European Monetary Union and (by David Laidler) on the quantity theory of money, which had been committed for publication elsewhere. Survey chapters on money and financial markets have been added.

M.P.T.

1 Introduction: Money and Financial Markets

Mark P. Taylor

The subject matter of this book is money and financial markets and the interface between them. It is split into four parts: on the literature, on money demand studies, on money and financial markets and on new developments in financial market research.

1 ASSESSING THE LITERATURE

The first part contains two survey chapters which serve to set the scene for the remaining contributions. The first, by **Keith Cuthbertson** and **David Barlow**, gives an outline of money demand analysis, starting with the early contributions of Pigou, Fisher and Keynes before moving on to survey more recent contributions such as the inventory and precautionary approaches, the mean-variance model and the consumer theory approach. Cuthbertson and Barlow also discuss the inadequate treatment of dynamics in theoretical monetary economics and the interface between theoretical and applied work on money demand. On the applied side, the authors provide a comprehensive discussion of the breakdown of money demand relationships on both sides of the Atlantic during the 1970s, and the resulting research efforts which have sought to explain or remedy this instability. In particular, they provide a discussion of the various buffer stock approaches to money demand and of the application of recently developed econometric techniques such as cointegration and rational expectations estimators to applied money demand analysis. Indeed, the authors argue that it is the application of new econometric techniques rather than advances in theoretical monetary economics which has provided the most informative research findings in recent years, despite the complexities of applied work concomitant with the high degree of financial innovation in the major economies over the same period.

The second survey chapter, by **Ronald MacDonald** and **Mark Taylor**, gives an outline of financial markets analysis. MacDonald and Taylor begin with a discussion of the theory and evidence pertaining to the efficient markets hypothesis (EMH). According to this hypothesis, prices in financial markets should reflect all pertinent information. After reviewing the literature on the EMH – in particular, evidence relating to the excess volatility of stock markets – the authors argue that the evidence is, on balance, not in favour of the hypothesis. They then discuss a number of issues pertaining to the rejection of efficiency, such as the stationarity of financial time series and time-varying real interest rates in the present value model, before going on to discuss phenomena such as explosive deviations from asset market fundamentals (speculative bubbles) and mean-reverting deviations from fundamentals (fads). The remainder of the survey contains an expository discussion of the theory and evidence relating to asset pricing, including the capital asset pricing model, the arbitrage pricing model and financial option pricing.

2 THE DEMAND FOR MONEY

The second part of the book is concerned with money demand studies. Each of the chapters has an applied orientation and each applies a relatively new econometric technique – cointegration. In one way, these chapters bear out Cuthbertson and Barlow's assertion that advances in money demand analysis are currently being made by the application of new econometric techniques rather than through theoretical breakthroughs. The cointegration technique, carefully applied, allows inferences on the long-run nature of empirical relationships to be drawn using short-run data, but with evidence of the *long-run* relationship providing a firm basis for the investigation of *short-run* dynamics (we give a brief outline of the cointegration technique below). In the Phylaktis-Taylor chapter, it is shown how cointegration techniques can be used to shed light on the short-run demand function without recourse to strong auxiliary assumptions concerning expectations formation.

The present editor (Taylor 1987) has characterized the empirical work on money demand relationships as falling into four partially overlapping phases: 'the years of hope' (1966–71), 'the years of despair' (1972–8), 'the period of Hendrification' (1978–86) and 'the years of uncertainty' (1980–6).[1] To this list it may now be fair to add a fifth phase, dating from the closing years of the 1980s: 'the years of resurrected hope'. The studies in this part suggest that stable, long-run money demand relationships exist for a variety of monetary aggregates, countries and historical periods. Moreover, this evidence largely echoes recent evidence on the long-run function which is only just beginning to emerge for other countries and periods (e.g. Hoffman and Rasche 1989; Hafer and Jansen 1989; Johansen and Juselius 1990;

Cuthbertson and Taylor 1990; Taylor 1990). At least two points are worth discussing in this connection.

First, to what extent is this new work simply hi-tech for the sake of it? One does not have to be the most cynical observer to conclude that many applied contributions to the journals have more to do with technique than economic content. Sensible applied work, in our view, should apply the simplest, most appropriate technique to the task in hand. Because of the constant tension in applied money demand work between long-run equilibrium and short-run dynamics, as well as the difficulty in specifying explicit, plausible methods of expectations formation or dynamic adjustment, the cointegration technique seems ideally suited to empirical investigation in this area, as the papers in this part demonstrate. Moreover, by its concentration on simple, linear relationships, the cointegration approach has much to recommend it both over the traditional practice of forcing the data into a preconceived framework such as partial adjustment or adaptive expectations, and also over the other extreme of general to specific modelling (Hendry et al. 1984). Those suspicious of the approach will argue that economic theory rather than the statistical properties of the data should be used in deciding the form of an estimating relationship. But such a view overlooks the possibility that the need to expand or adjust a theory can be deduced from the behaviour of the data in much the same way that the presence of hitherto uncharted heavenly bodies can be inferred from data on planetary motion. The contribution by the Bank of England team (chapter 5) is a particularly striking example of the subtle analysis of the time series properties of economic data in this fashion. Time will certainly tell whether the cointegration approach is of lasting significance or merely a passing fad; from the present viewpoint, it seems to provide an exciting avenue for applied research. The limits of the cointegration approach should not be overlooked, however. By going straight to the analysis of the long-run characteristics of the data, the short-run dynamics are implicitly treated as a black box; it is certain that the structure of the rest of the economy is crucial in determining their form. Although, as we describe below, the presence of cointegration does imply the existence of a dynamic error correction form relating the variables in question, there is nothing to guarantee that the error correction form is in fact a *structural relationship* which would remain invariant to shifts in the rest of the economic structure.[2]

Second, does the fact that the chapters in this part support the existence of stable long-run demand relationships thereby imply that the contributors or the editor have a monetarist bias? David Laidler (1982) has noted that monetarism, like beauty, tends to lie in the eye of the beholder. While belief in the existence of a stable, parsimonious money demand function has always been an important element of monetarism, it is very far from being the sole defining characteristic, as Laidler's discussion makes clear.

Economists of any school should be gratified by evidence which supports the existence of stable empirical relationships which are in accordance with economic reasoning.

As noted above, a major point of similarity among the contributions in this part is that they each employ an econometric technique - cointegration - on which published research has only appeared within the last three years or so (Engle and Granger 1987; Johansen 1988). Because of the recency of the cointegration literature, we provide below a *very* brief guide to the econometrics of cointegration.[3]

A time series, x_t say, is said to be integrated of order d, denoted $x_t \sim I(d)$, if it has a stationary, invertible, autoregressive moving average representation after differencing d times, so that $\Delta^d x_t \sim I(0)$. Thus a stationary series is by definition I(0), whilst the simplest example of an I(1) series is a random walk. It turns out that many economic and financial time series, such as output, money and interest rates, are I(1) series.

In general, any linear combination of two or more I(1) series will itself be I(1). If, however, there exists at least one linear combination of a set of I(1) series which is I(0), the series under consideration are then said to be *cointegrated.*

The economic interest of cointegration derives from the fact that although I(1) series will tend to drift over time - by definition they will have neither constant means nor variances - in a cointegrated set the series will tend to move *together* in the sense that there is at least one linear combination of them which does have a constant mean and a finite variance. Thus this linear combination can be thought of as corresponding roughly to a long-run equilibrium relationship towards which there is a constant tendency of the series to adjust.

More formally, consider an $N \times 1$ vector of time series, $\mathbf{x}_t$ say. For concreteness, $\mathbf{x}_t$ can be thought of as a vector containing observations on money, prices, income and interest rates. If each series in the vector needs to be differenced once to induce stationarity, then the vector is I(1). If there is some $N \times 1$ vector of constants $\boldsymbol{\alpha}$ such that $\boldsymbol{\alpha}'\mathbf{x}_t \sim I(0)$, then the elements of $\mathbf{x}_t$ are cointegrated. Moreover, the parameters of $\boldsymbol{\alpha}$ can be thought of as long-run money demand elasticities (if the relevant variables were expressed in logarithms and after normalization on the money coefficient). The linear combination itself, $\boldsymbol{\alpha}'\mathbf{x}_t$, can be thought of as the deviation from equilibrium, or equilibrium error, towards which the system tends to return.

The tendency of the system to return to equilibrium is formalized in the Granger representation theorem (Engle and Granger 1987), which states that if a vector of time series is cointegrated, then there must exist an error correction representation of its time series evolution. The error correction representation can be most simply expressed as a vector autoregression in the series, augmented by the lagged equilibrium error in at least one of the equations

$$\Phi(L)\Delta \mathbf{x}_t = \rho\alpha' \mathbf{x}_{t-1} + \epsilon_t \qquad (1.1)$$

where $\Phi(L)$ represents a matrix polynomial in the lag operator L, ρ is an $N \times 1$ vector of constants and ϵ_t is vector white noise. As noted by Cuthbertson and Barlow in chapter 2, the error correction representation has provided one of the most popular forms for applied money demand research during the 1980s, particularly but not exclusively in the UK.

In chapter 4, **James Boughton** applies the cointegration technique to examine the nature of long-run money demand functions in five large industrial countries - namely the US, the UK, France, Germany and Japan - under the hypothesis that the long-run functions have been stable but that the dynamic adjustment processes are more complex than those represented in many earlier models. In particular, Boughton reviews some of the key issues in applied money demand analysis which have dominated the literature over the past fifteen years or so - such as the use of unconstrained dynamic adjustment processes and buffer stock models - before going on to present and interpret error correction equations for broad and narrow money for the five countries. Boughton's results call into question some basic economic hypotheses about the nature of the demand function, such as homogeneity with respect to the price level.

In chapter 5 a Bank of England team, in the form of **Martin Brookes, Stephen Hall, Brian Henry** and **Glenn Hoggarth** (BHHG), apply the cointegration technique to an investigation of the long-run determination and short-run dynamics of the UK narrow (M0) and broad (M4) monetary aggregates. In common with Boughton, BHHG also bring into question some of the received hypotheses concerning the demand function. In particular, a striking finding of this research is that simple textbook money demand equations, in which money demand is viewed as a stable function only of prices, income and interest rates, are easily rejected. BHHG find, for example, that it is necessary to add a *cumulative* interest rate variable in order to induce long-run stability in their estimated demand function for narrow money. They argue that this term is significant because it captures the essence of a certain class of financial innovation: increases in interest rates provide incentives for cash saving technology and payments methods to be introduced. Once introduced, the new technology does not disappear as a result of interest rate falls, but is here to stay. Although they do not say so explicitly, BHHG thus succeed in incorporating *hysteresis* effects into the long-run demand function for narrow money. In modelling the long-run demand for broad money, BHHG find it necessary to include variables which reflect efficient portfolio management by individuals over a broad range of assets. They thus augment a standard demand function with variables such as personal sector gross wealth, both financial and tangible (the latter mainly reflecting the value of the owner-occupied housing stock), inflation, and the returns to holding equities (in the form of a series). BHHG demonstrate that their chosen long-run functions are empirically stable and admit satisfactory short-run dynamic error correction models.

In chapter 6, **Peter Westaway** and **David Walton** provide a detailed analysis of the long-run stability and short-run dynamics of UK narrow money (M0), again using cointegration techniques and again explicitly attempting to model the role of financial innovation in the demand for money. Westaway and Walton, in common with BHHG, reject simple textbook models of long-run demand for narrow money. They also find that exogenous measures of financial innovation - such as the number of cash dispensers in operation - are relatively unsuccessful in improving the empirical performance of their equation. Interestingly, they confirm the Bank of England finding of a hysteresis effect of financial innovation operating through interest rates, reflected in the need to incorporate a cumulative interest rate term in the long-run demand function.

In the following chapter, **Jonathan Slow, James Foreman-Peck** and **Andrew Hughes Hallett** (SFH) examine the demand for broad money (M3) for the UK, the US, France and Germany in the interwar period. One innovation of the SFH study is the use of monthly data, in an attempt to allow for the effects of financial crises and associated slumps, in contrast to previous analyses of this period which have used data of a lower frequency. In common with the other studies in this part, they also employ the cointegration technique to estimate long-run demand functions. Although SFH find reasonable support for a textbook long-run money demand function for each country - which serves as the basis for a satisfactory short-run error correction form in each case - the estimated scale variable elasticities are of a very small magnitude indeed. SFH argue that this is likely to be due to their use of series for industrial production as the scale variable, in the absence of monthly data on other income measures such as GDP or GNP.

In the final chapter in this part, **Kate Phylaktis** and **Mark Taylor** analyse the demand for money under conditions of very high inflation, drawing on the experience of Bolivia and Peru in the period 1975–87. The object of the chapter is to examine what light Cagan's classic (1956) model of money demand under hyperinflation can shed on the inflationary episodes of these two Latin American countries, notwithstanding that they do not formally qualify as hyperinflations. Phylaktis and Taylor begin by demonstrating that, under only very weak assumptions concerning expectations formation (the stationarity of forecasting errors), the Cagan model of money demand requires cointegration between real money balances and current inflation. Testing for cointegration between these variables thus constitutes a simple but unrestrictive test of the model. Applying this technique to the Bolivian and Peruvian data, the Phylaktis-Taylor results are supportive of the Cagan model. For both Bolivia and Peru, cointegration is found; the estimate of the semi-elasticity of money demand with respect to expected inflation is of plausible sign and magnitude; and the authors are unable to reject the hypothesis that the authorities, on average, expanded the money supply in such a way as to maximize the inflation tax revenue. Phylaktis and Taylor then use these first-stage estimates to test the stronger assumption of rational expectations in the context of the Cagan model. Here, the results differ significantly between the two countries: the hyperinflation model under rational expectations is easily rejected for Bolivia but not for Peru. Overall, although Phylaktis and Taylor find different results for the two countries when they go on to test the rational expectations version of the Cagan model, the research reported in this chapter is largely supportive both of the Cagan model under conditions of *high* as well as *hyper* inflation and of the hypothesis of inflation tax revenue-maximizing behaviour on the part of the authorities in both countries.

3 MONEY AND FINANCIAL MARKETS

The third part of the book is devoted to studies of financial markets or to some aspect of the relationship between money and financial markets.

In chapter 9, **Mark Taylor** and **Patricia Fraser** analyse the covered interest parity relationship using high-quality, high-frequency data on spot and forward exchange rates and Eurodeposit rates, recorded contemporaneously every five minutes for periods before and after the release of important UK and US economic figures. In an analysis of 6330 possible arbitrage opportunities, only 21 are found to be profitable. Of these, a number are found in the longer maturities (as also evidenced in Taylor 1989). Overall, however, the results support the covered interest parity relationship even during periods of significant turbulence in the markets. No econometrics are applied in this chapter. Rather, the authors rely on meticulous attention to data quality and institutional detail. It is thus an example of applied work which proceeds by carefully selecting the appropriate tools for the task in hand, rather than blindly wheeling out the latest techniques.

In chapter 10, **Stephen Hall** and **David Miles** do, however, apply another newly developed econometric technique in the form of generalized ARCH-in-mean (GARCH-m) modelling, to great effect. After a discussion of the various methods currently used to assess and control bank default risk, Hall and Miles outline a technique for measuring the market's perception of risk using the data on the market valuation of companies. Hall and Miles suggest applying the GARCH-m approach to estimate a capital asset pricing model with time-varying betas for the financial institution, from which the expected volatility of the market value of the capital funds can be inferred. Under the assumption of market efficiency, this should be equal to the 'best' expectation of the volatility in the underlying financial portfolio of the institution.[4] From this, the probability of default can be inferred. The authors then apply the technique to data on British banks and American banks, some of which did in fact default. Although the empirical results suggest that the markets may occasionally find it difficult to assess bankruptcy risk, Hall and Miles suggest that

> provided either that there is *some* information which stock market players have which is not available to regulators, or that some investors are better at analysing information than are regulators, then there should be some information of use to regulators in stock market prices. What this chapter provides is a technique for summarizing that information.

In the following chapter, a theoretical contribution by **Laurence Copeland** and **Richard Stapleton,** the interest rate volatility of equity prices is modelled using techniques that have been applied previously to the analysis of bond volatility. The central idea is that as interest rates change, the discounted value of the cash flows received by equity holders changes. The degree of change depends upon the duration (i.e. the Macaulay-Hicks average maturity) of the cash flows. Other important influences on equity volatility are shown to be the degree to which cash flows covary with real interest rates and inflation and the nature of the firm's capital structure. Models of equity volatility are of interest in the light of recent studies of excess volatility, and are important in the context of option valuation theory (on both of which see the MacDonald-Taylor survey, chapter 3).

Chapter 12, by **Jane Black** and **Ian Tonks,** is also a theoretical piece and is also concerned with equity price volatility. In particular, the authors investigate the conditions under which the managers of a firm would choose to disclose information about a production input (e.g. research and development expenditure) in order to minimize the variability of its share price. The theoretical model is a two-period rational expectations equilibrium with asymmetric information. The firm undertakes the first-best level of research and development, and trade takes place in the shares of the firm at the initial date. Following public disclosure or private acquisition of information about the level of research and development, retrading is allowed in the firm's shares. At the end of te second period the firm pays out the returns on the investment to its shareholders. In this framework, Black and Tonks demonstrate that the variability of the firm's share price could be reduced by a policy of not disclosing.

The following chapter, by **Ronald MacDonald** and **David Power,** applies disaggregated data on UK equities to examine the persistence of returns. As noted in the MacDonald-Taylor survey (chapter 3), a number of authors have demonstrated, using aggregate US data, that stock returns are predictable for both short and long horizons. There are good reasons, they argue, for investigating whether evidence of mean reversion is affected by the degree of aggregation. For example, arbitragers may be more skilled at perceiving mispriced individual securities than at taking positions in the entire market in order to exploit persistent over- or undervaluation. MacDonald and Power also test trading rules which seek to exploit any mean-reverting properties in equity returns.

Chapter 14, by **Michael Artis** and **Tamim Bayoumi,** examines the Feldstein-Horioka thesis that, as world capital markets become more integrated, the correlation between national savings and national investment should decline in international cross-section. Basically, the reasoning is that increased financial integration acts to reduce financial constraints and allows intertemporal consumption smoothing through the utilization of international capital flows. Artis and Bayoumi examine and extend these arguments before proceeding to an examination of savings and investment balances for the OECD countries. They demonstrate that the relevant correlation is in fact falling over time, although it still remains relatively high. They argue that this evidence reflects two factors: a commitment, weakening over time, by governments to target the current account, and a trend towards greater international financial integration.

In chapter 15, **Phil Davis** analyses four periods of instability in the Euromarkets - including the 1987 equity market crash, and interbank crises of the mid 1970s such as the Herstatt affair - in relation to a number of theories of financial crisis. This permits a qualitative evaluation of the alternative theories of crisis in the light of the available evidence for these periods. The chapter thus offers a literature survey of the recent theory of financial crisis and a comparative analysis of recent periods of financial disorder in the light of the survey. Davis draws together the various strands in the literature of financial crisis under five main groupings: a monetarist approach, a financial fragility approach, a rational expectations approach, an economic uncertainty approach and finally a credit rationing approach. Davis concludes on an eclectic note, arguing that the periods of financial disorder examined had a number of common strands, of which some would be important indicators of crisis according to some approaches and some according to others, before drawing out the implications of the research for financial regulators, for macroeconomic policy makers and for market participants.

4 NEW DIRECTIONS IN FINANCIAL MARKETS RESEARCH

The final part of the book contains two chapters, each of which provides an approach to financial market analysis which breaks with more traditional analyses.

Chapter 16, by **Paul Ormerod, John Taylor** and **Ted Walker,** reports the results of research on neural networks and financial markets. Neural network models are based on the structure and organization of neurons in the human brain. It is believed that, in the brain, information is processed principally via the dynamic change of connection strengths among neurons. In a neural network model, connection strengths are modelled by the weights associated with the links between processing elements. A key feature of a neural network is that the link weights can be varied over time. A learning role detects the precise mechanisms through which the network learns. The network is also capable of remembering previous sets of weights. The problem of parameter instability which is endemic to statistical investigations of financial asset prices thus seems ideally suited to a treatment within this framework.

In the final chapter, **Alan Kirman** extends the recent literature on noise trading and non-fundamental influences on financial markets (see e.g. De Long et al. 1987; Frankel 1990; Allen and Taylor 1990) to allow transmission and conversion of agents' views. Modifying the Frankel-Froot (1990) chartist-fundamentalist model of the foreign exchange market, Kirman allows conversion from one group to the other by encounter. Conversion is more likely to be to the prevalent market view (i.e. the one having the major influence on market price), and agents only act according to the view they supposedly hold when they perceive this to have become the majority view.

5 CONCLUDING COMMENTS

The studies collected together in this volume represent some of the most recent scholarship in the area of money and financial markets. This area is arguably one of the most dynamic subfields in economics, and presents substantial challenges to both theoreticians and applied workers. Readers must judge for themselves how well these challenges are met by the present contributions.

Notes

1 This taxonomy draws upon and extends a classification suggested by Grice and Bennett (1981).
2 A similar point is made concerning the role of lagged dependent variables in empirical money demand relationships by Laidler (1982).
3 For a more extensive discussion, see e.g. Cuthbertson et al. (1990).
4 The authors argue, however, that their technique is robust to certain departures from the efficient markets paradigm.

References

Allen, H. and Taylor, M. P. (1990) 'Charts, noise and fundamentals in the London foreign exchange market', *Economic Journal*, 100, 49–59.

Cagan, P. (1956) 'The monetary dynamics of hyperinflation', in M. Friedman (ed.), *Studies in the Quantity Theory of Money*, Chicago: University of Chicago Press.

Cuthbertson, K., Hall, S. G. and Taylor, M. P. (1990) *Techniques of Applied Econometrics*, Oxford: Philip Allan.

Cuthbertson, K. and Taylor, M. P. (1990) 'Money demand, expectations and the forward-looking model', *Journal of Policy Modeling*, forthcoming.

De Long, J. B., Shleifer, A., Summers, L. H. and Waldman, R. J. (1987) 'The economic consequences of noise traders', National Bureau of Economic Research, working paper 2395.

Engle, R. F. and Granger, C. W. J. (1987) 'Cointegration and error correction: representation, estimation and testing', *Econometrica*, 55, 251–76.

Frankel, J. A. (1990) 'Chartists, fundamentalists and trading in the foreign exchange market', *American Economic Review*, 80, 181–5.

Frankel, J. A. and Froot, K. (1990) 'Chartists, fundamentalists and the demand for dollars', in A. Courakis and M. P. Taylor (eds), *Policy Issues for Interdependent Economies*, Oxford: Oxford University Press.

Grice, J. and Bennett, A. (1981) 'The demand for sterling M3 and other aggregates in the United Kingdom', HM Treasury, working paper 20.

Hafer, R. W. and Jansen D. W. (1989) 'The demand for money in the United States: evidence from cointegration tests', Texas A & M University, mimeo.

Hendry, D. F., Pagan, A. R. and Sargan, J. D. (1984) 'Dynamic specification', in Z. Griliches and M. D. Intrilligator (eds), *Handbook of Econometrics*, Amsterdam: North-Holland.

Hoffman, D. and Rasche, R. H. (1989) 'Long-run income and interest elasticities of money demand in the United States', National Bureau of Economic Research, working paper 2949.

Johansen, S. (1988) 'Statistical analysis of cointegration vector', *Journal of Economic Dynamics and Control*, 12, 231–54.

Johansen, S. and Juselius, K. (1990) 'Maximum likelihood estimation and inference on cointegration – with applications to the demand for money', *Oxford Bulletin of Economics and Statistics*, 52, 169–210.

Laidler, D. E. W. (1982) *Monetarist Perspectives*, Oxford: Philip Allan.

Taylor, M. P. (1987) 'Financial innovation, inflation and the stability of the demand for broad money in the United Kingdom', *Bulletin of Economic Research*, 39, 225–33.

Taylor, M. P. (1989) 'Covered interest arbitrage and market turbulence', *Economic Journal*, 99, 376–91.

Taylor, M. P. (1990) 'Modelling the demand for UK broad money, 1871–1913', International Monetary Fund, Washington DC, forthcoming, *Review of Economics and Statistics*.

Part I
Assessing the Literature

2 Money Demand Analysis: an Outline

Keith Cuthbertson and David Barlow

1 INTRODUCTION

The search for a theoretically coherent yet empirically robust model of the demand for money is central to the transmission mechanism of monetary policy (Cuthbertson and Taylor 1987a). It is impossible to give an exhaustive account of work on the demand for money: we are therefore highly selective. An analysis of the demand for money provides an excellent example of how our knowledge has progressed because of the interaction between theory and evidence, and this provides the focus for this overview.[1] We begin in section 2 with an account of theories based on the motives approach; this is followed by the consumer demand approach, and finally we discuss buffer stock models. Theories of the demand for money almost invariably give rise to static equilibrium relationships, some of which contain expectations variables. We therefore briefly discuss the modelling of dynamic behaviour, expectations and risk in section 3. In section 4 we provide illustrative examples of the main empirical approaches to the demand for money, and we end with a brief summary.

2 THEORIES OF THE DEMAND FOR MONEY

Two characteristics of money provide the starting point for a number of theories of the demand for money. Its use as a universally acceptable means of exchange (at least in the domestic economy) leads to transactions models, of which some assume the level of transactions to be known (i.e. inventory models) and others treat net inflows as uncertain (i.e. precautionary demand models). Money also acts as a store of value; this gives rise to risk aversion models, where some assets in the choice set (e.g. equities, bonds) have an uncertain nominal return because capital gains and losses may occur. Thus considering the special characteristics of money results in theories that are based on explicit *motives* for holding money. In the theory of consumer demand, goods are held because the individual derives utility from them; however, we do not enquire into the specific motives for holding particular goods (Friedman 1956; Laidler 1985). The theory of consumer demand can be applied to the demand for a portfolio of assets all of which are assumed to yield utility, and this for want of a better term we label the consumer theory approach.[2] One general characteristic of nearly all the models considered is that optimization is usually over a single period.

2.1 Early theories of the demand for money

The Cambridge economist Pigou (1917) took the quantity theory identity of Fisher (1911), $MV = PY$, where M is the nominal money stock in circulation, P the aggregate price level, Y the level of transactions and V the velocity of circulation, and changed the focus of interest from a model where V is determined by the payments mechanism to one where agents have a *desired demand* for money. Implicitly this was a consumer theory approach with the model reduced to $M^d = kPY$, where M^d is the desired demand for money. It was recognized that k may depend on other variables in the consumer allocation problem, such as interest rates and wealth, but the main focus was the level of transactions. Broadly speaking, Keynes (1936) accepted the Cambridge view concerning the transactions demand but introduced two further motives for holding money: precautionary and speculative.

In Keynes's speculative model the individual is assumed to choose between a capital certain asset such as money and a risky asset, a bond. There are three main predictions from Keynes's theory. First, individuals do not hold a diversified portfolio of assets; they hold either all bonds or all money. Second, a downward sloping demand for money function with respect to the interest rate only occurs for the aggregate demand for money. Finally, in certain circumstances the elasticity of the demand for money with respect to the interest rate may become infinite; this is the liquidity trap.

2.2 The transactions demand for money

Inventory models

The key assumptions in the inventory-theoretic approach of Baumol (1952) are (a) the individual receives a known lump sum cash payment of T per period (say per annum) and spends it all, evenly over the period; (b) the individual may invest in bonds paying a known interest rate r per period, or hold cash (money) paying zero interest; (c) the individual sells bonds to obtain cash in equal amounts K, and incurs a (fixed) brokerage fee b per transaction. In the model all relevant information is known with certainty.[3] Agents minimize the sum of brokerage costs (bT/K) and interest income forgone ($rK/2$). The model yields a square root relationship between the demand for money and the level of income, the brokerage fee and the bond interest rate:

$$\ln(M^d/P) = 0.5[\ln(b/2) - \ln(T) + \ln(r)] \tag{2.1}$$

We have included a unit price elasticity in (2.1) because a doubling of the price level doubles both b and T and therefore doubles M (T and b must now be considered as real variables rather than nominal variables).

One can easily extend the simple inventory model to include interest payments on money, i:

$$M^d = K/2 = [(b/2)T/(r-i)]^{1/2} \tag{2.2}$$

The transactions elasticity is again 1/2 but the interest elasticity is now $E_r = -r/2(r-i)$. In principle, the above model may be easily estimated in log-linear form with coefficients of 1/2 expected on T and $(r-i)$; the demand for money now depends on the relative interest rate.

Sprenkle (1969, 1972) provides a damaging critique of the inventory model when applied to large firms. First, Sprenkle argues that cash holdings of large firms may be explained by the existence of multiple accounts as much as by optimal inventory behaviour. Second, it may not be profitable for firms to undertake optimal cash managment if the receipts of each branch of the firm are small; the firm can minimize costs by not purchasing any securities at all but keeping all its receipts in cash.

The fact that current (sight and deposit) accounts of UK companies increased by much less than those of the personal sector over 1960–80 is consistent with Sprenkle's view, since (nominal) sales would have also increased substantially over this period. For persons, however, the inventory model may have some relevance but the relationship between money, interest rates and transactions is likely to be more complex than in the simple Baumol (1952) model.

Extensions to the inventory model

There have been a number of refinements to the simple inventory model. Tobin (1956) introduced integer constraints and found that it may be worthwhile for some individuals to hold no earning assets at all (a corner solution); their demand for money is then proportional to the lumpy income receipts as in Fisher's model. Barro (1976) aggregated Tobin's corner solution and square root money holders (assuming a gamma distribution for the cross-sectional distribution of income) and found, not surprisingly, that the aggregate income elasticity lay between 1/2 and unity. Karni (1974) proposed that the brokerage free depended on the value of time. If the latter rises in proportion to real income, then the Baumol model yields an income elasticity of unity (1/2 from transactions and 1/2 from the brokerage fee). Feige and Parkin (1971) and Santomero (1974) introduce commodities into the choice set of the inventory framework. The expected rate of inflation then enters the determination of the demand for money (and bonds) but, somewhat surprisingly, its sign remains ambiguous (Grossman and Policano 1975). (Also Barro 1970 and Santomero 1974 endogenize the period between income receipts in the money-bonds-commodity inventory model.) Clearly, results vary depending on the assumptions used and it is dangerous to generalize.

Target threshold model

In Akerlof and Milbourne's (1980) model of the transactions demand for money, money holdings are only actively adjusted when they hit an upper or lower *threshold level.* This model is consistent with the stylized facts of empirical demand for money functions, since the model predicts that the short-run income elasticity is small (i.e. around zero) and may even take a small negative value.

There are two main variants of the Akerlof-Milbourne model. In the first there is no uncertainty but in the second the timing of lump sum expenditure plans by agents is uncertain.

In its simplest form, the model with certain net receipts assumes (a) a lump sum receipt of Y per period and (b) spending of C at a constant rate through the period. Money balances accumulate via savings, $S = Y - C$. When the money balance hits the upper threshold H^*, it is returned to C, so that money balances are exhausted by the next receipt date.

In their model with certain receipts, Akerlof and Milbourne obtain

$$\frac{\partial M}{\partial Y} = -s_y(Y)/4 \tag{2.3}$$

where M is *average* money holdings and $s_y = \partial S/\partial Y$ is the marginal propensity to save, which is assumed to be positively related to income. Hence, the short-run income elasticity is negative and takes a larger negative value the higher the level of income.

2.3 Precautionary models

Models of precautionary demand are based on the transactions motive for holding money, but in contrast to most inventory models we relax the assumption that receipts and payments are known with certainty. Precautionary demand models assume net receipts are uncertain but reduce the uncertainty to one of risk; that is, the probability distribution of receipts and payments is assumed known. The assumptions of the model are as follows. The firm incurs a brokerage cost b if net payments per period N (i.e. payments less receipts) are greater than money holdings M. The brokerage fee involves the costs of selling interest-bearing assets at short notice (e.g. time, inconvenience) and is usually assumed to be constant. The agent trades off expected brokerage fees against interest forgone (by not holding bonds) when deciding his optimal money holdings.

If the probability distribution of net payments is centred on zero and the probability of net payments exceeding money holdings (i.e. $N > M$) is p, then total expected brokerage costs are pb. Interest payments forgone are Mr, where r is the yield on the alternative asset. Thus expected total costs TC are

$$TC = Mr + pb \tag{2.4}$$

Precautionary demand models give different results depending upon the assumption made about the probability of illiquidity p, and the results involve reasonably complex derivations. For illustrative purposes consider Whalen's (1966) precautionary demand model (which assumes very risk-averse behaviour). It may be shown that the probability p of $N > M$ takes a maximum value $p = \sigma^2/M^2$, where σ is the standard deviation of net payments.[4] Substituting for p in (2.4) and minimizing TC with respect to M gives

$$M = (2\sigma^2 b/r)^{1/3} \tag{2.5}$$

and the second derivative $\delta^2 TC/\delta M^2 = \delta\sigma^2 b/M^4 > 0$ indicates a minimum.

As with the inventory models, we obtain the result that the individual's *mean* holdings of money (over some finite time interval) is positively related to the brokerage fee and negatively related to the interest rate on bonds (but with an interest elasticity of 1/3). The demand for money also increases with the (cube root) of the *variance* of expected net payments.

The Miller-Orr (1966, 1968) precautionary demand model is similar to the one described above but the individual only switches between bonds and money when upper or lower bounds for money are reached. The decision variable is then the amount transferred at these limiting points. This gives rise to a demand for money (assuming a binominal distribution for the net cash drain with a zero mean) of the form

$$M = \frac{4}{3}\left[\frac{3bm^2t}{4r}\right]^{1/3} \tag{2.6}$$

where m is the amount the cash balance is expected to alter (with a probability of 1/2) and t is the frequency of transactions. The variance of transactions is proportional to m^3t and therefore implicitly appears in the above formula.

Milbourne (1986) has examined the impact of financial innovation on monetary aggregates within the framework of the Miller-Orr model. For example, he finds that (for US definitions) M1 should be influenced more than M2 by a fall in transactions (brokerage) cost but that M1 should be largely unaffected by the introduction of interest-bearing capital safe assets (e.g. money market mutual funds). Sprenkle and Miller (1980) have extended the precautionary model to include the possibility of meeting an unexpected cash drain by (automatic) overdrafts at an interest cost r_0 as well as by running down liquid assets (with an interest rate r). The model is therefore particularly useful in analysing the demand for broad money (and bank advances) by large firms who have automatic overdraft facilities. Sprenkle and Miller are able to show that the demand for broad money depends on *relative* interest rates and that demand will rise *continuously* (in the form of increased overdrafts which appear on the liabilities side of the bank's balance sheet as money) as r, the rate of interest in non-monetary liquid assets, rises relative to the overdraft rate r_0, even when $r < r_0$.

This dependence of the demand for broad money on the relative interest rate $(r_0 - r)$ could account in part for the rapid rise in the broad money supply in the UK in some periods of the 1970s, and highlights the need to use relative interest rates in the demand function for broad money.

2.4 Risk aversion models

Risk aversion models deal with the problem of choice amongst a set of assets which have uncertain capital values. As the name suggests, these models assume that individuals maximize utility by trading off risk and return subject to a wealth constraint (Markowitz 1952, 1959; Borch 1969; Feldstein 1969). Holding more of the risky asset (bond) increases the return to be obtained on the whole portfolio but may also increase the riskiness of the portfolio owing to the possibility of capital gains and losses on the risky assets. Under such circumstances it may be worthwhile holding a capital safe asset such as money even if the latter does not earn interest. Risk aversion models allow the *individual* to hold a diversified portfolio including money and bonds which depends on expected returns, initial wealth and the variance-covariance matrix of returns.

The precise functional form for the asset demand functions depends on the particular parameterization for the utility function and the maximand chosen (the latter is usually assumed to depend either on the expected utility from the return on the total portfolio or on end of period wealth).[5] The most common functional forms for the utility function are the negative exponential, a power function, or the quadratic. End of period wealth may be nominal or real.

If all stochastic returns are regarded as normally distributed, or we disregard higher than second-order moments in the distribution of $\mathbf{W}_{t+1}$, then[6]

$$E[U(\mathbf{W}_{t+1})] = U(\mathbf{W}^e_{t+1}) + (1/2)U''(\mathbf{W}^e_{t+1})\mathbf{V}_{t+1} \quad (2.7)$$

If $\mathbf{m}^e$ is a $k \times 1$ vector of expected (proportionate) returns over the fixed holding period, $\mathbf{m}$ is the actual return (i.e. the known running yield plus the expected capital gain), $\mathbf{S}$ is the variance-covariance matrix of returns and $\mathbf{A}$ is a $k \times 1$ vector of desired assets holdings at time t, then $\mathbf{W}^e_{t+1} = (\mathbf{i} + \mathbf{m}^e)'\mathbf{A}$ and $\mathbf{V}_{t+1} = \mathbf{A}'\mathbf{S}\mathbf{A}$, the variance of $\mathbf{W}_{t+1}$. Maximizing (2.7) subject to a nominal wealth constraint $\mathbf{W}_t = \mathbf{t}'\mathbf{A}$ yields asset demand functions of the form

$$\mathbf{A}_t = (1/\theta)\mathbf{Q}(\mathbf{i} + \mathbf{m}^e)_t + \mathbf{B}\mathbf{W}_t \quad (2.8)$$

$$\theta = -U''(\mathbf{W}^e_{t+1})/U'(\mathbf{W}^e_{t+1}) \quad (2.9)$$

where $\mathbf{i}$ is the unit vector, $\mathbf{Q}$ and $\mathbf{B}$ are functions of $\mathbf{S}$, and θ is the coefficient of absolute risk aversion. The set of assets in $\mathbf{A}$ may contain at most one capital safe asset, namely money, and the asset demands satisfy the adding-up constraint. Results from here on depend on the explicit form of the utility function chosen (e.g. see Courakis 1989; Dalal 1983)[7] but the demand for assets (including the safe asset, money) in general depends on expected return, initial wealth, the variance-covariance matrix and the parameters of the utility function.

Although this *mean-variance model* has some desirable features, it is not universally applicable to all asset choices. Because assets are only distinguished according to their different variance-covariance characteristics, it allows only one safe asset. In a world where there exists a wide array of capital certain short-term assets with low transactions costs, these will dominate the low-interest asset termed narrow money, *for speculative purposes*. The mean-variance model therefore determines the demand for short-term assets but not the demand for narrow money; the latter is not held at all in a speculative model. (But see also Sprenkle 1974; Chang et al. 1983, 1984.)

In the empirical implementation of the mean-variance model it is usually assumed that the variance-covariance matrix of asset returns is constant over time. If the latter assumption is incorrect then coefficient instability will result. Time-varying covariances seem a definite possibility in time series data. For example, more volatile rates of inflation which are expected to be reflected in more volatile interest rate movements might alter the variance-covariance of asset returns (this is a form of the Lucas 1976 critique). Modelling second moments of returns is a yet largely uncharted territory is asset demand equations (but see Baba et al. 1988). There has been empirical work on asset price equations[8] where the time-varying variances and covariances have been estimated using the autoregressive conditional heteroscedastic (ARCH) model (Engle 1982; Bollerslev et al. 1988; Giovannini and Jorion 1987, 1988). Space constraints preclude discussion of this complementary strand of the literature, but the general conclusion appears to be that the variance-covariance matrix is time varying.

The informational requirements in using a mean-variance approach to asset holdings might limit the applicability of the model to sophisticated financial firms such as banks, insurance companies and pension funds. However, this covers the main agents who operate in risky financial markets; persons comprise only a small part of these markets. Alternatively one could assume that agents apply the mean-variance analysis to broad aggregates of homogeneous assets (e.g. gilts, equities, liquid assets).

2.5 Asset demands and consumer demand theory

Friedman, in his 1956 restatement of the quantity theory, argues that the demand for assets should be based on axioms of consumer choice. He focuses on the demand for money and presents a fairly long list of possible arguments of this function (i.e. a vector of expected returns, wealth and income) with signs to be determined primarily by the data. He eschews the idea of approaching the theory of demand for assets by considering explicit *motives* for holding money.

To keep the decision problem tractable and (some would argue) realistic, it is usual to invoke some separability assumptions. A variety of separability assumptions of either the utility function or the cost function can be made, but weak intertemporal substitutability and quasi-separability between blocks of assets (e.g. real assets, liquid capital certain, capital uncertain) are usually assumed when analysing the demand for financial assets.[9] The demand for a subset of assets then depends only on prices within the subset and the total wealth held in the subset. Having isolated a set of n separable assets (or liabilities) one can then apply the models of consumer choice to these assets.

Neoclassical demand theory is usually based either on maximization of utility subject to an expenditure constraint or on the equivalent dual of minimizing cost to achieve a given level of utility.[10] The axioms of consumer demand theory (e.g. negativity, transitivity) are met, for example, providing we choose a cost function that is quasi-concave and homogeneous of degree zero in prices and expenditure. Different functional forms for cost or (direct and indirect) utility functions yield different functional forms for demand functions. For example, Barr and Cuthbertson (1989a) use the almost ideal demand system (AIDS) cost function (Deaton and Muellbauer 1980),[11] which results in asset shares s_i given by

$$s_i = \alpha_i + \sum_j \gamma_{ij} \ln p^{\tau}_{jt} + \beta_i \ln \left(W^{\tau}/P^{*\tau} \right)_t \tag{2.10}$$

where $(s_{it} = a_{it}/W_t)$, $\ln P^{*\tau}_t = \Sigma \bar{s}_i \ln p^{\tau}_{it}$, a_{it} is nominal asset holdings, W_t is nominal wealth and $\ln p^{\tau}_{it} = \ln(1 + r_{it} - g_z)^{-1}$ is the *real* price or discount factor. It may be shown that the share equations (2.10) exhibit symmetry, homogeneity and negativity, all of which are testable restrictions.

The application of consumer demand theory to the demand for financial assets provides a tractable approach which allows testing of the key axioms of choice theory. It should therefore be considered as useful as the motives approaches to the demand for money discussed earlier.

2.6 Buffer stock money

In the recent literature there has been a revival of interest in the role of money as a buffer stock, that is as an asset that acts as a shock absorber enabling agents temporarily to postpone otherwise costly adjustments (to alternative economic variables such as employment, investment and output) and to economize on information (Laidler 1984, 1988). Running in tandem with the buffer stock notion has been the wide application in macroeconomics generally of the rational expectations (RE) hypothesis and the market clearing RE models of the New Classical School, where a key distinction is drawn between anticipated and unanticipated events. The latter concepts have been used in some buffer stock models.

There is also a recurring debate in the literature (Laidler 1982) concerning the interpretation of estimated demand for money functions: are they demand functions, or do they represent reparameterized real balance equations (where causation runs from money to the arguments of the demand for money function)? The notion that buffer holdings of money are voluntarily held in the short run and then dissipated in a slow real balance effect clearly has attractions both as an explanation of temporal instability in demand for money functions and in contributing to an explanation of the long and variable lags of monetary policy.

At a theoretical level, models of the precautionary demand for money (Miller and Orr 1966; Akerlof and Milbourne 1980; Milbourne 1983b; Milbourne et al. 1983; Smith 1986; Milbourne 1987) provide a useful framework in which to analyse certain aspects of the buffer stock approach.[12] In these models buffer money, in the short run, is willingly held at unchanged interest rates. However, in the empirical implementation of the buffer stock notion, the precautionary demand model provides an intuitively appealing framework rather than an explicit equation suitable for estimation. There are several types of model that may be given the generic title of 'buffer stock money'; we discuss these and their empirical results in section 4.

3 DYNAMICS, EXPECTATIONS AND RISK

3.1 Lag responses

Ideally one would like a theory of the demand for money (and other assets) in which all the costs of adjustment are included in a single constrained optimization problem. However, such complete theories quickly become analytically intractable.[13] As a result we are virtually forced to assume that the individual undertakes a two-stage decision process. First he decides on the long-run optimal amount of assets to hold in accordance with the theories set out in section 2. Second, he solves a completely separate optimization problem concerning the speed at which he wishes to adjust towards this equilibrium. Thus it is assumed that the adjustment path chosen does not influence the desired (optimal) long-run level of demand for the asset.

Partial adjustment

The partial adjustment model may be derived from minimizing (one-period) quadratic costs[14] of adjustment $(m_t - m_{t-1})^2$ and costs of disequilibrium $(m_t - m_t^*)^2$, where $m_t^*$is long-run money demand. This results in

$$m = \gamma m_t^* + (1 - \gamma) m_{t-1}$$

(Without loss, we may take m to be the logarithm of money balances, either real or nominal.) A defect of the first-order partial adjustment mechanism is that short-run money balances *continually* differ from long-run balances if $m_t^*$is rising, say owing to a continuous rise in real income.

We can also derive the basic *error feedback equation* (EFE) from minimizing quadratic costs (Nickell 1985):

$$\Delta m_t = \mu_1 (m_t^* - m_{t-1}) + \Psi \Delta m_t^*.$$

The simple EFE suffers from the underprediction problem if m_t^* is continually rising or falling. This may be solved by introducing an integral control term $\psi_1 \Sigma_{j=2}^{k} (m_{t-j}^* - m_{t-j})$. The change in m_t now depends upon *past* disequilibria (Hendry and von Ungern Sternberg 1983) and therefore on higher-order lags in m_t.

Interdependent asset adjustment

In the simple partial adjustment model the change in the short-run desired demand for money depends only on the disequilibrium in (long-run) money holdings, that is on $(m_t^* - m_{t-1})$. However, disequilibrium in money holdings must imply that at least one other asset is also in disequilibrium. In principle the speed of adjustment in money holdings might depend on the disequilibrium in other asset stocks (Brainard and Tobin 1968; Smith 1975) such as building society deposits. This is the basis of the interdependent asset adjustment model. Here individuals face (a) a wealth (budget) constraint $\Sigma A_i = W$ (where A_i is actual holdings of the ith asset and W is wealth) and (b) the rational desires hypothesis $\Sigma A_i^* = W$ (where A_i^* is the desired long-run stock of the ith asset).

In the Brainard-Tobin (1968) approach the adjustment of the ith asset A_i depends upon disequilibria in *other* assets, stocks as well as in the own asset stock:

$$\mathbf{A}_t = \mathbf{G}\mathbf{A}_{t-1} + (\mathbf{I} - \mathbf{G})\mathbf{A}_t^* \qquad (2.11)$$

where $\mathbf{I}$ is the identity matrix, $\mathbf{G}$ is a matrix of weights and $\mathbf{A}_t$ is a *vector* of assets (Christophedes 1976). The latter equation is easily generalized to produce an interdependent error feedback adjustment process (Anderson and Blundell 1982; Barr and Cuthbertson 1989a):

$$\Delta\mathbf{A}_t = \mathbf{C}\Delta\mathbf{A}_t^* + \mathbf{D}(\mathbf{A}_{t-1} - \mathbf{A}_{t-1}^*) \qquad (2.12)$$

where $\mathbf{C}$ is a comformable matrix of short-run adjustment parameters, and the parameters in the $\mathbf{D}$ matrix determine the path to long-run equilibrium.[15] Equation (2.12) may also be used to model changes in asset shares (or more generally asset ratios, e.g. the money–income ratio).

The interdependent asset demand approach has been frequently applied to the demand for assets for a wide variety of economic agents, such as banks, insurance companies and persons. While one can invoke quadratic cost minimization as a basis for the above adjustment mechanisms, the addition of lagged dependent variables to a static model is often simply viewed by applied economists as an *ad hoc* yet parsimonious method of capturing lag responses.

3.2 Estimation issues

One cannot adequately analyse empirical demand for money functions without knowledge of the impact of three major areas of applied research which have become prominent over the last ten years. These are the general to specific methodology (Hendry et al. 1984), cointegration (Hendry 1986; Granger 1986) and the estimation of equations containing expectations terms (Wallis 1980; Wickens 1982; Pagan 1984; Pesaran 1987). However, we can only give a brief résumé of the main elements of these ideas.

Hendry (1989) argues that preferred models should be *designed* to meet certain criteria which, broadly speaking, include theory consistency and data coherency. The latter criteria include an error term that is white noise (i.e. no serial correlation or heteroscedasticity) and an innovation with respect to the information set used; in addition, the model should have constant parameters. Hendry argues that since a theory tells us little about dynamics we should begin our specification search with a very general autoregressive distributed lag (ADL) model in the levels of the variables:

$$\mathbf{m}_t = \boldsymbol{\alpha}_1(L)\,\mathbf{m}_{t-1} + \boldsymbol{\alpha}_2(L)\,\mathbf{x}_t + \mathbf{u}_t \tag{2.13}$$

where $\mathbf{m}_t$ are money balances and $\mathbf{x}_t$ are independent variables of the long-run money demand function. $\boldsymbol{\alpha}_1(L)$ and $\boldsymbol{\alpha}_2(L)$ are lag polynomials of sufficient order to ensure $\mathbf{u}_t$ is white noise. Equation (2.13) is over-parameterized. A parsimonious model which is data acceptable and has sensible decision variables and theoretically consistent long-run parameters is obtained via a creative search procedure. This is the *general to specific* modelling strategy. The preferred equation is often an error correction model (ECM), for example

$$\Delta\mathbf{m}_t = \boldsymbol{\gamma}_1(L)\,\Delta\mathbf{m}_{t-1} + \boldsymbol{\gamma}_2(L)\,\Delta\mathbf{x}_t + \boldsymbol{\gamma}_3(\mathbf{m} - \boldsymbol{\beta}'\mathbf{x})_{t-j} + \mathbf{v}_t \tag{2.14}$$

with static equilibrium

$$\mathbf{m}_t = \boldsymbol{\beta}'\mathbf{x}_t \tag{2.15}$$

An alternative reparameterization of (2.14) is to search for common factors (Hendry and Mizon 1978) in the lag polynomials $\boldsymbol{\gamma}_i(L)$ $(i = 1, 2)$, which may result in a lower-order polynomial in the distributed lag terms plus an autoregressive error. Note therefore that it *is* possible statistically to discriminate between lagged adjustment and an *auto*regressive error using the common factor test;[16] this is ignored in much of the US applied literature, as we shall see below. Note that the previous point does not apply to moving average errors (or indeed to complex non-linear error structures) as these do not imply common factors.

Practitioners of the general to specific methodology, finding serial correlation in the *residuals* (but no common factors), will often include additional lagged variables to remove it. Critics argue that such additional lagged difference terms are not modelling a true lagged response but may be proxy variables for a complex error structure, e.g. authoregressive moving average (ARMA). Our ignorance is then merely represented by uninterpretable lagged variables rather than an (uninterpretable) error process. At a purely empirical level this argument may be resolved by testing the complex lag coefficients and the error parameters of the complex error process for temporal stability.

Under constant growth rates for the $\mathbf{x}$ variables, ECMs like (2.14) yield dynamic equilibrium solutions $\mathbf{m} - \boldsymbol{\beta}\mathbf{x} = \boldsymbol{\psi}\mathbf{g}_x$. There is often little economic rationale in assuming $\boldsymbol{\psi} \neq 0$. However, constraining $\boldsymbol{\psi}$ to be zero (even if accepted by the data) may radically alter the lag profile (Patterson and Ryding 1984). Notwithstanding these problems, the general to specific methodology has been widely applied in empirical work on the demand for money, particularly outside the US.

Cointegration (Granger 1986; Hendry 1986) has provided a sound statistical basis for the error feedback formulation. To simplify matters, let us assume that $\mathbf{m}_t$ and all the variables in $\mathbf{x}_t$ have a stochastic trend and must be differenced once to obtain a stationary series (i.e. broadly speaking one with no trend in mean and a finite variance). These variables are then said to be integrated of order one or I(1), and their first differences are stationary or I(0) variables. For a set of I(1) variables it *may* be possible to find a constant vector $\boldsymbol{\beta}$ which yields a stationary I(0) error ϵ_t:

$$\mathbf{m}_t - \boldsymbol{\beta}'\mathbf{x}_t = \epsilon_t \tag{2.16}$$

Since ϵ_t has no trend in mean, intuitively (2.16) implies that the I(1) variables in the trended set $(\mathbf{m}_t, \mathbf{x}_t)$ do not diverge over time. They are said to be cointegrated with cointegrating vector $\boldsymbol{\beta}$, which may not be unique and which may be obtained from an ordinary least squares (OLS) regression on (2.16). It follows that all the variables in (2.16) are I(0), ϵ_t is stationary; hence all statistical tests based on ϵ_t have the usual distributional properties. In fact, if a cointegrating vector $\boldsymbol{\beta}$ can be found (and tests are available) then this implies the existence of an error correction model of the form (2.16) (Engle and Granger 1987).

Using the idea of cointegrated series, *two-step procedures* have been used to discover a valid ECM (Engle and Granger 1987). A set of variables (e.g. income, wealth) of the same order of integration that could potentially be related to money are permuted until a cointegrating set of variables ensues (Johansen 1988). OLS on (2.16) then yields an estimate of $\hat{\beta}$ from this first-stage cointegrating regression. The lagged residuals from (2.16) then constitute the ECM term $(\mathbf{m} - \hat{\beta}\mathbf{x})_{t-j}$ in (2.14). Searches over the lag polynomials $\gamma_i(L)$ $(i = 1, 2)$ then determine the most parsimonious representation of the short-run dynamics, independently of the *fixed* long-run value of $\hat{\beta}$. This reduces the dimension of the second-stage search procedure - a useful practical outcome.

Direct estimation of (2.14) after applying the general to specific methodology will produce an alternative value for β, say $\hat{\beta}^*$. We should then check that $(\mathbf{m}_t - \hat{\beta}^*\mathbf{x}_t)$ is stationary. On practical grounds one would hope that $\hat{\beta}$ from the two-step method and $\hat{\beta}$ using the general to specific strategy are not too far apart. In practice, finite sample bias exists for both techniques and there is continuing debate as to the most useful method to adopt (Banerjee et al. 1986).[17]

3.3 Modelling expectations

Expectations about the rate of inflation, the level of income and the yield on assets appear in our theories of the demand for assets. Survey data on expectations and publicly available forecasts of economic variables may both be used directly in the asset demand functions. However, the most popular approaches used in the empirical literature for modelling expectations have been variants of the adaptive expectations hypothesis and more recently the rational expectations hypothesis (REH). Regressive and extrapolative expectations formation have not been widely used in empirical work. As far as estimation is concerned, the main feature of the adaptive expectations framework is that it introduces lagged dependent variables into asset demand functions.[18] The subjective expectations of Muth-RE agents (Muth 1961) are *assumed* to be identical to conditional mathematical expectations. The basic idea behind Muth-RE is that, in forming his expectations, the agent uses all the available information about the economy he finds it worthwile to collect.

The use of the REH in empirical work on asset demands is relatively recent. Two broad approaches have been adopted. The first invokes the unbiasedness property of RE, whereby the *actual* future value of the variable provides an unbiased predictor of the *expected* value and an errors in variables problem arises (e.g. McCallum 1976; Wickens 1982; Cumby et al. 1983; Hansen 1982). The second approach uses the fact that the REH predicts that the expected value of a variable is formed by the individual using forecasts from the economic model that is thought to generate the variable in question. A regression of the variable in question on the exogenous and predetermined variables from the whole model provides an equation for generating future expected values (Nelson 1975). This is known as weakly rational expectations. Full Muth rational expectations (Muth 1961) require the imposition of cross-equation parameter restrictions (Wallis 1980).

Expectations variables in money demand functions result in rather subtle estimation problems, and we only deal with a subset of these here. Consider estimating the following demand function (a simplified version of Cuthbertson 1988a):

$$\mathbf{m}_t = \boldsymbol{\Theta}_1 \mathbf{m}_{t-1} + \boldsymbol{\Theta}_2 \mathbf{n}_t + \boldsymbol{\Theta}_3 ({}_t\mathbf{x}^e_{t+1}) + \boldsymbol{\Theta}_4 ({}_t\mathbf{x}^e_{t+2}) + \mathbf{u}_t \tag{2.17}$$

where $\mathbf{n}_t$ are non-expectational variables in the demand for money function. A two-step procedure might involve regressing ${}_t\mathbf{x}_{t+j}$ ($j = 1, 2$) on a subset $\boldsymbol{\Lambda}_t$ of the complete information set $\boldsymbol{\Omega}_t$. The predictions $\hat{\mathbf{x}}_{t+j}$ ($j = 1, 2$) then replace $\mathbf{x}^e_{t+j}$ in (2.17), and OLS is applied to

$$\mathbf{m}_t = \boldsymbol{\Theta}_1 \mathbf{m}_{t-1} + \boldsymbol{\Theta}_2 \mathbf{n}_t + \boldsymbol{\Theta}_3 \hat{\mathbf{x}}_{t+1} + \boldsymbol{\Theta}_4 \hat{\mathbf{x}}_{t+2} + \mathbf{q}_t \tag{2.18}$$

$$\mathbf{q}_t = \mathbf{u}_t + \boldsymbol{\Theta}_3 (\mathbf{x}^e_{t+1} - \hat{\mathbf{x}}_{t+1}) + \boldsymbol{\Theta}_4 (\mathbf{x}^e_{t+2} - \hat{\mathbf{x}}_{t+2}) \tag{2.19}$$

There are several problems with this commonly used procedure. If $\mathbf{m}_{t-1}$ or $\mathbf{n}_t$ are excluded from $\boldsymbol{\Lambda}_t$ (e.g. $\hat{\mathbf{x}}_{t+j}$ is an extrapolative predictor based solely on $\mathbf{x}_{t-j}$ ($j = 1, 2, \ldots$)) but they influence $\mathbf{x}^e_{t+j}$, then OLS estimates of $\boldsymbol{\Theta}_i$ ($i = 1, \ldots 4$) are inconsistent (Nelson 1975). Regardless of the latter point, the usual standard errors from OLS on (2.18) are incorrect (Pagan 1984).

The inconsistency problem may be eliminated by using $\boldsymbol{\Lambda}_t$ and $(\mathbf{m}_{t-1}, \mathbf{n}_t)$ in the instrument matrix and applying the expected value model. However, the error term $\mathbf{q}_t$ then contains a moving average error due to the expectations forecasting error $(\mathbf{x}_{t+j} - {}_t\mathbf{x}^e_{t+j})$ and conventional corrections for serial correlation yield inconsistent estimators. Special corrections for serial correlation are required (see Hayashi and Sims 1983; Hansen 1982) which we do not pursue here. Thus there are some acute estimation problems when expectations terms enter the demand for money function. Pesaran (1987) argues that the conditions for identification in RE models are in general very stringent and are perhaps unlikely to be met in practice; this has not prevented applications in the money demand literature.

Learning and expectations formation

An alternative to the RE and (fixed coefficient) adaptive expectations schemes is to assume some updating or learning process by agents. A simple form of updating is to estimate the expectations equation by recursive least squares and to use parameter estimates and forecasts based only on information actually available to the agent. Models with unobservable components and models with time-varying parameters (Harvey 1981a, 1981b; Cuthbertson 1988b) have also been used to mimic optimal learning by agents (see Cuthbertson and Taylor 1987b, 1989).

If data are highly trended then expectations proxy variables are likely to be highly correlated with current and lagged values. Hence forward-looking expectations models and backward-looking error feedback models are likely to be difficult to distinguish empirically. Cross-equation rationality restrictions (Mishkin 1983; Abel and Mishkin 1983; Cuthbertson and Taylor 1987c) provide a further discriminating test, but again these may lack power in small samples. Hendry (1988) has recently proposed a rather ingenious test of a backward-looking versus forward-looking model based on parameter constancy tests. In short, Hendry (1988) argues that if we have a constant parameter backward-looking model *and* an auxiliary equation to generate expectations which is non-stable (based on any subset of information used by agents) then this rules out a structural expectations model such as (2.17). Cuthbertson (1991) argues that the test is useful against any *specific* expectations generation equation but lacks the universality claimed by Hendry. This is an important area of debate but definitive results are not yet available.

3.4 Modelling risk

The precautionary and risk aversion models suggest that risk is an important determinant of the demand for money. Riskiness is often measured by a moving sample variance (e.g. see Baba et al. 1988) although there are econometric problems with this approach (Pagan 1984; Pagan and Ullah 1988). Recently, Engle et al. (1987) have suggested that risk be modelled using a generalized ARCH (GARCH) process. To illustrate this approach, assume that bond prices $\mathbf{z}_t$ depend on a set of variables $\mathbf{Q}_t$ (this could constitute an inverted mean-variance asset demand system):

$$\mathbf{z}_t = \mathbf{Q}_t\gamma + \epsilon_t \qquad \epsilon_t \sim N(0, \mathbf{h}_t) \tag{2.20}$$

The variance of the prediction errors from (2.20), namely $\mathbf{h}_t$, is assumed to influence the demand for money:

$$\mathbf{m}_t = \mathbf{f}(x) + \beta\mathbf{h}_t + \mathbf{u}_t \tag{2.21}$$

We assume $\mathbf{h}_t$ responds slowly to past forecast errors (GARCH model, Bollerslev et al. 1988):

$$\mathbf{h}_t = \alpha_0\mathbf{h}_{t-1} + (1 - \alpha_0)\epsilon_{t-1}^2 \tag{2.22}$$

The set of equations (2.20)–(2.22) can be jointly estimated using maximum likelihood techniques. To date, ARCH and GARCH models have been mainly used in modelling time-varying risk premiums in the foreign exchange, bond and stock markets (e.g. Giovannini and Jorion 1988; Engel and Rodrigues 1987) but the approach is likely to provide a focus for future-work on the demand for assets as the above studies indicate that risk premiums may be time varying.

4 EMPIRICAL EVIDENCE

The empirical literature on the demand for money is vast. We do not attempt to give an exhaustive account of the empirical evidence; nor do we present a detailed econometric evaluation of specific equations. Rather, our aim is to provide illustrative examples of the different *approaches* adopted, concentrating on recent empirical work. Early empirical work provides illustrative examples of the partial adjustment and adaptive expectations approach. Recent work has utilized the error feedback and interdependent asset adjustment framework to model lag responses. There has been a revival of interest in modelling buffer stock money, and this provides the final approach discussed.

Data and definitional problems

Our theories of the demand for money do not give an unambiguous indication of what constitutes money. The inventory and precautionary models perhaps give the clearest indication, suggesting the use of 'cash plus demand deposits' as the appropriate definition since these are universally recognized as the means of exchange in most industrialized nations. However, even here recent innovations in financial markets have rendered this distinction less clear cut than previously. The risk aversion model gives no clear indication of the appropriate definition of money, since a wide variety of capital certain assets could be defined as acting as a store of value in nominal terms. The inventory and precautionary models yield demand functions for *average* money balances and therefore some form of time-average data is appropriate, while the consumer theory and mean-variance models determine money balances at a point in time. However, this distinction is often arbitrarily treated in empirical work.

Empirical work, in the main, has treated money as consisting of various elements of the liabilities of the banking system. M0 in the UK consists mainly of cash held by the non-bank private sector (NBPS) but also includes bankers' balances at the Bank of England. Although it is currently a targeted aggregate, it is of little operational significance for the UK (see Trundle 1982; Johnston 1984; and Hall et al 1989 for estimated M0 equations). These studies provide no evidence to support the assertion that M0 is an advance indicator of money GDP (Lawson 1986: p. 12). For the demand for currency in the US see the recent study by Dotsey (1988).

M1, the narrow definition, usually consists of cash and current (chequeing) accounts held by the non-bank private sector, and may often be further subdivided into interest-bearing and non-interest-bearing chequeing accounts (e.g. NIB M1 in the UK). M2 consists of M1 and usually also includes certain interest-bearing bank deposits of small denomination that are not marketable (e.g. seven-day time deposits), although in the UK it includes retail deposits held in building societies as well as banks. In the US M2 is often referred to as broad money, but in the UK (and some other European countries) the latter usually refers to a wider set of assets held by the NBPS. In the UK, until quite recently, £M3 was the most widely discussed of the broad monetary aggregates. It consists of M1 plus sterling time deposits plus certain large denomination fixed term deposits (wholesale deposits), some of which are marketable (e.g. certificates of deposit).[19] Prior to the 1970s it was generally the case that the various definitions of money gave similar conclusions concerning the appropriate form for the demand for money function, including the stability of such relationships. After 1970 the latter view became problematic and the appropriate definition of money became an empirical matter; that is, money was to be defined as that financial asset which had a stable demand function and which could be controlled by the authorities.

Many of the early empirical studies use annual data and therefore the issue of *adjustment* lags tends to play a minor role. Laidler (1985) provides a useful summary of this work, particularly for the US and the UK; it includes seminal papers by Meltzer (1963) using US data 1900–58, by Brunner and Meltzer (1963) and Laidler (1966) who refined this work for the US, and by Laidler (1971) and Barratt and Walters (1966) who repeated this kind of analysis for the UK. In these studies it is generally found that the demand for money appears to be related to a single representative interest rate. However, some early studies find that a wider set of interest rates influences the demand for money. For example, Lee (1967, 1969) and Hamberger (1966) find evidence in favour of the inclusion of the return on saving and loan association deposits and the return on equity as well as the time deposit rate (see also Klein 1974a, 1974b; Barro and Santomero 1972).

In summary, we note that studies for this early data period using annual data suggest a well-determined, fairly stable demand for money function. Broadly speaking, stability applies under different definitions of money, for different interest rates and over different data periods. As we shall see in subsequent sections, it appears to be the case that in recent years economists have become more circumspect concerning our knowledge of the demand for money.

4.1 Instability in the demand for money

Partial adjustment and adaptive expectations

Laidler and Parkin (1970) apply Feige's (1967) model to UK quarterly per capita data on M2 for 1956(2)–1967(4) and obtain ambiguous results concerning adjustment and expectations lags. They interpret the results in terms of permanent income rather than adjustment lags. The interest rate is statistically insignificant, and Laidler and Parkin argue that this arises because the Treasury bill rate does not provide a satisfactory proxy variable for the *relative* return on money – the omitted variable being the own rate on money. Artis and Lewis (1976) look at the stability of coefficient estimates as the sample period, which begins in 1963(2), is extended from 1970(4) to 1973(1). For broad money they include the interest *differential* between the own rate on money and the rate on long-term government debt; in *all* equations the variance of bond prices (measured as a moving average) is included to measure riskiness. Equations are presented with nominal and real balances as the dependent variables, and first-order partial adjustment is invoked. In all cases the equations fail the Chow test for parameter stability over the period 1971(1)–1973(1), and for broad money the equation is dynamically unstable over the long data period (as the lagged dependent variable exceeds unity). Thus a problem, namely instability of the demand for broad money (and to a lesser extent narrow money), arose after the introduction of the Competition and Credit Control policy in 1971, which allowed banks great freedom in setting deposit and loan rates and resulted in problems such as round tripping.[20]

It is probably fair to say that most work in the US using quarterly data on the demand for money has used and continues to use either (first-order) partial adjustment (in real or nominal terms) or, perhaps less frequently, the adaptive expectations hypothesis. There are few new analytic points to emerge from this work, and as recent empirical results are well documented elsewhere (Laidler 1980; Judd and Scadding 1982; Roley 1985) we content ourselves here with an overview of the main conclusions.

Over the period 1952(2)–1973(4) Goldfeld (1976) found a stable demand function for narrow money (M1) which was positively related to real GNP, was negatively related to a representative market short rate (e.g. the commercial bill rate) and the rate on time deposits, and incorporated first-order partial adjustment in nominal terms. However, this function seriously overpredicted money balances (in a dynamic simulation) over the period 1974–6 ('the case of the missing money') and was also found to be unstable over the 1979–81 period.

Attempts to account for the temporal instability by permutations of different interest rate and transactions variables have not proved wholly successful. Admittedly the use of bank debits as an additional transactions variable alongside GNP (which excludes intermediate transactions and transactions in financial assets but includes some imputed items for which no transactions take place) does improve matters somewhat (Judd and Scadding 1982). Also the use of the dividend price ratio (Hamberger 1977) improves the performance of the M1 equation (but other criticisms of this equation have been raised: see Hafer and Hein 1979; Laidler 1980).

The main candidates for the observed instability in the demand for money in the US since 1973 appear to be financial innovation, measurement problems, misspecified dynamics and the role of money as a buffer stock. We now deal with the first two items.

Financial Innovation

There has been a recent revival of interest in explaining secular changes in the velocity by structural variables as well as conventional variables (e.g. income, interest rates), using both cross-country and time series data. Bordo and Jonung (1987) provide an excellent source (for the US see also Mayer and Pearl 1984). They find evidence that such variables as the share of the labour force in non-agricultural pursuits (a measure of the monetization process) and the currency–money ratio (as a measure of the spread of commercial banking) influence long-run velocity for M2 in five countries (USA, Canada, UK, Sweden and Norway) for the period from 1880 to the mid 1970s. It should be noted, however, that cointegration techniques were not used and the estimated equations have severe first-order serial correlation with no common factor tests undertaken. The results must therefore be interpreted with caution.

Recently financial innovation has involved the banks offering interest-bearing accounts that are easily transferable to chequeing accounts and allowing the centralization of accounts (of different branches of the firm: cash concentration accounts). Ideally one would like direct measures of the change in brokerage fees (see Offenbacher and Porter 1982) and of the reduction in the variance of net cash flows facilitated by these innovations. These variables could then be used directly in the inventory and precautionary models of the demand for money. Unfortunately such direct measures are not readily available, and the most successful variables include the number of wire transfers and previous peak interest rates. The former reflects the increased use of cash management techniques by firms and the latter represents the increased incentive *to begin* using these services more frequently. When either of these variables is added to the demand for M1 it is statistically significant and the (outside sample) forecast errors of the equation post-1973 are reduced (Judd and Scadding 1982). In contrast to the above, the demand for narrow money in other industrialized countries does not appear to have been affected by financial innovation variables even though they also experienced high interest rates in the 1970s (Boughton 1981; Arango and Nadiri 1981). The pace of financial innovation appears to be accelerating in other industrialized nations and we may seem similar problems with instability in the demand for M1 in these countries in the near future. (There is already some evidence for this in the demand for M1 in the UK in 1983–4: Hall et al. 1989).

Measurement problems

Although there have been acute problems in finding a stable demand function for M1 in the US since 1973, the difficulties with M2 (which consists of M1 plus small savings accounts at commercial banks) have been far less severe. Laidler (1980) reports that the conventional demand function for M2 exhibits much greater outside sample temporal stability than does M1 and is less sensitive to alternative specifications of the arguments in the function (for a counter-argument see Hamberger 1980). Interest, however, tends to centre on M1 as this is the targeted aggregate in the US.

There has been an interesting attempt in the US to correctly measure money and the return on money using Divisia aggregates and to use these measures to test the stability of the partial adjustment model (Barnett et al. 1984). The approach recognizes that the components of the money supply (e.g. currency, demand and time deposits) may not be perfect substitutes for each other and should not be given equal weight as in official statistics on monetary aggregates. In the Divisia approach the separate components are weighted together according to their contribution to money services to form a consistent series for money. User costs measure the marginal money services yielded by each component and are proportional to the difference between the yield on a benchmark asset and the component's own yield. The share of each component's user cost in total user cost is used to weight each component in forming the Divisia aggregate.

In the demand for money function, conventional aggregates are replaced by their Divisia counterparts and interest rates are replaced by the user cost indices. On US data, for narrow money, there is no major improvement in the performance of the Divisia equation over the conventional function. However for broad agregates, where we expect conventional measures to incorrectly measure money services, the Divisia measures do produce a more stable demand function (e.g. Barnett et al. 1984; see Mills 1983 for some UK evidence). The approach is probably most useful where interest rates (which make up the user cost variables) are market determined rather than subject to regulation, and hence may prove useful in an increasingly competitive financial environment. However, use of Divisia aggregates does not appear to solve the missing money and great velocity decline of the 1980s (Lindsey and Spindt 1986).

4.2 The ADL-ECM approach

In this section we illustrate the approach using autoregressive distributed lag in error correction model form. The levels and ratio terms determine the long-run static equilibrium parameters of the asset demand function, while differenced variables model the short-run dynamics around this static equilibrium position. Broadly speaking the aim in this approach is to obtain a well-fitting (data coherent) equation that has good statistical properties, forecasts well outside its sample period of estimation, and conforms to the *a priori* notions given by the static equilibrium model (these issues are elaborated in Hendry 1983).

The demand for narrow money

Coughlan (1978) uses an unrestricted ADL model for narrow money, but Hendry (1979, 1985) provides a more recent econometric study of the demand for transactions balances M1 in the UK by the NBPS. In long-run equilibrium, the real demand for M1 is assumed to depend upon real income Y (i.e. GNP), the expected yield on alternative assets r (i.e. the local authority three-month rate) and the rate of inflation π. A long-run unit income elasticity is proposed. In obvious notation, the static long-run equilibrium is

$$(M/PY) = Kr^{\alpha} (\pi)^{\beta} \qquad \alpha, \beta < 0 \tag{2.23}$$

A general unrestricted ADL equation in the logarithms of the levels of Y_{t-j}, r_{t-j}, p_{t-j} and M_{t-j-1} ($j = 0, \ldots, 4$) is reparameterized and simplified to produce the following data-coherent dynamic error feedback equation or ECM:

$$\begin{aligned}\Delta(m-p)_t = \; & \underset{(0.16)}{0.4\Delta y_{t-1}} - \underset{(0.11)}{0.52R_t} - \underset{(0.17)}{0.86\Delta P_t} - \underset{(0.02)}{0.11(m-p-y)_{t-2}} \\ & - \underset{(0.09)}{0.26\Delta(m-p)_{t-1}} + \underset{(0.006)}{0.04}\end{aligned} \tag{2.23}$$

The data are from 1961(1) to 1977(1); the regression is OLS; the standard error is 1.5 per cent; and the test statistic for serial correlation is LM(3,43) = 0.4. The long-run static equilibrium is

$$m - p - y = 4.2 - 5.6 \ln(1 + R) - 1.9 \ln(1 + P^{a}) \tag{2.25}$$

giving unit income elasticity, and interest rate and annual inflation semi-elasticities of −5.6 and −1.9 respectively. The median lags for y and R are less than four quarters; the equation shows no sign of serial correlation of up to order three (i.e. the LM statistic is distributed as F under the null); and, most important, the equation exhibits parameter constancy when the data period is extended to 1982(4) and when estimated recursively over the period 1965(3) to 1982(4).

The inflation effect should probably be interpreted not as a switch from money into goods but rather as a lag response to a change in the price-level (Milbourne 1983a; Cuthbertson 1986a). In the spirit of the Miller-Orr (1966) 'bounds model', agents adjust money balances only when they hit an upper (or lower) threshold and this occurs after a lag.

The demand for M1 in the UK appears to have undergone some structural change in the second half of the 1980s. Cuthbertson and Taylor (1989) note that over the period 1968(1)–1985(2) there appears to be some instability in the long-run income elasticity. Hall et al. (1989) find evidence that the conventional variables in the demand for M1 do not form a cointegrating vector (although the addition of real financial wealth and a measure of stock market turnover tends to improve matters here).

After 1982 real M1 grew substantially owing to the growth in its interest-bearing component. During the 1970s less than 10 per cent of M1 was interest bearing: by the end of 1982 this rose to 30 per cent, and by the middle of 1987 the figure reached 65 per cent. Clearly, in principle we need data on the return from high-interest chequeing accounts (which are not readily available) and a measure of the growth in awareness of the existence of such accounts (see below for the Baba et al. 1988 attempt at modelling such learning behaviour). The latter will have to await further research to see if such additional variables can produce a cointegrating vector.

Longer data set

Hendry and Ericsson (1983) examine the demand for broad money of Friedman and Schwartz (1982) in the UK using annual data over the period 1867–1975. They find a shift in the money demand function over the period 1921–55 (as well as in the two World War periods); the equation also exhibits parameter instability over the period 1971–5 (but see also the results in Longbottom and Holly 1985, who subject the model to further detailed tests). In a subsequent paper Hendry and Ericsson (1988) utilize the Engle-Granger (1987) two-step procedure with a non-linear error correction term; this yields an equation with a long-run interest rate semi-elasticity of −7 and unit nominal income elasticity. Note that all of the above specifications fail parameter constancy tests over the period 1971–5 – an issue we return to later in this chapter. Taylor (1990a) fits a stable error correction model to UK data on broad money for the Gold Standard years, 1871–1913, and finds long-run price and income homogeneity. His equation also encompasses the Hendry-Ericsson equation over this period.

Artis and Lewis (1981) report studies on UK data on old M2 (excluding building society deposits) over the period 1880–1960, giving an income elasticity of unity and an interest elasticity with respect to the long rate between −0.3 and −0.8. Extending the data period to 1981, they uncover a 'rather jolly little nut' (Artis and Lewis 1984) whereby a very simple specification of the form $m - y = a + br + u_t$, where r is the consol rate (all variables in logarithms), fits rather well and suggests a fairly stable function except for 1973–6. Patterson (1987) demonstrates that in statistical terms we can improve on the Artis-Lewis equation by using an ADL-ECM model. However, broadly speaking the long-run results of Artis and Lewis remain intact (again this is not surprising given knowledge of cointegration techniques).

US demand for narrow money

Gordon (1984) applies the ADL-ECM approach to the demand for narrow money in the US but finds considerable instability in the equations estimated. Rose (1985) directly confronts the missing money problem for narrow money in terms of the restrictive (partial adjustment) lag structure used by previous investigators. By allowing the data to determine the appropriate lag structure within the ADL-ECM format, Rose finds a stable dynamic ECM for the missing money period (on seasonally adjusted and unadjusted data) with a long-run equilibrium solution (with constant inflation $g_p = \Delta p$)

$$m - p - y = k + \underset{(0.07)}{0.57y} - \underset{(0.05)}{0.12r} - \underset{(4.5)}{7.6g_p} \tag{2.26}$$

The income elasticity at 1.57 is higher than earlier representative results reported in Judd and Scadding (1982) but is not statistically very different from unity. However, an equation of the form (2.26) when estimated to 1977(4) exhibits parameter instability over the period 1978(1)–1981(4) (and poor diagnostics), which Rose conjectures may be caused by the monetary policy regime change (to monetary targeting) after 1979 and to general financial innovation.

Within the ADL-ECM framework Baba et al. (1988) provide the definitive empirical account of the behaviour of narrow money M1B in the US for 1960(2)–1984(2), covering the periods of missing money 1974(1)–1976(2) and the great velocity decline 1982(1)–1983(2). In the missing money episode, previous models had overpredicted the demand for money by some 8–12 per cent while similar models had in the main substantially underpredicted the growth in narrow money. Building on the basic ECM of Rose (1985), Baba et al. find that both the increase in the volatility of bond yields, and use of the appropriate learning adjusted after-tax *own yield* on M1 instruments, provide an empirical explanation for the rapid decline in velocity in the early 1980s. Volatility in bond yields has a local peak in 1971(3) and descends to a trough in 1974(1), and this accounts for the fall in the demand for money in the missing money period. (Note, however, that a (−1, +1) dummy variable for 1980(2) and 1980(3) to capture credit controls is needed for parameter stability after 1980.)

The volatility measure *AVA* is based on a yearly standard deviation of the monthly holding period yield. Financial innovation in the form of the introduction of new interest-bearing accounts is modelled by using a weighting system based on a (twenty-quarter) learning ogive applied to the return on new financial instruments (e.g. negotiable order of withdrawal (NOW) accounts from 1981(1), Super NOW accounts from 1983(1)). The actual return used is then the maximum of the previously available instrument (the passbook rate) and the *learning adjusted* yield on new accounts. Also, after-tax yields are used. Compared with Rose (1985) these are the main innovations in the Baba et al. model, and their dynamic ECM model has a static equilibrium solution

$$m - p = -2.4 + 0.5y - 12.4S - 4.7sz - 6.3rmz + 1.96rmocz - 1.3g_p + 0.03AVA + 1.1S^*AVA \quad (2.27)$$

where the symbols have the following meanings:

m	(logarithm of) nominal money (M1B)
y	(logarithm of) real GNP
p	(logarithm of) GNP deflator
S	bond–bill spread
sz	bill to learning adjusted M2 spread
rmz	learning adjusted highest prevailing yield on M2 accounts
$rmocz$	learning adjusted yield on chequeing accounts
AVA	moving standard deviation of holding period yield on long-term bonds
$S^*(AVA)$	max $[0, (R_t - r_t)\, AVA]$, where R_t is the yield on twenty-year Treasury bonds
r_t	yield on one-month Treasury bills
g_p	annual inflation rate

In the long run the demand for real money balances has a real income elasticity of 0.5 and an inflation elasticity of −1.3, and exhibits a negative relationship with the yield on alternative M2 instruments (*rmz* and *rmocz*). The bond volatility measure has a direct positive effect on the demand for

M1 (i.e. *AVA*) and an additional effect the higher the (positive) bond-bill spread (i.e. S^*AVA).

The policy implications, admittedly with hindsight, of the Baba et al. demand function are that the change in the Federal Reserve Bank's operating procedures in late 1979 caused an increase in the volatility of interest rates, which then led to a rise in the demand for M1 in the early 1980s (i.e. the great velocity decline). The increase in monetary growth was therefore indicative not of excess money, which might lead one to advocate a tightening of monetary policy, but merely of a change in desired money holdings by agents.

While one might not embrace all aspects of the results from Rose and Baba et al., one cannot avoid the inference that the ADL-ECM approach tells us more about the demand for narrow money in the US than working within the partial adjustment framework (but see Goodfriend 1985). Roley (1985) restricts himself to partial adjustment (and first-difference) equations for M1, and although he introduces a wide variety of other variables he is unable to make any positive inroads into the missing money and great velocity decline episodes.

Other countries

There is a substantial literature on the demand for money in hyperinflations (e.g. Cagan 1956; Barro 1970; Abel et al. 1979), and recently Taylor (1990b) has extended the analysis using cointegration and ECM techniques. In general the results support the view that real money demand is negatively related to the expected rate of inflation in these high-inflation periods (often 1920s data are used) across a number of countries (e.g. Germany, Austria, Hungary). The ECM approach has also been successful in modelling M1 and M2 definitions of money for West Germany, The Netherlands and France (Taylor 1986), Australia (Milbourne 1985) and Italy (Muscatelli and Papi 1988) since the 1960s. Thus, overall, the error feedback approach has yielded reasonable results for the demand for money in European countries.

The demand for broad money

Hendry and Mizon (1978) (see also Haache 1974) consider the demand for M3 (i.e. sight and interest-bearing deposits) by the UK *personal* sector. This work is extended by Grice and Bennett (1984) using a dynamic ECM model of the demand for £M3 by the UK NBPS over the 1960s and 1970s data. They introduce a dummy variable to proxy the large shift in demand after the introduction of Competition and Credit Control (CCC) (Goodhart 1984). They include gross financial wealth (i.e. total final expenditure) as a transactions variable, and also the *relative* return on money.

Taylor (1987), in an otherwise conventional ECM demand for money function for £M3, models financial innovation from 1984 by using the return on high-interest chequeing accounts (for deposits of between £2000 and £10,000). Prior to 1984 this own rate (RM) is the seven-day deposit rate. The preferred equation is

$$\begin{aligned}\Delta(m-p)_t = {} & \underset{(0.102)}{0.287}\Delta(m-p)_{t-2} - \underset{(0.006)}{0.019}(m-p-y)_{t-4} \\ & - \underset{(0.002)}{0.005}(RTB_{t-1} - RM_t) - \underset{(0.001)}{0.003}\Delta^2 RLB_{t-2} \\ & - \underset{(0.183)}{0.415}\Delta p_t + \underset{(0.007)}{0.03}\end{aligned} \tag{2.28}$$

The data are from 1964(2) to 1985(4); the regression instrumental variables; the standard error is 1.56 per cent; and LM(5, 73) = 1.24, HF(20) = 15.60, where LM and HF are test statistics for serial correlation and predictive accuracy respectively. RTB is the three-month Treasury bill rate, RLB is the rate on long bonds (i.e. gilt-edged stocks) and y is total final expenditure. The equation is homogeneous in the price level and real income, and is stable over the period 1979(4)–1985(4) [HF(20)] and over the period after the introduction of Competition and Credit Control. The term $\Delta^2 RLB$ is probably a proxy for a risk term on alternative capital uncertain assets.

Studies of gross liquidity (usually of the personal sector) are less numerous and the results are more mixed than those for narrow money or even £M3. Official liquidity aggregates for the UK include building society deposits. On UK data, gross liquidity depends on some measure of expenditure and wealth, but long-run interest rate effects are often not well determined (Johnston 1985; Currie and Kennally 1985; Spanos 1984). Cuthbertson and Barlow (1990) do find evidence for a set of interest rates influencing UK personal sector gross liquidity, but Hall et al. (1989) demonstrate the difficulties in obtaining a satisfactory (cointegration) equation for liquidity of the UK *private* sector when data to 1989 are included.

We conclude that the ADL-ECM approach in a single-equation context has proved most useful in advancing our knowledge of the behaviour of the demand for narrow money for a number of industrialized countries (but see Cover and Keeler 1987, who favour the first-difference model for US M1 but ignore the cointegration and ECM literature). Success with broader monetary aggregates has proved more elusive.

Systems approach

Estimating the demand for money as part of a system of asset demand equations has not proved as popular as single-equation studies, although this approach has proved successful in modelling asset demands other than money. Weale (1986), Hood (1987) and Barr and Cuthbertson (1990, 1991) consider the demand for UK personal sector liquid assets in a systems framework, while Barr and Cuthbertson (1989a, b, c) extend this approach to the company, other financial intermediary (OFI) and overseas sectors.

For example, Barr and Cuthbertson (1990) utilize an interdependent error feedback AIDS model for asset shares s_t for the UK personal sector:

$$\Delta \mathbf{s}_t = \mathbf{C}\Delta\mathbf{X}_t + \mathbf{L}(\mathbf{s} - \mathbf{s}^*)_{t-1} \tag{2.29}$$

where $\mathbf{s}_t^* = \mathbf{\Pi X}_t$; $\mathbf{s}_t$ is a $k \times 1$ vector of asset shares; $\mathbf{s}_t^*$ long-run desired asset shares; $\mathbf{X}_t$ is a $q \times 1$ vector of independent variables; $\mathbf{\Pi}$ is a $k \times q$ matrix of long-run parameters; $\mathbf{C}$ is a $k \times q$ matrix of short-run parameters; and $\mathbf{L}$ is a $(k-1) \times k$ matrix of adjustment parameters.

Barr and Cuthbertson estimate the system using the Engle-Granger two-step procedure and by conventional non-linear least squares. Although the estimated equations are highly disaggregated (e.g. notes and coin, sight deposits, time deposits), nevertheless one can derive the demand functions that are close to the conventional aggregate M1, M2, £M3 etc. In general they find that the system EFEs perform well statistically, and long-run homogeneity, symmetry and negativity restrictions are frequently accepted by the data. The above empirical results indicate that the demand for narrow and broad money depends on a *vector* of interest rates, wealth and expenditure, and the set of liquid assets is usually a net substitute. Keating (1985) used a highly restricted variant of the mean-variance model (e.g. diagonal and constant covariance matrix) to explain disaggregated holdings of financial assets in the UK. However, this particular systems approach did not yield satisfactory results (Courakis 1988a).

Particularly for the US and Canada, a systems approach to the demand for money has been widely utilized (see Feige and Pearce 1977 for a survey of early work). In general the evidence points to a low degree of substitutability (and sometimes even complementarity) between liquid financial assets that constitute narrow and broad money. This points to the need to model the demand for the *constituent parts* of M1, M2 etc. and to disaggregate by sector (e.g. persons, companies) where possible. Various functional forms (e.g. direct and indirect translog: see Donovan 1978, Serletis and Robb 1986, Serletis 1988 on Canadian data; Swofford and Whitney 1986, Ewis and Fisher 1984 on US data) have proved reasonably successful. Generally speaking such studies have used rather restrictive lag structures which may account for the failure of estimated equations to satisfy the axioms of consumer theory. Some studies (e.g. Barnett 1980; Serletis and Robb 1986) also compare Divisia and simple sum aggregates and find in favour of the former. What the above studies indicate is that a simple demand for money function containing only one opportunity cost variable and excluding a wealth variable may involve misspecification.

4.3 Buffer stock money: four approaches

The term 'buffer stock money' covers a number of different approaches, and below we classify these into four main types of model (Cuthbertson and Taylor 1987d; Milbourne 1988).

Single-equation disequilibrium money models

Estimates of demand for money functions for almost any developed country have a sizeable autoregressive component which has frequently been interpreted as reflecting slow adjustment of short-run to long-run desired money holdings. However, various authors (Artis and Lewis 1976; Laidler 1982) interpret these estimated demand for money parameters as representing a slow real balance effect and advocate inverting the demand for money function prior to estimation (for exmple, Artis and Lewis 1976; Laidler 1980; Goodhart 1984; Wren-Lewis 1984).

Artis and Lewis (1976) achieved some success when estimating inverted *long-run* demand for money functions assuming either slow adjustment in interest rates or nominal income, and find more stable demand for money parameters (for narrow and broad money) than those obtained when money is taken as the dependent variable. However, Hendry (1985) for UK M1 and MacKinnon and Milbourne (1988) for US narrow money clearly demonstrate that inverting a conventional *short-run* money demand function and taking the price level as the dependent variable yields exceedingly poor estimated price equations, over the 1960–85 period. They rightly conclude that price equations are not simply *short-run* 'money demand equations on their heads' (MacKinnon and Milbourne 1988).

Complete disequilibrium monetary models

In this type of buffer stock model, disequilibrium money holdings are allowed to influence a wide range of real and nominal variables. In this complete model approach the following types of equation frequently appear:

$$\Delta \mathbf{X}_t = \mathbf{f}(\mathbf{Z}_t) + \gamma(L)(\mathbf{M}_t^s - \mathbf{M}_t^d) \tag{2.30}$$

$$\mathbf{M}_t^d = \alpha_0 \mathbf{P}_t + \alpha_t \mathbf{R}_t + \alpha_2 \mathbf{Y}_t \tag{2.31}$$

$\mathbf{X}_t$ may be a set of real and nominal variables (for example output, prices, exchange rate); $\mathbf{Z}_t$ is a set of predetermined equilibrium variables; $\mathbf{M}_t^d$ is the *long-run* demand for money; and $\gamma(L)$ is a lag polynominal. As the money disequilibrium term appears in more than one equation, the model yields cross-equation restrictions on the parameters of the long-run demand for money function. This type of model has performed reasonably well for the US (Laidler and Bentley 1983), the UK (Davidson 1984; Hilliard 1980; Laidler and O'Shea 1980), Australia (Jonson and Trevor 1979) and Canada (Laidler et al. 1983). In some of these models the money supply is taken to be exogenous (for example, Laidler and Bentley 1983 for the US and Laidler et al. 1983 for Canada) and hence is not explicitly modelled, whereas for the UK (Davidson 1984) and Australia (Johnson and Trevor 1979) the money supply is determined by the financing of the public sector borrowing requirement. In some models of this type $\mathbf{M}_t^d$ is estimated using cointegration techniques and the residuals are viewed as disequilibrium money. The latter is then included as an additional variable in expenditure equations such as stockbuilding (Ireland and Wren-Lewis 1988) and non-durable consumption (Cuthbertson and Barlow 1991).

If the coefficients of long-run money demand are the investigator's parameters of interest, then the full systems approach has the drawback that any estimates of the latter are conditional on the correct specification of the whole model.

Shock absorber approaches

The third type of buffer stock model directly estimates the demand for money function, but it is assumed that shocks to the money supply are initially voluntarily held in transactions balances. The Carr-Darby (1981) version of this approach invokes the rational expectations hypothesis in that the monetary shock is the difference between actual money in circulation and the expected money supply. Some of these unanticipated balance $(m - m^a)_t$ are voluntarily held in money balances. On the other hand, anticipated changes in the money supply are immedialtely reflected in price expectations, and if prices are perfectly flexible then real money balances remain unchanged (Carr et al. 1985).

Carr and Darby (1981) report OLS estimates which appear to support the buffer stock or shock absorber hypothesis for a number of industrialized countries. However, see MacKinnon and Milbourne (1984) on US data.

Cuthbertson (1986b) using UK data finds that the shock absorber hypothesis is rejected using two-step estimation procedures. However, see Cuthbertson and Taylor (1988), who use a simple learning model and a Kalman filter to generate the m_t^a series and find evidence in favour of the Carr-Darby hypothesis.

Cuthbertson and Taylor (1986, 1988) note that, by using two-step methods, previous studies have neglected to test for the cross-equation rationality restrictions implicit in the Carr-Darby shock absorber hypothesis, and only if these are data acceptable can we accept the Carr et al. (1985) estimates. Cuthbertson and Taylor (1986, 1988) are easily able to reject the implicit cross-equation rationality restrictions using US and UK data (identical to those used in Cuthbertson 1986b). Overall, therefore, the Carr-Darby model of buffer stock money (including the RE assumption) appears to be rejected by the data. However, see Browne (1989) for an interesting application of the shock absorber approach which eschews a role for expectations.

A forward-looking buffer stock model

In determining their planned money holdings, agents may be influenced by their expected level of transactions, and in addition may temporarily hold unanticipated increases in money which they will perceive as innovations in nominal income (rather than in the aggregate money supply). These intuitively plausible ideas may be formalized in a tractable way by assuming that agents determine their planned money balances by minimizing a multiperiod quadratic cost function. The solution to this problem is an exercise in the discrete-time calculus of variations (see, for example, Sargent 1979), and results in a forward-looking model of the form

$$m_t = \lambda_1 m_{t-1} + (1 - \lambda_1)(1 - \lambda_1 D) \sum_0^{\infty} (\lambda_1 D)^s E_{t-1} m^*_{t+s} \qquad (2.32)$$

where $E_{t-1} m^*_{t+s}$ are the expected values of future long-run money balances, and λ_1 depends on the adjustment cost parameters and the discount factor D in the cost function. The buffer stock element arises because agents make decisions concerning m_t based on information in period $t-1$, and hence surprise increases in nominal income are partly held as buffer money. Hence if the long-run demand function is given by

$$m^*_t = c_0 p_t + c_1 y_t - c_2 r_t = c' x_t \qquad (2.33)$$

the estimating equation is (see Cuthbertson 1988a)

$$m_t = \lambda_1 m_{t-1} + \gamma (p - p^e)_t + \beta (y - y^e)_t - \delta (r - r^e)_t$$

$$+ (1 - \lambda_1)(1 - \lambda_1 D) c' E_{t-1} \sum_0^{\infty} (\lambda_1 D)^s x^e{}_{t+s} + u_t \qquad (2.34)$$

where we assume that monetary innovations are a linear combination of innovations in prices, income and interest rates, plus a catch-all disturbance u_t. The testable predictions of the demand for money function are that the weights on the expected future variables x^e_{t+s} decline geometrically as the time horizon is extended - an intuitively plausible restriction - and that these weights are related to the coefficients on the lagged dependent variables; the latter are referred to as the backward–forward restrictions. By explicitly modelling the expectations process, we go some way towards meeting the Lucas (1976) critique. Conventional demand functions that estimate a convolution of expectations and adjustment lags (for example, partial adjustment and error feedback equations) may exhibit instability because of instability in the expectations generating process.

Following Kannianien and Tarkka (1986), Muscatelli (1988) provides a variant of the above model. The main additional feature is that costs of adjustment apply to non-money asset holdings $(A_{t+s} - A_{t+s-1})^2$ rather than to money. Planned short-run money balances depend on expected forcing variables x^e_{t+s} as in (2.34) but in addition on expected future levels of saving.

Cuthbertson (1988a) uses a two-step procedure to estimate (2.34) for UK M1, with alternative autoregressive (AR) and vector autoregressive (VAR) forecasting schemes for the x variables (i.e. p, y, r). His results are encouraging; the backward–forward restrictions hold and the equation has stable parameters, with long-run unit expected price and income elasticities accepted by the data[21] (see also Cuthbertson and Taylor 1989). The inclusion of savings in the model creates additional estimation problems and does not appear to add appreciably to the empirical performance and theoretical interpretability of the model (Muscatelli 1988). Cuthbertson and Taylor (1987c) test the implicit cross-equation rationality restrictions assuming (y_t, p_t, r_t) are generated by a VAR process; they find in favour for the RE restrictions of the UK M1 definition of money. Cuthbertson and Taylor (1990c) also test the forward model using the Campbell-Shiller (1987) methodology, and find support for it when using £M3 over the postwar period (see also Muscatelli 1989; Cuthbertson and Taylor 1990a). Bagliano and Favero 1989 for Italian M2 find tentative evidence that an expectations model performs better than an error correction or feedback model after the monetary policy regime change which occurred in 1969–70. Similarly Cuthbertson and Taylor (1990b) for US narrow money find that the missing money period may be rationalized in terms of an expectations model with a shift in the expectations generation equation (see also Dutkowsky and Foote 1988 on US data). Taylor (1990a) applies the model to UK broad money data for the period 1871–1913 and finds that the backward–forward rationality restrictions cannot be rejected.

5 SUMMARY AND CONCLUSIONS

A great deal of ingenuity and creativity has been applied to the study of the demand for assets, and in particular money. On the theoretical side the inventory and precautionary approaches have yielded useful qualitative insights into the determinants of the demand for money, but provide only broad guidelines for applied work using aggregate time series data. The mean-variance model is only applicable to the demand for a single capital safe asset and hence to a broad definition of money; empirically it has not proved very successful. The consumer theory approach provides a useful framework for analysing the demand for money since it implicitly recognizes the interdependent nature of asset decisions. It also yields reasonably tractable estimating equations with testable restrictions (e.g. symmetry, homogeneity and negativity). Work on separability and non-parametric tests of the axioms of consumer theory also complement this approach. From the standpoint of the applied economist it has much to commend it.

A major weakness of all *theories* of the demand for money is a grossly inadequate treatment of dynamic adjustment. This is not a criticism of theorists, for clearly the detailed and complex transactions, information and learning costs faced by the representative agent are inherently difficult to formalize. In the *econometric modelling* of dynamic adjustment perhaps the main advance has been in the error correction model (ECM), and it is surprising that until recently this has been largely ignored in the US applied literature. Most US applied economists appear content to work within the highly restrictive partial adjustment framework (e.g. the survey by Roley 1985). Certainly one has to apply the general to specific and error feedback approach with due regard for theory consistency and plausible decision variables if one is to avoid the charge of data mining. However, it does appear to provide a very useful approach to dynamic modelling, with the laudable aim of yielding stable parameter estimates and testing any tentative empirical model extremely thoroughly against both the data and other competing models.

The new literature on unit roots (Dickey and Fuller 1979; Phillips and Park 1986) and cointegration provides a useful framework for analysing long-run relationships and can be satisfactorily combined with the ECM approach. It is bound to yield further insights concerning the demand for money (Engle and Yoo 1987; Johansen 1988; Hendry 1986).

Empirical work which employs variability measures such as time-varying variances of receipts on time-varying risk premiums is in its infancy, and we might expect to see applications of say the ARCH model in future work. To date, evidence for time-varying risk premiums has come from inverted asset demand functions, that is with the asset price (interest rate) as the dependent variable, or more directly form reduced from asset price equations (e.g. uncovered interest parity). However, the latter evidence points strongly to the need to investigate such effects in asset demand functions.

The problem of the lagged dependent variable in estimated money demand functions is not in my view an acute one, as long as one accepts the view that money has, in the past, been largely endogenous (in quarterly data) and that *all* agents do not react instantaneously (in say quarterly data). Admittedly the lagged dependent variable could be picking up all kinds of misspecification (e.g. aggregation problems, badly measured variables, wrong functional form) and in particular over-restrictive lag response in the partial adjustment model. However, given the limitations of the available data, empirical results from error correction models seem to me to yield plausible equations in the main, and in particular median lag responses are not unreasonable. However, none of the above is inconsistent with Laidler's (1982) argument that *if* the money supply is rigidly controlled by the authorities, then *estimated* ECM-type money demand functions should not be inverted to yield a solution for the interest rate, the price level etc. Similarly, adopting the error correction interpretation of past behaviour does not rule out the possibility that agents use money (somehow defined) as a buffer asset which responds to unanticipated events, or that some agents might not always be on their *long-run* demand function for (broad) money as in complete disequilibrium money models.

Whether expectations about future transactions or future bond prices play an important role in determining the demand for money is rather an open question, on which we have relatively little evidence. Our techniques for modelling expectations variables in aggregate data are rather crude. Expectations equations which incorporate learning by agents perhaps have greater intuitive appeal than fixed coefficient reduced forms, but ultimately it is difficult to distinguish models that incorporate expectations from backward-looking demand for money equations (however, Hendry 1988 provides a useful test procedure, notwithstanding the arguments in Cuthbertson 1991). Agents may base today's money holdings on expected transactions but, because of the highly autoregressive nature of aggregate transactions variables, this becomes largely indistinguishable from a current period transactions variable. Evidence that the demand for money depends on expectations (of income or bond prices) is rather weak. It therefore follows that, strictly, the Lucas (1976) critique may not be an important factor in interpreting most money demand equations; structural shifts in estimated demand for money equations are likely to have been caused by factors other than changes in the way agents form expectations.

The buffer stock notion has been implemented in a number of guises. To claim that surprises in nominal income and interest rates may result in changes in money balances seems largely uncontentious. First-difference terms in error feedback equations may act as proxy variables for such surprises. Modelling the impact of surprises is difficult but, as far as narrow money (M1) is concerned, such effects appear to be relatively small. The Carr-Darby shock absorber model does not appear to be a sensible way of modelling buffer stock effects, and certainly the rational expectations element of the hypothesis does not hold. For narrow money (e.g. M1) it is difficult to imagine agents being in prolonged disequilibrium since transactions costs in switching between M1 and other capital certain assets are relatively low. For broader monetary aggregates, and given general uncertainty, one can certainly entertain the possibility of disequilibrium money leading to changes in other economic variables. Complete disequilibrium models which use broad money are therefore useful in interpreting aspects of the transmission mechanism but are not the ideal vehicle for analysing the long-run demand for money. However, cointegration in systems of equations (Davidson and Hall 1988) may provide further insights into such models; disequilibrium in long-run money balances may lead to changes in short-run money holdings and in other variables such as prices and interest rates.

Financial innovation is clearly an important factor in influencing the demand for money. With financial innovation, the definition of what constitutes money becomes blurred. New financial instruments and the changes in transactions and information costs (widely defined) create acute problems in finding a stable demand for money function. It is quite remarkable in the face of such changes that we can still claim to know a great deal about the past behaviour of narrow and even broad money. Prediction of course is more hazardous, since it is difficult to forecast technological and institutional change.

Work on the demand for money has yielded reasonably satisfactory explanations of the past behaviour of the demand for narrow money for a number of industrialized nations (and in the US for broad money M2). This is despite the paucity of high-quality data, the major changes in economic variables and the pace of financial innovation. Recent advances have been made possible by new econometric approaches rather than new theory models. Less success has been achieved with the broader aggregates in the UK. Over the past decade financial markets and government policy have undergone substantial changes; yet applied monetary economists have managed to utilize economic theory and best-practice econometrics to considerably enhance our knowledge of the behaviour of the demand for money.

Notes

The authors are grateful to Mark Taylor for comments and suggestions on an earlier draft of this chapter, although the usual disclaimer applies.

1 We have therefore chosen to omit discussion of the legal restrictions theory of money (e.g. Wallace 1988; Hall 1982; Sargent and Wallace 1982) and cash in advance models (e.g. Lucas 1984; Hartley 1988) because they do not feature prominently in the applied literature. For a recent clear perspective on these and

other ideas in the 'new monetary economics' see Laidler (1988).

2 This distinction between the motives approach and the consumer theory approach is used for expositional purposes. Clearly, the underlying idea behind all of these models is that money yields utility in the general sense of the word, but consumer theory 'deliberately avoids any analysis of motivation and simply applies generalized notions about the determination of the demand for any good to the demand for money' (Laidler 1985). Barnett (1980) also applies this distinction.

3 Milbourne (1983b) provides an elegant synthesis of target threshold models, and demonstrates that Baumol-Tobin type inventory models may be viewed as special cases of the more general target threshold models (i.e. the Baumol-Tobin models have a fixed lower threshold and a non-stochastic cash inflow). However, for expositional purposes we have retained the distinction between inventory and precautionary models.

4 The result is based on Chebyshev's inequality. This states that the probability p of a variable x (net payments) deviating from its mean by t times its standard deviation σ is equal to or less than $1/t^2$; that is, $p(-t\sigma > x > t\sigma) \leq 1/t^2$. Net payments are assumed to have a zero mean, so the probability of net payments equal to M which is $M/\sigma = t$ standard deviations from zero is $p(N > M) \leq 1/t^2 = \sigma^2/M^2$.

5 Aggregation over risky assets is possible for any utility function for which the marginal utility of wealth is isoelastic in a linear function of wealth (Cass and Stiglitz 1972); the quadratic and negative exponential satisfy this property.

6 Tsiang (1972) argues that all we require for a second-order Taylor expansion around expected wealth to be a valid approximation to an acceptable utility function is that risk should remain small *relative to* the individual's total wealth.

7 Courakis (1988b) demonstrates the issues involved in extending the mean-variance approach when the maximand involves expected terminal *real* wealth. For the negative exponential, asset demands are not independent of the expected rate of price inflation (even though the zero row-sum condition holds), but for the power function the converse is the case.

8 This model is then usually interpreted as a version of a static capital asset pricing model (CAPM).

9 Varian (1983) provides formal non-parametric tests of separability, although these have not as yet been widely applied in the asset demand literature.

10 This also raises the question of aggregation over monetary assets. Consumer theory can be used to construct appropriate Divisia monetary aggregates (rather than simple sum aggregates). Space precludes discussion of the theoretical basis of Divisia aggregates (Barnett 1980; Barnett et al. 1984) but we do discuss empirical results using Divisia aggregates later in the chapter. Merton (1973), Diewert (1974) and Barnett (1980) examine the assumptions whereby the intertemporal maximization problem may be reduced to a single-period optimization problem.

11 Other popular functional forms for the direct and indirect utility functions are the translog (Christensen et al. 1975) and the generalized constant elasticity of substitution (GCES) (Chetty 1969). Space precludes a discussion of the relative

merits of the wide class of functional forms available.

12 Milbourne (1985), utilizing the Miller-Orr model, argues that average *quarterly* money holdings due to an unanticipated increase in exogenous money are likely to be relatively small for a narrow definition of money (e.g. M1). This provides a strong case for abandoning the Miller-Orr model as the basis for buffer stock ideas for M1. But note that Milbourne's results are weakened if (a) we use point-in-time money stock data; (b) different agents receive additional balances sequentially; (c) agents do not continuously monitor M1 balances because of time costs of information gathering; and (d) agents face generalized uncertainty and hence an ill-defined probability distribution. Assumptions (c) and (d) would of course violate the assumptions of the Miller-Orr model. See Laidler (1988) for a discussion of the importance of the precautionary demand for money in analysing the transmission mechanism, and in particular of how information costs and interest rates may interact to alter the distribution of cash flows in the Miller-Orr model.

13 For an interesting theoretically based adjustment model within the framework of the precautionary demand for money, see Milbourne et al. (1983) and Smith (1986). In these models the adjustment speed depends on a complex function of the mean and variance of net receipts, interest rate and brokerage fee; lagged money explicitly appears in the demand function. This approach has not been adopted in empirical work.

14 In practice, such costs are likely to be lump sum in the main. But search and information costs concerning the terms offered on non-money assets are likely to be very complex.

15 Friedman's (1979) optimal partial adjustment model is of the interdependent error feedback form.

16 For example, suppose the true model is *static* with an AR(1) error:

$$\mathbf{y}_t = \beta \mathbf{x}_t + \mathbf{u}_t \tag{2.35}$$

$$\mathbf{u}_t = \rho \mathbf{u}_{t-1} + \epsilon_t \tag{2.36}$$

These equations imply

$$\mathbf{y}_t = \boldsymbol{\pi}_0 \mathbf{x}_t + \boldsymbol{\pi}_1 \mathbf{x}_{t-1} + \boldsymbol{\pi}_2 \mathbf{y}_{t-1} + \epsilon_t \tag{2.37}$$

$$\boldsymbol{\pi}_0 = \beta, \quad \boldsymbol{\pi}_1 = -\beta\rho, \quad \boldsymbol{\pi}_2 = \rho$$

If we have an AR(1) error then in (2.37) the following common factor restriction holds: $(\boldsymbol{\pi}_1/\boldsymbol{\pi}_0) = -\boldsymbol{\pi}_2$. Hence if the $\boldsymbol{\pi}_i$ are statistically significant in (2.37) but the common factor restriction does *not* hold, we have a dynamic model; if the common factor restriction holds, we have the static model (2.35) (with an AR(1) error).

17 Note that in the presence of unit root I(1) series, inference may be hazardous in either the cointegration or the error correction formulation. Theoretical results from the unit root literature do not yet provide definitive answers to some of these inference problems (see, for example, West 1988; Banerjee et al. 1986; Phillips and Park 1986).

18 First-order adaptive expectations $\mathbf{x}_t^e - \mathbf{x}_{t-1}^e = \lambda(\mathbf{x}_{t-1} - \mathbf{x}_{t-1}^e)$ is only optimal if $\mathbf{x}_t$ is IMA(1,1); this is a property of numerous economic time series (Granger 1966).

19 Particularly with the rapid pace of financial liberalization, 'new' definitions of money frequently appear. In what follows we avoid the nuances of the various changes in definition that have occurred. In the UK major changes in definition have recently taken place and £M3 and M3 are no longer to be published (*Bank of England Quarterly Bulletin*, 29(3), August 1989, 352–3). However, in our discussion of the empirical work on UK broad money the reader will not be misled if he considers M3 and £M3 as synonymous.

20 'Round tripping' refers to the practice of borrowing on bank advances and redepositing the proceeds in wholesale deposits. The Sprenkle-Miller (1980) model indicates that this depends on the wholesale deposit to bank advance rate differential, even when this is non-positive.

21 Hendry (1988) demonstrates that if (a) a feedback ECM model for M1 is stable and (b) the AR and VAR forecasting schemes are unstable, then this implies rejection of the forward-looking model. Cuthbertson (1991) argues that one can only rescue the forward model either by searching for a stable (extended) VAR or by establishing that the feedback model is unstable (on the latter see Cuthbertson and Taylor 1990a; Hall et al. 1989). Note that in the face of (a) and (b), Hendry (1988) and Cuthbertson (1991) agree that instrumental variables (IV) estimation of the *structural* forward model (e.g. Hansen and Sargent 1982) is invalid. Hendry's (1988) article also has a bearing on Goodfriend's (1985) proposition (see also Grether and Maddala 1973) that a true *static* money demand function with serially correlated true income and interest rate variables which are subject to *measurement error* is consistent with an *estimated* model with *measured* income and interest rates and a significant lagged money variable (i.e. partial adjustment). Goodfriend's argument has, to our knowledge, not been examined empirically, but it can be cast in the Hendry (1988) framework since measurement error is the basis of weakly rational IV estimation procedures for expectations variables. Thus if Hendry's (a) holds for any (ADL) feedback money demand equation but auxiliary equations for the measurement error variables are non-constant, then this would discriminate between Goodfriend's static model with measurement errors and a dynamic model. However, unless a stochastic process for the form of the measurement error can be formulated, Goodfriend's assertion is untestable. Note also that as long as measurement errors are I(0) rather than I(1) then the parameter estimates from a cointegrating money demand equation are superconsistent (Cuthbertson and Taylor 1990d).

References

Abel, A., Dornbusch, R., Huizinga, J. and Marcus, A. (1979) 'Money demand during hyperinflation', *Journal of Monetary Economics*, 5, 97–104.

Abel, A. and Mishkin, F. S. (1983) 'An integrated view of tests of rationality, market efficiency, and the short-run neutrality of monetary policy', *Journal of Monetary Economics*, 11, 3–24.

Akerlof, G. A. and Milbourne, R. D. (1980) 'The short-run demand for money', *Economic Journal*, 90 (360), 885–900.

Anderson, G. J. and Blundell, R. W. (1982) 'Estimation and hypothesis testing in dynamic singular equation systems', *Econometrica*, 50 (6), 1559–71.

Arango, S. and Nadiri, M. I. (1981) 'Demand for money in open economies', *Journal of Monetary Economics*, 7 (1), 69–83.

Artis, M. J. and Lewis, M. K. (1976) 'The demand for money in the UK 1963–73', *The Manchester School*, 44, 147–81.

Artis, M. J. and Lewis, M. K. (1981) *Monetary Control in the UK*, Oxford: Philip Allan.

Artis, M. J. and Lewis, M. K. (1984) 'How unstable is the demand for money in the United Kingdom?', *Economica*, 51, 473–6.

Baba, Y., Hendry, D. F. and Starr, R. M. (1988) 'US money demand 1960–1984', Nuffield College, Oxford, discussion paper 27.

Bagliano, F. C. and Favero, G. A. (1989) 'Money demand instability, expectations and policy regimes: the case of Italy 1964–86', St Antony's College, Oxford, mimeo.

Banerjee, A., Dolado, J., Hendry, D. and Smith, G. (1986) 'Exploring equilibrium relationships in econometrics through static models: some Monte Carlo evidence', *Oxford Bulletin of Economics and Statistics*, 48 (3), 253–78.

Barnett, W. A. (1980) 'Economic monetary aggregates: an application of index number and aggregation theory', *Journal of Econometrics*, 14 (1), 11–48.

Barnett, W. A., Offenbacher, E. K. and Spindt, P. A. (1984) 'The new Divisia monetary aggregates', *Journal of Political Economy*, 92 (6), 1049–85.

Barr, D. G. and Cuthbertson, K. (1990) 'Modelling the flow of funds', in S.G.B. Henry and K. Patterson (eds) *Economic Modelling at the Bank of England*, Chapman and Hall.

Barr, D. G. and Cuthbertson, K. (1991) 'Neoclassical Consumer Demand Theory and the Demand for Money, forthcoming. *Economic Journal*.

Barr, D. G. and Cuthbertson, K. (1989a) 'An interdependent error feedback model of UK company sector asset demands', Bank of England, discussion paper, technical series.

Barr, D. G. and Cuthbertson, K. (1989b) 'A data based simulation model of the financial asset decisions of UK "other" financial intermediaries', Bank of England, discussion paper, technical series.

Barr, D. G. and Cuthbertson, K. (1989c) 'The demand for financial assets held in the UK by the overseas sector: an application of two-stage budgeting', Bank of England, discussion paper, technical series.

Barratt, C. R. and Walters, A. A. (1966) 'The stability of Keynesian and money multipliers in the UK', *Review of Economics and Statistics*, 48, 395–405.

Barro, R. J. (1970) 'Inflation, the payments period and the demand for money', *Journal of Political Economy*, 78 (6), 1228–63.

Barro, R. J. (1976) 'Integral constraints and aggregation in an inventory model of money demand', *Journal of Finance*, 31 (1), 77–88.

Barro, R. J. and Santomero, A. M. (1972) 'Household money holdings and the demand deposit rates', *Journal of Money, Credit and Banking*, 4, 397–413.

Baumol, W. J. (1952) 'The transactions demand for cash: an inventory theoretic approach', *Quarterly Journal of Economics*, 66, 545–56.

Bollerslev, T., Engle, R. F. and Wooldridge, J. M. (1988) 'A capital asset pricing model with time-varying covariances', *Journal of Political Economy*, 96 (1), 116–31.

Borch, K. (1969) 'A note on uncertainty and indifference curves', *Review of Economic Studies*, 36, 1–4.

Bordo, M. D. and Jonung, L. (1987) *The Long Run Behaviour of the Velocity of Circulation: The International Evidence*, Cambridge: Cambridge University Press.

Boughton, J. M. (1981) 'Recent instability of the demand for money: an international perspective', *Southern Economic Journal*, 47 (3), 579–97.

Brainard, W. C. and Tobin, J. (1968) 'Econometric models: their problems and usefulness: pitfalls in financial model building', *American Economic Review*, 58, 12–87.

Browne, F. X. (1989) 'A new test of the buffer stock money hypothesis', *The Manchester School*, 57, 2, 154–71.

Brunner, K. and Meltzer, A. H. (1963) 'Predicting velocity implications for theory and policy', *Journal of Finance*, 18, 319–54.

Cagan, P. (1956) 'The monetary dynamics of hyperinflation', in M. Friedman (ed.), *Studies in the Quantity Theory of Money*, Chicago: University of Chicago Press.

Campbell, J. Y. and Shiller, R. J. (1987) 'Cointegration and tests of present value models', *Journal of Political Economy*, 95, 1062–88.

Carr, J. and Darby, M. R. (1981) 'The role of money supply shocks in the short-run demand for money', *Journal of Monetary Economics*, 8 (2), 183–200.

Carr, J., Darby, M. R. and Thornton, D. (1985) 'Monetary anticipations and the demand for money: reply to MacKinnon and Milbourne', *Journal of Monetary Economics*, 16, 251–7.

Cass, D. and Stiglitz, J. E. (1972) 'Risk aversion wealth effects on portfolios with many assets', *Review of Economic Studies*, July, 331–53.

Chang, W. W., Hamberg, D. and Hirata, J. (1983) 'Liquidity preference as behaviour toward risk in a demand for short-term securities – not money', *American Economic Review*, 73, 420–7.

Chang, W. W., Hamberg, D. and Hirata, J. (1984) 'On liquidity preference again: reply', *American Economic Review*, 74 (4), 812–13.

Chetty, V. K. (1969) 'On measuring the nearness of near-moneys', *American Economic Review*, 59, 270–81.

Christensen, L. R., Jorgenson, D. W. and Lau, L. J. (1975) 'Transcendental logarithmic utility functions', *American Economic Review*, 65, 367–83.

Christophedes, L. N. (1976) 'Quadratic costs and multi-asset partial adjustment equations', *Applied Economics*, 8 (4), 301–5.

Coughlan, R. T. (1978) 'A transactions demand for money', *Bank of England Quarterly Bulletin*, 18 (March), 48–60.

Courakis, A. S. (1988a) 'Modelling portfolio selection', *Economic Journal*, 98, 619–42.

Courakis, A. S. (1988b) 'Anticipated inflation and portfolio selection', Institute of Economics and Statistics, Oxford, discussion paper 65.

Courakis, A. S. (1989) 'Does constant relative risk aversion imply asset demands?', Institute of Economics and Statistics, Oxford, discussion paper 78.

Cover, J. P. and Keeler, J. P. (1987) 'Estimating money demand in log-first-difference form', *Southern Economic Journal*, 53 (3), 751–67.

Cumby, R. E., Huizinga, J. and Obstfeld, M. (1983) 'Two-step two-stage least squares estimation in models with rational expectations', *Journal of Econometrics*, 21, 333–55.

Currie, D. and Kennally, G. (1985) 'Personal sector demands for liquid deposits', National Institute of Economic and Social Research, discussion paper.

Cuthbertson, K. (1986a) 'Price expectations and lags in the demand for money', *Scottish Journal of Political Economy*, 33 (4), 334–54.

Cuthbertson, K. (1986b) 'Monetary anticipations and the demand for money in the UK', *Bulletin of Economic Research*, 38, 257–70.

Cuthbertson, K. (1988a) 'The demand for M1: a forward looking buffer stock model', *Oxford Economic Papers*, 40, 110–31.

Cuthbertson, K. (1988b) 'Economics, expectations and the Kalman filter', *The Manchester School*, 56 (3), 223–46.

Cuthbertson, K. (1991) 'The encompassing implications of feedforward versus feedback mechanisms: a reply to Hendry', *Oxford Economic Papers*, forthcoming.

Cuthbertson, K. and Barlow, D. (1991) 'Disequilibrium, buffer-stocks and consumers' expenditure on non-durables', Review of Economics and Statistics, forthcoming.

Cuthbertson, K. and Barlow, D. (1990) 'The determination of liquid asset holdings of the UK personal sector', *The Manchester School*, LVIII (4), 348–60.

Cuthbertson, K. and Taylor, M. P. (1986) 'Monetary anticipations and the demand for money in the UK: testing rationality in the shock absorber hypothesis', *Journal of Applied Econometrics*, 1 (20), 1–11.

Cuthbertson, K. and Taylor, M. P. (1987a) *Macroeconomic Systems*, Oxford: Basil Blackwell.

Cuthbertson, K. and Taylor, M. P. (1987b) 'Monetary anticipations and the demand for money: some evidence for the UK', *Weltwirtschafliches Archiv*, 183, 509–20.

Cuthbertson, K. and Taylor, M. P. (1987c) 'The demand for money: a dynamic rational expectations model', *Economic Journal*, 97 (supplement), 65–76.

Cuthbertson, K. and Taylor, M. P. (1987d) 'Buffer stock money: an appraisal', in C. A. E. Goodhart, D. Currie and D. T. Llewellyn (eds), *The Operation and Regulation of Financial Markets*, London: Macmillan.

Cuthbertson, K. and Taylor, M. P. (1988) 'Monetary anticipations and the Demand for money in the US: further tests', *Southern Economic Journal*, 55 (2), 326–55.

Cuthbertson, K. and Taylor, M. P. (1989) 'Anticipated and unanticipated variables in the demand for M1 in the UK', *The Manchester School*, 57 (4), 319–39.

Cuthbertson, K. and Taylor, M. P. (1990a) 'The demand for M1: forward and backward looking models', *The Manchester School*, forthcoming.

Cuthbertson, K. and Taylor, M. P. (1990b) 'On the short-run demand for money: the case of the missing money; and the Lucas critique', *Journal of Macroeconomics*, forthcoming.

Cuthbertson, K. and Taylor, M. P. (1990c) 'Money demand, expectations and the

forward looking model', *Journal of Policy Modelling*, 12, 289–315.
Cuthbertson, K. and Taylor, M. P. (1990d) 'Money demand, expectations and the forward looking model: reply to Goodfriend', *Journal of Policy Modelling*, forthcoming.
Dalal, A. J. (1983) 'Comparative statics and asset substitutability/complementarity in a portfolio model: a dual approach', *Review of Economic Studies*, 50, 355–67.
Davidson, J. (1984) 'Monetary disequilibrium: an approach to modelling monetary phenomena in the UK', London School of Economics, mimeo.
Davidson, J. and Hall, S. G. (1988) 'Cointegration in recursive systems: the structure of wage and price determination in the United Kingdom', Bank of England, mimeo.
Deaton, A. and Muellbauer, J. (1980) *Economics and Consumer Behaviour*, Cambridge: Cambridge University Press.
Dickey, D. A. and Fuller, W. A. (1979) 'Distribution of the estimators for autoregressive time series with a unit root', *Journal of American Statistical Association*, 74, 427–31.
Diewert, W. E. (1974) 'Intertemporal consumer theory and the demand for durables', *Econometrica*, 42 (3), 497–516.
Donovan, D. J. (1978) 'Modelling the demand for liquid assets: an application to Canada', *IMF Staff Papers*, 25, 676–704.
Dotsey, M. (1988) 'The demand for currency in the United States', *Journal of Money, Credit and Banking*, 20 (1), 22–40.
Dutkowsky, D. H. and Foote, W. G. (1988) 'The demand for money: a rational expectations approach', *Review of Economics and Statistics*, 70 (1), 83–92.
Engel, C. and Rodrigues, A. P. (1987) 'Tests of the international CAPM with time-varying covariances', National Bureau of Economic Research working paper 2303.
Engle, R. F. (1982) 'Autoregressive conditional heteroscedasticity with estimates of the variance of UK inflation', *Econometrica*, 50, 987–1008.
Engle, R. F. and Granger, C. W. J. (1987) 'Cointegration and error correction: representation, estimation and testing', *Econometrica*, 55, 251–76.
Engle, R. F., Lilien, D. M. and Robbins, R. P. (1987) 'Estimating time-varying risk premia in the term structure', *Econometrica*, 55, 391–407.
Engle, R. F. and Yoo, S. B. (1987) 'Forecasting and testing in cointegrated systems', *Journal of Econometrics*, 35, 143–59.
Ewis, N. A. and Fisher, D. (1984) 'The translog utility function and the demand for money in the United States', *Journal of Money, Credit and Banking*, 16 (1), 34–52.
Feige, E. L. (1967) 'Expectations and adjustments in the monetary sector', *American Economic Review*, 57, 462–73.
Feige, E. L. and Parkin, J. M. (1971) 'The optimal quantity of money bonds, commodity inventories and capital', *American Economic Review*, 61 (3), 335–49.
Feige, E. L. and Pearce, D. K. (1977) 'The substitutability of money and near-monies: a survey of the time series evidence', *Journal of Economic Literature*, 15, 439–69.
Feldstein, M. S. (1969) 'Mean-variance analysis in the theory of liquidity preference

and portfolio selection', *Review of Economic Studies*, 36, 5–12.
Fisher, I. (1911) *The Purchasing Power of Money*, New York: Macmillan.
Friedman, B. M. (1979) 'Substitution and expectation effects on long-term borrowing behaviour and long-term interest rates', *Journal of Money, Credit and Banking*, 11 (2), 131–50.
Friedman, M. (1956) 'The quantity theory of money: a restatement', in M. Friedman (ed.), *Studies in the Quantity Theory of Money*, Chicago: University of Chicago Press.
Friedman, M. and Schwartz, A. J. (1982) *Monetary trends in the United States and the United Kingdom: their relationship to income, prices and interest rates 1867*–1975, Chicago: University of Chicago Press.
Giovannini, A. and Jorion, P. (1987) 'Interest rates and risk premia in the stock markets and in the foreign exchange market', *Journal of International Money and Finance*, 6, 107–23.
Giovannini, A. and Jorion, P. (1988) 'The time variation of risk and return in the foreign exchange and stock markets', Centre for Economic Policy Research, discussion paper 228.
Goldfeld, S. M. (1976) 'The case of the missing money', *Brookings Papers on Economic Activity*, 1, 683–739.
Goodfriend, M. (1985) 'Reinterpreting money demand regressions', in K. Brunner and A. H. Meltzer (eds), *Understanding Monetary Regimes*, Carnegie-Rochester Conference Series on Public Policy, vol. 22, Amsterdam: North-Holland.
Goodhart, C. A. E. (1984) *Monetary Theory and Practice: The UK Experience*, London: Macmillan.
Gordon, R. J. (1984) 'The short-run demand for money: a reconsideration', *Journal of Money, Credit and Banking*, 16 (4), 403–34.
Granger, C. W. J. (1966) 'The typical spectral shape of an economic variable', *Econometrica*, 34 (1), 150–61.
Granger, C. W. J. (1986) 'Developments in the study of co-integrated economic variables', *Oxford Bulletin of Economics and Statistics*, 48 (3), 213–28.
Grether, D. M. and Madala, G. S. (1973) 'Errors in variables and serially correlated disturbances in distributed lag models', *Econometrica*, 41 (2), 225–62.
Grice, J. and Bennett, A. (1984) 'Wealth and the demand for £M3 in the United Kingdom 1963–1978', *The Manchester School*, 52 (3), 239–71.
Grossman, H. I. and Policano, A. J. (1975) 'Money balances, commodity inventories and inflationary expectations', *Journal of Political Economy*, 83 (6), 1093–112.
Haache, G. (1974) 'The demand for money in the UK: experience since 1971', *Bank of England Quarterly Bulletin*, 14 (3), 284–305.
Hafer, R. W. and Hein, S. E. (1979) 'Evidence on the temporal stability of the demand for money relationship in the United States', *Federal Reserve Bank of St Louis Review*, 61 (2), 3–14.
Hall, R. (1982) 'Monetary trends in the United States and the United Kingdom: a review from the perspective of the new developments in monetary economics', *Journal of Economic Literature*, 20, 1552–5.
Hall, S. G., Henry, S. G. B. and Wilcox, J. (1989) 'The long run determination of the UK monetary aggregates', Bank of England, mimeo.

Hamberger, M. J. (1966) 'The demand for money by households, money substitutes and monetary policy', *Journal of Political Economy*, 74, 600–23.

Hamberger, M. J. (1977) 'The behaviour of the money stock: is there a puzzle?', *Journal of Monetary Economics*, 3, 265–88.

Hamberger, M. J. (1980) 'The demand for money in the United States: a comment', in K. Brunner and A. H. Meltzer (eds), *On the State of Macroeconomics*, Carnegie-Rochester Conference Series on Public Policy, vol. 12, Amsterdam: North-Holland, 273–85.

Hansen, L. P. (1982) 'Large sample properties of generalised method of moments estimators', *Econometrica*, 50, 1029–54.

Hansen, L. P. and Sargent, T. J. (1982) 'Instrumental variables procedures for estimating linear rational expectations models', *Journal of Monetary Economics*, 9, 263–96.

Hartley, P. (1988) 'The liquidity services of money', *International Economic Review*, 29, 1–24.

Harvey, A. C. (1981a) *Time Series Models*, Oxford: Phillip Allan.

Harvey, A. C. (1981b) *The Econometric Analysis of Time Series*, Oxford: Phillip Allan.

Hayashi, F. and Sims, C. (1983) 'Nearly efficient estimation of time series models with predetermined but not exogenous instruments', *Econometrica*, 51, 783–98.

Hendry, D. F. (1979) 'Predictive failure and econometric modelling in macroeconomics: the transactions demand for money', in P. Omerod (ed.), *Economic Modelling*, London: Heinemann.

Hendry, D. F. (1983) 'Econometric modelling: the consumption function in retrospect', *Scottish Journal of Political Economy*, 30 (3), 193–200.

Hendry, D. F. (1985) 'Monetary economic myth and econometric reality', *Oxford Review of Economic Policy*, Oxford: Oxford University Press.

Hendry, D. F. (1986) 'Econometric modelling with cointegrated economic variables: an overview', *Oxford Bulletin of Economics and Statistics*, 48 (3), 201–12.

Hendry, D. F. (1988) 'The encompassing implications of feedforward versus feedback mechanisms in econometrics', *Oxford Economic Papers*, 40, 132–9.

Hendry, D. F. (1989) 'PC-GIVE: an interactive econometric modelling system', Institute of Economics and Statistics, Oxford.

Hendry, D. F. and Ericsson, N. R. (1983) 'Assertion without empirical basis: an econometric appraisal of Friedman and Schwartz, *Monetary Trends in . . . the United Kingdom*', Bank of England, Panel of Academic Consultants, paper 22.

Hendry, D. F. and Ericsson, N. R. (1988) 'An econometric analysis of UK money demand in *Monetary Trends in the United States and the United Kingdom* by Milton Friedman and Anna J. Schwartz', Nuffield College, Oxford, mimeo.

Hendry, D. F. and Mizon, G. E. (1978) 'Serial correlation as a convenient simplification, not a nuisance: a comment on a study of the demand for money by the Bank of England', *Economic Journal*, 88, 549–63.

Hendry, D. F., Pagan, A. R. and Sargan, J. D. (1984) 'Dynamic specification', in Z. Griliches and M. D. Intriligator (eds), *Handbook of Econometrics*, vol. 2, Amsterdam: North-Holland.

Hendry, D. F. and von Ungern Sternberg, T. (1983) 'Liquidity and inflation effects on consumers' expenditure', in A. Deaton (ed.), *Essays in the Theory and Measurement of Consumers' Behaviour*, Princeton, NJ: Princeton University Press.

Hilliard, B. C. (1980) 'The Bank of England, small monetary model: recent developments and simulation properties', Bank of England, discussion paper 13.

Hood, W. (1987) 'The allocation of UK personal sector liquid assets', HM Treasury, Government Economic Service, working paper 94.

Ireland, J. and Wren-Lewis, S. (1988) 'Buffer stock money and the company sector', National Institute of Economic and Social Research, discussion paper.

Johansen, S. (1988) 'Statistical analysis of cointegration vectors', *Journal of Economic Dynamics and Control*, 12 (2/3), 231–54.

Johnston, R. B. (1984) 'The demand for non-interest bearing money in the United Kingdom', HM Treasury, Government Economic Service, working paper 66.

Johnston, R. B. (1985) 'The demand for liquidity aggregates by the UK personal sector', HM Treasury, Government Economic Service, working paper 81.

Jonson, P. D. and Trevor, R. (1979) 'Monetary rules: a preliminary analysis', Reserve Bank of Australia, discussion paper 7903.

Judd, J. P. and Scadding, T. (1982) 'The search for a stable demand for money function', *Journal of Economic Literature*, 20 (3), 993–1023.

Kahnianien, V. and Tarkka, J. (1986) 'On the shock-absorber view of money: international evidence from the 1960s and 1970s', *Applied Economics*, 18, 1085–101.

Karni, E. (1974) 'The value of time and the demand for money', *Journal of Money, Credit and Banking*, 6, 45–64.

Keating, G. (1985) 'The financial sector of the London Business School model', in D. Currie (ed.), *Advances in Monetary Economics*, London: Croom-Helm.

Keynes, J. M. (1936) *The General Theory of Employment, Interest and Money*, London: Macmillan.

Klein, B. (1974a) 'The competitive supply of money', *Journal of Money, Credit and Banking*, 6, 423–54.

Klein, B. (1974b) 'Competitive interest payments on bank deposits and the long-run demand for money', *American Economic Review*, 64, 931–49.

Laidler, D. E. W. (1966) 'The role of interest rates and the demand for money – some empirical evidence', *Journal of Political Economy*, 74, 545–55.

Laidler, D. E. W. (1971) 'The influence of money on economic activity: a survey of some current problems', in G. Clayton, J. C. Gilbert and R. Sedgwick (eds), *Monetary Theory and Policy in the 1970s*, Oxford: Oxford University Press.

Laidler, D. E. W. (1980) 'The demand for money in the United States – yet again', in K. Brunner and A. H. Meltzer (eds), *On the State of Macroeconomics*, Carnegie-Rochester Conference Series on Public Policy, vol. 12, Amsterdam: North-Holland.

Laidler, D. E. W. (1982) *Monetarist Perspectives*, Oxford: Phillip Allan.

Laidler, D. E. W. (1984) 'The buffer stock notion in monetary economics', *Economic Journal*, 94 (supplement), 17–34.

Laidler, D. E. W. (1985) *The Demand for Money: Theories, Evidence and Problems*, 3rd edn, New York: Harper and Row.

Laidler, D. E. W. (1988) 'Presidential address: taking money seriously', *Canadian Journal of Economics*, 21, 4, 687–713.

Laidler, D. E. W. and Bentley, B. (1983) 'A small macro-model of the post-war United States', *The Manchester School*, 51 (4), 317–40.

Laidler, D. E. W., Bentley, B., Johnson, D. and Johnson, S. T. (1983) 'A small macroeconomic model of an open economy: the case of Canada', in E. Claasen and P. Salin (eds), *Recent Issues in the Theory of Flexible Exchange Rates*, Amsterdam: North-Holland.

Laidler, D. E. W. and O'Shea, P. (1980) 'An empirical macromodel of an open economy under fixed exchange rates: the UK, 1954–70', *Economica*, 47, 141–58.

Laidler, D. E. W. and Parkin, J. M. (1970) 'The demand for money in the United Kingdom 1956–1967: some preliminary estimates', *The Manchester School*, 38, 187–208.

Lawson, N. (1986) 'Monetary policy', Lombard Association Speech, HM Treasury Press Release, 16 April.

Lee, T. H. (1967) 'Alternative interest rates and the demand for money: the empirical evidence', *American Economic Review*, 57, 1168–81.

Lee, T. H. (1969) 'Alternative interest rates and the demand for money: reply', *American Economic Review*, 59, 412–17.

Lindsey, D. E. and Spindt, P. (1986) 'An evaluation of monetary indices' Federal Reserve Board, Division of Research and Statistics, Special Studies Paper No 195 (March).

Longbottom, A. and Holly, S. (1985) 'Econometric methodology and monetarism: Professor Friedman and Professor Hendry on the demand for money', London Business School EFU, discussion paper 131.

Lucas, R. E. Jr (1976) 'Econometric policy evaluation: a critique in the Phillips curve and labour markets', in Carnegie-Rochester Conference Series on Public Policy, vol. 1, Amsterdam: North-Holland, 19–46.

Lucas, R. E. Jr (1984) 'Money in a theory of finance', in K. Brunner and A. H. Meltzer (eds), *Essays on Macroeconomic Implications of Financial and Labour Markets and Political Processes*, Carnegie-Rochester Conference Series on Public Policy, vol. 21, Amsterdam: North-Holland.

McCallum, B. T. (1976) 'Rational expectations and the estimation of econometric models: an alternative procedure', *International Economic Review*, 17, 484–90.

MacKinnon, J. G. and Milbourne, R. D. (1984) 'Monetary anticipations and the demand for money', *Journal of Monetary Economics*, 13, 263–74.

MacKinnon, J. G. and Milbourne, R. D. (1988) 'Are price equations really money demand equations on their heads?', *Journal of Applied Econometrics*, 3, 295–305.

Markowitz, H. (1952) 'Portfolio selection', *Journal of Finance*, 7, 77–91.

Markowitz, H. (1959) *Portfolio Selection: Efficient Diversification of Investment*, New York: Wiley.

Mayer, T. H. and Pearl, L. R. (1984) 'Life cycle effects, structural change and long-run movements in the velocity of money', *Journal of Money, Credit and Banking*, 160, 175–84.

Meltzer, A. H. (1963) 'The demand for money: the evidence from the time series', *Journal of Political Economy*, 71, 219–46.

Merton, R. C. (1973) 'An intertemporal asset pricing model', *Econometrica*, 41 (5), 867–89.

Milbourne, R. (1983a) 'Price expectations and the demand for money: resolution of a paradox', *Review of Economics and Statistics*, 65 (4), 633–8.

Milbourne, R. (1983b) 'Optimal money holding under uncertainty', *International Economic Review*, 24 (3), 685–98.

Milbourne, R. (1985) 'Distinguishing between Australian demand for money models', *Australian Economic Papers*, June, 154–68.

Milbourne, R. (1986) 'Financial innovation and the demand for liquid assets', *Journal of Money, Credit and Banking*, 18 (4), 506–11.

Milbourne, R. (1987) 'Re-examining the buffer stock model of money', *Economic Journal*, 97 (supplement), 130–42.

Milbourne, R. (1988) 'Disequilibrium buffer stock models: a survey', *Journal of Economic Surveys*, 2 (3), 187–208.

Milbourne, R. Buckholtz, P. and Wasan, N. T. (1983) 'A theoretical derivation of the functional form of short run money holdings', *Review of Economic Studies*, 50, 531–41.

Miller, M. and Orr, D. (1966) 'A model of the demand for money by firms', *Quarterly Journal of Economics*, 109, 68–72.

Miller, M. and Orr, D. (1968) 'The demand for money by firms: extension of analytic results', *Journal of Finance*, 23, 735–59.

Mills, T. C. (1983) 'The information content of UK monetary components and aggregates', *Bulletin of Economic Research*, 35 (1), 25–46.

Mishkin, F. S. (1983) *A Rational Expectations Approach to Macroeconometrics*, Chicago: Chicago University Press.

Muscatelli, V. A. (1988) 'Alternative models of buffer stock money: an empirical investigation', *Scottish Journal of Political Economy*, 35 (1), 1–21.

Muscatelli, V. A. (1989) 'A comparison of the rational expectations and general to specific approach to modelling the demand for M1', *Oxford Bulletin of Economics and Statistics*, forthcoming.

Muscatelli, V. A. and Papi, L. (1988) 'Cointegration and "general to specific": an example of the demand for money in Italy', University of Glasgow, mimeo.

Muth, J. F. (1961) 'Rational expectations and the theory of price movements', *Journal of Political Economy*, 29 (6). Reprinted in R. E. Lucas Jr and T. J. Sargent (eds) (1981), *Rational Expectations and Econometric Practice*, London: Allen and Unwin.

Nelson, C. R. (1975) 'Rational expectations and the estimation of econometric models', *International Economic Review*, 16, 555–61.

Nickell, S. (1985) 'Error correction, partial adjustment and all that: an expository note', *Oxford Bulletin of Economics and Statistics*, 47 (2), 119–30.

Offenbacher, E. and Porter, R. (1982) 'Update and extensions on econometric properties of selected monetary aggregates', Board of Governors of the Federal Reserve System, mimeo.

Pagan, A. (1984) 'Econometric issues in the analysis of regressions with generated regressors', *International Economic Review*, 25 (1), 221–48.

Pagan, A. and Ullah, A. (1988) 'The econometric analysis of models with risk terms', *Journal of Applied Economics*, 3 (2), 87–106.

Patterson, K. D. (1987) 'The specification and stability of the demand for money in the United Kingdom', *Economica*, 54 (1), 41–55.

Patterson, K. D. and Ryding, J. (1984) 'Dynamic time series models with growth effects constrained to zero', *Economic Journal*, 94, 137–43.

Pesaran, M. H. (1987) *The Limits to Rational Expectations*, Oxford: Basil Blackwell.

Phillips, P. C. B. and Park, J. Y. (1986) 'Statistical inference in regressions with integrated processes: part I', Cowles Foundation, paper 811.

Pigou, A. C. (1917) 'The value of money', *Quarterly Journal of Economics*, 37, 38–65.

Roley, V. V. (1985) 'Money demand predictability', *Journal of Money, Credit and Banking*, 17 (2), 611–41.

Rose, A. K. (1985) 'An alternative approach to the American demand for money', *Journal of Money, Credit and Banking*, 17 (4), 439–55.

Santomero, A. M. (1974) 'A model of the demand for money by households', *Journal of Finance*, 29 (1), 89–102.

Sargent, T. J. (1979) *Macroeconomic Theory*, New York: Academic Press.

Sargent, T. J. and Wallace, N. (1982) 'The real bills doctrine and the quantity theory: a reconsideration', *Journal of Political Economy*, 90, 1212–36.

Serletis, A. (1988) 'Translog flexible functional forms and substitutability of monetary assets', *Journal of Business and Economic Statistics*, 6, 59–67.

Serletis, A. and Robb, A. L. (1986) 'Divisia aggregation and substitutability among monetary assets', *Journal of Money, Credit and Banking*, 18, 430–46.

Smith, G. (1975) 'Pitfalls in financial model building: a clarification', *American Economic Review*, 65, 510–16.

Smith, G. (1986) 'A dynamic Baumol-Tobin model of money demand', *Review of Economic Studies*, 53, 465–9.

Spanos, A. (1984) 'Liquidity as a latent variable: an application of the MIMIC model', *Oxford Bulletin of Economics and Statistics*, 46 (2), 125–43.

Sprenkle, C. M. (1969) 'The uselessness of transactions demand models', *Journal of Finance*, 4, 835–47.

Sprenkle, C. M. (1972) 'On the observed transactions demand for money', *The Manchester School*, 40 (3), 261–7.

Sprenkle, C. M. (1974) 'An overdue note on some "Ancient but popular" literature', *Journal of Finance*, 29, 1577–80.

Sprenkle, C. M. and Miller, M. H. (1980) 'The precautionary demand for narrow and broad money', *Economica*, 47, 407–21.

Swofford, J. L. and Whitney, G. A. (1986) 'Flexible functional forms and the utility approach to the demand for money: a non-parametric analysis', *Journal of Money, Credit and Banking*, 18 (3), 383–9.

Taylor, M. P. (1986) 'From the general to the specific: the demand for M2 in three European countries', *Empirical Economics*, 11, 243–61.

Taylor, M. P. (1987) 'Financial innovation, inflation and the stability of the demand for broad money in the United Kingdom', *Bulletin of Economic Research*, 39 (3), 225–33.

Taylor, M. P. (1990a) 'Modelling the demand for UK broad money, 1871–1913', International Monetary Fund, Washington DC, forthcoming, *Review of Economics and Statistics*.

Taylor, M. P. (1990b) 'The hyperinflation model of money demand revisited', International Monetary Fund, Washington DC, forthcoming *Journal of Money, Credit and Banking*.

Tobin, J. (1956) 'The interest elasticity of transactions demand for cash', *Review of Economics and Statistics*, 38, 241–7.

Trundle, J. M. (1982) 'Recent changes in the use of cash', *Bank of England Quarterly Bulletin*, 22 (4), 519–29.

Tsiang, S. C. (1972) 'The rationale of the mean – standard deviation analysis, skewness preference and the demand for money', *American Economic Review*, 62, 354–71.

Varian, H. R. (1983) 'Non-parametric tests of consumer behaviour', *Review of Economic Studies*, 50, 99–110.

Wallace, N. (1988) 'A suggestion for oversimplifying the theory of money', *Economic Journal*, 98 (conference papers), 267–74.

Wallis, K. F. (1980) 'Econometric implications of the rational expectations hypothesis', *Econometrica*, 48 (1), 49–73.

Weale, M. (1986) 'The structure of personal sector short-term asset holdings', *The Manchester School*, 54 (2), 141–61.

West, K. D. (1988) 'Asymptotic normality when regressors have a unit root', *Econometrica*, 56 (6), 1397–417.

Whalen, E. L. (1966) 'A rationalisation of the precautionary demand for cash', *Quarterly Journal of Economics*, 80 (May), 314–24.

Wickens, M. R. (1982) 'The efficient estimation of econometric models with rational expectations', *Review of Economic Studies*, 49, 55–67.

Wren-Lewis, S. (1984) 'Omitted variables in equations relating prices to money', *Applied Economics*, 16, 483–96.

3 Financial Markets Analysis: An Outline

Ronald MacDonald and Mark P. Taylor

1 INTRODUCTION

This chapter provides an outline of the theoretical and empirical literature relating to the study of financial markets. Because it is an *outline*, it should not be treated as a comprehensive literature survey.[1] In particular, because of space constraints, we cover only the most salient topics in financial markets analysis: the efficient markets view of the determination of stock prices, asset pricing models and the pricing of contingent claims (option pricing). We use the available space, however, to *exposit* rather than merely catalogue the relevant literature.

The outline of the remainder of this chapter is as follows. In section 2 the efficient markets view of stock returns is reviewed, along with the corresponding extant empirical evidence. Explanations for departures from the efficient markets paradigm are also considered in section 2 in terms of time-varying real interest rates, bubbles and fads. Asset pricing models are discussed in sections 3 and 4. In particular, we consider the capital asset pricing model and the arbitrage pricing theory and the empirical evidence on both of these models. The pricing of contingent claims is the topic of section 5. The particular derivative security considered is an option, and we consider the binomial option pricing model, derive the famous Black-Scholes formula, discuss put-call parity and outline some empirical evidence on option pricing.

2 THE EFFICIENT MARKETS MODEL OF STOCK RETURNS: A MODERN OVERVIEW

In this section we provide an overview of the efficient markets hypothesis and alternatives to the efficient markets view, concentrating on recent research on the excess volatility of stock prices.[2]

A financial market is said to be informationally efficient if all available information is discounted into current asset prices. Although there is no precise agreement over what is meant by the efficient markets model, we shall now present a model which is widely referred to as such in the finance literature.[3] The efficient markets (EM) view of the stock market (see, for example, Shiller 1987) states that the real return r_t on stocks is unforecastable and that all information about future prices is efficiently incorporated into the current price. The model is usually written as

$$E(r_t | I_t) = \pi \tag{3.1}$$

$$r_t = (p_{t+1} - p_t + d_t) p_t^{-1} \tag{3.2}$$

where the total return r_t of holding stocks between t and $t+1$ consists of capital gain $p_{t+1} - p_t$ plus dividend income d_t expressed as a proportion of the initial price p_t (prices and dividends are expressed in real terms). $E(.|.)$ denotes the mathematical conditional expectations operator; I_t denotes the information set containing all publicly available information at time t; and π denotes the opportunity cost of using the funds, which may include a risk premium over the safe rate of return, and which we assume constant for the time being. Equation (3.1) represents a simple random walk model for the dividend adjusted price of stocks. On rearranging (3.1) we get

$$p_t = \delta E_t d_t + \delta E_t p_{t+1} \quad \delta = (1 + \pi)^{-1} \tag{3.3}$$

where we have used the shorthand notation $E_t = E(.|I_t)$. By recursively substituting the price term on the right hand side of (3.3) (i.e. step 1 gives $\delta E_t d_t + \delta^2 E_t d_{t+1} + \delta^2 E_t p_{t+2}$) and assuming that the transversality condition holds (that is, $\delta^n E_t p_{t+n} \to 0$ as $n \to \infty$), we obtain

$$p_t = \sum_{k=0}^{\infty} \delta^{k+1} E_t d_{t+k} \tag{3.4a}$$

or

$$p_t = E_t p_t^* \tag{3.4b}$$

where $p_t^* = \Sigma_{k=0}^{\infty} \delta^{k+1} d_{t+k}$. In words, p_t^* is the present value, discounted at the constant rate π, of actual future real dividends. It is interpreted as the perfect foresight (or *ex post* rational) price: it is that price which would obtain if all investors knew with certainty what future dividends would be and if the EM model is correct. So p_t is the optimal forecast of p_t^*.

If we define the forecast error φ_t as being equal to $p_t^* - p_t$, and noting that φ_t must be orthogonal to p_t (which it must be if p_t is a rational forecast), then

$$\mathrm{var}(p_t^*) = \mathrm{var}(\varphi_t) + \mathrm{var}(p_t) \tag{3.5}$$

Since variances cannot be negative, it must be the case that

$$\mathrm{var}(p_t) \leq \mathrm{var}(p_t^*) \tag{3.6a}$$

or

$$\mathrm{var}(p_t)/\mathrm{var}(p_t^*) \leq 1 \tag{3.6b}$$

The variance inequality, or variance ratio, has become an extremely popular way of testing the EM model of stock prices.

2.1 Some empirical evidence on the efficient markets model

A large amount of empirical work has been conducted in an attempt to gauge the validity of the model outlined in the previous section. Perhaps the simplest type of test conducted has involved comparing the actual historical values of p_t with some measure of p_t^*. Shiller (1981) conducted such an experiment using the Standard and Poor's composite stock price index and associated dividend series (both series are transformed into real terms). An important aspect of his work – and this shall be discussed in more detail below – is the fact that he detrends both the p_t and d_t series using a deterministic trend. p_t^* is calculated as the present discounted value of the actual subsequent real dividends (the discount rate π was taken as the average real return for the index over the sample period). In figure 3.1 both p_t and p_t^* are plotted; the striking feature of their relationship is that p_t^* is considerably less volatile than p_t, and this would suggest that the inequality (3.6a) is dramatically violated by these data. Indeed, when Shiller formally computes a number of variance bounds tests he finds that the left hand side of (3.6a) is always at least five times as great as the right hand side. Similar findings to Shiller's are reported by LeRoy and Porter (1981).

2.2 Explaining the rejection of the efficient markets model

Stationarity issues

Perhaps the earliest explanation for the rejection of the EM model concerned the stationarity assumptions invoked by Shiller. Thus, both Kleidon (1986) and Marsh and Merton (1986) argue that the results noted above may simply be a reflection of the assumption, implicitly made in Shiller's 1981 paper, that the price and dividend series do not contain unit roots. However,

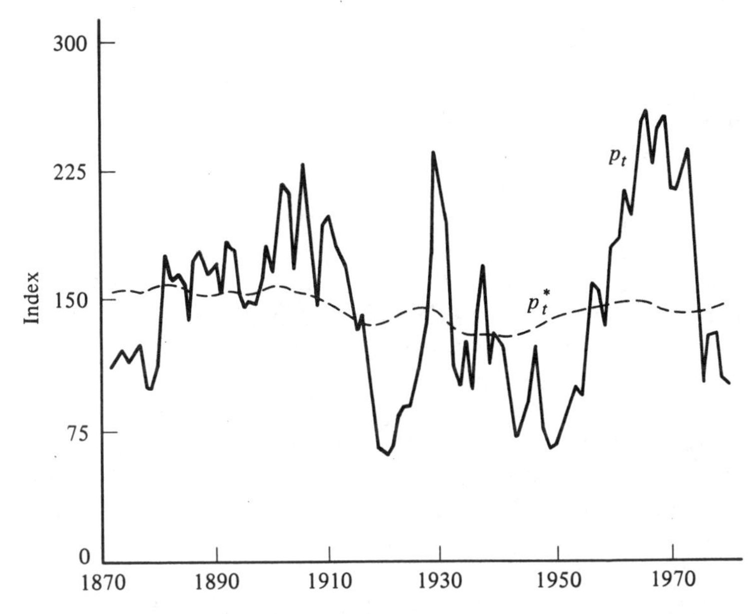

Figure 3.1 Real Standard and Poor's composite stock price index p_t and *ex post* rational price p_t^*, 1871–1979, both detrended by dividing by a long-run exponential growth factor (Shiller 1981)

when allowance is made for stochastic non-stationarity, by using arithmetic or logarithmic differences of d_t and p_t, the inequality (3.6a) still tends to be violated, although by a lesser magnitude (Kleidon 1986; Shiller 1983). Perhaps one of the neatest, and currently most popular, ways in which the non-stationarity issue has been handled is that proposed by Campbell and Shiller (1987). Their insight is to note that if both d_t and p_t series contain unit roots then (3.4a) implies that d_t and p_t must be cointegrated (Engle and Granger 1987) with a cointegration parameter $\gamma = \delta(1 - \delta)^{-1}$; that is, the variable $p_t - \gamma d_t$ is stationary. The intuition for this result is that if both d_t and p_t contain unit arithmetic roots, subtracting some multiple of d_t from p_t removes the linear trend in p_t and gives a stationary random variable.

For example, on subtracting γd_t from both sides of (3.4a), and on defining $S_t = p_t - \gamma d_t$ as the spread, we obtain

$$S_t = E_t S_t^* \tag{3.7}$$

where

$$S_t^* = \gamma \sum_{k=1}^{\infty} \delta^k \Delta d_{t+k} \tag{3.8}$$

In words, (3.7) simply states that S_t is an optimal forecast of a geometric weighted sum of future values of Δd_t, conditional on the agents' full information set. Campbell and Shiller (1987) purpose testing this version of the model in a number of ways. First, if d_t and p_t *are* cointegrated it is well known (Engle and Granger 1987) that S_t and Δd_t (or Δp_t) will have a vector autoregressive (VAR) representation. Standard restriction tests may be performed on this system in order to gauge the validity of the hypothesis captured by (3.4a) or, equivalently, (3.7) and (3.8). Furthermore, the VAR representation allows one to test, in a straightforward fashion, the idea that S_t should Granger-caused Δd_t (i.e. if S_t is an optimal forecast of future values of Δd_t it should have explanatory power, over and above the past history of Δd_t; see Campbell and Shiller 1987). A second advantage of the VAR framework is that it can be used to generate measures of the model's *economic* importance (in addition to its statistical significance as described by the restrictions tests). Such measures can be implemented by constructing the theoretical spread S_t', which is defined as the unrestricted VAR forecast of the present value of future changes in dividends ((3.7) and (3.8)), and comparing it graphically with the actual spread; if the model is valid the two series should be closely related. Additionally, the variance ratio $\text{var}(S_t)/\text{var}(S_t')$ may be computed and should, as before, equal unity if the model is valid; if the ratio is larger than one, then the spread is too volatile relative to information about future dividends.

Campbell and Shiller (1987) implement this approach using annual US data (Standard and Poor's real composite indices) over the period 1871–1986. Their tests for cointegration between p_t and d_t give somewhat mixed results in that the Engle-Granger (1987) ξ_2 statistic (a Dickey-Fuller statistic computed on the residuals from the cointegrating regression) is significant, allowing rejection of the null of no cointegration, whereas the ξ_3 statistic (the augmented Dickey-Fuller statistic) is insignificant. Since the latter is the more robust statistic in the presence of autocorrelation, this would tend to cast some doubt on the validity of the model (we shall discuss this finding in more detail in the section on speculative bubbles). Despite this finding, Campbell and Shiller implement the VAR model and find that, although the spread Granger-causes dividend changes, the model is rejected at standard significance levels. Additionally, the computed variance ratios for the spreads are dramatically different from one (although high standard errors imply that they do not differ significantly from one) and graphically the theoretical spread does not track the actual spread in a satisfactory way. Hence even accounting for non-stationarity in this rather sophisticated way does not appear to save the simple efficient markets model.

Time-varying real interest rates

Perhaps one of the earliest rationalizations (see e.g. Shiller 1981) for the violation of simple inequality tests was in terms of the non-constancy of expected returns. Thus on replacing (3.1) with $E_t(r_t - \pi_t) = \chi$, where π_t denotes the *ex post* real interest rate and χ is a constant, we obtain

$$p_t = E_t p_t^{r*} \tag{3.9}$$

$$\begin{aligned} p_t^{r*} = {} & d_t/(1 + \pi_t + \chi) + d_{t+1}/[(1 + \pi_t + \chi)(1 + \pi_{t+1} + \chi)] \\ & + d_{t+2}/[(1 + \pi_t + \chi)(1 + \pi_{t+1} + x)(1 + \pi_{t+2} + \chi)] + \ldots \end{aligned} \tag{3.10}$$

Shiller (1987) computes p_t^{r*} for the Standard and Poor's data noted above and demonstrates graphically that there is virtually no correlation between it and p_t. A somewhat different approach is taken in Shiller (1981) in that he calculates the variability of real returns that would be necessary to explain his reported violation of the variance inequality; an implausible standard deviation of real returns greater than 4 per cent (per annum) is required to save the model.

Both West (1988) and Poterba and Summers (1988) present even larger estimates of how much expected real returns would have to move to save the model for the case where p_t and d_t contain unit roots, instead of the deterministic trends assumed by Shiller. Since the postulated movements tend to be much larger than the actual historical movements of real interest rates for the samples considered, the explanation for excess volatility does not seem to lie with time-varying expected returns.

However, the failure of the above noted extensions to the basic model to save the efficient markets model may simply reflect the poor measure of real interest rates chosen. More specifically, the *ex post* real interest rate may not be a particularly good proxy for the *ex ante* real interest rate. In a bid to provide an alternative measure of time-varying returns, researchers have turned their attention towards non-financial data, particularly consumer expenditure. The usefulness of consumption in modelling real interest rate movements may be illustrated by considering a simple model in which a representative agent (or more appropriately investor) is attempting to maximize an expected utility function of the form

$$V = E\sum_{t=0}^{\infty} \beta^t u(c_t) \tag{3.11}$$

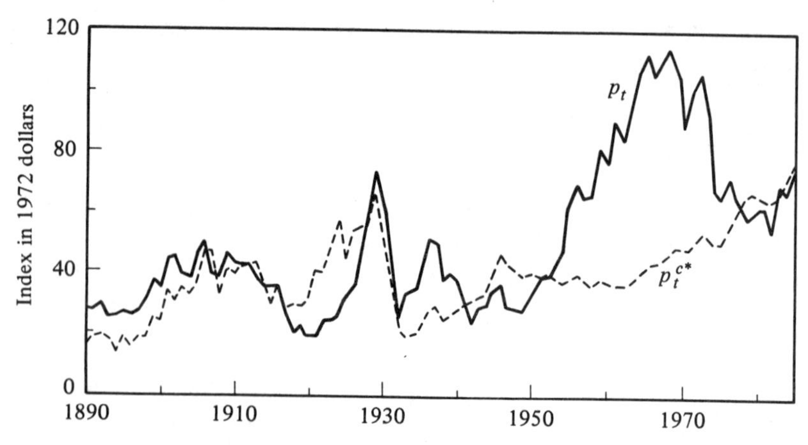

Figure 3.2 Real Standard and Poor's composite stock price index p_t and *ex post* rational price p_t^*, 1889–1985, computed using consumption-based time-varying real interest rates (Shiller 1987)

where c_t denotes consumption during period t, $u(c_t)$ denotes the utility from that consumption and β denotes the rate at which future consumption is discounted relative to present consumption ($= (1 + \sigma)^{-1}$, where σ is the subjective rate of time discount). Maximization of (3.11) subject to a standard budget constraint gives the Euler condition $u'(c_t) = \beta E_t[(1 + r_t) u'(c_{t+1})]$, where $u'(.)$ denotes marginal utility. Thus if in period t there is a unit decrease in consumption, the loss in utility is $u'(c_t)$, whilst in period $t + 1$ the agent has $1 + r_t$ units of extra consumption, giving a discounted increase in expected utility of $\beta E_t(1 + r_t) u'(c_{t+1})$. On rearranging the Euler condition we obtain an expression for $(1 + r_t)^{-1}$ as

$$\delta^c = (1 + r_t)^{-1} = u'(c_{t+k})/[u'(c_t)(1 + \sigma)^{k+1}] \tag{3.12}$$

which has the interpretation of the intertemporal marginal rate of substitution between c_t and c_{t+k}. In order to implement this approach some functional form must be assumed for $u(c_t)$, and it is usual to adopt the constant relative risk aversion model $u(c_t) = c_t^{1-\alpha}/1 - \alpha$, where $\alpha \geq 0$ is the relative degree of risk aversion (assumed to be constant). Using the expression for δ^c, p_t now becomes

$$p_t = E_t p^{c*} \tag{3.13}$$

$$p_t^{c*} = \sum_{k=0}^{\infty} \delta^{c,k+1} d_{t+k} \tag{3.14}$$

Shiller (1987) computes (3.14) for the Standard and Poor's composite index over the period 1889–1985, and its value along with actual p_t is graphed in figure 3.2. This figure indicates that although p_t^{c*} and p_t appear to be positively correlated up to around 1950, thereafter there is little correlation. Shiller attributes this pattern to the well-known correlation of the business cycle (reflected in consumption behaviour) with the stock market, a correlation which has decreased since the 1950s. One interesting feature of Shiller's implementation of this version of the model is that on using p_t^{c*} the variance ratio is not violated; however, the support for the model which may be adduced from this result is questionable since an implausibly high value of the risk aversion parameter is used. Campbell and Shiller (1987) implement the model (3.11)–(3.14) in VAR form (see the discussion in the previous section) using Standard and Poor's data over the period 1909–1986. The VAR consists of the dividend–price ratio (i.e. on the basis of our discussion above this should be stationary), the change in dividends and the change in consumption (all variables are in logarithms). The restrictions implied by the model are easily rejected by the data; the forecastability of consumption growth does not help to explain the behaviour of the dividend–price ratio; and their estimate of α is wrongly signed.[4] West (1988) also uses the consumption-based asset pricing model to generate expected returns and finds that the variance ratio is strongly violated (it lies in the range of 5 to 30 times its theoretical value).

Speculative bubbles

A device which has been widely cited as rescuing the EM model is that of a rational speculative bubble: an otherwise extraneous event which affects stock prices because everyone expects it to do so. In this section we discuss speculative bubbles and attempt to assess whether they do indeed save the EM model. We return, for simplicity, to the constant returns version of the model (see Flood and Hodrick 1987 for a discussion of rational bubbles with time-varying returns).

It is well known from the rational expectations literature that, in the absence of an appropriate transversality condition, (3.4b) has multiple solutions each of which may be written in the form

$$p_t = E_t p_t^* + b_t \tag{3.15}$$

where b_t is the bubble term. It is straightforward to demonstrate that if $b_t = \delta^{-1} E_t b_{t+1}$ then (3.15) is a solution to (3.4b). If b_t is a constant equal to b then (3.15) says that, even if dividends are constant, the stock price will grow at the rate $b\delta^{-1}$. This is a pure capital gain unrelated to fundamentals and there are an infinite number of such paths, one for each value of b. If everyone believes that share prices will rise at some common rate, unrelated to fundamentals, the price will go up by that amount; prices can rise through speculation and, moreover, those expectations will be fulfilled.

The deterministic bubble b is perhaps the simplest example, but casual empiricism would suggest that it is not very realistic. The South Sea bubble and the Tulipmania bubble (see Garber 1989) are both examples of asset price movements which are not consistent with a deterministic process; furthermore, those bubbles eventually burst. A more attractive family of bubbles has been suggested by Blanchard (1979). For example, a collapsing bubble may be modelled from the following structure:

$$b_{t+1} = \begin{cases} b_t(\delta\pi)^{-1} & \text{with probability } \pi \\ 0 & \text{with probability } 1-\pi \end{cases}$$

This structure satisfies $E_t b_{t+1} = b_t$ and therefore satisfies as a solution to (3.4b). The bubble has a probability of collapse at any point in time, and once it collapses it is over since all future b_ts are zero. However, with probability π it does not collapse and continues growing.

Note that the existence of bubbles can explain the empirical finding that variance ratios are violated. Thus on using (3.15) and our earlier result that $p_t^* = E_t p_t^* + \varphi_t$, we obtain

$$\text{var}(p_t^*) = \text{var}(p_t) + \text{var}(b_t) + \text{var}(\varphi_t) - 2\text{cov}(p_t, b_t) \qquad (3.16)$$

Because there is no *a priori* reason to exclude the possibility that p_t and b_t are positively correlated, inequalities like (3.6a) cannot be derived from (3.15); evidence of excess volatility is *prima facie* evidence for the presence of speculative bubbles. However, a number of theoretical issues and also empirical evidence lead us to seriously doubt that it is bubbles which explain the rejection of the EM model.

From a theoretical perspective the existence of bubbles is somewhat questionable. First, it is theoretically impossible to have negative bubbles (i.e. $b_t < 0$). This is because such a bubble would imply a stock price below its fundamental value, a capital gain when the bubble bursts and therefore the requirement of a potential capital loss as the bubble moves downwards. However, since stock prices cannot be negative, there must be some (low) price which precludes further capital loss and which therefore must also be inconsistent with a bubble; by backward deduction, any higher price must also be inconsistent (since it inevitably leads to the low price) and therefore there cannot be a negative bubble. Positive bubbles, which are the kind usually discussed in the literature, also have a rather thin theoretical basis. Tirole (1982) has demonstrated, in an infinite horizon model, that positive bubbles cannot arise. The idea is that an agent who sells a stock at a price higher than its fundamental value and leaves the market passes on a stock with a negative present value; this is clearly not an attractive investment for a rational maximizing agent. In finite horizon, overlapping generations, perfect foresight models, positive bubbles may exist in steady-state equilibrium as long as the rate of growth in the economy is greater than the return on the stock (see, for example, Tirole 1986). West (1988), however, indicates that this relationship does not find support is US data. Other empirical evidence is also not particularly well disposed towards the bubbles hypothesis.

In testing for bubbles an econometrician is immediately faced with the problem of distinguishing them from other phenomena. For example, Hamilton (1986) gives some illustrations of how an econometrician might incorrectly conclude that there exists a speculative bubble when there is an expected regime change of which he is unaware (i.e. the so-called peso problem first noted by Krasker 1980). Diba and Grossman (1985) suggest testing for bubbles by checking the orders of integration of d_t, p_t and S_t. Thus the addition of the bubble term to (3.4a), as in (3.15), would generate explosive behaviour of p_t and therefore the existence of bubbles would suggest different orders of integration of p_t and d_t. However, even if p_t and d_t are integrated of the same order this does not rule out bubbles. In particular, the existence of a bubble term in (3.7) would generate non-stationary behaviour in S_t (i.e. the absence of cointegration between p_t and d_t) and, by implication, in Δp_t. Hence a further test of the no-bubbles hypothesis would be to test for the stationarity of Δp_t and the cointegration of p_t and d_t. Campbell and Shiller (1988) test for the order of integration of the Standard and Poor's composite (real) price index and corresponding (real) dividend series 1871–1986, and cannot reject the null hypothesis that each contains a unit root. However, as we noted above, Campbell and Shiller do not find that p_t and d_t are cointegrated and this would tend to indicate the existence of a bubble.

West (1986) tests for bubbles using a version of the Hausman (1978) specification idea. In particular, by assuming dividends follow an AR(1) process of the form

$$d_t = \phi d_{t-1} + v_t, \quad |\phi| < 1 \tag{3.17}$$

where v_t is a white noise process, a closed form solution for (3.4a) may be obtained as

$$p_t = \gamma d_t \tag{3.18}$$

where $\gamma = \delta\phi/(1 - \delta\phi)$. Ordinary least squares (OLS) estimates of (3.17) and (3.18) will yield point estimates of δ and ϕ which will be consistent in the absence of speculative bubbles, but inconsistent in the presence of such bubbles (if the bubble is correlated with dividends). However, a consistent estimate of δ may be obtained, even in the presence of a bubble, by estimating the arbitrage condition (3.3) using McCallum's (1976) instrumental variables technique; i.e.

$$p_t = \delta(d_t + p_{t+1}) + u_t \tag{3.19}$$

Thus Hausman's specification test may be used to test whether the estimate of δ obtained from (3.19) differs significantly from that obtained from (3.17) and (3.18); if it does then this suggests the presence of a speculative bubble. West tests this proposition using the data described in Shiller (1981) (see above) and reports some striking (and significant) differences between the two estimates of δ. But as West recognizes (see also his later paper: West 1988) his tests do not have great power in discriminating between bubbles and fads (see below). (See also Summers 1986 for evidence on the power of these kinds of tests.)

One other problem with the validity of the bubbles story is worth noting. As Flood and Hodrick (1987) have pointed out, some of the stock market efficiency tests conducted (most notably those by Mankiw et al. 1985) already allow for speculative bubbles under the null hypothesis and therefore the reported rejections must be due to some other factor.

Fads

Given that rational speculative bubbles do not seem to provide a viable way of explaining excess volatility findings, some attention has focused on the idea that uninformed, naive or noise traders may be at least partially to blame for this empirical finding. Anecdotal evidence on noise trading is widespread; the most famous discussion is probably Keynes's (1936) analogy of the stock market with a beauty contest. More recently, DeBondt and Thaler (1985) and Shiller (1984), among others, have argued that noise trading may be at the root of excess asset price volatility.

A simple way of analysing a fads model would be to add a fads term, f_t say, to what would otherwise be the rational or fundamental price:

$$p_t = E_t p_t^* + f_t \tag{3.20}$$

This will, in general, lead to a violation of the variance inequality (3.6a) in the same way as the presence of bubbles (compare (3.20) and (3.15) and replace b with f in (3.16)). Superficially, this is indeed very similar to the case of rational bubbles, as discussed above. The important difference, however, is that the fads term is assumed to be mean-reverting: the price will have a tendency to return to fundamentals. For example, we might have

$$f_t = \kappa f_{t-1} + \epsilon_t \tag{3.21}$$

where $|\kappa| < 1$ and ϵ_t is stationary white noise. Another, more sophisticated example would be (West 1988)

$$f_{t+1} = \begin{cases} (\kappa/\pi) f_t + \epsilon_{t+1} & \text{with probability } \pi \\ \epsilon_{t+1} & \text{with probability } (1-\pi) \end{cases} \tag{3.22}$$

where $|\kappa| < 1$ and ϵ_{t+1} is stationary white noise and, in particular, $E_t \epsilon_{t+1} = 0$. Thus $E_t f_{t+1} = \kappa f_t$, and the deviation from fundamentals is stationary or mean-reverting. Such a model would seem to capture behaviour which, although mean-reverting, is similar in some ways to that which would be generated by speculative bubbles.

One way of reconciling the concept of fads with market rationality is to argue that, although a large proportion of trading is done by naive speculators or so-called noise traders, a significant proportion is in fact undertaken by informed speculators. Informed speculators, in turn, *do* drive the market price to a *risk adjusted* equilibrium, but the extra risk which is generated by the presence of noise traders is not captured by standard models (see e.g. De Long et al. 1987).

Apart from anecdotal evidence on the presence of fads, formal evidence at the level of individual equity prices is provided by DeBondt and Thaler (1985, 1987), Lehmann (1987), Camerer (1987) and MacDonald and Power (1990). These papers demonstrate that abnormally high returns can be generated by shorting stocks which have recently performed well and buying stocks which have recently performed poorly – thus providing evidence of mean reversion in prices.

At the aggregate market level, evidence of mean-reverting behaviour in stock prices is provided by, *inter alios*, Lo and McKinley (1987), Fama and French (1988), Poterba and Summers (1988), Campbell and Shiller (1988) and MacDonald and Power (1991). In particular, these studies demonstrate that the fads term is predictable, using variables such as lagged dividend–price ratios or earnings.

As noted by West (1988), however, evidence of mean reversion and predictability in stock prices is at best *suggestive* of the presence of fads; it does not *prove* that they are present. Indeed, the most compelling argument presently available in support of the fads hypothesis is that they are the major viable alternative explanation of excess volatility findings, given that neither traditional models nor rational bubbles appear to be satisfactory in this respect. Further research on fads might thus concentrate on more direct, testable implications of fads models.

3 MEAN-VARIANCE ANALYSIS AND THE CAPITAL ASSET PRICING MODEL

As was evident in our discussion of efficient markets, equilibrium in financial markets inevitably involves some sort of tradeoff between risk and return. In the models discussed in the previous sections, the required or expected rate of return on stocks was largely taken for granted. In a world in which individuals are risk-averse, the required return to a risky asset will, *in general*, differ from that to a riskless asset. This difference may be thought of as a *risk premium*. A large part of the theory of finance is devoted to explaining risk premiums, i.e. the expected or required excess return of risky assets over risk-free assets. Much of this literature is derived from a particular approach to the theory of portfolio selection - *mean-variance analysis*. The foundations of mean-variance models of portfolio selection were laid by Hicks (1946), Tobin (1958) and Markowitz (1959). The justification for focusing on the return mean and variance given by these authors is that either agents' utility functions are quadratic[5] or the distribution of returns is normal (so that the mean and variance are sufficient statistics to characterize the entire distribution). Given these assumptions, risk-averse agents will seek to maximize the overall expected return to their portfolio for any given level of variance. In that sense, therefore, the overall variance of a market portfolio becomes a sufficient statistic for the risk attached to that portfolio. Because the variance of return is measured in units which are the squared percentages, it is often useful, however, to think of the market risk as being measured by the *standard deviation* of market return (i.e. the positive square root of the variance).

Building on the early work on mean-variance analysis, Sharpe (1964), Lintner (1965) and Mossin (1966) each developed, independently, an equilibrium model of the required excess return on an individual risky asset which became known as the *capital asset pricing model* (CAPM).

Consider a portfolio of say *n* risky assets, such that the expected return and variance on the *i*th asset are $E(R_i)$ and σ_{ii}^2 respectively and the covariance between the returns on asset *i* and those on asset *j* is σ_{ij}^2. If the proportion of total wealth held in asset *i* is W_i ($\Sigma_{i=1}^n W_i = 1$), the expected return and variance on the portfolio are

$$E(R_p) = \sum_{i=1}^{n} W_i E(R_i) \tag{3.23}$$

$$\sigma_{pp}^2 = \sum_{i=1}^{n} \sum_{j=1}^{n} W_i W_j \sigma_{ij}^2 \tag{3.24}$$

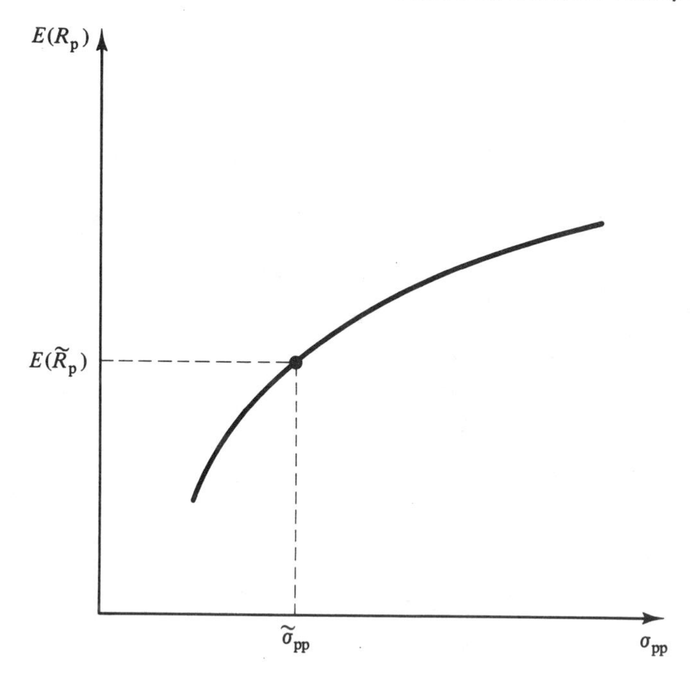

Figure 3.3 The efficient frontier

It can be demonstrated that as the number n of assets in the portfolio gets larger and larger, the variance of the portfolio return, as defined in (3.24), approaches the average covariance between assets in the portfolio (this is demonstrated empirically by Fama 1976). Thus in a large, well-diversified portfolio the covariance terms are extremely important.

It can be shown that choosing the weights W_i in order to minimize the portfolio variance for any given level of expected portfolio return results in a locus of points in (σ_{pp} $E(R_p)$ space with a shape similar to that given in figure 3.3. This is called the *efficient frontier*. For any given level of expected return, the locus indicates the minimum portfolio variance which is feasible given the set of means, variances and covariances for the individual asset returns. For example, suppose a portfolio return of $E(\tilde{R}_p)$ is desired; then the efficient frontier in figure 3.3 tells us that the minimum portfolio return variance that can be attained for this level of expected return is $\tilde{\sigma}^2_{pp}$ (corresponding to a portfolio return standard deviation of $\tilde{\sigma}_{pp}$).

Clearly, a risk-averse individual will always choose a portfolio on the efficient frontier. In general, however, two individuals with different attitudes towards risk will choose different portfolios. For example, in figure 3.4 individual 1 chooses portfolio 1 because this allows him to get on to his highest indifference curve (i.e. to attain the highest level of utility).

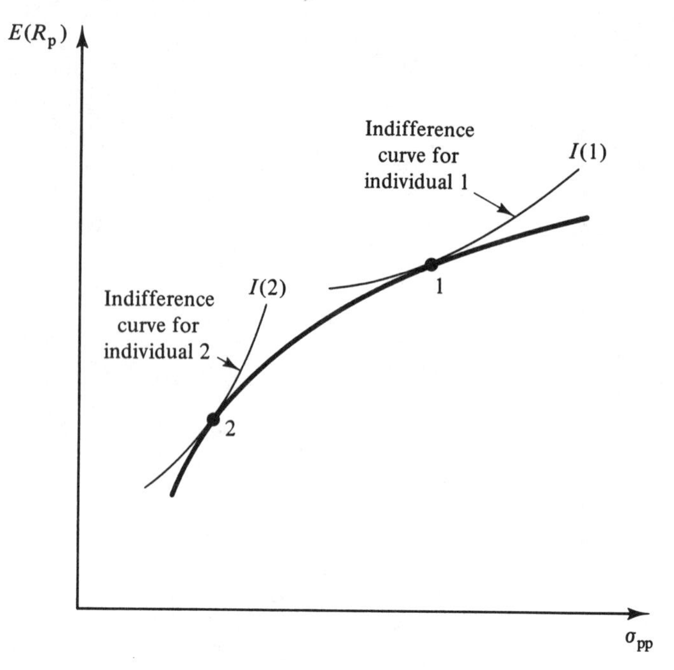

Figure 3.4 Portfolio selection and attitudes to risk

For similar reasons, however, individual 2, who is more risk-averse than individual 1, will choose portfolio 2.

Now suppose there is a risk-free asset (i.e. one whose return variance is zero) which can be borrowed or lent at a rate R_f. In the absence of such an asset, individuals can locate anywhere on (or within) the efficient frontier. Once such a risk-free asset is available, however, individuals can locate anywhere in a set bounded above by a line from the point R_f on the vertical axis which is just tangential to the upper part of the efficient frontier. In figure 3.5, for example, by placing some of his wealth in the risk free asset and the remainder in portfolio M, individual 2 can attain the risk–return pairing at point A. The less risk-averse individual 1, however, prefers to borrow the risk-free asset and use it to purchase more of portfolio M (i.e. he takes a levered position) in order to get to point B. Clearly, utility-maxizing individuals will always locate somewhere on the line going through R_f and M. This line is termed the *capital market line*. The capital market line gives the relationship between risk and return for efficient portfolios of assets. It is easy to establish that its equation is given by

$$E(R_p) - R_f = \left[\frac{E(R_m) - R_f}{\sigma_{mm}}\right]\sigma_{pp} \qquad (3.25)$$

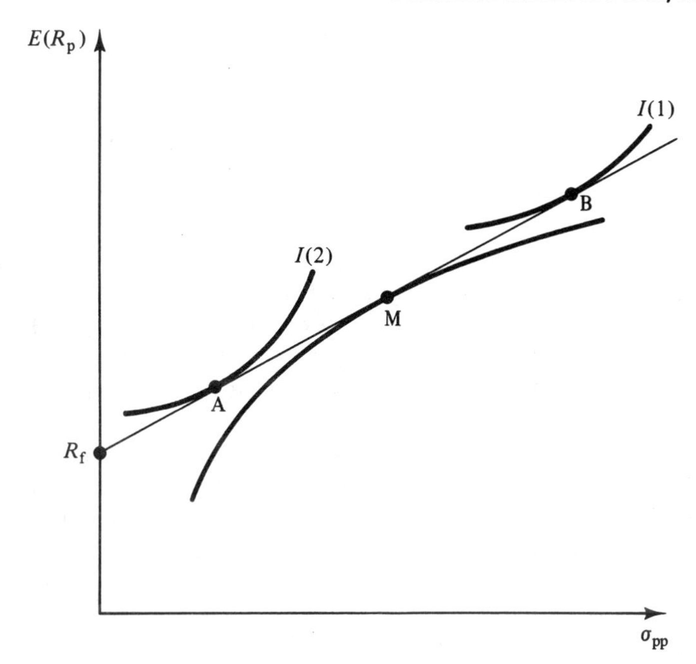

Figure 3.5 The capital market line

where $E(R_m)$ and σ^2_{mm} are the mean and variance of the return on the market portfolio.

The preceding analysis leads to two remarkable conclusions. The first is that all individuals, regardless of their attitudes towards risk, will choose to hold some of their wealth in the risk-free asset and some of it in portfolio M.[6] This result is known as *two-fund separation*. The second implication is that the subjective marginal rate of substitution between risk and return (given by the slope of the indifference curve, say MRS_i for the ith individual) is the same for all individuals and is equal to the technically feasible marginal rate of transformation of risk into return (given by the slope of the efficient frontier, say MRT). Moreover, each of these must be equal in equilibrium to the slope of the capital market line. From (3.24) we therefore have, in equilibrium,

$$MRS_i = MRS_j = MRT = \left[\frac{E(R_m) - R_f}{\sigma_{mm}}\right] \tag{3.26}$$

The term in brackets in (3.26) can be thought of as the *market price of risk*. If we take the standard deviation of the market portfolio return as a measure of overall risk, then this term indicates the amount of excess return which is required in equilibrium to compensate for one unit of market risk. Indeed, the capital market line (3.25) simply indicates how much excess return on a portfolio is required for a unit increase in its risk (measured by σ_{pp}). Relation (3.26) says that all individuals, regardless of their attitude towards risk, will agree on the market price of risk – providing their perceptions of the means and variances of asset returns are the same.

The portfolio M is known as the *market portfolio*. The proportionate weighting W_i given to the ith asset in the market portfolio is equal to the ratio of the market value of the ith asset to the market value of all assets.

In a sense, the final step in deriving the CAPM simply exploits (3.26). Let us derive the marginal rate of substitution of risk for return for any individual in equilibrium. The above analysis showed that the equilibrium holding of asset i is W_i, the ratio of the market value of holdings of asset i to the total market capitalization. Now consider increasing the percentage of wealth held in asset i. The variance of the market return is σ^2_{mm} and of asset i is σ^2_{ii}. Thus, if an extra percentage of wealth γ is put into asset i (so that only $1 - \gamma$ is left in the market portfolio), the expected return on the new portfolio becomes

$$E(R_p) = \gamma E(R_i) + (1 - \gamma) E(R_m) \tag{3.27}$$

and the standard deviation of the return on the new portfolio is

$$\sigma_{pp} = [\gamma^2 \sigma^2_{ii} + (1 - \gamma)^2 \sigma^2_{mm} + 2\gamma(1 - \gamma)\sigma_{im}]^{1/2} \tag{3.28}$$

Taking the derivatives of (3.27) and (3.28) with respect to γ and setting γ equal to zero (as it must be in equilibrium), we have

$$\left.\frac{\partial E(R_p)}{\partial \gamma}\right|_{\gamma=0} = E(R_i) - E(R_m) \tag{3.29}$$

$$\left.\frac{\partial \sigma_{pp}}{\partial \gamma}\right|_{\gamma=0} = \frac{\sigma^2_{im} - \sigma^2_{mm}}{\sigma_{mm}} \tag{3.30}$$

Dividing (3.29) by (3.30), we can then find the marginal rate of substitution of risk for return of any individual at the market equilibrium:

$$MRS_i = MRS_j = \frac{E(R_i) - E(R_m)}{(\sigma^2_{im} - \sigma^2_{mm})/\sigma_{mm}} \tag{3.31}$$

Equating this to the slope of the capital market line as suggested by (3.25), and rearranging, we then have

$$E(R_i) - R_f = \beta_i[E(R_m) - R_f] \tag{3.32a}$$

where

$$\beta_i = \sigma_{im}^2 / \sigma_{mm}^2 \tag{3.33}$$

Equations (3.32a) and (3.33) are the equations of the capital asset pricing model. They say that the required excess return on a risky asset will be proportional to the required excess return on the market portfolio (3.32a), the coefficient of proportionality being given by the *asset beta* (3.33) which measures the covariation between the asset return and the market return and a proportion of total market return variance.

It is straightforward to demonstrate that the variance of the return to the market portfolio can be expressed as

$$\sigma_{mm}^2 = \sum_{i=1}^{n} W_i \sigma_{im}^2$$

so that

$$\frac{\partial \sigma_{mm}^2}{\partial W_i} = \sigma_{im}^2 \tag{3.34}$$

Thus the marginal contribution to the portfolio risk, as measured by the portfolio variance, is given by the covariance of the asset return with the market return. Expressing this as a proportion of total market risk (as measured by return variance) gives the asset beta (3.33).

The CAPM thus implies that the required excess return - or risk premium - associated with an asset will be a function not of the total variance of the asset return, but of the covariance of the asset return with the market return. That part of the total asset variance which is orthogonal with the market return is termed the *unsystematic risk*. Unsystematic risk can be diversified away by holding a well-diversified, efficient portfolio. Thus there is no reward to bearing this kind of risk; an asset whose return had zero covariance with the market return would have zero beta and thus, in equilibrium, would earn only the safe rate of return. This is fair because, as (3.34) shows, the marginal contribution of such an asset to the overall risk of the market portfolio would be zero.

The degree to which an asset's return covaries with the market portfolio is termed the *systematic risk* attached to the asset. Clearly, systematic risk cannot be diversified away and thus must be rewarded. The bigger the systematic risk of an asset (i.e. the covariation of its return with the market return), the bigger its beta and hence the bigger the risk premium.

Although our derivation of the CAPM relied on the existence of a risk-free asset, Black (1972) has shown that the CAPM can still be derived in the absence of such an asset. In this case, the expected return on the minimum-variance zero-beta portfolio plays the role of the risk-free return.

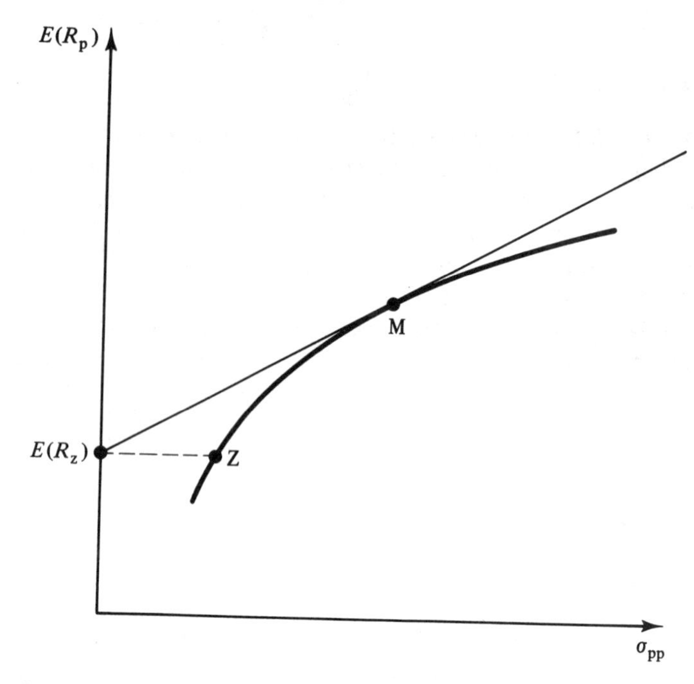

Figure 3.6 The two-factor model

In figure 3.6, for example, portfolio Z is the minimum-variance zero-beta portfolio associated with the market portfolio. We know that Z is zero-beta because its expected return lies at the intersection of a tangent to the efficient frontier at M and the vertical axis. We know that it is minimum-variance among the class of zero-beta portfolios because its risk–return pairing lies on the efficient frontier. Proceeding precisely as before but with $E(R_z)$ playing the role of R_f, we can derive a version of the CAPM which does not rely on the existence of a risk-free asset:

$$E(R_i) - E(R_z) = \beta_i [E(R_m) - E(R_z)] \tag{3.32b}$$

This version of the CAPM is sometimes termed the *two-factor model.* The two-factor model relies, however, on the assumption that there are no constraints on short sales; the zero-beta portfolio can be sold short in order to raise cash to take a levered position on the market portfolio. Ross (1977) has shown that when short-sales restrictions are imposed, the linear CAPM can no longer be derived.

3.1 Empirical evidence on the CAPM

A number of researchers have carried out empirical tests of the CAPM, e.g. Friend and Blume (1970), Black et al. (1972), Miller and Scholes (1972), Blume and Friend (1973), Fama and MacBeth (1973), Reinganum (1981a), Litzenberger and Ramaswamy (1979), Banz (1981), Gibbons (1982), Stambaugh (1982), Shanken (1985a), Bollerslev (1988) and Hall et al. (1989). Most of these studies use monthly total returns (dividends reinvested) on listed common stocks.

A common way of testing the CAPM is to estimate the beta for a number of securities over a five-year holding period by regressing the asset return on to a market index.[7] Next the securities are ranked by beta and placed into ten or twenty portfolios, and the returns and betas on these portfolios are then calculated over a second five-year period. The reason for this grouping is to reduce the measurement error resulting from estimating individual asset betas. The excess return is then regressed on to the estimated betas in cross-section across the portfolios, in an empirical equation such as

$$(R_p - R_f) = \alpha_0 + \alpha_1 \beta_p + \zeta \tag{3.35}$$

where β_p is the measured beta for portfolio P and ζ is a residual term. The term on the left hand side of (3.35) is the *ex post* excess return on the portfolio. The final term on the right hand side of (3.35) is the *ex post abnormal return* – that part of the excess return which is not explained by the asset beta.

The CAPM predicts that, in a relationship such as (3.35), the intercept term α_0 should be zero and the slope coefficient α_1 should be equal to the excess market return. In general, however, empirical studies have tended to find that the intercept term is insignificantly different from zero and the slope coefficient is less than the excess market return. This implies that low-beta securities earn more than would be consistent with the model and high-beta securities earn less.

Researchers have also reported that other factors besides beta are significant in explaining excess returns. Thus the following factors have been found to have a positive association with excess returns: low price–earnings ratios (Basu 1977); small firm size (Banz 1981; Reinganum 1981a); and high dividend yields (Litzenberger and Ramaswamy 1979). Keim (1983, 1985) reports a significant seasonal effect in stock returns.

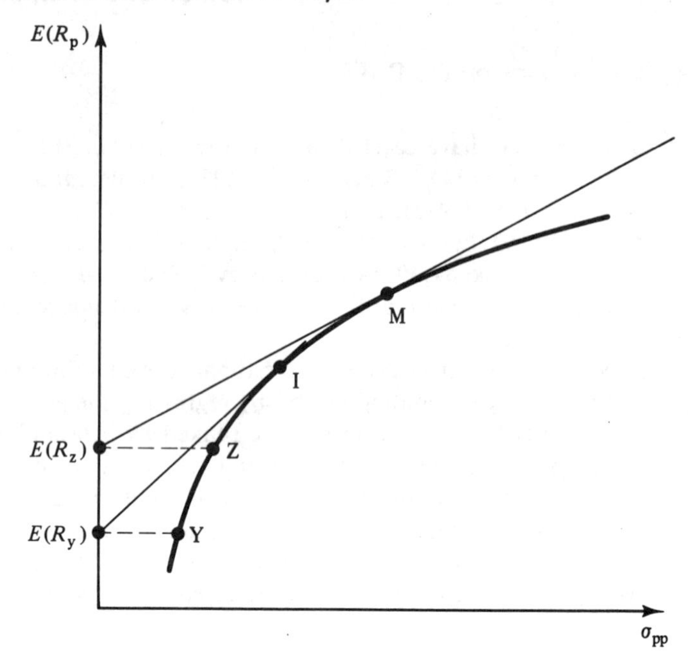

Figure 3.7 Roll's critique

3.2 Roll's critique

Roll (1977) pointed out that it is always possible to write the expected return on an asset as a linear function of its beta measured relative to *some* efficient market index. In figure 3.7, for example, portfolio Z is the zero-beta portfolio associated with the market portfolio, so that we can derive the two-factor version of the CAPM as in equation (3.35). However, consider any other efficient portfolio, I say. Portfolio I will also have a minimum-variance zero-beta portfolio associated with it – portfolio Y. We can therefore derive an equation precisely analogous to (3.35) for any asset i:

$$E(R_i) - E(R_Y) = \tilde{\beta}[E(R_I) - E(R_Y)] \tag{3.36}$$

where

$$\tilde{\beta}_i = \sigma_{iI}^2 / \sigma_{II}^2$$

Equation (3.36) is a consequence of the mean-variance efficiency of portfolio I; it is *not*, however, a representation of the CAPM *unless* I is in fact the true market portfolio. Since, in practice, researchers *always* use some proxy for the market portfolio (such as a market index of listed stocks) when attempting to test the CAPM, Roll's critique implies that they are not really testing the CAPM but simply whether their proxy portfolio is mean-variance efficient.[8] Indeed, the logical implication of Roll's critique is that the only valid test of the CAPM is whether or not the true market portfolio is mean-variance efficient. Unfortunately, the true market portfolio will be hard if not impossible to observe, since it will typically contain all of the various assets which individuals hold - not only stocks but also bonds, houses, non-tradable assets such as human capital, and so on. Roll (1977: 129–30) concludes:

> The two-parameter model is testable *in principle*; but arguments are given here that: (a) no correct and unambiguous test of the theory has appeared in the literature, and (b) there is practically no possibility that such a test can be accomplished in the future.

3.3 Extending the CAPM beyond a single period

The CAPM as derived above is a single-period model. A number of authors have worked on extending the model to an intertemporal setting.

Merton (1973) developed an intertemporal capital asset pricing model (ICAPM) in which required excess return are a function, at each point in time, not only of the asset beta with respect to the market return but also of the asset betas with respect to each of the state variables which describe the economic environment at a particular point in time. A similar model was advanced by Ross (1975). Lucas (1978) presents an intertemporal CAPM model in which the distribution of prices is determined endogenously. Perhaps the most general presentation of the intertemporal CAPM, involving a continuous-time rational expectations general equilibrium framework, is given by Cox et al. (1985).

Breeden (1979) simplified the Merton ICAPM model by assuming that agents' preferences can be described by intertemporally additive utility functions. This allows the ICAPM to be collapsed into a single-beta model - the consumption CAPM. In the consumption CAPM, excess returns are shown to be a function of the beta between an asset's return and aggregate consumption.

4 THE ARBITRAGE PRICING THEORY

The arbitrage pricing theory (APT) was developed by Ross (1976) and is the most general model of asset valuation, including the CAPM as a special case.

The APT is based on elegant reasoning concerning arbitrage portfolios.[9] An arbitrage portfolio is a portfolio which involves no commitment of either wealth or risk. Financial returns can only logically accrue for two reasons: either as a reward for the commitment of wealth (the time value of money) or as a reward for bearing risk. Thus arbitrage portfolios – which involve no commitment of wealth and which are riskless – should have a zero return.

The APT starts from a general assumption concerning the evolution of asset returns – that they are a linear function of a finite number of, say, k factors:

$$R_i = E(R_i) + \beta_{i1}\delta_1 + \beta_{i2}\delta_2 + \ldots + \beta_{ik}\delta_k + e_i \tag{3.37}$$

Equation (3.37) states that the return to asset i is a linear function of k factors $\{\delta_j\}_{j=1}^k$ plus an asset-specific term e_i, with the amount of influence exerted by each individual factor on the return to asset i given by the *factor loadings* $\{\beta_{ij}\}_{j=1}^k$.

The factors are not specified *a priori* in the theoretical development of the APT. In empirical work on the APT, researchers have assumed that the factors are macroeconomic and financial variables such as the market return, short- and long-term interest rates on government debt, the inflation rate, the growth rate of industrial production, the aggregate consumption rate, and so on (see e.g. Chan et al. 1985; Chen et al. 1986). It is useful to think of the factors as being in mean deviation form, so that $E(\delta_j) = 0$.

The idiosyncratic term e_i is a zero-mean ($E(e_i) = 0$) stochastic term affecting the return to asset i.

As it stands, (3.37) is purely a *statistical* model: it merely states a quite general relationship between the excess return on an asset and the economic and financial environment. The APT follows from an application of the properties of arbitrage portfolios to this equation.

Consider an arbitrage portfolio consisting of n assets, where n is assumed to be much larger than the number of factors k. Let the weight attached to the ith asset in the portfolio be ω_i. The first property of an arbitrage portfolio is that it involves a zero commitment of wealth. Thus a long position in any asset must be counterbalanced by a short position in one or more of the other assets. This means that the portfolio weights must sum to zero:

$$\sum_{i=1}^{n} \omega_i = 0 \tag{3.38}$$

The second property of arbitrage portfolios is that they are riskless. This means, first, that any particular arbitrage should be sufficiently well diversified to remove the *non-systematic* risk attached to each asset:

$$\sum_{i=1}^{n} \omega_i e_i = 0 \tag{3.39}$$

and, second, that the *systematic risk* attaching to each asset from any particular factor should be diversified away:

$$\sum_{n=1}^{n} \omega_i \beta_{ik} = 0 \quad \text{for all } k \tag{3.40}$$

Given that the portfolio return, R_p say is a weighted average of the individual asset returns, we then have

$$R_p = \sum_{i=1}^{n} \omega_i R_i$$
$$= \sum_{i=1}^{n} \omega_i E(R_i) + \sum_{j=1}^{k} \delta_j \sum_{i=1}^{n} \omega_i \beta_{ij} + \sum_{i=1}^{n} \omega_i e_i$$

So, using (3.39) and (3.40) and the fact that the return to an arbitrage portfolio must be zero:

$$\sum_{i=1}^{n} \omega_i E(R_i) = 0 \tag{3.41}$$

Relations (3.39), (3.40) and (3.41) can be satisfied simultaneously if the expected return on an asset is a linear function of each of the factor coefficients:

$$E(R_i) = \lambda_0 + \lambda_1 \beta_{i1} + \lambda_2 \beta_{i2} + \ldots + \lambda_k \beta_{ik} \tag{3.42}$$

To see this, multiply (3.42) by ω_i, sum over $i = 1, \ldots n$ and apply (3.39) and (3.40) to yield (3.41).

Because the factor loadings associated with the risk-free asset must be zero, and since by definition $E(R_f) = R_f$, substituting $i = \text{f}$ in (3.42) yields $\lambda_0 = R_f$. Thus

$$E(R_i) = R_f + \lambda_1 \beta_{i1} + \lambda_2 \beta_{i2} + \ldots + \lambda_k \beta_{ik} \tag{3.43}$$

Equation (3.43) is one representation of the arbitrage pricing theory.[10] The required excess return to an asset is viewed as a function of k risk premiums $\{\lambda_j\}_{j=1}^{k}$, each of which is associated with a particular factor.

It is immediately seen that the CAPM is a very special case of the APT (set $\lambda_1 = E(R_m) - R_f$ and $\lambda_j = 0,\ j > 1$). The same is also clearly true for the consumption CAPM. The APT can also be thought of as a snapshot of the ICAPM in which the factors represent innovations in the underlying state variables.

4.1 Empirical evidence on the APT

Empirical work on the APT involves identifying (at least implicitly) a set of factors, estimating the factor loading matrix (i.e. all the β_{ij}s) and then testing (3.43). Broadly speaking, three approaches have been employed to estimate the factor loading matrix in empirical work.

The first involves determining the factor loadings without explicit reference to the factors themselves, by working back from the restrictions implicitly imposed on the covariance matrix of asset returns by the APT. Thus investigators have used either principal component analysis (e.g. Chamberlain and Rothschild 1983) or factor analysis (e.g. Roll and Ross 1980; Chen 1983; Lehmann and Modest 1985a, b).

The second approach to estimating the factor loading matrix involves identification of potential factors from visual inspection of the covariance matrix of asset returns. Thus, for example, Huberman and Kandel (1985) use indices of small, medium and large firms as factors after noting that returns to equities in firms of similar size appear to be more highly correlated than returns to equities in firms of dissimilar size.

The third approach simply involves the researcher in using his or her judgement to write down a set of factors which are then used to estimate the factor loadings empirically (see e.g. the studies by Chan et al. 1985 and Chen et al. 1986 mentioned above).

Once the factor loading matrix has been estimated, the APT is generally tested either by testing it against the CAPM (a set of zero restrictions on (3.43)) or by testing for the significant explanatory power of additional variables such as firm size and the asset return variance (add these variables into (3.43) and test for zero coefficients on them).

In general, empirical studies have found that the CAPM is easily rejected against the alternative of the APT. There is, however, mixed evidence of a small-firm effect whereby smaller firms appear to earn systematically higher returns than larger firms even when factor loading differences are controlled for; that is, a firm size variable is sometimes found to be a significant additional variable in (3.43). Thus although Chen (1983), Chan et al. (1985), Chen et al. 1986 and Huberman and Kandel (1985) cannot reject the hypothesis that factor loadings alone explain cross-sectional variations in assets' mean returns, studies by Reinganum (1981b), Cannor and Korajczyk (1986) and Lehmann and Modest (1985a) are able to do so.

Note that any empirical test of the APT must be a *joint* test of the linear pricing relation (3.43) and of the correct identification of the full set of factors. Just as Roll (1977) argues that the CAPM cannot be tested empirically, Shanken (1982) argues that the APT cannot be tested because the factors are not specified by the theory. This has generated some debate in the literature (see e.g. Dybvig and Ross 1985; Shanken 1985b).

Perhaps the best that can be said is that the APT seems to explain asset returns better than other models currently available.

5 PRICING CONTINGENT CLAIMS: FINANCIAL OPTIONS

A financial option is a *derivative security* (see e.g. Rubinstein 1987) which gives the holder the *right* but not the *obligation* either to buy (if it is a call option) or to sell (if it is a put option) a specified amount of the underlying security at a specified price, either *on* a certain future date known as the expiration date (a European option) or at any time between the purchase of the option and the expiration date (an American option)[11].

Clearly, a put option will only be worth something at the expiration date if the price at which it can be exercised, the *strike price*, exceeds the market (cash) price of the underlying asset, i.e. it is 'in the money'. A call option will only have a non-zero value if its strike price is less than the market price of the underlying asset. An option will have a positive value before the expiration date even if it is not in the money, because there is always a non-zero probability that it will move into the money by the expiration date.

The classic article on option pricing is due to Black and Scholes (1973). The Black and Scholes approach is, however, technically very demanding and the Black-Scholes formula can be derived as a limiting case in a simpler approach due to Cox et al. (1979), which we outline here.

5.1 The binomial option pricing model

We shall illustrate the binomial option pricing model for the simple case of a call option on an equity, assuming no dividend is payable during the period of analysis.[12] We shall then show how the Black-Scholes option pricing formula can be derived from the binomial model.

We start by assuming that the current, cash market price of the equity is S. In one period from now, we expect the price either to rise to uS with probability q, or to fall to dS with probability $1 - q$.[13] We assume that the riskless one-period interest rate is R_f. In order to avoid riskless arbitrage opportunities we require

$$u > 1 + R_f > d \tag{3.44}$$

If (3.44) did not hold, then money could be risklessly made either by borrowing money to purchase the equity or by selling the equity short and lending at the rate R_f.

Now consider a one-period call option on the equity which costs C. Let the strike price be K. After one period, the call option will only be exercised if the strike price is less than the market price of the equity at that time, so that a profit can be made. Otherwise, the option will expire worthless. Thus, if the price goes to uS, the value of the call option will then be

$$C_u = \max[0, uS - K] \tag{3.45}$$

Similarly, if the price falls to dS, the value of the option will be

$$C_d = \max[0, dS - K] \tag{3.46}$$

We now employ a standard tactic in finance theory to work out the equilibrium price of an asset: namely, we construct an equivalent portfolio and equate the rates of return.

Suppose we held one unit of the equity and *wrote m* call options against it, and we chose m such that the payoff was the same after one period regardless of what happened to the price of the equity. The cost of this portfolio is initially $S - mC$, i.e. the cost of the equity less the revenue from writing the m call options. If the equity price goes to uS then after one period the portfolio will be worth uS *less* the value mC_u of the m call options which we have written, i.e. $uS - mC_u$. Conversely, if the equity price falls to dS, the portfolio will be worth $dS - mC_d$. Since we choose m such that the payoff is state invariant after one period, we have

$$uS - mC_u = dS - mC_d \tag{3.47}$$

This implies a *hedge ratio m* given by

$$m = \frac{S(u - d)}{C_u - C_d} \tag{3.48}$$

Now, because the return to holding this portfolio is riskless, in order to avoid risk-free arbitrage it must be the case that the cost of borrowing money to purchase the portfolio is just equal to its return. If we borrow $S - mC$, we have to repay $(1 + R_f)(S - mC)$ after one period. Therefore, to preclude arbitrage,

$$(1 + R_f)(S - mC) = uS - mC_u \tag{3.49}$$

Solving (3.49) for C:

$$C = \frac{S[(1 + R_f) - u] + mC_u}{m(1 + R_f)} \tag{3.50}$$

Substituting for the hedge ratio from (3.48) in (3.50):

$$C = \frac{\pi C_u + (1 - \pi)C_d}{1 + R_f} \qquad (3.51)$$

where

$$\pi = \frac{(1 + R_f) - d}{u - d} \qquad (3.52)$$

Equation (3.51) is a very simple option pricing formula for the one-period case: given u, d, S and R_f we can work out what the fair price for the call option is (note that S is required for C_u and C_d). It is remarkable for at least three reasons.

First, the option price does not depend on q, the probability that the price of the equity will rise; thus bulls and bears can agree on the price of the option. Second, the option price depends only on the safe rate and on the current cash price of the equity and on no other asset returns such as the market portfolio return. One should remember, however, that a financial option is a derivative security; the market's views concerning the likely future course of equity prices will already be reflected in S and R_f and the required returns to other assets should also be reflected in S (e.g. through the CAPM or the APT). Third, we made no assumptions concerning agents' attitudes towards risk. The only assumptions that were made were that agents prefer more to less and that risk-free arbitrage opportunities are eliminated in equilibrium.

Note that π must always be between zero and unity (by virtue of (3.44) and assuming $R_f > 0$), and so it can be interpreted as a probability. In fact, if agents were risk-neutral, then we would have to have $\pi = q$ in equilibrium. To see this, note that the expected value of the equity after one period is $quS + (1 - q)dS$. If agents were risk-neutral, they would require only the expectation of the risk-free rate of return. Thus

$$(1 + R_f)\,S = quS + (1 - q)\,dS$$

So

$$q = \frac{(1 + R_f) - d}{u - d} = \pi$$

If this were indeed the case, then (3.51) would simply define the value of the call option as the discounted present value of its expected value next period. On reflection, this is not surprising. Since the simple option pricing model must hold for the whole range of attitudes towards risk, it must hold in particular for the case of risk neutrality. In general, however, agents are not risk-neutral.

We now extend this simple one-period option pricing model to many

Table 3.1 Value of the equity after one and two periods

Initial value	Value after one period	With probability	Value after two periods
S	uS	q	u^2S
S	uS	q	udS
S	dS	$1 - q$	duS
S	dS	$1 - q$	d^2S

periods. After the first period, the cash value of the equity will be either uS or dS. We assume that the state probabilities remain the same. There is now a probability q of the equity rising by a factor u to the end of the second period, and a probability $1 - q$ of it falling by a factor d. The set of possible outcomes is listed in table 3.1.

It is clear from table 3.1 that the equity can only take one of three values at the end of the second period: u^2S, udS or d^2S. We might thus write the range of possible option values at the end of the second period as

$$C_{uu} = \max[0, u^2S - K] \tag{3.53}$$

$$C_{ud} = \max[0, udS - K] \tag{3.54}$$

$$C_{dd} = \max[0, d^2S - K] \tag{3.55}$$

The question we now address is: given this range of possible outcomes, what would be the fair value of the option at the end of the first period? The solution to this problem is formally identical to the solution to the one-period problem given above. Assume first that the equity price has gone to uS, and as before denote by C_u the value of the call option given that this has occurred. Given that the equity price is uS after one period, it can then go either to u^2S with probability q, or to udS with probability $1 - q$ in the remaining period. Proceeding precisely as before, the fair value of C_u is given by

$$C_u = \frac{\pi C_{uu} + (1 - \pi)C_{ud}}{1 + R_f} \tag{3.56}$$

with π defined as in (3.52). Similarly, the fair value of the call if the equity price is dS after one period is given by

$$C_d = \frac{\pi C_{ud} + (1 - \pi)C_{dd}}{1 + R_f} \tag{3.57}$$

Substituting (3.34) and (3.35) into (3.51) yields the fair price for the call option in the initial period:

$$C = \frac{\pi^2 C_{uu} + 2\pi(1-\pi)C_{ud} + (1-\pi)^2 C_{dd}}{(1+R_f)^2} \tag{3.58}$$

with C_{uu}, C_{ud} and C_{dd} defined as in (3.53)–(3.55). Equation (3.58) can again be interpreted as the discounted present value of the expected value of the call option after two periods, given risk neutrality.

The extension of this formula to the general n-period case involves, in principle, solving back from period n to the initial period. A more straightforward route, however, is to exploit the interpretation of the option pricing formula under the assumption of risk neutrality.[14]

Suppose, after n periods, the equity price has gone up by a factor u exactly j times, and has fallen by a factor d exactly $n-j$ times. The value of the equity at the end of period n must then be $u^j d^{n-j} S$, and thus the value of the call option at the end of the nth period must be $\max[0, u^j d^{n-j} S - K]$. The probability of this occurring is (recalling the fact that $q = \pi$ in equilibrium, assuming risk neutrality) $\pi^j (1-\pi)^{n-j}$. Finally, we observe that the total number of possible combinations of j ups and $n-j$ downs over n periods is

$$\frac{n!}{(n-j)!j!}$$

where $g! = gx(g-1) \times (g-2) \times \ldots \times 3 \times 2 \times 1$ for any integer g.

Putting these observations together, and noting that j can take any integer value between 0 and n, the expected value of the call option at the end of period n, $E[C(n)]$ say, given risk neutrality, must then be

$$E[C(n)] = \sum_{j=0}^{n} \frac{n!}{(n-j)!j!} \pi^j (1-\pi)^{n-j} \max[0, u^j d^{n-j} S - K] \tag{3.59}$$

Equation (3.59) can be further simplified by deleting the cases where the call option is 'out of the money' at the end of period n, i.e. $\max[0, u^j d^{n-j} S - K] = 0$. Let a be the smallest number of ups such that the option is in the money at the end of period n, i.e. a is the smallest non-negative integer such that

$$u^a d^{n-a} S > K \tag{3.60}$$

Solving inequality (3.60), a is the smallest non-negative integer which satisfies

$$a > \log(K/Sd^n)/\log(u/d) \tag{3.61}$$

Using this, the zero terms in (3.59) can be deleted so that $E[C(n)]$ becomes

$$E[C(n)] = \sum_{j=a}^{n} \frac{n!}{(n-j)!j!} \pi^j (1-\pi)^{n-j} (u^j d^{n-j} S - K) \tag{3.62}$$

Under risk neutrality, the present value of $E[C(n)]$, discounted at the risk-free rate, must be equal to the fair value of the call in the initial period. Thus

$$C = \left\{ \sum_{j=a}^{n} \frac{n!}{(n-j)!j!} \pi^j (1-\pi)^{n-j} (u^j d^{n-j} S - K) \right\} (1 + R_f)^{-n}$$

or

$$C = S \left\{ \sum_{j=a}^{n} \frac{n!}{(n-j)!j!} \pi^j (1-\pi)^{n-j} \frac{u^j d^{n-j}}{(1+R_f)^n} \right\}$$
$$-K(1+R_f)^{-n} \left\{ \sum_{j=a}^{n} \frac{n!}{(n-j)!j!} \pi^j (1-\pi)^{n-j} \right\} \tag{3.63}$$

Under risk neutrality, the first bracketed expression in (3.63) is the discounted present value of the equity at the end of period n, given that the call ends in the money. Similarly, the second bracketed term is, under risk neutrality, the present value of the strike price of the call, multiplied by the probability that the call will finish in the money. Thus, under risk neutrality, (3.63) can be interpreted as the expected present value of the profit from the call option.

Since we know that a fair option price must be invariant with respect to all attitudes towards risk (including risk neutrality), we know that this formula must hold even when agents are not risk-neutral.

The above assumes a binomial distribution for the equity price: in each period the equity price can either go up (multiply by u) with probability q, or down (multiply by d) with probability $1 - q$. The *complementary binomial distribution function* $B(j \geq a | n, \pi)$ is the probability that the sum of j random variables, each of which can take the value 1 with probability π and 0 with probability $1 - \pi$, will be greater than or equal to some non-negative integer a after n binomial trials. It is defined as

$$B(j \geq a | n, \pi) = \sum_{j=a}^{n} \frac{n!}{(n-j)!j!} \pi^j (1-\pi)^{n-j} \tag{3.64}$$

If we write

$$\pi' = \frac{u}{1 + R_f} \tag{3.65}$$

then (3.63) can be written, using (3.64), as

$$C = SB(j \geq a|n, \pi') - K(1 + R_f)^{-n}B(j \geq a|n, \pi) \tag{3.66}$$

This is the form in which the binomial call option pricing formula is normally expressed.

To see how the binomial formula relates to the classic formula derived by Black and Scholes (1973), we observe the limiting value of (3.66) as we shift to continuous time.

5.2 The Black-Scholes option pricing formula

In the analysis in the previous section, we assumed there were n periods to the expiration of the option. In order to derive the option pricing formula of Black and Scholes (1973), we must shift to continuous time. This means that, although the total time to expiration remains fixed - at, say, T units of calendar time (e.g. years) - the number - of subperiods (e.g. hours, minutes or seconds) gets larger and larger and, in the limit, tends to infinity.

First, consider the way in which the future value of the option must be discounted in continuous time. Above, R_f was defined as the one-period risk-free interest rate. We now redefine it as the annualized rate available for the maturity of the option, which is compounded continuously. Thus, if the total number of years is T (or fraction of a year if $T < 1$), and there are n periods in T, then the one-period rate is now TR_f/n. Thus, if we compound at this rate over the whole period to expiration,[15]

$$\lim_{n \to \infty} (1 + TR_f/n)^n = e^{TR_f} \tag{3.67}$$

Conversely, if we continuously discount at this rate, we have a discount factor of

$$\lim_{n \to \infty} (1 + TR_f/n)^{-n} = e^{-TR_f}$$

Next, we consider the continuously compounded rate of return on the equity. We denote the market value of the equity at expiration by S^*. If, over the time to maturity of the option there have been j upward moves and $n - j$ downward moves in the equity price, then we have $S^* = u^j d^{n-j} S$, so that one plus the continuously compounded rate of return is given by

$$\log (S^*/S) = j \log u + (n - j) \log d \tag{3.68}$$

Thus, since j is the only random variable in (3.68),

$$E[\log(S^*/S)] = E(j)[\log(u/d)] + n \log d \tag{3.69}$$

$$\text{var}[\log(S^*/S)] = \text{var}(j)[\log(u/d)]^2 \tag{3.70}$$

Since j is binomially distributed, its mean and variance are given by nq and $nq(1-q)$ respectively (see e.g. Larson 1974). Thus

$$E[\log(S^*/S)] = [q \log(u/d) + \log d]n \tag{3.71}$$
$$= \hat{\mu}n, \quad \text{say}$$

$$\operatorname{var}[\log(S^*/S)] = q(1-q)[\log(u/d)]^2 n \tag{3.72}$$
$$= \hat{\sigma}^2, \quad \text{say}$$

Equations (3.71) and (3.72) are expressions for the mean and variance of the return to holding the equity, expressed as a multiple n of the one-period mean and variance. As we shift to continuous time, n tends to infinity ($n \to \infty$). Suppose that, as a matter of fact, the mean and variance of the equity return over the period of length T calendar units are given by μT and $\sigma^2 T$ respectively. Cox et al. (1979) point out that if we let

$$u = e^{\sigma\surd(T/n)}, \quad d = e^{-\sigma\surd(T/n)}, \quad q = (1/2) + (1/2)(\mu/\sigma)\surd(T/n) \tag{3.73}$$

then

$$\lim_{n \to \infty} \hat{\mu}n = \mu T$$

$$\lim_{n \to \infty} \hat{\sigma}^2 n = \sigma^2 T$$

Note that μ and σ^2 denote the *instantaneous* mean and variance of the return to holding the equity.

Given (3.73) and with π and π' as defined in (3.52) and (3.65) repsectively, Cox et al. (1979) prove that, under weak regularity conditions,

$$\lim_{n \to \infty} B(j \geq a|n, \pi) = N(d_1) \tag{3.74}$$

$$\lim_{n \to \infty} B(j \geq a|n, \pi') = N(d_2) \tag{3.75}$$

where

$$d_1 = \frac{\log(S/K) + R_f T}{\sigma\surd T} + \frac{1}{2}\sigma\surd T \tag{3.76}$$

$$d_2 = d_1 - \sigma\surd T \tag{3.77}$$

and where $N(x)$ denotes the cumulative standard normal distribution function evaluated at x, i.e. the probability that a normally distributed random variable with mean zero and variance unity will be less than or equal to x.

Thus Black and Scholes show that the continuously compounded rate of return to holding the equity, S^*/S, will have a limiting log-normal distribution, i.e. log (S^*/S) is normally distributed.

Thus, using (3.68) and (3.74)–(3.77), we can see that as n tends to infinity and time becomes continuous, expression (3.66) for the value of the call option approaches the limit

$$C = SN(d_1) - K\,e^{-R_f T}N(d_2) \tag{3.78}$$

with d_1 and d_2 defined as in (3.76) and (3.77).

Equation (3.78) is the expression derived by Black and Scholes (1973) for the fair value of a call option. To interpret (3.78), consider the probability that the call option will finish in the money,

$$\begin{aligned}\Pr\{\text{in the money}\} &= \Pr\{S^* \geq K\}\\ &= \Pr\{\log(S^*/S) \geq \log(K/S)\}\end{aligned}$$

Since S^*/S has a log-normal distribution with mean μT and variance $\sigma^2 T$, the random variable $[\{\log(S^*/S) - \mu T\}/\sigma\sqrt{T}] = z$ will have a standard normal distribution. Thus

$$\Pr\{\text{in the money}\} = \Pr\{z \geq [\log(K/S) - \mu T]/\sigma\sqrt{T}\}$$

and, by the symmetry of the normal distribution,

$$\Pr\{\text{in the money}\} = \Pr \leq z < -\ [\log(K/S) - \mu T]/\sigma\sqrt{T}\} \tag{3.79}$$

Now, by the properties of the log-normal distribution, we have

$$\log E(S^*/S) = \mu T + (1/2)\sigma^2 T \tag{3.80}$$

Moreover, if agents are risk-neutral, then the expected return to holding the equity $E(S^*/S)$ must be just equal to the continuously compounded safe return $e^{R_f T}$. Thus, using (3.80), we have

$$\mu T = R_f T - (1/2)\sigma^2 T \tag{3.81}$$

Using (3.81) in (3.79), we have

$$\begin{aligned}\Pr\{\text{in the money}\} &= \Pr \leq z < [\log(S/K) + R_f T -\\ &\quad (1/2)\sigma T^2]/\sigma\sqrt{T}\}\\ &= N(d_2)\end{aligned} \tag{3.82}$$

Thus the second term in the Black-Scholes option pricing model (BSOPM) (3.78) can be interpreted as the present value of paying the strike price of the call option at maturity, given that the call is in the money and assuming that agents are risk-neutral, as we demonstrated for the binomial pricing model. By a similar procedure, the first term in the BSOPM can be shown to be equal to the present value of the expected value of the market value of the equity, given that the option expires in the money and again assuming risk neutrality. Thus (3.78) can be interpreted as the present value of the expected payoff at maturity to holding the call option, given risk neutrality.

5.3 The relationship between puts and calls: put-call parity

For a European put option on an equity which pays no dividends before the expiration date of the option, we can derive an arbitrage relationship between the fair value of puts and calls so that the option price formulas developed above can also be used to price put options.

Suppose an investor formed a portfolio by writing one call option on an equity (at price C), buying one put option on the equity (at price P) and buying one unit of the equity (at price S). The put and call options are assumed to be of the same maturity T and to have the same strike price K. The cost of this portfolio is therefore $P + S - C$. At the expiration of the options, let the market price of the equity be S^*. At this time, we have either $S^* \leq K$ so that the put option is in the money but the call option expires worthless, or else $S^* > K$ so that the call option expires in the money but the put option expires worthless.

In the first case, $S^* \leq K$, the put option is in the money and so will be exercised. This gives the portfolio a revenue of $K - S^*$. The call option is worthless and so will not be exercised. The equity is now worth S^*. Thus the total value of the portfolio at expiration of the options is

$$K - S^* + 0 + S^* = K \tag{3.83}$$

In the second case, $S^* > K$, the put option will expire worthless while the call option will be in the money and will thus be exercised. This results in a payout by the investor to the holder of the call option of $S^* - K$. The value of the equity will be S^*, as before. Thus in this case the value of the portfolio will be

$$0 - (S^* - K) + S^* = K \tag{3.84}$$

Comparing (3.83) and (3.84), we can see that the value of the portfolio at maturity is state invariant: it is equal to K whatever the value of the equity. Since the portfolio is riskless, in order to preclude arbitrage, its fair value initially must be just equal to the present value of its payoff at expiration, i.e. $e^{-R_f T}K$. Since the cost of the portfolio is $P + S - C$, we therefore have

$$P + S - C = e^{-R_f T}K \tag{3.85}$$

Equation (3.85) is the put-call parity relationship. Given the formula derived for the fair value of a call option in previous sections, (3.85) can be used to determine the fair value of a put.

5.4 Some empirical evidence on option pricing

As in much of empirical financial economics, tests of the option pricing model are generally joint tests of the model and of a market efficiency condition. For example, one method of testing the BSOPM is to identify options which are under- or overvalued according to the formula and then to write or buy the options while going long or short of the equivalent amount of the underlying equity. This yields a riskless hedge portfolio which, if the BSOPM is correct and the market is efficient, ought to yield a return no larger than the risk-free rate (at least, once transaction costs and taxes are taken into account). Equivalently, the beta of a hedge portfolio ought to be zero. If the excess return is non-zero, then this may be due to a failure of the BSOPM, to a failure of market efficiency or to both.

Black and Scholes (1973) applied this technique to price data from the over-the-counter option market for contracts written on 545 securities between 1966 and 1969. Taking transaction costs into account, their results were consistent with the BSOPM and market efficiency. A similar finding was obtained by Galai (1977), using data from the Chicago Board of Options Exchange for each option traded between 26 April 1973 and 30 November 1973.

Chiras and Manaster (1978) compute implied equity price volatilities by inverting the option pricing formulas, and find that they are good predictors of future actual variances.

MacBeth and Merville (1979) found some tendency for the BSOPM to overprice out of the money options and to underprice in the money options, although Geske and Roll (1984) have argued that this effect disappears if the statistics are reformulated. The finding of bias in the BSOPM is, however, corroborated by Rubinstein's (1985) non-parametric study, although Rubinstein is unable to find an alternative model which explains all of the various biases all of the time.

Chiras and Manaster (1978) compute implied equity price volatilities by inverting the option pricing formulas and find that they are good predictors of future actual variances.

6 CONCLUSION

In this chapter we have outlined the salient topics in the literature on financial markets, including the theory and evidence on efficient markets, on the major models of asset price determination and on the pricing of contingent claims, i.e. option pricing. The outline is intended as an introduction to the literature, and we hope that it will serve as a primer for the chapters in this book concerned with financial markets.

Notes

1 See MacDonald and Taylor (1990) for a more comprehensive coverage of the financial markets literature.
2 In this chapter we follow American usage and take the terms 'stock' and 'equity' as synonyms for 'company share'.
3 For example, Fama's (1976) working definition of an efficient market is 'a market in which prices always "fully reflect" available information'.
4 Campbell and Shiller (1987) use two alternative measures of expected returns, namely the return on short-term debt plus a constant, and the return on short-term debt plus a term that depends on the conditional variances of stock returns. However, neither of these alternatives results in a significant improvement of the model's performance.
5 Pratt (1964) and Arrow (1965) show that the quadratic utility function has the undesirable property that the degree of risk aversion increases as wealth increases. Markowitz (1959) argues, in essence, that mean-variance analysis requires only that the quadratic surface should be taken as a local approximation around current (single-period) wealth and may be allowed to vary from portfolio to portfolio. The Pratt-Arrow objections apply only if a quadratic approximation is fitted around current wealth at some instant in time and used in subsequent analysis.
6 Of course, if agents borrow the risk-free asset, their holding of that asset will be negative.
7 This is sometimes called the *market model*; see Fama and MacBeth (1973).
8 In fact, because returns can only be measured *ex post*, they are testing the *ex post* efficiency of the proxy portfolio.
9 Varian (1987) gives a lucid introduction to the arbitrage principle.
10 Some authors term this the *exact arbitrage pricing* relationship, to distinguish it from more general versions of the APT in which this equation holds to a small approximation.
11 In most of what follows we shall be concerned with European options.
12 It can be shown that an American call option on an equity which pays no dividend during the period of analysis will never be exercised before the expiration date (see e.g. Cox and Rubinstein 1986, ch. 5). Thus it is not necessary to distinguish between European and American calls in this context.
13 Although we shall find it convenient to speak as if $d < 1$, nothing in what follows rests on this. In fact, we require only the weaker condition that $d < 1 + R_f < u$.
14 This route will only be correct so long as we know that the option will not be exercised before maturity, i.e. if it is a European option or if it is an American call on an equity which pays no dividend between now and the expiration date.

Otherwise, the formula must be derived recursively, as we did in the two-period analysis above.

15 Symbol e is the exponential constant 2.71821828. . .the base of natural logarithms.

References

Arrow, K. (1965) *Aspects of the Theory of Risk Bearing*, Helsinki: Yrjö Jahnsson Foundation.

Banz, R. W. (1981) 'The relationship between return and market value of common stocks', *Journal of Financial Economics*, 9, 3–18.

Basu, S. (1977) 'Investment performance of common stocks in relation to their price–earnings ratios: a test of the efficient markets hypothesis', *Journal of Finance*, 32, 663–82.

Black, F. (1972) 'Capital market equilibrium with restricted borrowing', *Journal of Business*, 45, 444–55.

Black, F., Jensen, M. and Scholes, M. (1972) 'The capital asset pricing model: some empirical tests', in M. C. Jensen (ed.), *Studies in the Theory of Capital Markets*, New York: Praeger.

Black, F. and Scholes, M. (1973) 'The pricing of options and corporate liabilities', *Journal of Political Economy*, 81, 637–54.

Blanchard, O. J. (1979) 'Speculative bubbles, crashes and rational expectations', *Economics Letters*, 3, 387–9.

Blume, M. and Friend, I. (1973) 'A new look at the capital asset pricing model', *Journal of Finance*, 28, 19–34.

Bollerslev, T., Engle, R. F. and Wooldridge, J. M. (1988) 'A capital asset pricing model with time-varying covariances', *Journal of Political Economy*, 96, 116–31.

Breeden, D. T. (1979) 'An intertemporal asset pricing model with stochastic consumption and investment opportunities', *Journal of Financial Economics*, 7, 265–96.

Camerer, C. (1987) 'Bubbles and fads in asset prices: a review of theory and evidence', University of Pennsylvania, mimeo.

Campbell, J. Y. and Shiller, R. J. (1987) 'Cointegration and tests of present value models', *Journal of Political Economy*, 95, 1062–88.

Campbell, J. Y. and Shiller, R. J. (1988) 'The dividend–price ratio and expectations of future dividends and discount factors', *Review of Financial Studies*, 1, 195–228.

Chamberlain, G. and Rothschild, M. (1983) 'Arbitrage, factor structure and mean-variance analysis on large asset markets', *Econometrica*, 51, 1281–304.

Chan, K. C., Chen, N. and Hsieh, D. (1985) 'An exploratory investigation of the firm size effect', *Journal of Financial Economics*, 14, 451–71.

Chen, N. (1983) 'Some empirical tests of the theory of arbitrage pricing', *Journal of Finance*, 38, 1393–414.

Chen, N., Roll, R. and Ross, S. A. (1986) 'Economic forces and the stock markets', *Journal of Business*, 59, 383–403.

Chiras, D. P. and Manaster, S. (1978) 'The information content of option prices and a test of market efficiency', *Journal of Financial Economics*, 6, 213–34.

Connor, G. and Korajczyk, R. A. (1986) 'Performance measurement with the arbitrage pricing theory: a framework for analysis', *Journal of Financial Economics*, 15, 373–94.

Cox, J. C. Ingersoll, J. and Ross, S. A. (1985) 'An intertemporal general equilibrium model of asset prices', *Econometrica*, 53, 363–84.

Cox, J. C., Ross, S. A. and Rubinstein, M. (1979) 'Option pricing: a simplified approach', *Journal of Financial Economics*, 7, 229–63.

Cox, J. C. and Rubinstein, M. (1986) *Options Markets*, Englewood Cliffs, NJ: Prentice-Hall.

DeBondt, W. F. M. and Thaler, R. (1985) 'Does the stock market overreact?', *Journal of Finance*, 40, 793–808.

DeBondt, W. F. M. and Thaler, R. (1987) 'Further evidence on investor overreaction and stock market seasonality', *Journal of Finance*, 42, 557–81.

De Long, J. B., Schleifer, A., Summers, L. M. and Waldmann, R. J. (1987) 'The economic consequences of noise traders', National Bureau of Economic Research, working paper 2395.

Diba, B. T. and Grossman, H. I. (1985) 'Rational bubbles in stock prices?', National Bureau of Economic Research, working paper 1779.

Dybvig, P. H. and Ross, S. A. (1985) 'Yes, the APT is testable', *Journal of Finance*, 40, 1173–88.

Engle, R. F. and Granger, C. W. J. (1987) 'Co-integration and error correction: representation, estimation and testing', *Econometrica*, 55, 251–76.

Fama, E. F. (1976) *Foundations of Finance*, New York: Basic Books.

Fama, E. F. and French, K. R. (1988) 'Permanent and temporary components of stock prices', *Journal of Political Economy*, 96, 246–73.

Fama, E. F. and MacBeth, J. (1973) 'Risk, return and equilibrium: empirical tests', *Journal of Political Economy*, 81, 607–36.

Flood, R. P. and Hodrick, R. J. (1987) 'Asset price volatility, bubbles and process switching', *Journal of Finance*, 41, 831–42.

Friend, I. and Blume, M. (1970) 'Measurement of portfolio performance under uncertainty', *American Economic Review*, 70, 561–75.

Galai, D. (1977) 'Tests of market efficiency of the Chicago Board of Options Exchange', *Journal of Business*, 50, 167–97.

Garber, P. (1989) 'Tulipmania', *Journal of Political Economy*, 97, 535–60.

Geske, R. and Roll, R. (1984) 'Isolating the observed biases in call option pricing: an alternative variance estimator', University of California at Los Angeles, working paper.

Gibbons, M. R. (1982) 'Multivariate tests of financial models: a new approach', *Journal of Financial Economics*, 10, 3–28.

Hausman, J. A. (1978) 'Specification tests in economics', *Econometrica*, 46, 1251–72.

Hall, S. G., Miles, D. K. and Taylor, M. P. (1989) 'Modelling asset prices with time-varying betas', *The Manchester School*, 57, 340–56.

Hamilton, J. D. (1986) 'On testing for self-fulfilling speculative price bubbles',

International Economic Review, 27, 545–52.

Hicks, J. R. (1946) *Value and Capital*, 2nd edn, Oxford: Oxford University Press.

Huberman, G. and Kandel, S. (1985) 'A size-based stock returns model', Center for Research in Security Prices, University of Chicago, working paper 148.

Keim, D. (1983) 'Size-related anomalies and stock return seasonality: further empirical evidence', *Journal of Financial Economics*, 12, 13–32.

Keim, D. (1985) 'Dividend yields and stock returns', *Journal of Financial Economics*, 14, 474–89.

Keynes, J. M. (1936) *The General Theory of Employment, Interest and Money*, London: Macmillan.

Kleidon, A. W. (1986) 'Variance bounds tests and stock price valuation models', *Journal of Political Economy*, 94, 953–1001.

Krasker, W. (1980) 'The peso problem in testing the efficiency of forward exchange markets', *Journal of Monetary Economics*, 6, 269–76.

Larson, H. J. (1974) *Introduction to Probability Theory and Statistical Inference*, New York: Wiley.

Lehmann, B. (1987) 'Fads, martingales and market efficiency', Columbia University, mimeo.

Lehmann, B. and Modest, D. (1985a) 'The empirical foundations of the arbitrage pricing theory I: the empirical tests', Department of Economics, Columbia University, working paper 291.

Lehmann, B. and Modest, D. (1985b) 'The empirical foundations of the arbitrage pricing theory II: the optimal construction of basis portfolios', Department of Economics, Columbia University, working paper 292.

LeRoy, S. F. and Porter, R. (1981) 'The present value relation: test based on implied variance bounds', *Econometrica*, **49**, 555–674.

Lintner, J. (1965) 'The valuation of risky assets and the selection of risky investments in stock portfolios and capital budgets', *Review of Economics and Statistics*, **47**, 13–37.

Litzenberger, R. and Ramaswamy, K (1979) 'The effects of personal taxes and dividends on capital asset prices: theory and empirical evidence', *Journal of Financial Economics*, 8, 163–95.

Lo, A. W. and McKiney, A. C. (1987) 'Stock market prices do not follow random walks: evidence from a simple specification test', University of Pennsylvania, mimeo.

Lucas, R. E. Jr (1978) 'Asset prices in an exchange economy', *Econometrica*, 46, 1429–45.

MacBeth, J. and Merville, L. (1979) 'An empirical examination of the Black-Scholes call option pricing model', *Journal of Finance*, 34, 1173–86.

McCallum, B. T. (1976) 'Rational expectations and the estimation of econometric models: an alternative procedure', *International Economic Review*, 17, 484–90.

MacDonald, R. and Power, D. (1991) 'Persistence in UK stock market returns: aggregated and disaggregated perspectives', Chapter 13 of this volume.

MacDonald, R. and Taylor, M. P. (1990) 'Financial markets: an introduction', in R. MacDonald and M. P. Taylor (eds), *Financial Markets*, Aldershot: Edward Elgar.

Mankiw, N. G., Romer, D. and Shapiro, M. D. (1985) 'An unbiased reexamination of stock price volatility', *Journal of Finance*, 40, 677–88.

Markowitz, H. (1959) *Portfolio Selection: Efficient Diversification of Invetsments*, New York: Wiley.

Marsh, T. A. and Merton, R. C. (1986) 'Dividend variability and variance bounds tests for the rationality of stock market prices', *American Economic Review*, 76, 483–98.

Merton, R. C. (1973) 'An intertemporal capital asset pricing model', *Econometrica*, 41, 867–87.

Miller, M. and Scholes, M. (1972) 'Rates of return in relation to risk: a re-examination of some recent findings', in M. C. Jensen (ed.) *Studies in the Theory of Capital Markets*, New York: Praeger.

Mossin, J. (1966) 'Equilibrium in a capital asset market', *Econometrica*, 34, 768–83.

Poterba, J. M. and Summers, L. H. (1988) 'Mean reversion in stock prices: evidence and implications', *Journal of Finance*, 43, 27–59.

Pratt, J. W. (1964) 'Risk aversion in the small and in the large', *Econometrica*, 32, 122–36.

Reinganum, M. R. (1981a) 'Misspecification of capital asset pricing: empirical anomalies based on earnings yields and market values', *Journal of Financial Economics*, 8, 19–46.

Reinganum, M. R. (1981b) 'The arbitrage pricing theory: some simple tests', *Journal of Finance*, 36, 313–21.

Roll, R. (1977) 'A critique of the asset pricing theory's tests', *Journal of Financial Economics*, 4, 129–76.

Roll, R. and Ross, S. A. (1980) 'An empirical investigation of the arbitrage pricing theory', *Journal of Finance*, 35, 1073–103.

Ross, S. A. (1975) 'Uncertainty and the heterogeneous capital good model', *Review of Economic Studies*, 42, 133–46.

Ross, S. A. (1976) 'The arbitrage theory of capital asset pricing', *Journal of Economic Theory*, 13, 341–60.

Ross, S. A. (1977) 'The capital asset pricing model (CAPM), short-sale restrictions and related issues', *Journal of Finance*, 32, 177–83.

Rubinstein, M. (1985) 'Non-parametric tests of alternative option pricing models', *Journal of Finance*, 40, 455–80.

Rubinstein, M. (1987) 'Derivative assets analysis', *Journal of Economic Perspectives*, 1, 73–93.

Shanken, J. (1982) 'The arbitrage pricing theory: is it testable?', *Journal of Finance*, 19, 1129–40.

Shanken, J. (1985a) 'Multivariate tests of the zero-beta CAPM', *Journal of Financial Economics*, 12, 327–48.

Shanken, J. (1985b) 'A multi-beta CAPM or equilibrium APT?: a reply', *Journal of Finance*, 40, 1189–96.

Sharpe, W. (1964) 'Capital asset prices: a theory of market equilibrium under conditions of risk', *Journal of Finance*, 19, 425–42.

Shiller R. J. (1981) 'Do stock prices move too much to be justified by subsequent changes in dividends?', *American Economic Review*, 71, 421–36.

Shiller, R. J. (1983) 'Reply', *American Economic Review*, 73, 236–7.

Shiller, R. J. (1984) 'Stock prices and social dynamics', *Brookings Papers on Economic Activity*, 14, 457–98.

Shiller, R. J. (1987) 'The volatility of stock market prices', *Science*, 235, 33–7.

Stambaugh, R. (1982) 'On the exclusion of assets from tests of the two-parameter model: a sensitivity analysis', *Journal of Financial Economics*, 9, 237–68.

Tirole, J. (1982) 'On the possibility of speculation under rational expectations', *Econometrica*, 50, 1163–81.

Tirole, J. (1986) 'Asset bubbles and overlapping generations', *Econometrica*, 53, 1071–100.

Tobin, J. (1958) 'Liquidity preference as behavior towards risk', *Review of Economic Studies*, 25, 65–86.

Varian, H. (1987) 'The arbitrage principle in financial economics', *Journal of Economic Perspectives*, 1, 55–72.

West, K. D. (1986) 'A specification test for speculative bubbles', National Bureau of Economic Research, working paper 2067.

West, K. D. (1988) 'Bubbles, fads and stock price volatility tests: a partial evaluation', *Journal of Finance*, 43, 639–60.

Part II
Money Demand Studies

4 Money Demand in Five Major Industrialized Countries: Estimating and Interpreting Error Correction Models

James M. Boughton

The recent revival of interest in estimating aggregate money demand functions has resulted in part from the promising results that have been obtained with error correction models. As a modelling approach, the estimation of cointegrating relationships together with largely unconstrained dynamic adjustment processes has proved to be a useful generalization of the partial adjustment and buffer stock models that had dominated the literature in the 1970s and early 1980s. Specific applications, however, have frequently been controversial, as it has been difficult to deflect criticisms of data mining and of the opaqueness of many of the estimated equations. This chapter reviews some of the key issues that have arisen in this literature, presents error correction equations for narrowly and broadly defined monetary aggregates in each of five large industrial countries, and discusses the implications of this approach for interpreting the long-run demand for money in these countries.

1 ISSUES IN ESTIMATING ERROR CORRECTION MODELS

As a starting point for reviewing some of the interesting features of error correction models of the demand for money, consider the following equation for M1 in the United States, from a widely cited paper by Baba *et al.* (1988), based on quarterly data 1960–84:

$$\Delta(m-p) = -0.144\mu_{-2} - 0.758rma + 0.117rmoc_{-1}$$
$$-0.457S - 0.574S_{-3} - 0.363s_{-3} + 0.005V_{-3}$$

$$-0.174\Delta(m-p)_{-4} + 0.450\Delta rmoc - 0.454\Delta s_{-1}$$
$$- 0.902\Delta p + 0.359\Delta Ay + 0.050\Delta^2 S^* V_{-1} \qquad (4.1)$$

where the symbols have the following meanings:[1]

m	logarithm of the nominal money stock
p	logarithm of the GNP deflator
y	logarithm of real GNP
μ	$= m - p - 0.5y$
rma	after-tax maximum yield on instruments included in M2 but not in M1
$rmoc$	after-tax maximum yield on instruments included in M1
S	difference between after-tax yields on twenty-year Treasury bonds (r) and one-month Treasury bills (i)
s	difference between i and rma
V	three-year moving standard deviation of r
S^*V	$= (\max(0,S))V$
Ay	$= \frac{2}{3}y + \frac{1}{3}y_{-1}$

The first RHS term (in μ) is the error correction term, which has been specified prior to estimating the rest of the equation. The rest of the static terms in the equation complete the steady-state representation, which may be interpreted as characterizing the long-run demand for money. If the steady state is further restricted to one in which interest rate ceilings are non-binding (i.e. $rma = rmoc = i$; also $s = V = 0$), then the long-run demand function may be simplified to

$$m - p = 0.5y + 2.71i - 7.16r \qquad (4.2)$$

As with most earlier models, this equation was estimated subject to the prior constraint – in this case based on initial estimation of a simplified equation – that the long-run price elasticity was unity. The real income coefficient was initially estimated to be close to 0.5, and that value was then imposed as being consistent with the simple version of the Baumol-Tobin model.

These steady-state parameters appear to be non-controversial; for comparison, the steady state estimated by Goldfeld (1976), using a much more restricted specification and an earlier (1952–73) data sample, was[2]

$$m - p = 0.629y - 5.618i \qquad (4.3)$$

The main departure that (4.2) makes from the conventional approach as represented by (4.3) is the inclusion of both short- and long-term interest rates, with short-term rates serving as a proxy for the own yield on the interest-bearing component of M1. In the earlier sample period, very little of M1 bore interest, and what yields there were tended to be low and invariant; that property no longer holds in the United States or in the other countries examined below. But there is also an econometric reason for including both rates in equations such as (4.1) but not in the more restricted equations that prevailed until recently. When the demand function is estimated with all arguments entering contemporaneously, it is very difficult to sort out the effects of different interest rates, owing to collinearity. In a more general specification, in which short and long rates might, for example, enter with different lags, disentangling their effects could be enhanced.[3] This appears to be the case with (4.1).

Although the steady state of (4.1) seems straightforward and reasonable, the full equation is rather more complex to interpret, because the dynamics are based on the data rather than imposed *a priori*. For example, one probably would not have thought *a priori* that there should be a three-quarter lag before a rise in the volatility of bond yields, or a shift in the term structure, would affect portfolio decisions. It also may be surprising to note that the adjusting variable, in effect, is not real but nominal money balances, since the coefficient on the inflation rate (Δp) is approximately -1.[4] In other words, the impact effect of a shift in the demand for money is to change the nominal money stock in the same direction, which is suggestive of an accommodating monetary policy in the short run. Although most of the properties of (4.1) are interpretable in terms of money demand theory, the very complexity of the equation is bound to raise doubts about its robustness: would a different researcher, or even the same researcher working with (say) a slightly longer data sample, derive this same specification?

It may be instructive to compare (4.1) with a few samples drawn from studies of money demand in other large industrial countries.[5] It should be noted that these comparisons are not intended as criticisms of the selected papers, but rather as illustrations of the issues that arise in evaluating error correction models of money demand.

Yoshida (1990) derived the following equation for M2 in Japan, using quarterly data over 1968–85:[6]

$$\Delta(m - p) = 0.79\mu_{-1} - 0.84\mu_{-2} + 1.17\Delta y_{-1} - 0.7\Delta r - 0.18\Delta p - 0.82\Delta^2 p + 0.05\sum_{i=1}^{4} EQV_{-1} \quad (4.4)$$

where $\mu = m - p - 1.4y$, r is the coupon rate on five-year bank debentures and EQV is the coefficient of variation on stock prices.

Equation (4.4) has an unusual feature in that the error correction term appears with both a one-period and a two-period lag. Yoshida does not present tests for whether the two coefficients are significantly different in absolute value; if not, then the error correction form may vanish, in the sense that there is no statistically significant steady-state solution. In any event, the adjustment lags will be extremely long. Also, there is no interest rate effect in the steady state; that could simply reflect the use of a broader definition of money, or it could be an inappropriate restriction in the specification. Overall, while the error correction term is similar to that used in (4.1) except for the rather higher income elasticity (1.4 against 0.5), the dynamic structure is quite different. It is striking, however, that in (4.4), as in (4.1), the impact effect is on nominal rather than real balances. That is, $0.18\Delta p + 0.82\Delta^2 p = \Delta p - 0.82\Delta p_{-1}$, so the dependent variable may be rewritten as Δm rather than $\Delta(m - p)$, with the appropriate transformations on the RHS.

Bordes and Strauss-Kahn (1989) have estimated an error correction model for French M1, using quarterly data over the period 1971–88:

$$\Delta(m - p) = -0.23\mu_{-1} - 0.32\Delta i_{-2} - 0.40\Delta^2 p - 0.20\Delta^2 p_{-1} - 0.18\Delta^2 p_{-2} \quad (4.5)$$

where $\mu = m - p - 0.45y + 0.46i + 0.25\Delta p$ and i is the overnight call-money rate ('le taux de l'argent au jour le jour'). There is a subtle difference in the estimation procedure between (4.5) and the equations discussed above. Both Baba et al. and Yoshida (1990) constrained the coefficients in the error correction term (principally by excluding interest and inflation rates) before specifying the dynamic equation, while Bordes and Strauss-Kahn used the residuals from the unconstrained cointegrating regression. That difference in part reflects disagreement regarding whether nominal interest rates are cointegrated with real money balances and real income. But it also reflects disagreement about the stationarity of inflation rates. If Δp is I(1) (integrated of order 1, or stationary in first differences), then it may be appropriate to include it in the cointegrating equation. If, however, the price *level* is I(1) – i.e. if the inflation rate is stationary – then one might envisage a multivariate cointegrating relationship among the I(1) variables, i.e. nominal money, price level, real income and nominal interest rates. Unfortunately, the order of integration of aggregate price indices is ambiguous, depending on the test that is used.[7]

As a final example, consider the error correction equation for M1 in the United Kingdom estimated by Muscatelli (1989) using data over the period 1963–84:[8]

$$\Delta m = -0.172(m - p)_{-1} - 0.610i + 0.267y - 0.164y_{-3} - 0.177\Delta m_{-3} + 0.406\Delta_3 p_{-1} \quad (4.6a)$$

This functional form differs from those discussed above in that the levels of each variable appear with different lags: one-quarter for real balances, no lag for the interest rate, and contemporaneous and three-quarter lag on real income. If (4.6a) were transformed into a more standard error correction form, one would obtain

$$\Delta m = -0.172\mu_{-1} - 0.610\Delta i + 0.267\Delta y + 0.164\Delta_2 y_{-1} - 0.177\Delta m_{-3} + 0.406\Delta_3 p_{-1} \tag{4.6b}$$

where $\mu = m - p - 0.6y + 3.55i$. Note, however, that the implied coefficients on the dynamic variables Δi, Δy and $\Delta_2 y_{-1}$ have been estimated subject to constraints. Thus the choice between specifying an error correction term with a single lag structure (as in the other equations discussed above) or allowing the lag structure to be data-based (as in (4.6a)) is non-trivial.

In general, any equation in levels and differences can be transformed into one in which the levels all appear with the same lag, simply by adding the appropriate difference terms subject to constraints on the parameters. To take a simple example, the equation

$$\Delta y = -\beta_1 y_{-2} + \beta_2 x_{-1} \tag{4.7}$$

may be transformed as

$$\Delta y = -\beta_1 y_{-1} - \beta_1 \Delta y_{-1} + \beta_2 x_{-1} \tag{4.8a}$$

or as

$$\Delta y = -\beta_1 \mu_{-1} - \beta_1 \Delta y_{-1}, \quad \text{where } \mu = y - \beta_2 x \tag{4.8b}$$

Imposition of a single lag structure is equivalent to estimating (4.8a) or (4.8b) without the constraint. Especially in the context of the general to specific model reduction process that is an inherent part of the specification of error correction models, that procedure is inefficient and may lead the researcher to drop terms that would be (implicitly) significant in (4.7). In this example, one would be likely to find the coefficient on Δy_{-1} to be insignificant; dropping it, however, would produce an equation that would be encompassed by (4.7).

This highly selective review suggests several issues that are important for evaluating error correction models of money demand:

(a) Is it appropriate to impose constraints on the error correction term during the first stage of the specification process, such as forcing elasticities to take on certain values or excluding certain variables?
(b) Is two-stage estimation (first estimating a cointegrating equation and then using the residuals as an argument in a dynamic equation) necessarily superior to a single-stage specification process?
(c) Does the typical specification search avoid data mining sufficiently to yield equations that are both stable (in the sense that the parameters

of a given specification would not change significantly over time) and robust (in the sense that a different search procedure or a different sample period would not substantially alter the selected specification)?

(d) Are the estimated dynamic relationships sufficiently parsimonious to be both analytically transparent and robust across data sets?

(e) Are the estimated steady states consistent with generally accepted theories of the demand for money?

The first two issues are examined in section 2, and the other three are then taken up in section 3. The conclusions are summarized in section 4.

2 METHODOLOGY

2.1 Alternative approaches

There are several methods available for specifying and estimating error correction models.[9] At the most general level, there is a choice between the two-stage procedure advocated by Engle and Granger (1987) and single-stage estimation in which the coefficients on levels and differences are estimated simultaneously. The latter lacks the super-consistency of the former (see Stock 1987) and is difficult to evaluate because the standard errors may not be evaluated by the standard t distribution if (some of) the regressors have unit roots (see Dickey and Fuller 1981). It may nonetheless be a more efficient use of data in small samples, especially where (as in the present case) it is necessary to derive a data-based specification of the equation's dynamics; in general, one will not arrive at the same model when the steady state is constrained.

2.2 Two-stage estimation

If one chooses to use the two-stage procedure, the cointegrating equation will generally not be unique, as Engle and Granger noted and as Johansen (1988) has stressed. That is, there is a variety of methods for obtaining the first-stage equation – and, in the multivariate case, there may be as many as $n - 1$ valid cointegrating vectors – and there is no clear basis for choosing among them. As alternatives to simple static estimation (as originally proposed by Engle and Granger), one could directly estimate the steady state of a distributed-lag function, or one could arbitrarily select one of the vectors estimated by Johansen's vector autoregression (VAR) methodology, or one could impose prior values on the coefficients. Choosing among the results raises issues of both efficiency and identification.

Regardless of how the first stage is obtained, the second stage is to estimate a dynamic money demand relationship, which might initially have the form

$$\Delta m = \alpha + \beta_1 L(p) + \beta_2 L(y) + \beta_3 L(i) + \beta_4 L(r) - \gamma \mu_{-1} + \epsilon \quad (4.9)$$

where L is the lag operator and μ is the time series of residuals from the cointegrating vector. Equation (4.9) can then be reduced to a parsimonious equation through the elimination of insignificant terms and the imposition of constraints that hold to a reasonable approximation. If and only if the levels of all variables vanish in this reduction process will the initial estimate of the cointegrating vector be accepted as the steady state (i.e. the long-run demand function). Hence the specification of the dynamics cannot be treated as recursive to the specification of the steady state.[10]

The initial development of cointegration analysis was aimed at bivariate models. In that context, the question is whether a single relationship exists and, if so, how it is parameterized. In the case of money demand functions, the model is multivariate and there may exist multiple cointegrating vectors linking some or all of the included variables. Johansen (1988) has devised a general procedure for the multivariate case, and the test statistics have been generalized in Johansen and Juselius (1990). For this test, consider a VAR on the detrended logarithms of money, price level and real income, plus short- and long-term interest rates:

$$\beta_0 L(m) + \beta_1 L(p) + \beta_2 L(y) + \beta_3 L(i) + \beta_4 L(r) - \alpha = \mu \quad (4.10)$$

The null hypothesis is that there are five unit roots in this system (no cointegrating vectors). If that hypothesis is rejected, one tests sequentially for additional cointegrating vectors. For the present problem, it is also interesting to examine the coefficients of any significant vectors to determine if they have the signs and order of magnitude that are expected for a long-run money demand relationship.

A complication that arises is that the steady-state demand function, if it exists, may exclude one or both interest rates. In that case, the five-variable VAR may still be characterized by one or more cointegrating vectors, none of which might have the desired characteristics. Furthermore, there is a strong likelihood of multiple cointegrating vectors, because – in addition to the presumed long-run money demand relationship – the two interest rates are normally linked with each other and possibly with other included variables through related demand functions. The procedure followed here is therefore also to examine subsystems that exclude first one interest rate (generally the short rate, which is less likely to enter the long-run function)[11] and then both interest rates.

The results of this exercise, with four lags included in each VAR, are

Table 4.1 Tests for the existence of cointegrating vectors

	Number of significant vectors[b]	Preferred vector[c]	Elasticities[a]			
			Price level	Real income	Short rate	Long rate
United States						
M1	3 of 5	3 *	0.760	1.084	0.110	−0.027
M1	2 of 4	2 *	0.885	0.895		−0.045
M2	2 of 5	1 ***	0.791	2.013	0.140	−0.153
M2	2 of 4	2 *	1.091	0.917		−0.016
Japan						
M1	4 of 5	2 ***	1.198	0.962	0.027	−0.028
M2	1 of 5	1 ***	0.625	1.423	0.038	−0.079
Germany						
M1	5 of 5	1 ***	0.976	1.061	0.041	−0.036
M3	3 of 5	1 ***	0.533	2.123	0.033	−0.027
M3	2 of 3	1 ***	0.876	1.630		
France						
M1	3 of 5	2 ***	0.862	0.816	0.030	−0.050
M2	3 of 5	1 ***	1.272	0.821	0.024	−0.060
United Kingdom						
M1	2 of 5	2 *	0.752	1.709	0.125	−0.154
M3	2 of 5	1 ***	0.534	3.280	0.090	−0.079

[a] Semi-elasticities for interest rates.
[b] The first number is the number of vectors for which the trace of the eigenmatrix exceeds the 90 per cent significance level, as reported in table A2 in Johansen and Juselius (1990). The second number is the maximum number (when the matrix is full rank), i.e. the number of variables included in the VAR.
[c] The first vector is the one with the highest eigenvalue (and significance level), and so forth. *, ** and *** indicate significance levels of 90, 95, and 99 per cent, respectively.

summarized in table 4.1.[12] The interpretation of this table may be illustrated by taking the first two rows (M1 for the United States) as an example. For the full five-variable VAR, there are three significant cointegrating vectors (at the 90 per cent level or higher), of which the third (i.e. the least highly significant of those three) comes closest to matching the prior values on the coefficients. This vector is not very satisfying, however, because the price elasticity is low. Consequently, a second test has been conducted without the short-term interest rate. In the second row, two of the four cointegrating vectors are significant, of which the second looks reasonably as expected. Overall, the results shown in table 4.1 do support the hypothesis that these data sets are characterized by error correction representations, with steady states that could be interpreted as conventional money demand relationships. There are, however, a few exceptions. First, for both M2 in Japan and M3 in the United Kingdom the estimated long-run price elasticities are well below unity (0.6 and 0.5, respectively). Second, for M1 in Germany the matrix may be full rank;[13] in this case, although there is a steady state, there may not be a stable dynamic adjustment process.

One way to employ these results would be to take the vectors in table 4.1 as point estimates of the steady state, and incorporate the lagged residuals from those equations as arguments in a dynamic Engle-Granger equation linking changes in money to changes in the other variables. There are, however, a number of difficulties with that procedure. First, as already noted, the key parameters are not always consistent with conventional priors regarding the shape of the long-run demand function. Second, compounding this first problem, it is not always obvious which of perhaps several candidates should be selected as the most relevant cointegrating vector. Third, the estimated steady state may change in the context of a more fully specified model, especially when constraints have been imposed at the initial stage.

Another variant of the two-stage procedure is to impose some or all of the coefficients of the error correction term *a priori*. In particular, since all theoretical models of money demand hypothesize long-run homogeneity with respect to prices, it is natural to consider imposing a unitary price elasticity. In addition, a number of theoretical models imply constraints on the range of acceptable values for the real income elasticity. Commonly considered possibilities would include a simple velocity model, used by, among others, Hendry and Ericsson (1989) for M2 in the United Kingdom and Hall et al. (1989) for M1 in the United Kingdom, namely $\mu = m - p - y$; and the Baumol-Tobin model of economies of scale, used by Baba et al. (1988) for M1 in the United States, namely $\mu = m - p - 0.5y$. As with the Johansen procedure, the imposition of prior coefficients in this manner (even if they closely approximate coefficients in an unconstrained static regression) raises the possibility that the error correction term will not adequately capture the cointegrating relationships; when the full dynamic model is specified, the steady-state income and price elasticities may turn out to be different from those that were initially imposed, and interest and inflation rates may be additional arguments in the long-run function.

2.3 Single-stage estimation

An alternative to the two-stage procedure is to estimate the steady state implicitly, through a general to specific regression strategy along the lines advanced by David Hendry (e.g. 1987). That is, starting from a distributed-lag equation such as

$$m = \alpha + \sum_{i=1}^{T} \beta_{0,i} m_{-i} + \sum_{j=1}^{k} \sum_{i=0}^{T} \beta_{j,i} x_{j,-i} + \epsilon; \quad x = (p, y, i, r) \qquad (4.11)$$

one can eliminate the least significant current or lagged elements and reduce the system to a more parsimonious equation in levels and differences, and then solve directly for the steady state of that equation. There are two main differences between this approach and the two-stage procedure. First, as noted above in the discussion of Muscatelli's model, the error correction term need not be limited to contemporaneous observations. Second, because the extraneous elements in the original regression are eliminated and restrictions may be imposed on the coefficients, there may be a substantial gain in degrees of freedom. While neither of these differences is likely to be consequential asymptotically, both may be important in small samples. The extension to non-contemporaneous observations turns out to be especially important for the problem at hand.

The specification of general dynamic equations is subject to criticism as a form of data mining, especially when the results are as eclectic as the examples discussed in section 1. This danger is present for the second stage of the two-stage procedures just discussed, but it is especially important when the steady state is estimated simultaneously with the specification of the dynamics.

There is, of course, no firm line that can be drawn between data mining and using a data set properly to compare alternative models; the proof is in the pudding, which in this case is in the robustness of the estimated model. Most studies of robustness of error correction models have, however, been quite limited, in that they have taken the final (derived) specification as given. That is, if the specification of a regression is derived by experimentation, it is not sufficient to test whether the parameters of that equation are stable over time; it is necessary to test as well for whether the specification itself would have been different if it had been derived over a different sample period or over a different data set.

For the tests discussed below, the dynamic regressions have been specified according to a specific algorithm, in order to minimize the possibility of over-parameterizing through experimentation. This process involves eliminating insignificant variables and imposing constraints that hold approximately in an initial unconstrained regression, but it does not permit other constraints, or the addition of variables other than those in the long-run function. The algorithm, which is otherwise rather arbitrary but commonsensical, is as follows. First, estimate (4.11) with $T = 4$. Second, for each variable, drop the lag (or the current value) with the lowest t ratio, as long as the ratio is less than unity. Repeat this operation as necessary. Third, eliminate further lags if t ratios are below the 5 per cent level, taking due account of interactions and of the effects on the final specification.[14]

If eliminating a variable has a noticeable effect on other coefficients or would qualitatively alter the steady-state solution, further testing (including F tests) may be needed to determine if the variable should be retained. Fourth, test to determine whether two or more lags can be combined to form simple or compound differences. For example, if x_t has a positive coefficient and x_{t-i} has a negative coefficient of similar magnitude, test to see if the two can be replaced by $\Delta_i x_t$ without significantly raising the standard error of the estimate. At each step, account is taken of the shape of the equation residuals; problems such as instability, autocorrelation, heteroscedasticity or skewness may reflect a misspecification.

2.4 Evaluation of the various approaches

In view of the variety of methods available for estimating error correction models of money demand, it is necessary to find a means of selecting among them. The range of possible estimates of steady-state relationships for M1 in the United States 1964(1)–1988(4) is suggested by the following:

Simple static equation:

$$m = 0.960p + 0.629y + 0.017i - 0.006r \tag{4.12}$$

Static solution to autoregressive distributed lag:

$$m = 0.615p + 1.424y + 0.022i - 0.030r \tag{4.13}$$

Four-variable Johansen vector from table 4.1:

$$m = 0.885p + 0.895y - 0.045r \tag{4.14}$$

Steady state from two-stage estimation with (4.14) as error correction term:

$$m = 0.669p + 1.293y + 0.014i - 0.029r \tag{4.15}$$

Steady state from single-stage estimation:

$$m = 0.652p + 1.338y + 0.015i - 0.030r \tag{4.16}$$

Single-stage estimation with p as dependent variable:

$$m = 0.522p + 1.544y + 0.021i - 0.040r \tag{4.17}$$

Single-stage estimation with $m - p$ as dependent variable:

$$m = 0.648p + 1.364y + 0.013i - 0.030r \tag{4.18}$$

Two-stage estimation with $m - p - y$ as error correction term:

$$m = 0.825p + y + 0.018r - 0.037r \tag{4.19}$$

Single-stage estimation with trend included:

$$m = 1.761p + 5.004y - 0.041t \tag{4.20}$$

It is immediately apparent that the choice of estimation strategy makes a substantial difference. These estimates allow for non-homogeneity with respect to the price level, and in most cases the elasticity is estimated to be significantly less than unity. Exceptions to that result are the simple static equation (4.12), and (4.20) in which a trend is included. Note that even when the error correction term is constrained so that the price elasticity is unity, as in (4.19), the price level is found to have a significant negative effect in the second-stage regression, and the long-run elasticity is thus again found to be less than unity.

Most of the estimates (4.12)–(4.20) generate a real income elasticity that exceeds unity and a positive coefficient on the short-term interest rate, but these results also are not completely robust. Even the finding of a negative steady-state relationship with the long-term interest rate, which is supported by almost all models, is overturned when the trend is included.

Space precludes a detailed discussion of the full dynamic regressions underlying the nine equations summarized above. Suffice it to say that there is little or no uniformity of specification that emerges from the algorithm described. In other words, the choice of methodology has a substantial effect not only on the qualitative properties of the long-run demand function, but also on the form of the dynamic adjustment process. To illustrate with the two most closely related models, the second-stage regressions that were derived starting from (4.13) and (4.14) are respectively as follows:

$$\Delta m = -0.83\mu_{-1} + 0.245\Delta y - 0.280\Delta_2 p_{-2} - 0.254\Delta_2 i - 0.354\Delta_3 r_{-1} \tag{4.21}$$

$$\Delta m = -0.113\mu_{-1} + 0.045y - 0.025p_{-1} + 0.160i_{-3} + 0.181r_{-3} - 0.318\Delta i - 0.290\Delta r_{-3} - 0.292\Delta_3 p_{-1} \tag{4.22}$$

where μ in each equation is defined as the residual from the corresponding static equation. The presence of the levels of each variable in (4.22) accounts for the differences between (4.14) and (4.15). The dynamic effects of inflation and interest rates are fairly similar in these two equations, but changes in real income are significant only in the first.[15]

Larger differences in structure are found in comparisons with single-stage estimation or with specifications derived over different sample periods. For example, when the same specification algorithm for single-stage estimation is applied to the same US M1 data, but ending the sample three years apart, one obtains for 1964–88

$$\Delta m = -0.101m_{-2} + 0.066p_{-1} + 0.135y + 0.150i - 0.304r_{-1}$$

$$-0.240\,\Delta_3 p_{-1} - 0.369\Delta i - 0.207\Delta_3 r_{-1} \qquad (4.23)$$

and for 1964–85

$$\Delta(m-p) = -0.058(m-p)_{-2} - 0.029p_{-3} + 0.095y_{-1} - 0.544\Delta_3 p$$

$$-0.217\Delta_3\Delta i - 0.520(\Delta r_{-1} + \Delta r_{-3}) + 0.250\Delta_3\Delta y$$

$$-0.228\Delta(m-p)_{-2} \qquad (4.24)$$

A Chow test for parameter stability of (4.24) over the twelve omitted quarters strongly rejects the null hypothesis.[16] Obviously, in this case one's perception of both the steady-state and dynamic properties is almost completely determined by the sample period. The demand for US M1 is perhaps the least stable of all the aggregates examined in this chapter, and other comparisons would be less stark. The point of this exercise is simply to illustrate the necessity of examining the robustness of the equation's structure as well as the stability of its parameters.

The various models from which the steady states (4.12)–(4.20) were drawn are almost all non-nested, so an appropriate test for dominance is the procedure developed by Davidson and MacKinnon (1981). In this test the predictions from one model are added to another; if the predictions from model 1 are significant in model 2, but those of model 2 are insignificant in model 1, then model 1 is preferred over model 2.[17]

Tests comparing several models for M1 in the United States and the United Kingdom, and the two basic approaches (single- and two-stage estimation) for the other aggregates, are summarized in table 4.2. It would have been a pleasant surprise to find that these tests conclusively favoured one approach over the others; more realistically, they do broadly support unconstrained single-stage estimation (model ECl) over most alternatives. For M1 in the United States, the conclusion is unambiguous: model ECl is preferred over all other estimates. For M1 in the United Kingdom, the tests imply that a more general model may be required, since the predictions of model ECl are significant when added to the other three estimates, but the estimates from the other models are also significant when added to model ECl. Comparisons of single-stage and two-stage estimation for the other eight aggregates indicate that the single-stage estimates are preferred in four cases; the two-stage estimates in two cases (both of the French aggregates); and a more general model in the remaining two. Thus with the exception of France, relatively little seems to be gained – and a possibly heavy cost could be incurred – by two-stage estimation. The submodels included for the United States in table 4.2 are also of interest. Constraining

Table 4.2 Encompassing tests for non-nested models, 1964–88 (*F* statistics)[a]

Basic model	Additional model AD2	PV2	JV2	EC1	EC1a	EC1b	EC1c
United States M1							
AD2	–	0.55	2.27	2.89*	2.08	2.85*	0.25
PV2	2.87*	–	3.49*	4.41**	1.47	4.82**	0.00
JV2	5.26**	4.86**	–	4.20**	4.18**	5.34**	0.55
EC1	2.09	1.63	0.01	–	–	2.15	0.03
EC1a	4.44**	1.48	1.30	3.00*	–	5.04**	0.02
EC1b	4.65**	4.03**	2.15	4.27**	3.99**	–	0.00
EC1c	5.45**	4.34**	1.26	3.59*	3.62*	4.79**	–
United Kingdom M1							
AD2	–	0.90	0.51	4.91**			
PV2	3.21	–	2.34	5.75**			
JV2	2.58	3.45*	–	6.27**			
EC1	6.02**	4.72**	4.86**	–			

Other aggregates

	AD2 versus EC1	EC1 versus AD2
United States		
M2	20.36***	5.45**
Japan		
M1[c]	10.43***	2.33
M2	62.73***	0.01
Germany		
M1	19.76***	6.46**
M3[d]	12.63***	1.80
France		
M1	0.84	6.26**
M2	0.24	7.64***
United Kingdom		
M3	17.01***	2.59

[a] Test of the significance of adding the predictions from the additional model to the regression of the basic model; see Davidson and MacKinnon (1981). The null hypothesis is that the information from the additional model is already in the basic model. The symbols *, ** and *** indicate rejection of the null hypothesis at the 0.10, 0.05 and 0.01 levels, respectively. The models are as follows:

AD2 Two-stage estimation, with first stage estimated as (4.11) with $T = 4$
PV2 same procedure as AD2 except first stage imposed, with unitary elasticities on prices and real income and both interest rates omitted
JV2 same procedure as PV2 except that long-term interest rate included, and coefficients taken from table 4.1
EC1 single-stage general to specific modelling, starting from (4.11)
EC1a EC1 with real income elasticity constrained to unity
EC1b EC1 with trend included
EC1c EC1 with real balances as dependent variable

[b] For this aggregate, EC1a is nested in EC1.
[c] Estimated in first differences.
[d] Estimated with real balances as the dependent variable.

the real income elasticity to unity (model ECla) has little effect one way or another,[18] but estimating the model with real rather than nominal money balances as the dependent variable (model EClc) makes matters decidedly worse. Inclusion of a trend (model EClb) is either neutral or superior to all other models except for the unconstrained single-stage model.

The clearest conclusion to be drawn from this exercise is that there does exist at least one cointegrating vector linking the variables that are expected to enter the long-run demand function. This conclusion holds for all ten data sets (two aggregates in each of five countries) being examined. There is thus a *prima facie* case for estimating error correction models of the demand for these aggregates. It is also clear that the imposition of prior constraints leads, in most cases, to inferior performance. In spite of the very strong theoretical prior for price homogeneity, the imposition of that constraint can be quite misleading. Whether a single- or a two-stage estimation strategy is to be preferred is, however, less clear.

3 FINAL ERROR CORRECTION ESTIMATES

The procedure adopted here for estimating error correction models for each of these aggregates is to pursue at least two approaches - the general single-stage and two-stage strategies discussed above - and then to select between them on the basis of both encompassing tests and the plausibility of the parameters. If both models have serious problems, then related models are also estimated and compared.

The results of this approach are summarized in table 4.3; the complete dynamic regressions are available upon request. With two exceptions, one or the other of the two basic models has been successfully estimated for each aggregate. For M3 in Germany, single-stage estimation failed to confirm the existence of an error correction model; the final equation contained only differences in the variables, except for the level of the long-term interest rate. Two-stage estimation generated an acceptable steady state, but the error correction term was non-stationary (i.e. the hypothesis that the data are not cointegrated could not be rejected), and the dynamic equation was encompassed by other models. The preferred estimate was taken to be that of model EClc: single-stage estimation starting with real balances as the dependent variable. For M1 in Japan, none of the models produced an acceptable error correction equation, so the basic models were rerun in first-difference form.

The most striking finding from this exercise is that six of the ten aggregates have long-run price elasticities that are significantly less than unity. The reasons for this anomaly are not obvious, but there are two explanations that probably account for at least part of it. The first is the possibility of

Table 4.3 Long-run elasticities: final estimates

		Elasticity		Semi-elasticity	
Aggregate	Model[a]	Price level	Real income	Short-term interest rate	Long-term interest rate
United States					
M1	EC1	0.652	1.338	0.487	−3.013
M2	EC1	1.0	1.0	−0.779	-
Japan					
M1	EC1d	0.831	0.831	-	−2.628
M2	EC1	0.387	1.604	1.777	−5.572
Germany					
M1	AD2	1.0	1.199	−2.447	−1.482
M3	EC1c	0.418[b]	2.240	2.180	−3.183
France					
M1	AD2	1.0	0.434	−1.226	0.960
M2	AD2	0.685	1.965	−1.280	-
United Kingdom					
M1	EC1	1.0	3.332	−10.343	-
M3	EC1	0.699	3.281	-	−3.441

[a] AD2 Two-stage estimation, with first stage estimated as (4.11) with $T = 4$
EC1 single-stage general to specific modelling, starting from (4.11)
EC1c EC1 with real balances as dependent variable
EC1d EC1 estimated in first differences
[b] Insignificantly different from zero.

aggregation bias. For four of the five countries, the estimated price elasticity is much closer to unity for narrow money than for the broad aggregate; for the United States, the opposite holds. It may be, therefore, that excessive (or, in the US case, insufficient) aggregation is introducing errors in the parameter estimates. If, for example, the output elasticities differ across components of the aggregates, constraining them to be equal could bias the estimates.

The second likely explanation for the low price elasticities is the shortness of the data sample (25 years). If the true underlying price elasticity is unity but adjustment of the stock of money to repeated inflationary shocks has been incomplete over the data sample, then the estimated elasticity would be less than unity. To the extent that the central bank has responded to increases in the price level by reducing the money stock or that the price level has responded slowly in response to monetary policies, lags would be increased and the downward bias would be aggravated. In this case, the discrepancy would be greatest for the aggregates that were the primary focus of monetary policy; this story would thus suggest that US monetary policy had been concerned more with M1 during this period, while other countries had focused more on M2. Sorting out the importance of these various factors would require further research.[19]

There is virtually no evidence here in support of economies of scale in cash holdings. That is, the microeconomic theories pioneered by Baumol and Tobin do not seem to apply to the aggregate data: for eight of the ten aggregates, the real income elasticities are unity or higher.

In all but one case (M1 in France), the total effect of interest rates (the effect of a combined change in short and long rates) is negative, as expected. In several cases, however, there is a significant term structure relationship. In three cases, short-term interest rates have a positive effect on money holdings in the long-run, offset by a somewhat larger negative effect from long-term rates.

4 CONCLUSIONS

This chapter has examined the long-run properties of money demand equations for five large industrial countries and has compared the performance of error correction models specified under various approaches. These estimates raise questions about the robustness of both the long-run demand function and the dynamic adjustment properties, and they suggest that some of the most commonly accepted restrictions employed in the money demand literature may be inconsistent with the data. These questionable properties include homogeneity with respect to the price level, unitary or less than unitary elasticities with respect to real income, and restriction of the set of included interest rates to either short- or long-term rates, to the exclusion of the other.

In view of the apparent dependence of the specification of the error correction equations on the estimation strategy, the data sample and the particular monetary aggregate, it would be premature to attempt to derive specific recommendations for a research strategy from this exercise. One might have very strong priors about certain properties of the demand functions, such as price homogeneity, and be willing to impose those priors regardless of the unconstrained estimates. But it seems important to recognize that even the most fundamental hypotheses may not hold - at least in small samples - when the specification is data-based and unconstrained. In most cases examined in this chapter, regressions derived according to an Engle-Granger two-stage procedure are outperformed (encompassed) by a less restricted single-stage general to specific process. But it has not been possible to demonstrate that one approach is always preferred to the others; nor has it emerged that any of the properties of the estimates are invariant with respect to that choice. If error correction modelling is to become widely accepted, the robustness of the estimates, and especially of the specification of the regressions, will have to be subjected to more rigorous tests than those applied so far.

Notes

The author wishes to thank Neil Ericsson, George Tarlso, and Mark Taylor for helpful comments. Any remaining errors are the author's responsibility.

1 The equation also includes a constant term and a dummy variable for the temporary imposition of credit controls in 1980. These are omitted here to simplify the presentation; constant terms are also ignored in the equations discussed below. Some of the other notation has been simplified from that in the original paper.

2 This is derived from equation (5.1) in Goldfeld (1976), holding the yield on time deposits (r_{td}) fixed. Alternatively, if $r_{td} = i$, the steady-state coefficient on i would rise to 25.281. Over Goldfeld's sample period, however, r_{td} showed very little variation.

3 For the United States over the period 1963–88, the correlation coefficient between the quarterly first differences of short- and long-term interest rates (the six-month commercial paper rate and the yield on long-term government bonds) is 0.73. When one rate is lagged by one-quarter, the correlation drops to 0.15.

4 The standard error on the coefficient (0.902) is 0.102.

5 Other papers in which error correction models are estimated for money demand in the United States include Cuthbertson and Taylor (1988), Ebrill (1988), Mehra (1989) and Rose (1985). For international comparisons, see Boughton and Tavlas (1990) and Domowitz and Hakkio (1990).

6 Corker (1990) also presents error correction equations for Japanese money demand.

7 See, for example, Boughton et al. (1989).

8 For other error correction models of UK money demand, see *inter alia* Cuthbertson and Taylor (1990), Hall et al. (1989), Hendry and Ericsson (1989), Hendry and Richard (1983) and Taylor (1987). Muscatelli also included seasonal dummies, not shown here. The article did not specify the interest rate that was used. The notation is $\Delta_i x_j = x_{-j} - x_{-j-i}$.

9 This section is based in part on Boughton (1991).

10 If the constraints in the cointegrating vector are valid, then μ_{-1} should capture all of the relationships among the levels of the variables (see Engle and Granger 1987). But if the researcher imposes restrictions that seem to hold approximately (such as price homogeneity) or omits key variables (such as interest rates), or if there are different lags linking the levels, then μ may not be a sufficient characterization of the steady state. These complications are discussed below. For further evidence on the difficulties that can arise with application of the two-step methodology, see Banerjee et al. (1986).

11 In most cases, bivariate tests indicate that short- and long-term interest rates are cointegrated; the apparent exception is the United Kingdom, where the Dickey-Fuller test just fails at the 90 per cent level to reject the null hypothesis of no cointegration. The long-term rates, however, have stationarity properties that come closer to those of the other variables in the system; specifically, the levels of short-term rates have somewhat higher Durbin-Watson statistics.
12 All of the estimates presented in this paper have been made using PC-GIVE; see Hendry (1989).
13 If significance were restricted to the 95 per cent rather than the 90 per cent level, then only four of the five vectors would pass the test.
14 Since some of the regressors will have unit roots, this criterion may be unduly strict; the danger is that one or more variables in the cointegrating relationship may be improperly excluded. It is thus helpful to compare the results with direct estimates of the cointegrating equation.
15 An F test (1,89) for adding Δy to (4.22) gives a value of 2.61, which is insignificant at the 10 per cent level. Its t ratio is 1.62, compared with 2.88 in (4.21).
16 $F(12,68) = 4.64$, significant at the 0.01 level.
17 See Hendry (1989) for a summary of several other encompassing tests. Those tests are programmed into PC-GIVE, but only for smaller data sets than those used here.
18 Unconstrained estimation yields a long-run real income elasticity of 1.34, which is close to that in most other estimates; see (4.12)–(4.20). However, an F test fails to reject (at 95 per cent) the hypothesis that the true coefficient is unity.
19 Other factors may also help to explain the lack of homogeneity in the regression estimates. First, the aggregate price indices may not measure the true prices on which asset holders' decisions are based. Second, there may be inflationary expectations effects that have not been modelled, such that a rise in the price level would cause the desired stock of real balances to fall. These factors, however, would not explain why the irregularity is present much more for one aggregate than for the other in each country.

References

Baba, Y., Hendry, D. F. and Starr, R. M. (1988) 'US money demand 1960–1984', Nuffield College, Oxford, discussion paper 27.

Banerjee, A., Dolado, J. J., Hendry, D. F. and Smith, G. W. (1986) 'Exploring equilibrium relationships in econometrics through static models: some Monte Carlo evidence', *Oxford Bulletin of Economics and Statistics*, 48 (3), 253–78.

Bordes, C. and Strauss-Khan, M.-O. (1989) 'Coïntégration et demande de monnaie en France', *Cahiers Economiques et Monétaires*, 34, Banque de France, 161–97.

Boughton, J. M. (1991) 'Long-run money demand in large industrial countries', *IMF Staff Papers*, 38 (March), 1–32.

Boughton, J. M., Branson, W. H. and Muttardy, A. (1989) 'Commodity prices and inflation: evidence from seven large industrial countries', National Bureau of Economic Research, working paper 3158.

Boughton, J. M. and Tavlas, G. S. (1990) 'Modeling money demand in large industrial countries', *Journal of Policy Modeling*, 12 (summer), 433–61.

Corker, R. (1990) 'Wealth, financial liberalization, and the demand for money in Japan', *IMF Staff Papers*, 37 (2), 418–32.

Cuthbertson, K. and Taylor, M. P. (1988) 'Monetary anticipations and the demand for money in the US: further results', *Southern Economic Journal*, 55 (2), 326–35.

Cuthbertson, K. and Taylor, M. P. (1990) 'Buffer-stock money, expectations, and feedback models of demand for financial assets', *Journal of Money, Credit and Banking*, forthcoming.

Davidson, R. and MacKinnon, J. G. (1981) 'Several tests for model specification in the presence of alternative hypotheses', *Econometrica*, 49, 781–93.

Dickey, D. A. and Fuller, W. A. (1981) 'Likelihood ratio statistics for autoregressive time series with a unit root', *Econometrica*, 49 (4), 1057–72.

Domowitz, I. and Hakkio, C. S. (1990) 'Interpreting an error correction model: partial adjustment, forward-looking behavior, and dynamic international money demand', *Journal of Applied Econometrics*, 5 (1), 29–46.

Ebrill, L. (1988) 'Money demand in the United States', International Monetary Fund, working paper WP/88/86.

Engle, R. F. and Granger, C. W. J. (1987) 'Cointegration and error correction: representation, estimation, and testing', *Econometrica*, 55 (2), 251–76.

Goldfeld, S. M. (1976) 'The case of the missing money', *Brookings Papers on Economic Activity*, 1, 577–646.

Hall, S. G., Henry, S. G. B. and Wilcox, J. B. (1989) 'The long run determination of the UK monetary aggregate', Bank of England, discussion paper 49.

Hendry, D. F. (1987) 'Econometric methodology: a personal perspective', in T. F. Bewley (ed.), *Advances in Econometrics*, vol. 2, Cambridge: Cambridge University Press, 29–48.

Hendry, D. F. (1989) 'PC-GIVE: an interactive econometric modelling system', version 6.0/6.01, University of Oxford.

Hendry, D. F. and Ericsson, N. R. (1989) 'An econometric analysis of UK money demand in *Monetary Trends in the United States and the United Kingdom* by Milton Friedman and Anna J. Schwartz', 81 (1), 8–38.

Hendry, D. F. and Richard, J.-F. (1983) 'The econometric analysis of economic time series', *International Statistical Review*, 51, 111–63.

Johansen, S. (1988) 'Statistical analysis of cointegration vectors', *Journal of Economic Dynamics and Control*, 12, 231–54.

Johansen, S. and Juselius, K. (1990) 'Maximum likelihood estimation and inference on cointegration – with applications to the demand for money', *Oxford Bulletin of Economics and Statistics*, 52 (May), 169–210.

Mehra, Y. P. (1989) 'Some further results on the source of shift in M1 demand in the 1980s', Federal Reserve Bank of Richmond *Economic Review*, 75 (5), 3–13.

Muscatelli, V. A. (1989) 'A comparison of the "rational expectations" and "general-to-specific" approaches to modelling the demand for M1', *Oxford Bulletin of Economics and Statistics*, 51 (4), 353–75.

Rose, A. K. (1985) 'An alternative approach to the American demand for money', *Journal of Money, Credit and Banking*, 17 (4), 419–55.

Stock, J. H. (1987) 'Asymptotic properties of least squares estimators of cointegrating vectors', *Econometrica*, 55 (5), 1035–56.

Taylor, M. P. (1987) 'Financial innovation, inflation and the stability of the demand for broad money in the United Kingdom', *Bulletin of Economic Research*, 39 (3), 225–33.

Yoshida, T. (1990) 'On the stability of the Japanese money demand function: estimation results using the error correction model', *Bank of Japan Monetary and Economic Studies*, 8 (1), 1–48.

5 Modelling Broad and Narrow Money: A Study Using Cointegration

Martin Brookes, Stephen Hall, Brian Henry and Glenn Hoggarth

1 INTRODUCTION

In this chapter we investigate the long-run determination of both narrow and broad monetary aggregates using M0 and M4 respectively. We do this by constructing models of the demand for these aggregates which focus primarily on the long-run properties of the data using cointegration techniques. That is to say, most of the effort in this chapter is devoted to ensuring that we have a sufficiently large set of variables that are, at least in principle, able to explain the long-run movements in the monetary aggregate concerned. It is our contention that many previous studies have worked with sets of explanatory variables that are too limited and which cannot capture the richness of the institutional changes which have occurred over the last twenty years. Hence we argue that the failure of these econometric models is a direct result of this omission.

If our contention is correct then cointegration techniques can play a significant role in obtaining models which more fully represent actual behaviour. Cointegration sets a standard for a model which must be met if the model is to be an adequate representation of the data. For a model to pass tests of cointegration it must contain a sufficiently rich set of variables for a potentially convincing long-run explanation of the trends in the data to occur. So we see a very close link between the structural failure of many existing money demand studies and the non-cointegration of the sets of variables used in these studies. A progressive strategy would therefore focus heavily on the long-run concepts emphasized in cointegration analysis and build models which stress this property as a prerequisite for any dynamic model. Of course establishing cointegration does not guarantee that we have the true model, or even a good one, but tests of cointegration do rule out many other models as inadequate. We will argue that this is a powerful approach at the current time simply because many existing models are ruled out at this stage.

Modelling the demand for money has received considerable attention over many years. Recently various new approaches have been tried. The buffer stock model has been widely discussed; see, for example, Carr and Darby (1981), Cuthbertson (1986) and Cuthbertson and Taylor (1987a, 1987b, 1990). The estimation of complete systems has been considered by Davidson (1987) and Davidson and Ireland (1987). A Bayesian approach to modelling the monetary aggregates has been used by Lubrano. et al. (1986). More conventional approaches have been adopted by Trundle (1982), Hendry and Mizon (1978), Hendry (1979), Hendry and Ericsson (1983), Johnston (1984), Artis and Lewis (1984) and Patterson (1987). Despite the fact that many of these studies claim to offer structurally stable demand functions, subsequent studies often proceed by demonstrating the inadequacies of their predecessors.

This chapter draws on the work of Hall, Henry and Wilcox (1989) (hereafter HHW), who examined a broad range of monetary aggregates. Here we focus on only two for illustrative purposes: M0 and M4. Although this chapter closely follows the procedures used in HHW, it presents additional evidence on the structural stability of the estimated demand for money functions. HHW presented evidence on the stability of their estimated equations. We repeat that here. But as there are now additional data, we also provide genuine *ex ante* stability tests of the models reported in the earlier work. We argue that these results together provide impressive evidence of parameter stability, and that this is an important finding given our earlier remarks about the lack of such stability in other studies.

As noted above, use is made of the new cointegration tools provided by Engle and Granger (1987) and Johansen (1988) and illustrated by Hall (1986, 1988) in modelling these monetary aggregates. This procedure enables us to concentrate at the first stage on testing that the set of explanatory variables used is sufficient to adequately model the series. So, for example, when this procedure is used on a simple demand for money equation for each aggregate, using only real income, prices and an interest rate as explanatory variables, the inability of this limited set of variables to capture the movements in the series becomes transparent. Attempting to model the dynamics of monetary adjustment using these variables may merely serve to obscure this basic problem. If a valid dynamic model of money demand of any form is to exist, including an error correction model or a forward-looking buffer stock model, it must contain a set of variables which satisfy the tests of cointegration which are applied at the first stage. If this is not the case then the model will be subject to the Granger and Newbold (1974) spurious regression problem and we would not expect it to be structurally stable.

We have chosen to examine M0 and M4 because they present an interesting contrast: M0 is primarily a transactions-based aggregate, while M4 is essentially one asset in the agent's wealth portfolio. Hence we might expect the underlying behaviour and modelling problems to be quite different as between the two aggregates. We will adopt a similar modelling strategy in each case, however. First we examine the possibility of forming a cointegrating regression for the aggregate using only the price level, real income and an interest rate as explanatory variables. For both aggregates this simple textbook model fails to provide a cointegrating vector. This original set of variables is then augmented by a wealth term and by variables capturing financial innovation. It is shown that this larger set of variables is capable of providing a cointegrating set for each of the aggregates. Once this is done it proves relatively easy to derive dynamic equations for both M0 and M4.

This chapter has the following plan. Section 2 discusses the technique of cointegration and defines the time series properties of the data to be used in subsequent sections. Then the original demand equations for each of the monetary aggregates M0 and M4 obtained by HHW are briefly described in sections 3 and 4. The discussion provides new regression results on extended samples. The final section draws some general conclusions.

2 COINTEGRATION AND LONG-RUN PROPERTIES

The concept of cointegration, first proposed in Granger and Weiss (1983) and extended in Engle and Granger (1987), is fundamental to the use of the error correction model (ECM) formulation. In particular, the Granger representation theorem establishes that for a valid ECM to exist the set of variables must cointegrate, and if the variables do cointegrate then a valid ECM form of the data must exist. The importance of this result to general estimation procedures is that if an ECM model is estimated for a set of variables which do not cointegrate then this regression will be subject to all the well-known problems of spurious regression outlined in Granger and Newbold (1974). This suggests that tests for cointegration should be a necessary component of estimation exercises conducted with ECM models. Further, the super-convergence proof due to Stock (1985) and generalized by Phillips and Durlauf (1986) and Park and Phillips (1986) suggests that very precise estimates of the levels terms can be obtained in the cointegrating regression (although some doubts about this are raised by Banarjee et al. 1986, which may in fact be relevant here).

We will not attempt to summarize the background theory of cointegration, however, as recent surveys are provided by Hendry (1986) and Granger (1986) and an application is given in Hall (1986). Some of the analysis

Table 5.1 The time series properties of the variabales

	Test for I(0)		Test for I(1)		Test for I(2)	
	DF	ADF	DF	ADF	DF	ADF
LM0[a]	−2.3	−2.4	−6.6	−1.8	−16.4	−5.7
LM4[a]	3.1	0.9	−3.6	−2.6	−14.0	−6.5
LGDP[a]	−1.2	−1.1	−11.9	−5.4		
LPGDP[a]	0.9	−0.4	−4.1	−2.6	−14.6	−4.8
LQCE[a]	0.3	0.4	−11.7	−3.7		
LCPI[a]	0.9	−0.9	−2.9	−1.7	−11.5	−5.18
LTFE[a]	−0.9	−0.6	−10.8	−4.9		
LPTFE[a]	0.7	−0.8	−2.9	−1.7	−12.6	−4.3
RTB[a]	−2.4	−2.4	−8.9	−5.3		
BSSR[a]	−1.6	−1.6	−8.5	−4.6		
CC[b]	1.3	1.9	−4.9	−2.4		
CDA[b]	11.5	2.5	−1.7	0.5		
LCAP[b]	2.7	0.9	−2.1	−1.9		
BSSR[c]	13.9	1.8	−1.6	−1.6		
SND[d]	−1.2	−2.7	−4.6	−3.7		

[a]1963(Q2)–1987(Q2). [b]1966(Q1)–1986(Q4). [c]1975(Q2)–1987(Q2).
[d]1968(Q1)–1986(Q4)

LM0 log of M0
LM4 log of M4
LGDP log of real gross domestic product
LPGDP log of the GDP deflator
LQCE log of real total consumption
LCPI log of consumer price index
LTFE log of total final expenditure
LPTFE log of TFE deflator
RTB three-month Treasury bill rate
BSSR building society average share rate
CC number of credit cards issued
CDA number of cash dispensers in use
LCAP log of the number of current accounts per head of the population
LFTI log of the *Financial Times* ordinary share index (used in SND)
SND defined in section 4

presented below will also rely on the maximum likelihood approach of Johansen (1988). Before any estimation work can properly begin within this framework we first need to establish the properties of the series we are dealing with. This is because, in principle, it is only possible for certain combinations of series to cointegrate, so if the set of series under consideration does not fall within this set there is simply no point in proceeding with estimation. Table 5.1 presents the Dickey-Fuller (DF) and the augmented Dickey-Fuller (ADF) tests for the series we will be considering throughout this chapter. The tests for integration of order zero, I(0), are tests carried out on the level of the variables; the tests for integration of order one, I(1), are carried out on the first difference of the variables. The DF and ADF tests are constructed as t tests with a non-standard distribution which is tabulated in Dickey and Fuller (1979).

In broad terms the conclusions which follow from table 5.1 are that the measures of real output (LGDP, LQCE and LTFE) and the interest rate variables (RTB, BSSR) are clearly I(1) variables. The measures of money (LM0 and LM4) and prices (LPGDP, LCPI and LPTFE) are probably I(2) variables, although they are often close to the critical value of the I(1) test and so might be I(1). This conforms well with our theoretical priors as it suggests that money and prices must cointegrate I(2,1), and then this series can cointegrate with the remaining variables (income, interest rates etc.) to produce a stationary residual process. The implication of this is that we might well be able to work in terms of real money which is I(1) rather than nominal money and prices.

3 AN EXERCISE FOR M0

This section briefly describes the approach and the results of HHW, before giving additional tests of their model. Previous work reported in HHW noted the correspondence between periods for which real M0 falls more rapidly and periods of sluggish growth in real consumers' expenditure; thus the ratio of M0 to consumption shows a smoother downward trend than real M0. This suggests that the widely held belief that real expenditure and price movements cannot by themselves explain the demand for cash over the past twenty years is correct. They examined this assertion by running tests of cointegrability on the variables concerned (see table 5.2).

Table 5.2 Test of cointegrating vectors involving LM0

	(5.1)	(5.2)	(5.3)	(5.4)
LCPI	0.7	1.00	1.00	1.00
LQCE	0.47	0.88	1.00	0.50
BSSR	0.007	−0.009	−0.039	−0.031
CRDW	0.32	0.14	0.06	0.06
DF	−2.3	−1.7	1.1	0.79
ADF	−2.1	−2.6	1.3	0.87
R^2	0.99	0.71	0.12	0.13

Sample 1969(Q3) to 1986(Q4).
CRDW is the cointegrating regression Durbin-Watson statistic.

Table 5.3 Johansen procedure and likelihood ratio test for variables in table 5.2

Eigenvalue	Eigenvector			
	LM0	LCPI	LQCE	BSSR
0.18	−30.27	26.67	− 6.14	−0.59
0.16	−44.35	31.91	27.83	0.28
0.05	18.89	−10.14	−22.74	0.04
0.0007	−39.22	27.91	−0.53	1.57

r	LR	5% critical value
0	30.2	38.6
1	16.0	23.8
2	3.8	12.0
3	0.05	4.2

These simple tests show that the unrestricted transactions demand for money equation (5.1) partly captures the upward trend in velocity by an unacceptably low price elasticity. When the price elasticity is restricted to one, as in (5.2), the income elasticity becomes unacceptably low. When both price and income elasticities are restricted, as in (5.3) and (5.4), the equations fail the cointegrability tests even more noticeably than the first two equations.

Hence the ordinary least squares (OLS) results strongly suggest that no cointegrating vector exists amongst this set of variables. Indeed, the Johansen procedure confirms this; the procedure yields the result in table 5.3. The likelihood ratio test that there are at most r cointegrating vectors is also shown in table 5.3. This test suggests that we are unable to reject the hypothesis that there are no cointegrating vectors. So the Johansen procedure confirms the OLS suggestion that cointegration does not exist between the variables in this set. It is interesting to note that the eigenvectors corresponding to the two largest eigenvalues produce parameter estimates which are similar to the OLS results in (5.1) and (5.2) in table 5.2.

3.1 Financial innovation and the demand for cash

The failure of these simple models of the demand for money functions is quite well known, and a number of additional factors have been adduced to try to overcome their failure. One plausible explanation for the decline in the ratio of M0 to nominal consumers' expenditure is financial innovation. Over the period we are considering it is true that transactions technology

Table 5.4 Tests of cointegrating vectors involving LM0 – LCPI – LQCE

	Equation (5.5)	(5.6)	(5.7)
BSSR	−0.0012	0.0012	-
ΣBSSR	−0.0013	−0.0008	−0.0013
Time	-	−0.004	-
CRDW	0.67	0.73	0.65
DF	−3.8	−3.8	−3.7
ADF	−2.9	−2.9	−2.8
R^2	0.99	0.99	0.99

Sample 1969(Q3) to 1986(Q4).

has changed considerably, with the widespread introduction of cash dispensers and credit cards, and a substantial increase in the number of bank current accounts. (Johnston 1984 attempts to assess the impact of these variables on narrow money holdings.) HHW tested whether direct measures for these three variables (numbers of cash dipensers, credit cards and current accounts) produced a cointegrating vector when introduced into the examples in table 5.2, but concluded they did not.

So they decided on an alternative approach to direct measures of innovation which in essence is an attempt to model the innovation process. This approach noted two distinct interest rate effects. The first implies that, for a given transactions technology, a rise (fall) in the rate will lead to an increase (decrease) in velocity. The second effect, however, is that (for example) an increase in the rate of interest provides an incentive for cash saving technology and payments methods to be introduced. Such changes are likely to be asymmetric and, once implemented, are unlikely to be repeated exactly or reversed, e.g. the introduction of cash dispensers. Furthermore, such changes alter the transactions technology and hence the likely magnitude of the first effect noted above.

In summary, HHW used a cumulative interest rate variable ΣBSSR as their measure of the effect of interest rates on the innovation process. This variable proved to be fairly successful in improving the cointegrating properties of the demand for money equation. Table 5.4 (taken from HHW) shows the results of using the innovation variable in the restricted equation. In this case, because the additional lags in the ADF test statistic were not significant, the simple DF statistic is the more relevant. Hence these results indicate that the simple form of innovation variable provides a cointegrating vector with the log of the ratio of M0 to nominal consumers' expenditure. (More general forms of the innovation variable show little improvement on (5.7).)

Table 5.5 Johansen procedure and likelihood ratio test for variables in table 5.4

Eigenvalue	Eigenvector	
	LM0 − LCPI − LQCE	ΣBSSR
0.16	58.26	0.0769
0.017	−20.28	−0.037

r	LR	5% critical value
0	13.3	12.0
1	1.14	4.2

The Johansen procedure, this time applied to the two variables LM0 − LCPI − LQCE and ΣBSSR to establish whether a cointegrating vector exists, gave the results shown in Table 5.5 The test that there are at most r cointegrating vectors is also shown. This, then, was suggestive that a cointegrating vector exists. Further, HHW noted that if the first eigenvector is normalized on money it gives a coefficient of −0.0013 on BSSR, which is identical to the OLS estimate in (5.7) in table 5.4.

Given the agreement between the OLS results and the Johansen results (5.7) was used in the subsequent dynamic model. The second-stage equation as estimated by HHW is as follows:

$$\begin{aligned}\Delta \text{LM0}_t = \; & \underset{(4.4)}{0.01} + \underset{(4.1)}{0.39}\,\Delta \text{LM0}_{t-1} + \underset{(2.2)}{0.30}\Delta\,\Delta \text{LCPI}_{t-1} \\ & \underset{(3.1)}{0.18}\,(\widehat{\text{LM0}}_{t-1} - \text{LM0}_{t-1}) + \underset{(6.1)}{0.05}\,\text{DUM}\,711_t \end{aligned} \tag{5.8}$$

where $\widehat{\text{LM0}}$ denotes the fitted value of LM0 from (5.7) and DUM711 is a dummy variable for decimalization. The diagnostic statistics, detailed in HHW, were as follows:

$\sigma = 0.010$, DW = 2.3, ARCH(1) = 0.09
LM(1) = 1.86, LM(2) = 3.90, LM(4) = 4.6, LM(8) = 9.3
LB(1) = 1.52, LB(2) = 3.75, LB(4) = 4.4, LB(8) = 12.9
RESET(4) = 7.0, BJ(2) = 1.7
FORC(8) = 4.9, FORC(12) = 4.8, FORC(24) = 16.7

The sample was 1967(Q1) to 1986(Q4).

The model, although simple, passes a wide range of diagnostic tests of its error process, functional form and stability. Given the notorious structural

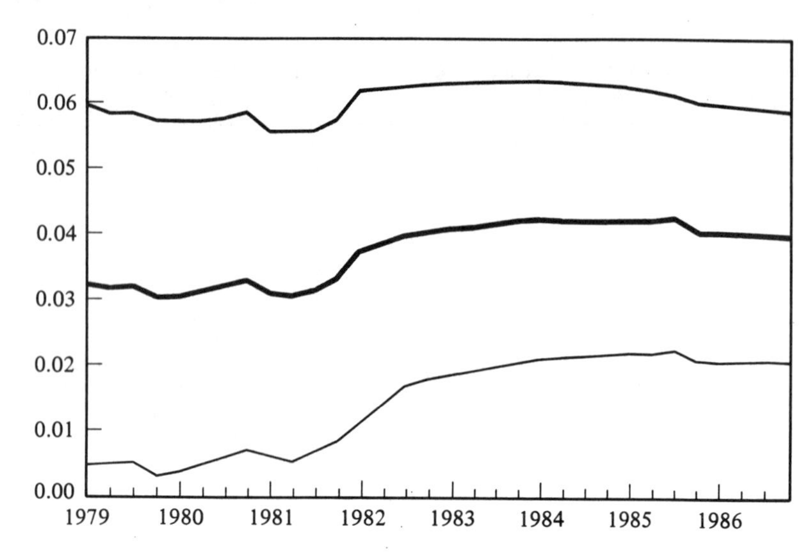

Figure 5.1 Recursive estimation time series of $\Delta LM0_{t-1}$

instability of money equations which has already been noted, the next section provides an investigation of the structural stability of this equation more methodically than is allowed by simple forecasting tests.

3.2 Structural stability tests

The first set of exercises undertaken to investigate the structural stability of the preferred model was recursive estimation for the period 1979(Q1)–1986(Q4). The resulting parameter estimates are presented in figures 5.1 to 5.4. In all cases the parameters are remarkably stable and in no case move outside the standard error band. Figure 5.5 shows a sequential one-period-ahead Chow test; this also does not reach the 5 per cent critical value at any point over this period. Figure 5.6 shows the CUSUMSQ statistic.

These results show that the M0 equation has a remarkable degree of stability over the period 1979–86. One further exercise, however, is to test the stability of parameters with additional data. What we show next is the preferred equation re-estimated over the period 1970(Q3)–1989(Q2), the long-run solution being shown first. Since the original estimation by HHW we have obtained additional data, and much of the data have been revised. So a re-estimation of the original model (for M0 and, subsequently, for M4) on the new extended data set is a stringent test of its properties in an *ex ante* situation.

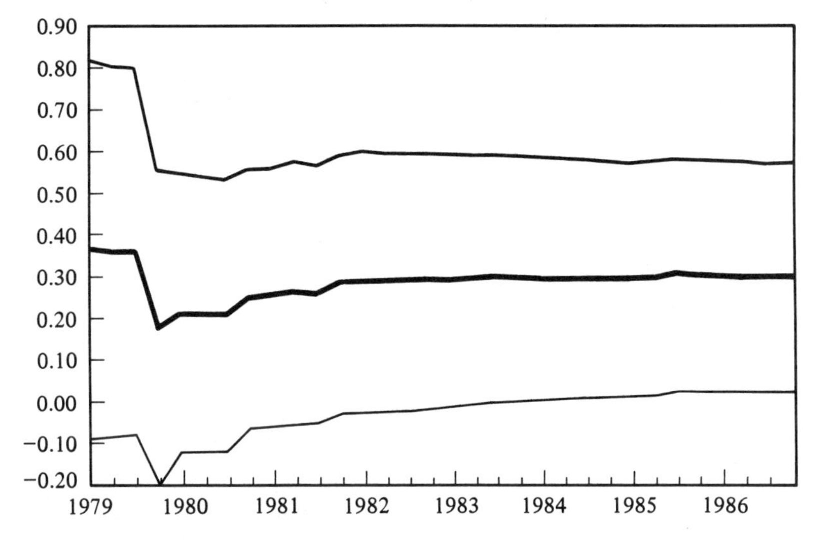

Figure 5.2 Recursive estimation time series of $\Delta\Delta LCPI_{t-1}$

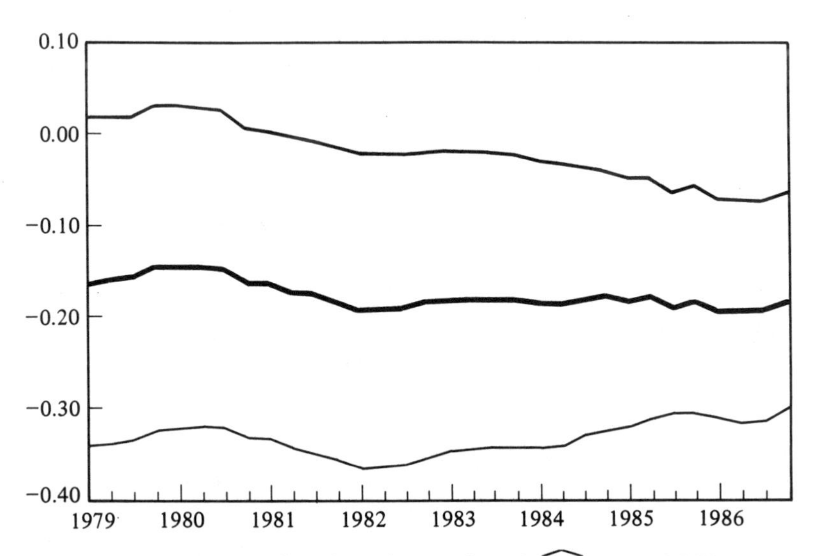

Figure 5.3 Recursive estimation time series of $\widehat{LM0}_{t-1} - LM0_{t-1}$

First, for a sample 1969(Q2) to 1989(Q2), we obtained

$$LM0_t - LCPI_t - LQCE_t = 0.562 - 0.0014\Sigma BSSR_t \tag{5.9}$$

$DF = -4.02, ADF = -3.1$

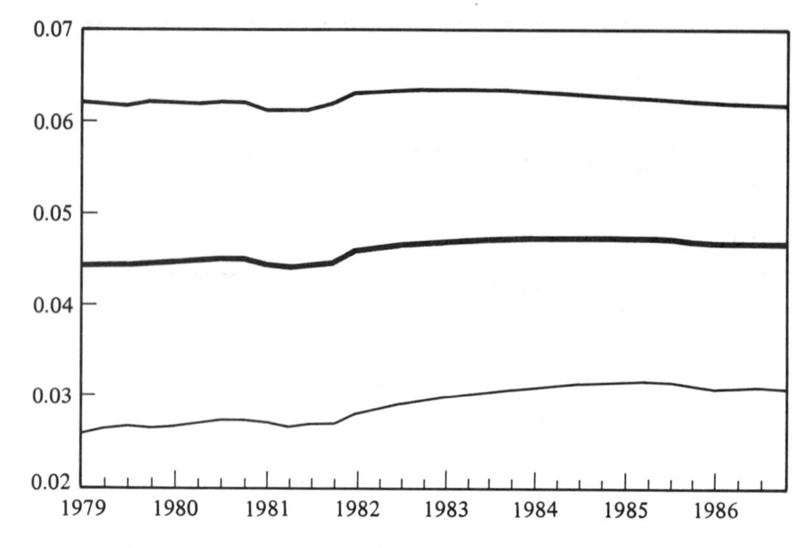

Figure 5.4 Recursive estimation time series of DUM711

Second, for a sample 1970(Q3) to 1989(Q2), we obtained

$$\begin{aligned}\Delta \text{LM0}_t = \underset{(3.2)}{0.02} + \underset{(2.99)}{0.31}\Delta \text{LM0}_{t-1} + \underset{(2.2)}{267}\Delta\Delta \text{LCPI}_{t-1} \\ + \underset{(3.09)}{0.185}(\widehat{\text{LM0}}_{t-1} - \text{LM0}_{t-1}) + \underset{(5.99)}{0.044}\text{DUM711}_t \qquad (5.10)\end{aligned}$$

where $\widehat{\text{LM0}}$ denotes the fitted value of LM0 from (5.9). Here: $R^2 = 0.544$, DW = 2.24

$\sigma = 0.009$, ARCH(1) = 0.01
LM(1) = 3.42, LM(2) = 3.49, LM(4) = 5.79, LM(8) = 10.6
LB(1) = 1.39, LB(2) = 1.58, LB(4) = 4.35, LB(8) = 13.54,
RESET(4) = 4.99, BJ(2) = 0.84

What this shows is that the empirical result is almost the same as the original HHW estimate. Thus, from this exercise we can also conclude that the equation is stable.

4 A MODEL OF M4

We now present similar material for the broader aggregate M4, again briefly noting the original HHW tests of the co-integrating properties of a simple money demand equation. Table 5.6 gives the relevant results for M4. As one

Table 5.6 Testing the simple model of M4

		Equation	
	(5.11)	(5.12)	(5.13)
LPGDP		0.819	
LPTFE	0.807		
LCPI			0.80
LGDP		2.613	
LTFE	2.27		
LQCE			2.43
RTB	−0.011	−0.0081	−0.005
CRDW	0.25	0.34	0.665
DF	−2.11	−2.4	−3.9
ADF	−1.46	−1.3	−2.6
R^2	0.992	0.991	0.997

Sample 1969(Q3) to 1986(Q4).

might expect, the simple set of variables considered in table 5.6 does not provide a cointegrating set. HHW in consequence focused on various forms of financial innovation as additional explanations of the demand for M4. They added a number of additional variables to the set considered in table 5.6, including wealth, inflation and the rates of return on assets.

The role of wealth in many key macroeconomic relationships is at present receiving renewed attention. Although wealth might be thought the crucial scaling variable if the demand for money is seen as part of a wider portfolio decision, many demand for money equations have omitted such a variable (for an exception see Grice and Bennett 1984). Wealth plays a crucial role in determining the demand for money in the equations below; this is particularly important in explaining developments since 1980, when both wealth and broad money have grown rapidly. The wealth variable used by HHW was personal sector gross wealth, both financial and tangible; the latter mainly reflects the value of the owner-occupied housing stock.

A second variable added to the initial list is inflation (see, for example, Taylor 1987). This variable could have a number of influences, including an allowance for the tendency for nominal rates not to move in line with expected inflation. In part, it could reflect front-end loading which occurred in debt markets during periods of high inflation and high nominal interest rates. During such periods the real value of debt fell noticeably and the constraints associated with front-end loading could have resulted in consumers running down liquid assets to maintain consumption levels.

HHW also used variables reflecting rates of return on assets. These were

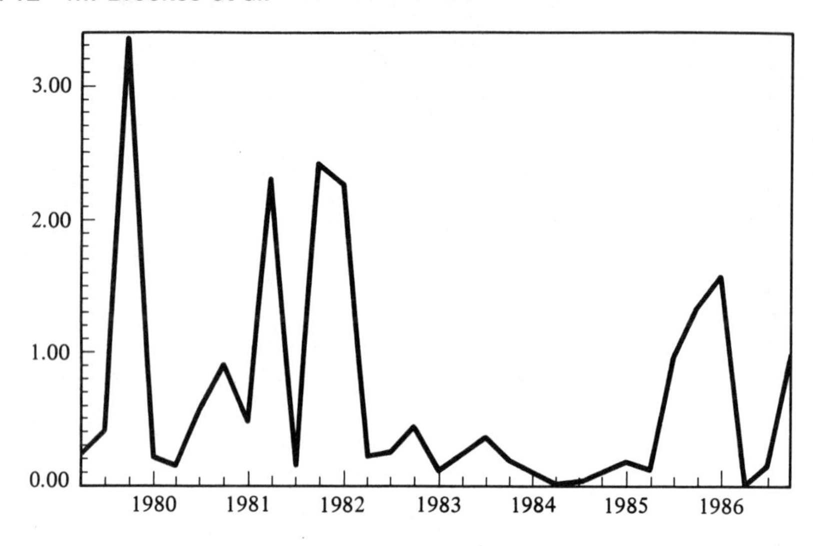

Figure 5.5 Sequential one-period-ahead Chow test for dynamic M0 equation

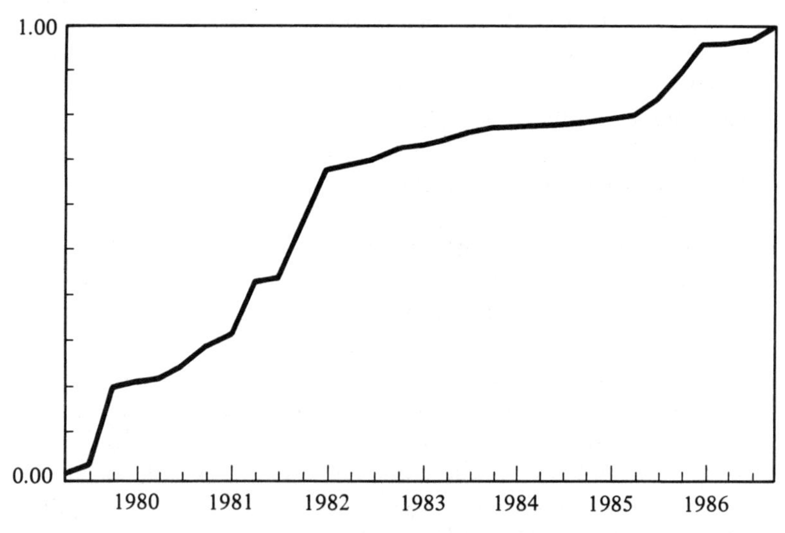

Figure 5.6 CUSUMSQ statistic for dynamic M0 equation

found to be unimportant, with one exception. They found that a two-year moving average of the quarterly change in stock market prices could be used as a proxy for expected capital gains, when entered as a moving average of the falls in the index.

Table 5.7 A cointegrating vector for M4

	Equation		
	(5.14) LM4	(5.15) LM4 – LPGDP	(5.16) LM4 – LPGDP – LGDP
LPGDP	0.99		
LGDP	1.07	1.05	
Δ_4LPGDP	−0.71	−0.71	−0.71
LPW – LGDP – LPGDP	0.71	0.71	0.72
SND	−0.20	−0.20	−0.20
DCCC	0.09	0.09	0.10
CRDW	1.30	1.30	1.30
DF	−6.00	−6.00	−6.00
ADF	−5.1	−5.1	−5.0
R^2	0.99	0.99	0.96

Sample 1968(Q1) to 1987(Q2).

LPW log of personal sector real and financial wealth
LFTI log of *Financial Times* ordinary share index
DCCC dummy variable for CCC: value 0 prior to 1971(4), value 1 thereafter

$$\text{ND} = \min(\Delta\text{LFTI},0) \qquad \text{SND} = \sum_{i=0}^{7} \text{ND}(t-i)$$

The final variable added to the set was a dummy variable to capture the introduction of Competition and Credit Control (CCC). With tehse additions it proved possible to form a cointegrating vector. Table 5.7 shows the HHW results. These results provide a plausible cointegrating vector for M4. The parameter values show only minor variation as the restriction of unit elasticity is applied. In (5.16) the demand for M4 has an income elasticity of 0.28 and a wealth elasticity of 0.72. The inflation effect plays a powerful role, with an increase of 1 per cent in the inflation rate leading to a reduction in desired money holdings of 0.7 per cent. The stock market term implies that if falls in the index over the previous two years amounted to 1 per cent then money holding would be 0.2 per cent larger than if no falls in the index had occurred.

Equation (5.16) can be verified as a cointegrating vector, as well as considering its uniqueness, by applying the Johansen procedure to this set of variables. The Johansen procedure suggested that there may exist two

Table 5.8 Johansen procedure all likelihood ratio test for (5.16)

	Eigenvector				
Eigenvalue	LM4-LPGDP-LGDP	Δ_4LPGDP	LPW−LGDP−LPGDP	SND	DCCC
0.391	4.82	25.6	−4.05	−1.53	−2.23
0.281	−92.5	−80.33	66.68	11.03	10.13

r	LR	5% critical value
0	78.9	57.2
1	42.1	38.6
2	17.7	23.8
3	7.3	12.0
4	1.14	4.2

cointegrating vectors but that there is unlikely to be more than two; the relevant test statistics are shown in table 5.8. In this case the eigenvector corresponding to the second eigenvalue is almost identical to the OLS results given in table 5.7. The eigenvector corresponding to the larger eigenvalue is quite implausible as a causal relationship for M4, and given the large coefficient on inflation it seems likely that this cointegrating vector is actually determining inflation. So this procedure again finds a set of results which broadly support the OLS findings.

The dynamic model for M4 is therefore based on the cointegrating regression (5.16) given in table 5.7, and is

$$\underset{}{\Delta \text{LM4}} = \underset{(4.8)}{0.016} + \underset{(5.2)}{0.512\,\Delta \text{LM4}_{t-1}} - \underset{(2.4)}{0.15\,\text{RES}_{t-1}} \tag{5.17}$$

where RES is residuals from the cointegrating regression (5.16), the data period is 1969(Q1) to 1987(Q2), and the remaining parameters are as follows:

$\sigma = 0.0096$, $R^2 = 0.30$, DW = 1.98
ARCH(1) = 0.27, RESET(4) = 6.5, BJ(2) = 0.32
LM(1) = 0.57, LM(4) = 10.8, LM(8) = 10.7
LB(1) = 0.12, LB(4) = 2.45, LB(8) = 3.02
CHISQ(8) = 6.1, CHISQ(12) = 6.4, CHISQ(24) = 11.4

4.1 Stability tests for the model

As in the case of M0 we now summarize the stability properties of (5.17), using recursive estimation over 1979(Q1)–1987(Q2) and a re-estimation of the whole equation over a longer sample period.

Recursive estimation over the period 1979(Q1) to 1987(Q2) again shows these parameters to be very stable. We present figures of a sequential one-period-ahead Chow test and the CUSUMSQ statistic, both of which clearly emphasize this stability (figures 5.7 and 5.8).

This stability is also confirmed when we re-estimate the original equation over a different sample period. Estimating our preferred equation (5.16) again, over the period 1968(Q1)–1989(Q1), gave the following result:

$$\begin{aligned} \mathrm{LM4} - \mathrm{LPGDP} - \mathrm{LGDP} = & -0.74\Delta_4\,\mathrm{LPGDP} + 0.73 \\ & (\mathrm{LPW} - \mathrm{LGDP} - \mathrm{LPGDP}) \\ & - 0.20\,\mathrm{SND} + 0.11\,\mathrm{DCCC} \end{aligned} \qquad (5.18)$$

$R^2 = 0.97$, DF $= -5.6$

The dynamic model (5.17) becomes

$$\underset{}{\Delta\mathrm{LM4}} = \underset{(5.17)}{0.017} + \underset{(5.3)}{0.50\,\Delta\mathrm{LM4}_{t-1}} - \underset{(2.29)}{0.12\,\mathrm{RES}_{t-1}} \qquad (5.19)$$

$\sigma = 0.0094$, $R^2 = 0.30$, DW $= 1.93$
ARCH(1) $= 0.03$, RESET(4) $= 5.4$, BJ(2) $= 1.03$
LM(1) $= 0.2$, LM(4) $= 4.0$, LM(8) $= 4.13$
LB(1) $= 0.07$, LB(4) $= 2.4$, LB(8) $= 2.67$

This result is further confirmation that the M4 model, like the M0 one, is structurally stable.

5 CONCLUSION

In this chapter we have investigated the long-run determination of two of the historically more important monetary aggregates, M0 and M4, based on earlier work by Hall et al. (1989). Econometric modelling experience has found a stable money demand function to be one of its more elusive goals, and we might characterize the attitude of many practitioners as being highly sceptical that such a stable function even exists. In this study we have found that the simple set of variables which have traditionally formed the backbone of most models can easily be rejected as a suitable cointegrating vector to use as a base for model building. Given this fundamental flaw in these models

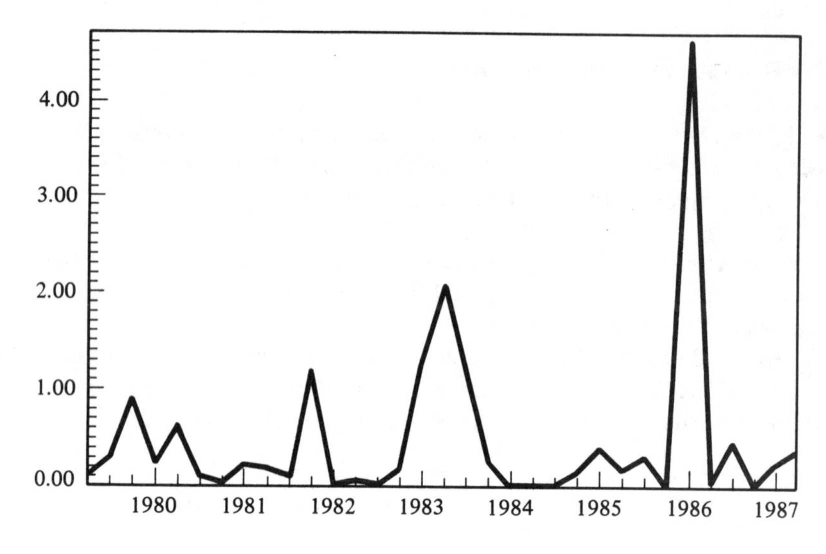

Figure 5.7 Sequential one-period-ahead Chow test for dynamic M4 equation

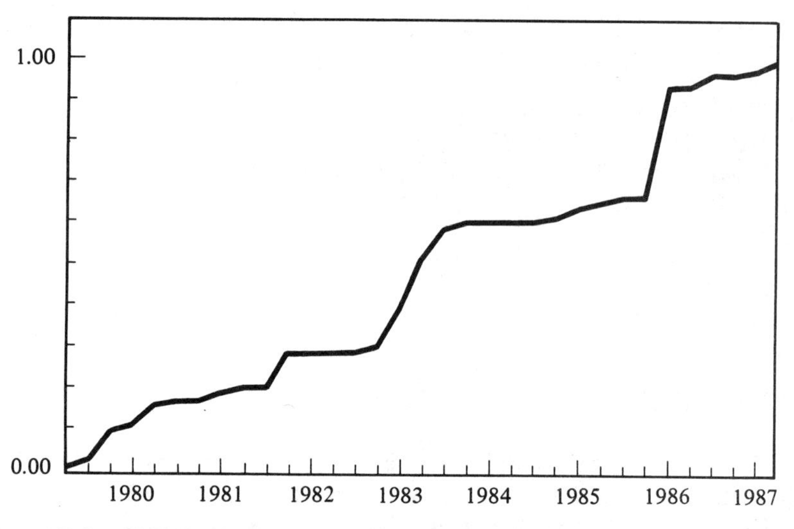

Figure 5.8 CUSUMSQ statistic for dynamic M4 equation

we would not expect them to be structurally stable, and so the observed failure of models based on them is far from surprising.

Practitioners in the field of monetary economics have tended to explain the changes in the simple velocity relationship in terms of financial innovation and liberalization. In terms of narrow money this means more effective ways of making transactions, and in terms of broad money it means the increasing efficiency of the market in managing and allocating its portfolio of wealth. In their previous study Hall et al. (1989) found that introducing these effects into models of the demand for money does allow the models to meet the basic criteria of cointegration; and, further, that once these effects are added a satisfactory dynamic model can be derived which is remarkable both for its stability and for its simplicity. This former feature has been further investigated here, and the results confirm that the models are indeed stable.

Note

The views expressed are those of the authors and not necessarily those of the Bank of England. The authors are grateful to Mark Taylor for comments on an earlier draft; the usual disclaimer applies.

References

Artis, M. J. and Lewis, M. K. (1984) 'How unstable is the demand for money function in the UK?', *Economica*, 51, 473–6.

Banerjee, A., Dolado, J. J., Hendry, D. F. and Smith, G. W. (1986) 'Exploring equilibrium relationships in econometrics through static models: some Monte Carlo evidence', *Oxford Bulletin of Economics and Statistics*, 48 (3), 253–78.

Carr, J. and Darby, M. (1981) 'The role of money supply shocks in the short-run demand for money', *Journal of Monetary Economics* 8, 183–200.

Cuthbertson, K. (1986) 'Price expectations and adjustment lags in the demand for money', *Scottish Journal of Political Economy*, 33 (4), 334–54.

Cuthbertson, K. and Taylor, M. P. (1987a) 'Buffer stock money: an appraisal', in C A. E. Goodhart, D. Currie and D. T. Llewellyn (eds), *The Operation and Regulation of Financial Markets*, London: Macmillan.

Cuthbertson, K. and Taylor, M. P. (1987b) 'The demand for money: a dynamic rational expectations model', *Economic Journal*, 97 (supplement), 65–76.

Cuthbertson, K. and Taylor, M. P. (1990) 'Money demand, expectations, and the forward looking model', *Journal of Policy Modelling*, 12, 289–315.

Davidson, J. (1987) 'Disequilibrium money: some further results with a monetary model of the UK', in C. A. E. Goodhart, D. Currie and D. T. Llewellyn (eds), *The Operation and Regulation of Financial Markets*, London: Macmillan.

Davidson, J. and Ireland, J. (1987) 'Buffer stock models of the monetary sector', *National Institute Economic Review*, August, 67–71.

Dickey, D. A. and Fuller, W. A. (1979) 'Distribution of the estimation for autoregressive time series with a unit root', *Journal of the American Statistical Association*, 74, 427–31.

Engle, R. F. and Granger, C. W. J. (1987) 'Cointegration and error correction: representation, estimation and testing', *Econometrica*, 55 (12), 251–76.

Granger, C. W. J. (1986) 'Development in the study of cointegrated economic variables', *Oxford Bulletin of Economics and Statistics*, 48 (3), 213–28.

Granger, C. W. J. and Newbold, P. (1974) 'Spurious regression in econometrics', *Journal of Econometrics*, 2, 111–20.

Granger, C. W. J. and Weiss, A. A. (1983) 'Time series analysis of error correcting models', in S. Karlin, T. Amemiya and L. A. Goodman (eds), *Studies in Econometrics, Time Series and Multivariate Statistics*, New York: Academic Press.

Grice, J. and Bennett, A. (1984) 'Wealth and the demand for £M3 in the United Kingdom 1975–81', *The Manchester School*, 52 (3), 239–71.

Hall, S. G. (1986) 'An application of the Granger and Engle two-step estimation procedure to UK aggregate usage data', *Oxford Bulletin of Economics and Statistics*, 48 (3), 229–40.

Hall, S. G. (1988) 'Maximum likelihood estimation of cointegrating vectors: an example of the Johansen procedure', *Oxford Bulletin of Economics and Statistics*, forthcoming.

Hall, S. G., Henry, S. G. B. and Wilcox, J. (1989) 'The long run determination of the monetary aggregates', Bank of England, discussion paper 41.

Hendry, D. F. (1979) 'Predictive failure and econometric modelling', in P. Ormerod (ed.), *Macroeconomics: The Transactions Demand for Money*', London: Heinemann.

Hendry, D. F. (1986) 'Econometric modelling with cointegrated variables: an overview', *Oxford Bulletin of Economics and Statistics*, 48 (3), 201–13.

Hendry, D. F. and Ericsson, N. (1983) 'Monetary trends in the UK' paper presented to the 22nd Meeting of the Bank of England Panel of Academic Consultants.

Hendry, D. F. and Mizon, G. E. (1978) 'Serial correlation as a convenient simplification not a nuisance: a comment on a study of the demand for money by the Bank of England', *Economic Journal*, 88, 49–63.

Johansen, S. (1988) 'Statistical analysis of cointegrating vectors', *Journal of Economic Dynamics and Control*, 12 (2/3), 231–54.

Johnston , R. B. (1984) 'The demand for non-interest bearing money in the UK', HM Treasury working paper 28.

Lubrano, M., Pierse, R. G. and Richard, J. F. (1986) 'Stability of a UK money demand equation: a Bayesian approach to testing exogeneity', *Review of Economic Studies*, 53 (4), 603–34.

Park, J. Y. and Phillips, P. C. B. (1986) 'Statistical inference in regressions with integrated processes: part 1', York University, discussion paper 811.

Patterson, K. D. (1987) 'The specification and stability of the demand for money in the UK', *Economica*, 54, 41–55.

Phillips, P. C. B. and Durlauf, S. N. (1986) 'Multiple time series regression with integrated processes', *Review of Economic Studies*, 53, 473–95.

Stock, J. H. (1985) 'Asymptotic properties of least squares estimates of cointegrating vectors', Harvard University, mimeo.

Taylor, M. P (1987) 'Financial innovation, inflation and the stability of the demand for broad money in the United Kingdom', *Bulletin of Economic Research*, 39, 225–33.

Trundle, J. (1982) 'The demand for M1 in the UK', Bank of England, mimeo.

6 Endogenous Financial Innovation and the Demand for M0

Peter Westaway and David Walton

1 INTRODUCTION

This chapter is concerned with the determination of M0, the narrow money aggregate first introduced as a target by the government in the 1984 budget. Outside official circles, M0 has always been treated with some degree of scepticism, partly because of its tendency to grow much more slowly than other monetary aggregates and also because of its small magnitude compared with other broader measures of liquidity. Even for the government, the operational status of this aggregate in the overall framework of monetary policy has often been ambivalent. The 1987 Financial Statement and Budget Report suggested that the movement of M0 outside its target range was a clear signal to change interest rates; by 1988, its role was relegated to one among many indicators. Nevertheless the recent unintended expansion of demand and upsurge in inflation has coincided with an overshooting of M0 outside its target range again, suggesting that it may have an important role to play in the assessment of monetary conditions.

If M0 is to be accorded this role, it is crucial that there should be a clear understanding of both why it matters and how it is determined. On the first question, it has wrongly been argued that M0 matters because it constitutes the high-powered money base and hence ultimately causes inflation. In fact, this would not be appropriate in the UK since M0 purely reflects the demand for cash balances and is *not* supply determined. The government has never cited this argument, or indeed seriously claimed that M0 causes inflation. Instead, they argue that because of its timely availability it serves as a useful contemporaneous and possibly leading indicator of current activity. If this line of argument is correct, a stable econometric explanation of the behaviour of M0 must exist. As figure 6.1a shows, it is certainly true that the velocity of M0 with respect to consumer spending has seemed to behave in

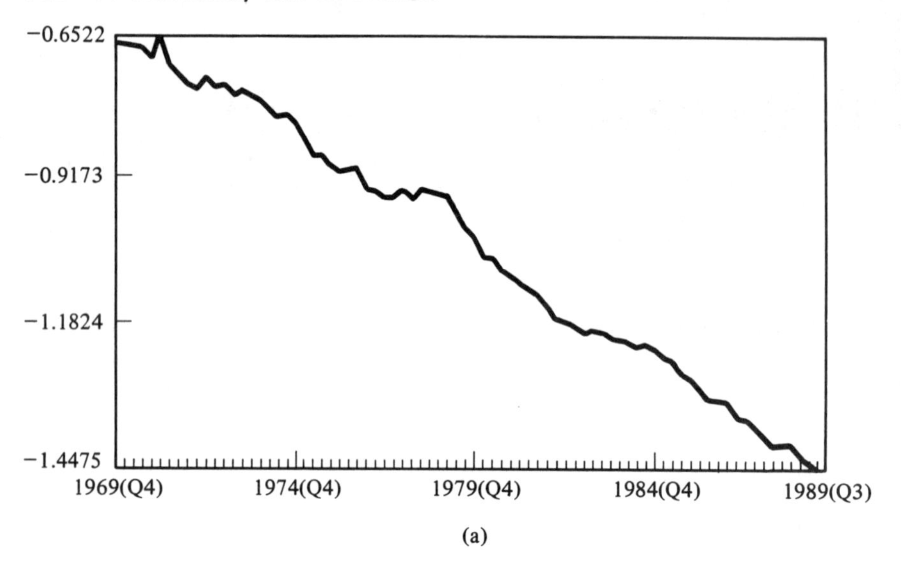

(a)

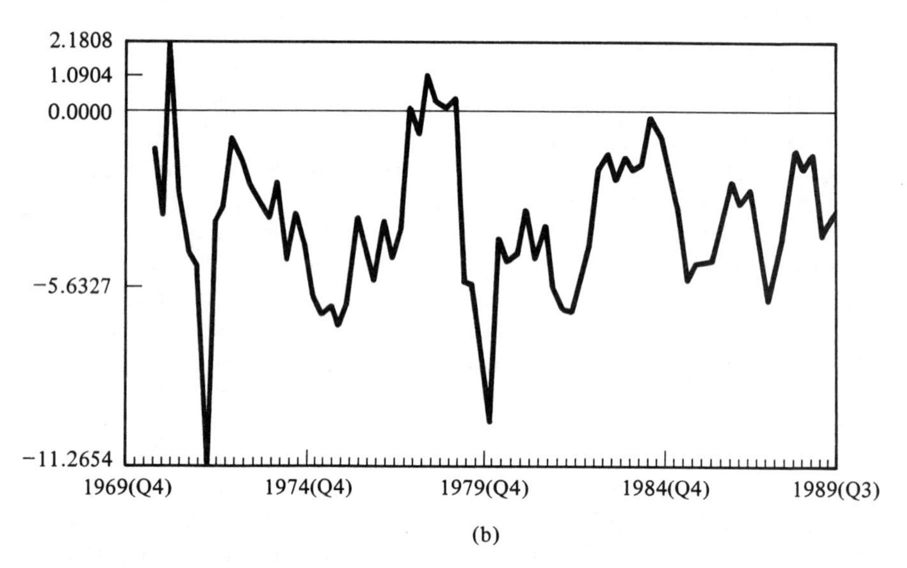

(b)

Figure 6.1 (a) Velocity of M0 relative to non-durable consumption (LCNDVEL); (b) Annual change in velocity (ΔLCVEL)

a fairly predictable manner, trending downwards consistently over the last twenty years, in contrast to the more erratic behaviour of the broader monetary aggregates. However, this figure alone can be somewhat misleading. Figure 6.1b shows the annual growth of this velocity measure, which has clearly been fairly volatile and which obviously must be explained if M0 growth is to be accounted for. Nevertheless, we shall see that the evidence for a stable relationship is fairly strong although not unequivocal; the rest of the chapter is concerned with this question. It is important to note, however, that the existence of a stable econometric relationship is only a necessary condition for M0 being a reliable monetary indicator, not a sufficient one. This also requires that new M0 data provide *extra* information on economic activity compared with that already available, including forecasts. To our knowledge, this has never been demonstrated to be the case for M0. We do not address this important question here.

The plan of the rest of this chapter is as follows. The next section discusses the main factors which are likely to determine M0 and notes and coin. After a review of the institutional details appropriate in the UK context, the standard inventory-theoretic approach to the transactions demand for money is outlined, highlighting in particular the crucial role of financial innovation. The problems in adequately capturing these exogenous forms of innovation are noted, and an alternative approach is suggested which is based on the idea that many types of innovation are endogenous, increasing more rapidly for example at times of high interest rates. A brief theoretical justification for this type of approach is given. Section 3 describes the econometric results, which exploit cointegration analysis. Previous attempts to model the demand for notes and coin are reviewed and compared with a new preferred specification which appears to have properties which are both data coherent and consistent with the theory. Section 4 concludes.

2 THE DETERMINATION OF M0

2.1 Institutional details

M0 consists of notes and coin in circulation outside the Bank of England and bankers' operational deposits with the Bank. The latter are non-interest-bearing deposits retained voluntarily by banks at the Bank of England in excess of their non-operational cash ratio deposits, which are set at 0.5 per cent of monetary sector institutions' eligible liabilities. (Cash ratio deposits are excluded from the definition of M0.) Since notes and coin account for around 99 per cent of M0, the movement in M0 closely tracks that of notes and coin over time.[1]

Before discussing the theoretical background to the demand for notes and coin, it is worth considering those institutional factors which are likely to be important in determining the path for M0. The first point noted above is that the published figures for M0, leaving aside bankers' operational deposits with the Bank of England, simply reflect the demand for cash balances. M0 is not and never has been supply determined. No attempt has ever been made in modern times to limit the supply of notes and coin available to the public, despite the fact that the authorities obviously could exert control by setting production quotas on note printing and coin minting. To apply such limits would serve no purpose as people would simply use alternative means of payment. Similarly, the Bank of England does not control the level of bankers' operational deposits held at the Bank. Money market operations which the Bank undertakes primarily accommodate market pressures and very rarely inject or withdraw reserves by an amount substantially different from normal daily clearing requirements. Monetary policy shifts are therefore usually signalled by the interest rate at which assistance is supplied to the money market and not by the amount of assistance itself. In this way, the UK authorities do not operate either a control on the supply of notes and coin or a system of monetary base control. To switch to a system of monetary base control would almost certainly make short-term money market interest rates more volatile, and this has historically been seen as undesirable.

2.2 The theory of the demand for notes and coin

In explaining the demand for the main component of M0, notes and coin, it is clearly necessary to focus on demand factors. Furthermore, since around 90 per cent of notes and coin outside the monetary sector are held by individuals and households, it is individuals' behaviour that we need to explain.

Since notes and coin are only likely to perform the medium of exchange function of money, we must assume that the major motive for holding any notes and coins at all is to facilitate economic transactions. These payments tend to be irregular in both size and timing and therefore cannot be easily coordinated with income receipts, which tend to come in a relatively small number of large lump sums. Hence money – in this case notes and coin – is held as an inventory to adjust as necessary when receiving income or making payments. This inventory-theoretic approach to the transactions demand for money was first developed by Baumol (1952) and Tobin (1956). Most previous attempts to explain the demand for notes and coin in the UK (for example Johnston 1984; HM Treasury 1988; Hall et al. 1989) can be said to a lesser or greater extent to have fallen within this framework.

In its simplest form, Baumol-Tobin models derive the well-known square root rule which predicts that holdings of transactions balances M are proportional as $\sqrt{(2b/i)}$ to the square root of the value of transactions (T), where b represents the transactions costs of withdrawing money (the brokerage fee) and i gives the opportunity cost of the interest payments forgone by holding money in non-interest-bearing form. More complicated models imply a transactions elasticity greater than 0.5 (see Fisher 1978) and in the case of notes and coin will differ importantly as b varies through time as financial innovation causes agents to economize on cash holding.

Additionally, it is important to note that for many individuals this 'rational' approach to money holding will not be appropriate, since notes and coin will comprise most if not all of their financial assets. This is likely to apply to the surprisingly large number of individuals who hold no form of bank account at all. This figure is related to the proportion of the population paid in cash, which has fallen from 75 per cent in 1960 and 59 per cent in 1976 to around 30 per cent today.[2] Consequently, any discussion of the demand for notes and coin must take into account not only how individuals would behave within the inventory-theoretic framework but also what proportion of cash holders will fall outside this category. This is obviously related to the question of how financial innovation affects M0, to which we return below.

Despite the simplicity of the framework outlined so far, it allows us to separate the main influences on the demand for notes and coin: the choice of transactions variable, the role of interest rates and the role of financial innovation.

The transactions measure

Early studies of the demand for M0 used a measure of real disposable income as the scale variable in empirical work (see Johnston 1984). More recent work has, more sensibly in our view, focused on different measures of consumers' expenditure, a better measure of actual transactions (see HM Treasury 1988; Hall et al. 1989). Recent econometric work by the Treasury has in fact found that M0 is most closely related to a subsection of consumers' expenditure, namely that on non-durable goods (excluding services). Intuitively this seems reasonable since spending on durable goods and services is much more likely to be made by cheque or credit card. Clearly, the appropriate choice of category is closely related to the question of financial innovation in the means of payment, as described below. Importantly, the Treasury specification also imposes a long-run unit elasticity on this consumption measure. As argued above, there are no good theoretical grounds for doing this. In fact, we find there is no case on econometric grounds either.

Interest rates

Higher interest rates make it attractive to hold interest-bearing (IB) financial assets instead of non-interest-bearing (NIB) money, including cash. In practice, however, it is difficult in econometric work to find a statistically robust specification for interest rates in an M0 equation. This may be because the relevant marginal decision for M0 may be between holding cash or an NIB current account, while interest rates only affect the decision to hold NIB or IB bank accounts.[3] Thus the effect on cash from a change in interest rates will only ripple through if individuals wish to hold a constant proportion of their NIB assets as cash. In empirical work, the Treasury's equation has a lag structure imposed which has a long-run elasticity of minus one, but many other specifications would also be accepted by the data.

Moreover, the most obvious way in which changes in interest rates have an impact on the demand for cash is via their impact on consumers' expenditure. Thus to some extent the effect of interest rates is already embodied in an M0 equation by including consumers' expenditure as an explanatory variable.

Financial Innovation

That is not to argue that the direct effects of interest rates are wholly unimportant for explaining M0, however. There has been a substantial shift in personal sector behaviour in recent years towards holding wealth in the form of liquid interest-bearing bank and building society accounts. The ready accessibility of these accounts, particularly given the development of automatic cash dispensers, has encouraged individuals over time to economize on cash holdings. As a consequence, the ratio of cash to personal disposable income or consumers' expenditure has fallen steadily. In other words, financial innovations have led to an increase in the velocity of circulation of cash. This trend has been aided by developments such as the move away from cash payments to employees and the increased acceptance of a variety of forms of payment in shops etc. other than cash (e.g. credit cards, cheques).

What is also interesting to note is that the velocity of circulation has not risen at a constant rate over time. From figure 6.1b it is possible to see that on two occasions there has been a sharp increase in the velocity of circulation – between 1974 and 1976 and between 1978 and 1980. These coincided with periods of rapid inflation and of a sharp move upwards in nominal interest rates. This would be consistent with the notion of ratchet effects in the demand for money (see Goldfeld 1970 and Johnston 1984 for an unsuccessful empirical attempt to capture this effect). That is,

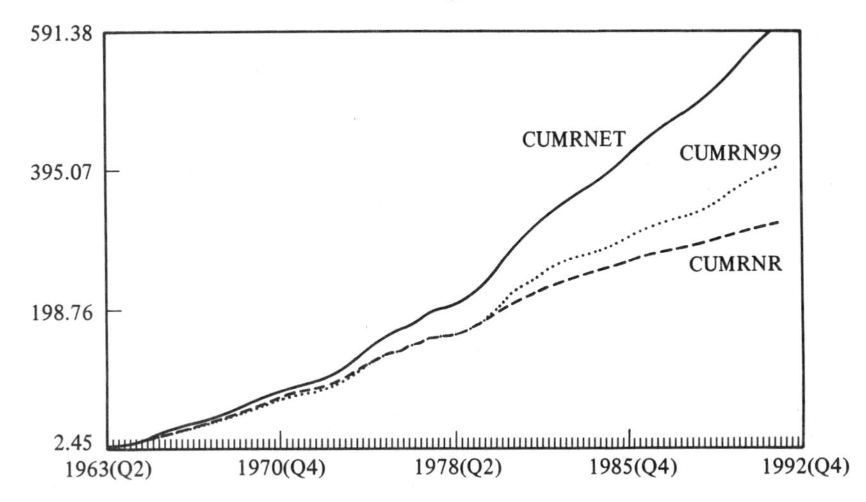

Figure 6.2 Different measures of cumulated interest rates

suppose that there are fixed costs in altering cash management techniques. People will only change to more efficient cash management methods when they find it worthwhile to do so, such as when inflation picks up or when there is a jump in interest rates. Once the new efficient cash management techniques are adopted, though, people are unlikely subsequently to abandon them when either inflation or interest rates drop back. This behaviour may be modelled either by including the rate of inflation in a demand for cash equation or by introducing a variable which cumulates the path of interest rates over time (see also Hall et al. 1989). (The intuition behind this latter variable is that when interest rates rise sharply, the slope of this variable becomes steeper, reflecting a change in the incentive to economize on cash.) Figure 6.2 illustrates the profile of three such cumulated interest rate terms which use discount rates of unity (CUMRNET), 0.99 (CUMRN99) and the interest rate itself (CUMRNR), respectively.

A number of arguments can be made against this approach. First, there is an absence of any clear theoretical basis for the choice of the discount rate. While it is clear that some discounting or more accurately reversal of financial innovation should occur, it is not obvious how quick this should be. In our empirical work, we experiment with different rates to find the one which is most coherent with the data. Second, it is possible that the results will change depending on where the process of cumulation begins; we have found that this makes little difference in practice. Third, and most importantly, it can be argued that this type of financial innovation is supposed to be picking up the behaviour of those individuals who are opening bank accounts for the first time. Since these accounts are likely to be NIB, it is unclear why their decision should be affected by the interest rate (unless of course they open a deposit account). This argument suggests that our endogenous innovation measure may instead be capturing the effect of interest rates via their effect on the supply side, that is on the behaviour of banks themselves. Since banks' profits on current accounts may rise when interest rates are higher, they will have an extra incentive to encourage more people to open bank accounts, through increased expenditure on advertising for example. This seems more plausible than the demand side motivation. The theoretical basis of this argument will be developed in further work and will not be pursued here.

Whatever the motivation for these constructed proxy innovation series, the advantage of using inflation and the cumulative path of interest rates as proxies for financial innovation is that financial innovation then becomes endogenous to the determination of the demand for cash. By contrast, the measures of financial innovation used at various times in econometric research by the Treasury – such as the ratio of the number of bank current accounts to the total population, the ratio of the number of building society accounts to the total population, the total number of cash dispensers, the proportion of manual workers in the population (as a proxy for trends in the payment of cash to employees) and the number of credit cards – are all treated as being exogeneously determined. Figure 6.3 illustrates two of these quantities. But the trends in all of these measures are almost certainly influenced by prevailing financial conditions.

A further problem with these exogenous measures of financial innovation is that they are highly collinear; in other words, they all move fairly closely together over time. This induces problems in an econometric specification of the demand for M0. If all of the measures of financial innovation are included in a regression, almost all will appear to be statistically insignificant. In the equation for notes and coin in the latest public version of the Treasury model, this is resolved by proxying all the different types of financial innovation by including just the number of cash dispensers and the proportion of manual workers in the population. However, this gives the rather implausible conclusion that each additional cash dispenser will reduce the demand for cash by £0.25 million. Conclusions such as this are avoided if financial innovation is treated endogenously.

3 EMPIRICAL RESULTS

3.1 Estimation methodology

This section uses the ideas described in the theoretical discussion to investigate empirically the demand for notes and coin. The estimation technique

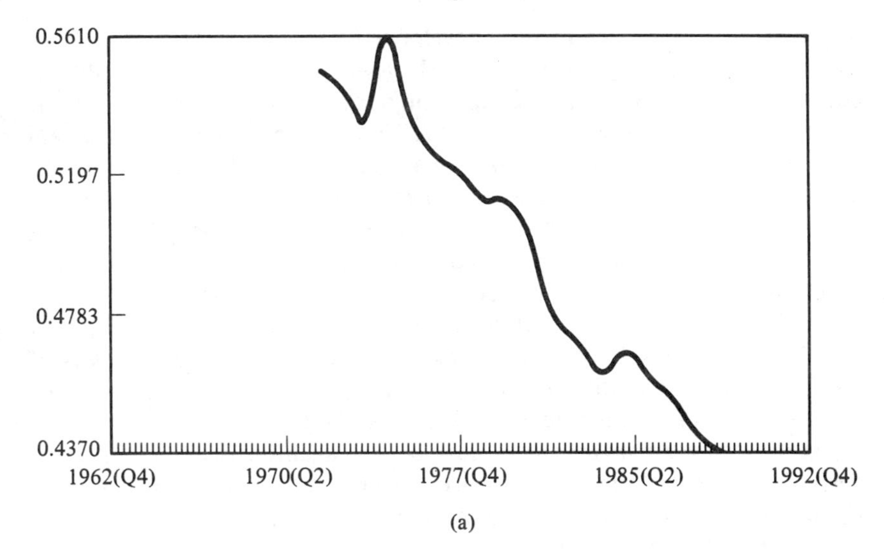

(a)

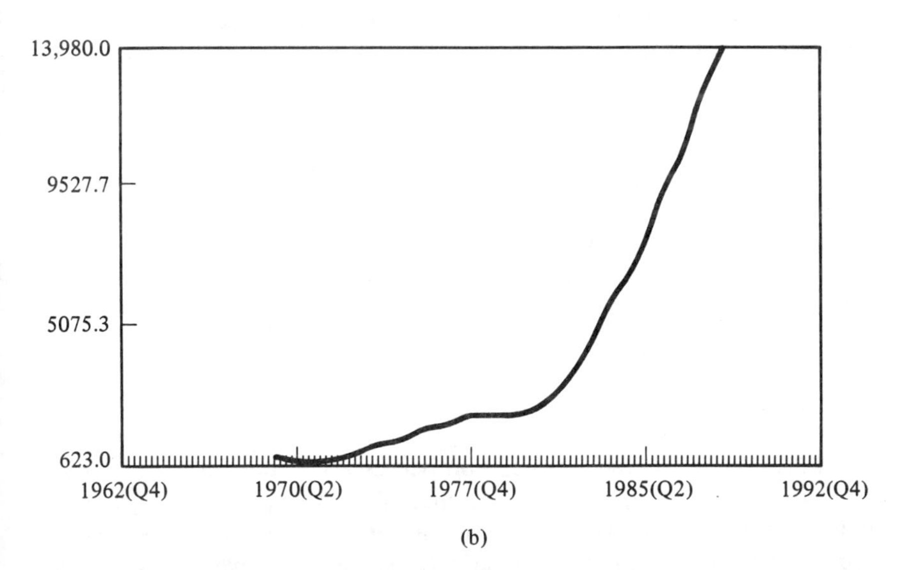

(b)

Figure 6.3 Exogenous measures of financial innovation (a) Proportion of manual workers in working population (PROMP); (b) Number of cash dispensers (CDISP)

employed is the two-step method developed by Engle and Granger (1987). In the first-stage, a regression among the levels of the trending variables is conducted. This allows the determination of the long-run relationship to be separated from the specification of the short-run dynamics. Of course a seemingly satisfactory relationship may emerge simply because of the common trend in a number of variables. This is known as the spurious regression problem (Granger and Newbold 1974). If, however, the variables in the long-run relationship can be combined in an equation with stationary residuals, then the variables are said to be cointegrated. These cointegration tests therefore form an important necessary step (though not a sufficient one) in testing the validity of any long-run solution. For recent surveys of the theory of cointegration analysis see Hendry (1986), and for an overview of how the theory should be applied see Hall and Henry (1988).

In practice, two main arguments may be used against this approach. First, despite the superior super-convergence properties of the first stage estimates (Stock 1985), small-sample bias has been shown to be a problem by Banerjee et al. (1986). This may be why other researchers (e.g. HM Treasury 1988) have eschewed these techniques in favour of a more conventional one-stage approach. While this argument may be correct, the sample of 80 quarters used here is not particularly small for macroeconomic empirical work. In any case even a small sample still needs a careful study of the time series properties of the variables used. To avoid this criticism, conventional one-stage estimates of our preferred specification are presented in addition to our two-stage estimates.

The second argument concerns the non-uniqueness of the cointegrating vector (see Johansen 1988). We suggest that this is unlikely to be a problem using the chosen specification, and hence that the long-run relationship found is likely to be uniquely defined.

3.2 The data

Table 6.1 summarizes the time series properties of the data used in this study. This throws interesting light on the estimation problems since it suggests that unlike many studies, where all of the long-run variables are integrated of order 1 or I(1), many of the key relationships are I(2) or marginally so. This is important since if one variable in the long-run relationship is I(2) then this must combine with another I(2) variable to form an I(1) variable, which itself must combine with at least one more I(1) variable to create a stationary I(0) residual.

Taking the ADF as the guiding criterion (critical value −2.93 at 95 per cent significance level) then nominal cash and prices are certainly I(2), as are the exogenous measures of financial innovation and some of the cumulated

Table 6.1 Tests on time series properties

	I(0)			I(1)			I(2)		
	CRDW	DF	ADF	CRDW	DF	ADF	CRDW	DF	ADF
LCASH	0.0	−3.5	−2.0	1.5	−6.7	−2.0	3.1	−16.7	−6.0
LCPI	0.0	0.7	−0.7	0.4	−3.7	−2.2	2.6	−14.0	−6.0
LRMC	0.0	−0.9	−1.4	1.5	−6.8	−2.9	3.0	−15.0	−5.3
LCND	0.0	1.96	0.9	1.9	−9.2	−2.8	3.2	−19.5	−6.6
LCNDI	0.0	0.3	−0.1	1.9	−8.6	−3.0	3.0	−15.3	−6.7
LC	0.0	1.1	0.8	2.1	−9.7	−2.8	3.1	−17.4	−6.5
RNET	0.1	−2.0	−2.4	1.5	−8.4	−5.4			
CUMRNR	0.0	0.1	−0.7	0.2	−2.6	−3.3	1.4	−7.9	−5.3
R3R	0.2	−2.3	−2.7	1.6	−8.5	−5.2			
CUMR3R	0.0	−12.3	−3.3	0.1	−1.3	−1.6	1.5	−8.0	−4.9
R3M	0.1	−1.9	−2.3	1.6	−8.1	−5.2			
CUMR3M	0.0	−4.8	−2.1	0.2	−2.0	−2.7	1.4	−7.6	−5.0
PROPM	0.0	0.2	0.1	0.4	−2.6	−2.5	0.9	−4.3	−3.8
CDISP	0.0	14.7	1.5	0.1	−1.1	−0.3	1.4	−7.2	−7.0

CRDW cointegrating regression Durbin-Watson statistic
DF Dickey-Fuller statistic
ADF augmented Dickey-Fuller statistic

LCASH log M0 excluding bankers' balances
LCPI log consumer price index
LRMC LCASH − LCPI
LCND log real non-durable consumption of goods and services
LCNDI log real non-durable consumption of goods
LC log real consumption
RNET RBDEP × (1 −composite rate tax)
RBDEP weighted bank deposit rate (HM Treasury definition)
CUMRNR cumulated RNET discounted by $(1 + RNET/100)^{1/4}$ per period
R3R three-month interbank rate
CUMR3R cumulated R3R discounted by R3R as above
R3M three-month interbank rate net of income tax
PROPM proportion of manual workers in working population
CDISP (number of cash dispensers)/100,000

interest rate terms. On the same basis, real cash is still marginally I(2) while the consumption measures are marginally I(1). Study of the relevant correlograms (see figures 6.4a and b) confirm that real cash and the endogenous innovation terms are difficult to reject as I(2) variables. As is conventionally found, our results show, perhaps counter-intuitively, that interest rates and inflation are I(1), consistent with the view that these variables follow a random walk.

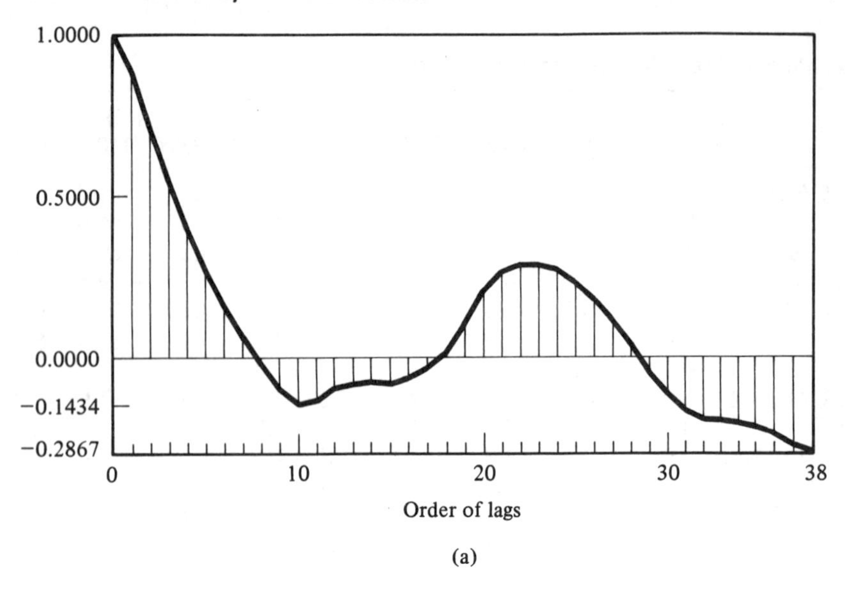

(a)

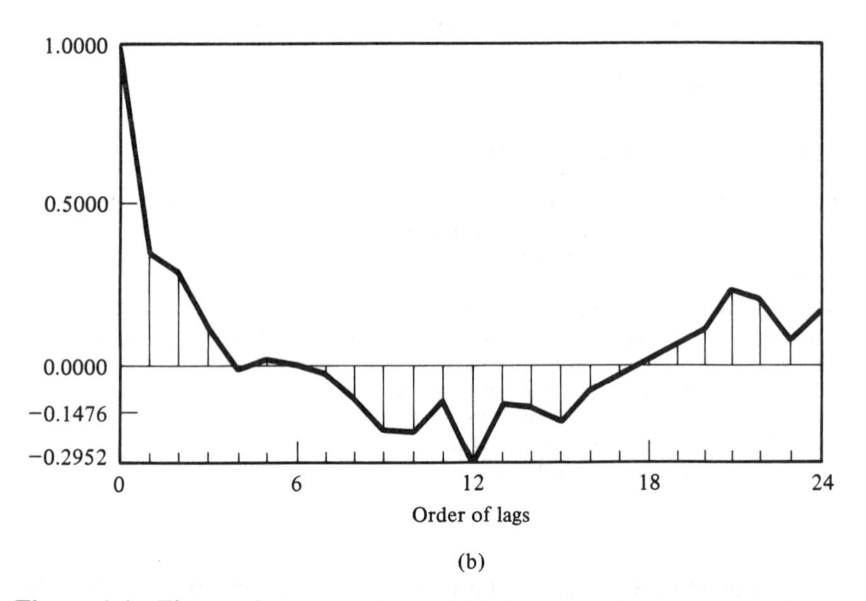

(b)

Figure 6.4 Time series properties of CUMRNR and LRM0 (first differences) (a) Autocorrelation function of ΔCUMRNR; (b) Autocorrelation function of ΔLRMC

These time series properties imply that if real M0 is I(2), then at least one I(2) financial innovation variable is required in the long-run relationship.

3.3 Testing for a long-run relationship

The results in this section are presented in the form of first-stage cointegrating regressions. This type of analysis should be carried out carefully for a number of reasons. First, the *t* statistics give a biased estimate of the significance of the variables included in the long-run solutions. Second, if the sample size is too small to justify using cointegration methods (see Banerjee et al. 1986), it will be dangerous to base model selection on these criteria. This reservation applies even more strongly if the long-run relationship postulated does not form a cointegrating vector.

However, in practice this approach invariably allows valuable insights into model specification without necessitating time-consuming general to specific specification searches on the full dynamic model. (In cases where the cointegration analysis results are not clear cut, such a dynamic specification will still be necessary.)

In particular, variables included which attract very low *t* statistics are likely to have very little effect on the time series properties of the residual and hence can be rejected.

In table 6.2, regression (6.1) confirms the point made in Hall et al. (1989) that conventional variables used in studies of the demand for money but excluding financial innovation do not cointegrate. Regressions (6.2a) and (6.2b) illustrate that the variables used in the HM Treasury specification (with and without a unit consumption elasticity) do not cointegrate. Regressions (6.3a) and (6.3b) introduce the cumulated interest rate term CUMRNR. This is seen to be highly significant, seemingly dominating the exogenous financial innovation measures. In table 6.3, regressions (6.4a) and (6.4b) confirm that the consumption of non-durable goods dominates other transactions variables such as total consumption and consumption of all non-durables.

In table 6.4, regressions (6.5a) to (6.5c) show that the RNET measure of interest rates dominates other cumulated terms. This would seem to suggest albeit weakly that the demand-based explanation of endogenous innovation dominates the supply-led influence (which would probably be better explained by the three-month interbank rate). Regression (6.5d) also shows that price homogeneity is not exactly accepted. This can be explained as a cumulated inflation effect. In table 6.5, regressions (6.6a) and (6.6b) give our preferred specifications for the long-run solution. Real cash is explained by real consumption of non-durable goods with an elasticity of 0.8, in line with the theory; there is an effect from discounted cumulated

Table 6.2 Cointegrating equations (6.1)–(6.3), dependent variable LRMC: 1971(Q4) to 1988(Q4)

	(6.1)	(6.2a)	(6.2b)	(6.3a)	(6.3b)
CON	16.34	−2.1	−2.8	0.05	−0.6
	(14.5)	(1.6)	(29.0)	(0.1)	(0.9)
LCNDI	−0.65	0.92	1.0	0.99	1.05
	(5.9)	(7.2)	(-)	(12.8)	(15.6)
RNET	−0.01	−0.0007	−0.0013	−0.0017	-
	(2.1)	(0.4)	(0.8)	(1.5)	-
Δ_4LCPI	0.35	−0.87	−0.86	-	-
	(1.7)	(10.5)	(10.5)	-	-
CUMRNR	-	-	-	−0.0026	−0.0026
				(20.6)	(22.2)
PROPM	-	4.92	4.93	0.1	0.2
	-	(26.6)	(26.8)	(0.5)	(1.0)
CDISP	-	−0.47	0.61	−0.25	−0.4
	-	(1.6)	(4.1)	(1.4)	(2.7)
$\bar{R}^2$	0.58	0.963	0.999	0.987	0.987
SE	0.079	0.022	0.022	0.022	0.013
CRDW	0.104	0.615	0.648	0.757	0.744
DF	−1.1	−3.3	−3.45	−3.88	−3.86
ADF	−2.0	−2.8	−2.7	−3.4	−3.1

CON constant
SE standard error

Table 6.3 Cointegrating equations (6.4), dependent variable LRMC: 1969(Q3) to 1989(Q3)

	(6.4a)	(6.4b)
CON	1.67	1.69
	(4.2)	(4.4)
LCNDI	0.84	0.83
	(19.8)	(21.0)
CUMRNR	−0.0027	−0.0027
	(41.0)	(42.0)
CRAT	0.02	-
	(0.2)	-
CNDRAT	-	−0.03
		(0.3)
$\bar{R}^2$	0.985	0.985
SE	0.015	0.015
CRDW	0.779	0.772

CRAT = LCNDI - LC
CNDRAT = LCNDI - LCND

Table 6.4 Cointegrating equations (6.5), dependent variable LRMC: 1969(Q3) to 1989(Q3)

	(6.5a)	(6.5b)	(6.5c)	(6.5d)
CON	1.70	1.74	1.05	1.85
	(4.3)	(4.4)	(1.1)	(4.5)
LCNDI	0.83	0.83	0.90	0.81
	(21.1)	(20.8)	(9.3)	(18.7)
CUMRNR	−0.0027	−0.0026	−0.0024	−0.0024
	(8.5)	(17.1)	(4.2)	(11.6)
CUMRN99	0.000	-	-	-
	(0.09)	-	-	-
CUMR3R	-	0.000	-	-
	-	(0.5)	-	-
TIME	-	-	−0.001	-
	-	-	(0.6)	-
LCPI	-	-	-	−0.024
	-	-	-	(1.1)
$\bar{R}^2$	0.985	0.985	0.985	0.985
SE	0.015	0.95	0.016	0.015
CRDW	0.776	0.777	0.801	0.774
DF	−4.4	−4.4	−4.4	−4.4
ADF	−3.46	−3.46	−3.46	−3.46

Table 6.5 Cointegrating equations (6.6), dependent variable LRMC: 1969(Q3) to 1989(Q3)

	(6.6a)	(6.6b)
CON	1.69	1.81
	(4.4)	(5.1)
LCNDI	0.84	0.82
	(21.6)	(22.9)
CUMRNR	−0.0026	−0.0027
	(46.9)	(49.0)
RNET	-	0.0036
		(3.6)
Δ_4LCPI	-	−0.1
		(2.8)
$\bar{R}^2$	0.985	0.988
SE	0.015	0.014
CRDW	0.776	0.944
DF	−4.4	−5.1
ADF	−3.5	−3.94

interest rates. Regression (6.6b) includes separate effects from the level of interest rates and inflation; these are included because they are I(1) variables which ought to be included in the cointegrating vector. The residuals on this specification are close to stationarity; figure 6.5 plots the correlogram. The ADF statistic is still marginally failed, however (see Engle and Yoo 1987). Nevertheless, figures 6.6a–d suggest that the specification is remarkably stable as shown by the recursive estimates of the coefficients.[4] Overall, these results provide evidence, albeit rather weak, for the long-run relationhip between M0, consumption, cumulated interest rates, inflation and interest rates. Even so, this cointegrating vector may not be unique (see Johansen 1988). However, preliminary work using the Johansen maximum likelihood estimation technique has suggested that while the null hypothesis that there are no cointegrating vectors between the variables used in (6.6b) is rejected, the null hynothesis that there are at most one cannot be. Encouragingly the coefficient estimates on the relevant eigenvector are similar to these found above using OLS, although given the relatively weak status of our original cointegrating vector we would not expect them to be identical. This aspect of our work is in the process of further research and is not discussed further here.

3.4 Specifying short-run dynamics

In table 6.6, regression (6.7) gives our model of the short-run dynamics, where the residual from the cointegrating vector in (6.6b) is included with other I(0) variables (the first differences of the I(1) variables in the cointegrating vector) and regressed on the first difference of the dependent variable. This specification passes all the standard diagnostic tests for serial correlation (using the Lagrange multiplier tests for serial correlation of first order and up to fourth order), functional form (using Ramsey's RESET test) and heteroscedasticity (based on the regression of squared residuals on squared fitted values). Regression (6.8) is a similar specification derived from a testing-down procedure using a conventional one-stage estimation technique. This yields almost identical long-run coefficients on the cumuated interest rate term and only a slightly higher elasticity of 0.88 on consumpion. The one-stage dynamic specification also easily passes a parameter stability test (splitting the sample half-way through the data set and applying a Chow test).

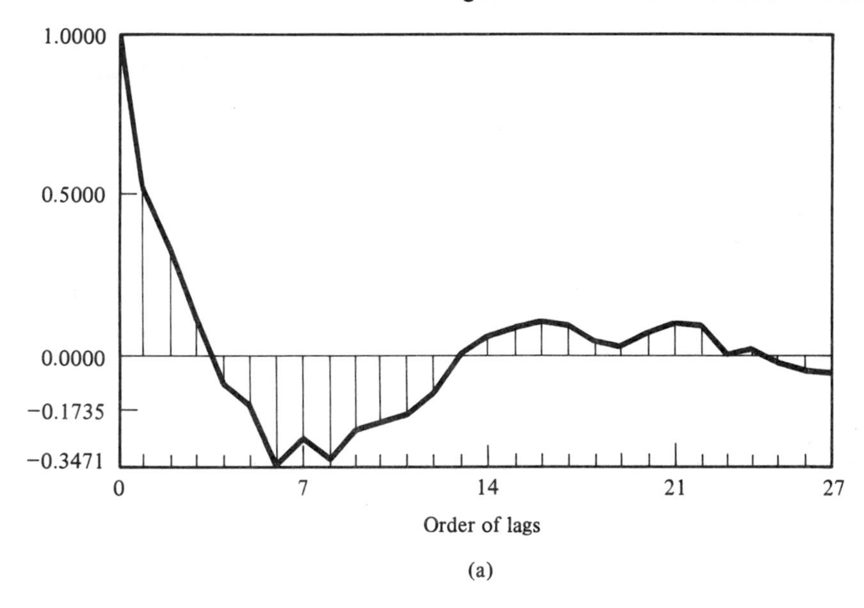

(a)

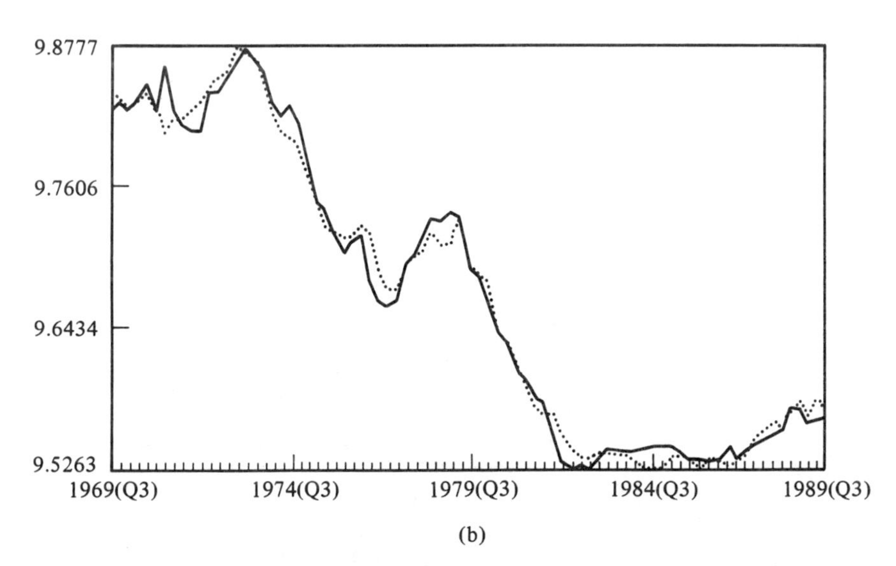

(b)

Figure 6.5 Long-run solution to preferred specification (a) Autocorrelation function of RES; (b) Plot of CRMC actual (____) and fitted (.....) values

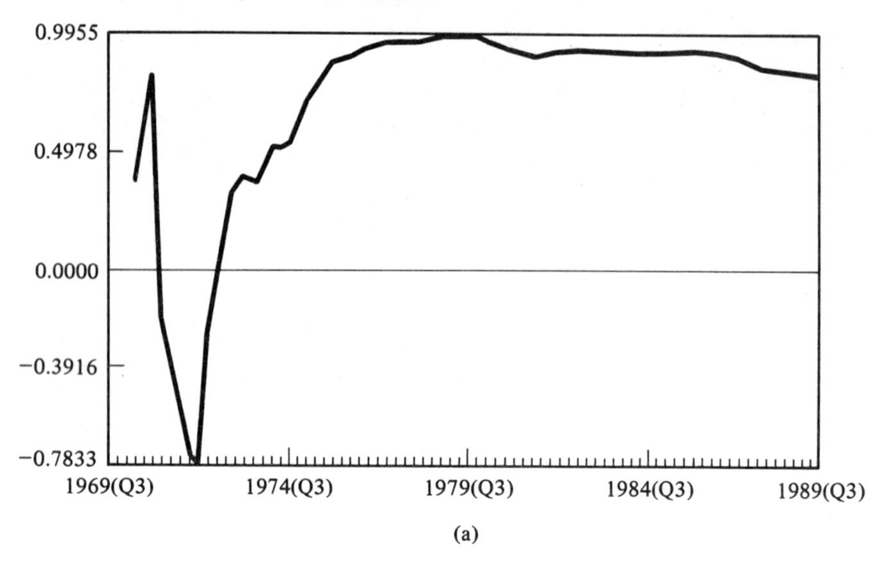

(a)

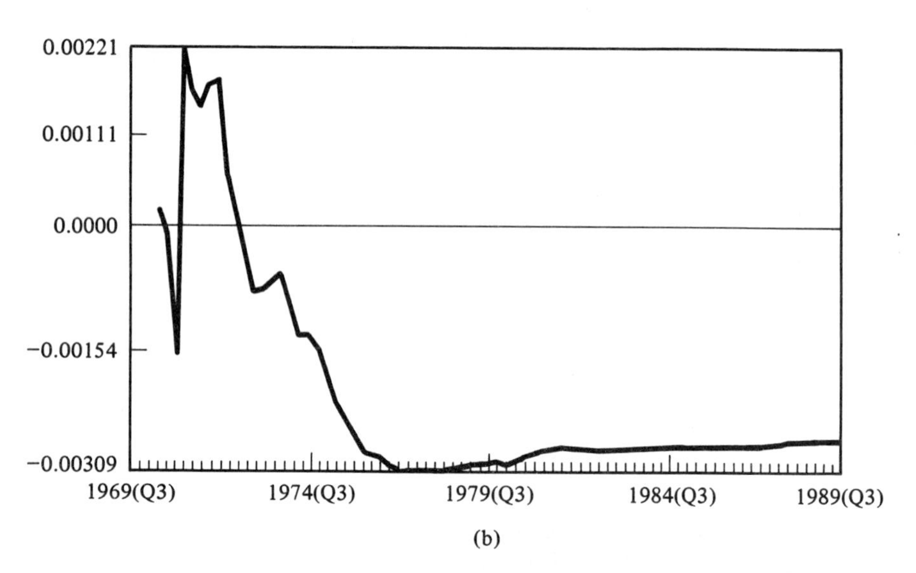

(b)

Figure 6.6 Recursive estimates for preferred specification (a) Plot of the coefficient of LCNDI based on recursive regression; (b) Plot of the coefficient of CUMRNR based on recursive regression; (c) Plot of the coefficient of RNET based on recursive regression; (d) Plot of the coefficient of Δ_4LCPI based on recursive regression

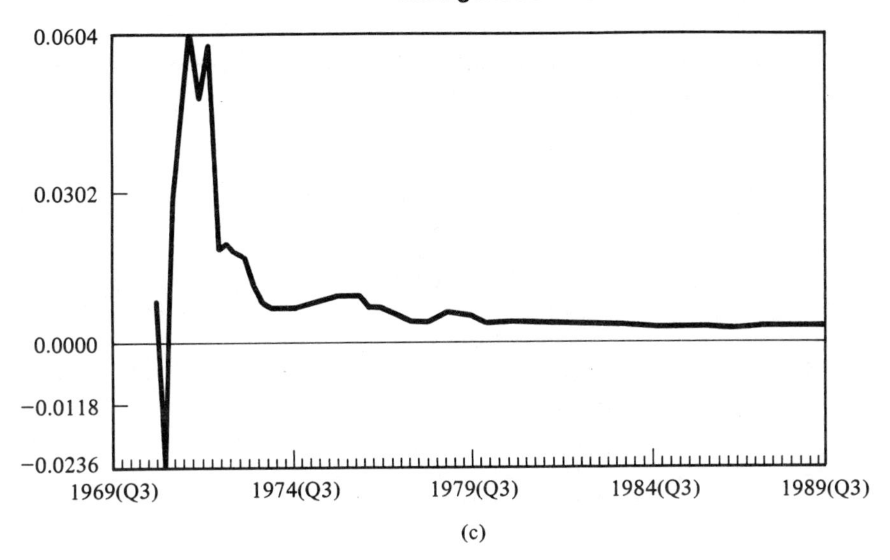

0.0604
0.0302
0.0000
−0.0118
−0.0236
1969(Q3)
1974(Q3)
1979(Q3)
1984(Q3)
1989(Q3)

(c)

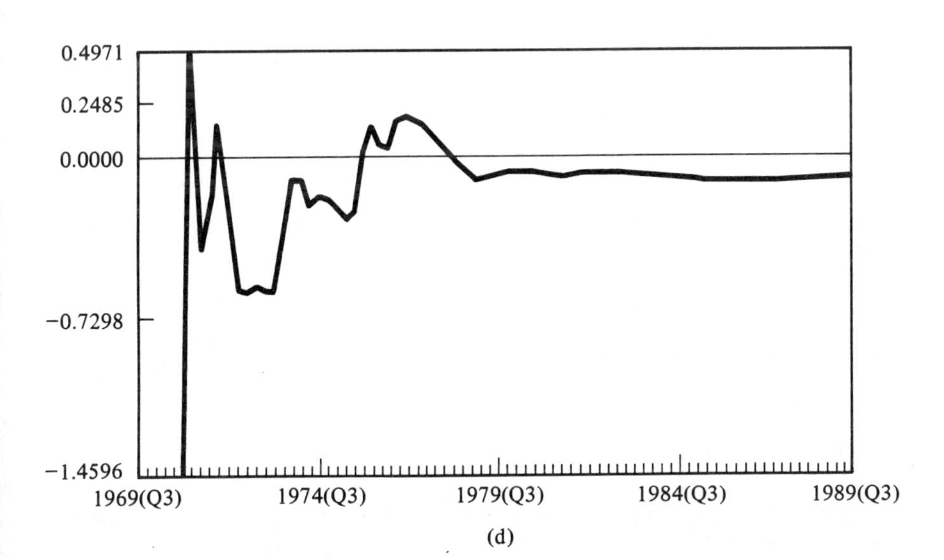

0.4971
0.2485
0.0000
−0.7298
−1.4596
1969(Q3)
1974(Q3)
1979(Q3)
1984(Q3)
1989(Q3)

(d)

Table 6.6 Dynamic regressions on (6.6b), dependent variable DLRMC: 1969(Q4) to 1989(Q3)

	(6.7)	(6.8)
CON	−0.0085	0.41
	(5.7)	(1.27)
ECM from (6.6b)	0.447	-
	(4.7)	-
LRMC(−1)	-	−0.34
		(3.7)
LCNDI(−1)	-	0.30
		(3.8)
CUMRNR(−1)	-	−0.0009
		(3.7)
Δ_4LCPI(−1)	-	−0.11
		(3.8)
RNET(−1)	-	−0.0017
	-	(2.1)
ΔLC	0.51	0.29
	(4.7)	(2.5)
ΔLC(−1)	0.44	-
	(3.73)	-
Δ_1LCPI	−0.60	−0.46
	(3.73)	(3.1)
$\bar{R}^2$	0.4457	0.54
SE	0.011	0.010
LM(4)	6.8	6.6
RESET(1)	1.71	0.32
HET(1)	0.003	0.008
Split sample Chow	0.088 (dynamics only)	0.54

4 CONCLUSIONS

This chapter has attempted to validate the contention that a stable econometric relationship for M0 can be found. This we have done, although it should be noted that the specification derived is somewhat different from that used by HM Treasury, which we found could not be supported by the data.

In deriving our preferred specification, we have also attempted to draw attention to a number of interesting theoretical issues regarding the determination of notes and coin which in the past have received scant attention. First, we have suggested that endogenous proxy measures for financial innovation may explain past behaviour more satisfactorily than exogenous measures which anyway prove problematical. Second, we have emphasized that holders of notes can comprise two different types of economic agent, only one of which will behave according to the inventory-theoretic model. This, in turn, motivates the search for an explanation of how individuals move between the groups. We have suggested that this type of financial innovation may be initiated from the supply side rather than the demand side. Finally, given the unusual time series properties of the data in this area, we have illustrated that cointegration analysis casts useful light on the plausibility of competing long-run models.

Notes

An earlier version of this chapter was presented at a Money Study Group Spring Workshop on Money at LSE. We are grateful to participants at the Workshop, and in particular to Mark Taylor, for useful comments and suggestions, although responsibility for the final version rests with us.

1 Over shorter periods, however, the extreme volatility of bankers' operational deposits can sometimes cause a divergence between the growth rates of M0 and cash.
2 Source: National Opinion Poll data and International Banking Research Organization (IBRO).
3 This is similar to the point made in Taylor (1987) where the marginal rate relevant for moving between broad money and less liquid assets is captured by the interest rate on high-interest chequeing accounts.
4 We argue that it is relevant to analyse the structural stability of the estimated cointegrating vector. By contrast, and somewhat irrelevantly in our view, Hall et al. (1989) analyse the structural stability of the second-stage dynamics taking the first-stage CV as given. This is only a valid test of the stability of the dynamics if the long-run solution is structurally stable; this is likely to be the case if the long-run solution cointegrates.

References

Banerjee, A., Dolado, J. J., Hendry, D. F. and Smith, G. W. (1986) 'Exploring equilibrium relationships in econometrics through static models: some Monte Carlo evidence', *Oxford Bulletin of Economics and Statistics*, 48 (3), 253–78.

Baumol, W. J. (1952) 'The transactions demand for cash: an inventory theoretic approach', *Quarterly Journal of Economics*, 66, 545–56.

Engle, R. F. and Granger, C. W. J. (1987) 'Cointegration and error correction: representation, estimation and testing', *Econometrica*, 55 (12), 251–76.

Engle, R. F. and Yoo, B. S. (1987) 'Forecasting and testing in cointegrated systems', *Journal of Econometrics*, 35 (1), 143–60.

Fisher, D. (1978) *Monetary Theory and the Demand for Money*, Oxford: Martin Robertson.

Goldfeld, S. M. (1970) 'The case of the missing money', *Brookings Papers on Economic Activity*, 3, 577–638.

Granger, C. W. J. and Newbold, P. (1974) 'Spurious regression in econometrics', *Journal of Econometrics*, 2, 111–20.

Hall, S. and Henry, B. (1988) *Macroeconomic Modelling*, Amsterdam: North-Holland.

Hall, S., Henry, B. and Wilcox, J. (1989) 'The long run determination of the UK monetary aggregates', Bank of England, discussion paper 41.

Hendry, D. F. (1986) 'Econometric modelling with cointegrated variables: an overview', *Oxford Bulletin of Economics of Statistics*, 48 (3), 201–13.

HM Treasury (1988) HM Treasury Public Model Documentation.

Johansen, S. (1988) 'Statistical analysis of cointegrating vectors', *Journal of Economic Dynamics and Control*, 12 (2/3), 231–45.

Johnston, R. B. (1984) 'The demand for non-interest bearing money in the United Kingdom', HM Treasury, working paper 28.

Stock, J. H. (1985) 'Asymptotic properties of least squares regression with integrated processes', *Review of Economic Studies*, 53, 473–95.

Taylor, M. P. (1987) 'Financial innovation, inflation and the stability of the demand for broad money in the United Kingdom', *Bulletin of Economic Research*, 39 (3), 225–34.

Tobin, J. (1956) 'The interest elasticity of the transactions demand for cash', *Review of Economics and Statistics*, 38, 241–7.

7 The Demand for Money in Four Countries in the Interwar Period: A Study Using Monthly Data

Jonathan Slow, James Foreman-Peck and
Andrew Hughes Hallett

1 INTRODUCTION

This chapter presents results of an empirical study of the demand for money in the interwar period for four countries: the United Kingdom, the United States, France and Germany. It is novel, we believe, in two ways. First, it directly estimates such relationships for this period using recently developed econometric techniques which deal directly with the relationship between long-run equilibrium and short-run dynamics (Engle and Granger 1987). Second, we are using a higher-frequency data set (monthly) than previously utilized for this period to try and capture the effects of financial crises and associated slumps.

The results are only a small part of a much larger project which considers the transition mechanism across countries of the Great Depression and associated financial crises. One point that appears to crop up constantly is that the banking crises were generally preceded by falls in industrial production. In other words, real phenomena led to monetary problems and not necessarily the other way around. Similarly, some countries (especially Germany and the United States) appear to have been heading into recession before the Wall Street Crash of October 1929. Whilst these points remain conjecture at present, they will be examined in greater detail in future research.

Because financial crises tend to come and go quite quickly, they can best be analysed using higher-frequency data. The monthly data set we use is the most reliable higher-frequency set available for the interwar period that we know of.

We apply best-practice econometric techniques to assess whether the standard textbook approaches to money demand functions apply to the interwar period, or whether they are lacking (as Hall et al. 1989 find for recent United Kingdom data). Consequently, we have focused on the cointegration and error correction model (ECM) outlined by Engle and Granger (1987), which separates out the decision process into long- and short-run components.

We utilize two types of cointegration technique: that of Engle and Granger (1987) and that of Johansen (1988). For applications of both see Cuthbertson and Slow (1989), Hall (1986, 1989) or Taylor (1990).

The plan of the chapter is as follows. Section 2 discusses the role of cointegration in this analysis and presents the results for all four countries: the United States, the United Kingdom, France and Germany. We examine the individual series used for each country for non-stationarity and then look for cointegration between them. We find that in all cases there exists at least one cointegrating vector, and that the ordinary least squares (OLS) and maximum likelihood (ML) results are generally not too dissimilar. Section 3 examines the dynamic properties of the data given our findings in section 2. This also lends support to our models being a good representation of the data generation process, although the case for Germany is a little weaker. Section 4 presents some conclusions and pointers for future research.

2 COINTEGRATION RESULTS

When utilizing the ECM formulation set out above, it is essential to consider the cointegrating properties of our proposed series. Essentially, cointegration is based on the idea of a group of variables stochastically moving together over time (see Granger and Weiss 1983; Granger and Engle 1985; Engle and Granger 1987). In other words, the steady-state difference between such variables is finite. Moreover, following the Granger representation theorem (see Engle and Granger 1987), providing a valid cointegrating vector exists then underlying this process there is an ECM. Conversely, for an ECM to be valid, a cointegrating vector must exist. Therefore before using ECMs we must test for cointegration amongst our proposed variables. Once we have established cointegration (if it exists) we can appeal to the super-consistency results of Stock (1985, 1987), generalized by Phillips and Durlauf (1986) and Park and Phillips (1986), to ensure that estimated coefficients of the level terms are very precise. In other words, the coefficients estimated in the (static) cointegrating regression converge to their true values faster than standard estimates.[1] This, however, may be bought at the cost of some small-sample bias (Banerjee et al. 1986).

There seems to be little point in summarizing the theoretical background to cointegration here when it has been extensively studied elsewhere (Hendry 1986; Granger 1986; Perman 1989; for applications see Hall 1986; Cuthbertson and Slow 1989). One of the techniques we apply is more recent and uses a maximum likelihood approach to assess the number and estimates of cointegrating vectors. This is based on the work of Johansen (1988) and Johansen and Juselius (1990); it is summarized by Hall (1989) and applied in Taylor (1990) and Cuthbertson and Slow (1989).

Table 7.1 lists the variables proposed as possible candidates for cointegration and assesses their orders of integration using two tests: the Dickey-Fuller (DF) test (Dickey and Fuller 1979; Fuller 1976) and the augmented Dickey-Fuller (ADF) test (Dickey and Fuller 1981; Said and Dickey 1984). The tests for I(0) behaviour are carried out on the levels of the variables, and the tests for I(1) are performed on the first differences. The country prefixes on the variables (UK, US, F, G) are dropped from tables 7.2 and 7.3 for convenience.

The results seem quite promising, with the proposed variables all appearing to be I(1) for all four countries. One exception to this rule is the risk terms MOVSD. We would expect these to be stationary over time (i.e. fluctuating around a constant mean value). However, only in France do we have evidence that this might be the case, as opposed to having a deterministic component. This highlights some of the problems of the Dickey-Fuller approach outlined in Banerjee et al. (1986) and Engle and Granger (1987), and in the work below we treat this variable as being I(0).[2]

2.1 United Kingdom

The results for the UK are shown in table 7.2a. The variables appear to form a cointegrating regression. The test statistics DF and ADF, testing for non-stationarity of the cointegrating residuals, appear to reject this hypothesis.[3] Further support is given by the statistic CRDW (cointegrating regression Durbin-Watson) (see Sargan and Bhargava 1983; Bhargava 1980). The correlogram of the cointegrating residuals also appears stationary, adding informal support to our hypothesis of cointegration.

The estimated coefficients assess the economic significance of our results. All variables have the correct *a priori* signs, and the coefficients on the inflation term ΔLP and the interest rate R are plausible in magnitude (see Laidler 1977; Cuthbertson and Taylor 1987; Taylor 1990). The dummy variable is included to capture the effects of the UK abandoning the Gold Standard in September 1931 and moving to a flexible exchange rate.

Also in table 7.2a are the results of the Johansen likelihood ratio test. Again, we strongly reject the hypothesis of no cointegration, although

Table 7.1 Variables for cointegration

	Test for I(0)		Test for I(1)	
	DF[a]	ADF[b]	DF[a]	ADF[b]
UKLM3	−0.77	−2.41*	−9.05	−3.23*
UKΔLP	−1.25	−0.83*	−11.31	−3.45*
UKIBA	0.26	−0.86	−10.52	−1.93
UKR	−2.43	−1.81	−14.29	−3.59
UKMOVSD	−0.39	−0.62*	−1.84	−8.17*
USLM3	−0.88	−1.47	−8.60	−3.58*
USΔLP	−0.86	−2.32	−5.37	−4.01
USIP	−0.92	−0.49	−5.92	−2.97
USR	0.94	−2.51	−9.81	−3.96*
USMOVSD	−1.30	−1.30*	0.13	−14.28*
FRLM3	−2.08	−1.84*	−9.19	−1.26
FRΔLP	1.90	1.27*	−8.19	−6.59*
FRIP	−1.76	−2.08	−6.55	−2.67
FRR	−3.03	−1.98	−9.99	−2.60
FRMOVSD	−2.09	−3.23*	0.16	−15.47*
GLM3	−2.76	−2.83	−12.49	−2.04
GΔLP	−1.67	−1.46	−15.29	−2.83*
GIP	−1.43	−2.26*	−3.39	−1.39
GR	−1.70	−2.29*	−7.16	−3.72*
GMOVSD	−1.00	−1.46*	0.10	−14.32*

[a] The DF test is based on $\Delta X_t = C + \alpha X_{t-1} + U_t$. The test is based on the statistical significance of α: on $X = >$ I(0); on $\Delta X = >$ I(1); etc.

[b] The ADF test is as for the DF test but adds $\Delta X_{t-i} i = 1, \ldots, p$ to the right hand side to capture more dynamics. p is large enough to make U_t white noise. The test is again of the significance of α. A twelfth-order lag was generally sufficient.

The * implies the ADF statistic is more valid because it contains significant ΔX_{t-1} variables. In other cases, the ADF is over-parameterized and the DF is more useful.

UKLM3	log[(Bank of England notes andd coins + nine clearing bank deposits/RPI] (LCES)
UKΔLP	Δ[log (RPI)] (LCES)
UKIBA	*Economist* index of business activity
UKR	yield on day-to-day interest rate ($=R/(1 - R/1200)$) (FED)
UKMOVSD	moving standard deviation of long-run consol yield. Measure is twelve-month forward-looking, but the results are virtually unchanged if a six-month forward- , six-month backward-looking model is used (FED)
USLM3	log (Friedman-Schwartz series) (FS, LON)
USΔLP	Δ[log (finished prices)] (FED, LON)
USIP	index of industrial production (FED, LON)
USR	yield on US short interest rate (FED)

USMOVSD	as for UKMOUSD on US data
FRLM3	log (note circulation + private deposits of Bank of France + demand deposits of other French banks)/wholesale prices index] (FED, LCES)
FRΔLP	Δ[log (wholesale price index)] (FED)
FRIP	index of industrial production (LCES, LON)
FRP	yield on private Paris discount rate (FED, LON)
FRMOVSD	as for UKMOVSD for French data
GLM3	log [(note circulation including other notes and coinage + deposits of six Berlin banks)/index of prices, all items] (LCES, FED)
GΔLP	Δ[log (index of prices, all items)] (LCES, FED)
GIP	German industrial production (LON)
GR	official Reichsbank rate (FED)
GMOVSD	as for UKMOVSD for German data

Sources:

FED	*Federal Reserve Monthly Bulletin*
LCES	London and Cambridge Economic Service
LON	League of Nations monthly statistical bulletin
FS	Friedman and Schwartz (1982)

the cointegrating vector may not be unique. Upon normalizing the estimated Johansen vectors and assessing their relationship to the OLS cointegrating regression, we find the relationship is not particularly good. The coefficients are different in all cases. However, the signs are correct. The main difference concerns the income elasticity, which jumps from (the implausibly low) 0.03 to (the implausibly high ?) 2.5 (see Laidler 1977). Both cointegration vectors were tried at the second stage of estimation, the estimated short-run dynamic models, and their statistical performance was very similar.

2.2 United States

For the sake of brevity, we report that the results for the US (table 7.2b) are similar to those for the UK. In other words, we reject the hypothesis of non-cointegration between these variables. Analysis of the DF and ADF statistics, although not conclusive, is strengthened when the correlogram is examined. Moreover, the likelihood ratio procedure confirms that there are as many as three cointegrating regressions.[4] Of even more importance is the comparison between the estimated coefficients of the OLS and Johansen methods: the interest rate terms are very similar, and although there is a difference in the inflation term, both estimates are within a plausible range.[5] Also the estimated coefficients have the correct *a priori* signs.

2.3 France

The results for France are shown in table 7.2c. Both estimation methods confirm cointegration and the estimated coefficients are very close. However, the dummy variable is necessary for sensible cointegration. In other words, when it is dropped, although the maximum likelihood approach still indicates cointegration, the elasticities are implausibly large for both the scale variable and inflation.

2.4 Germany

The situation for Germany (table 7.2d) is, however, not as promising as for the other three countries. The OLS method implies cointegration according to the DF and ADF statistics. Moreover, the signs and the sizes of the interest rate and inflation terms are plausible. However, the low $\bar{R}^2$ implies that there may well be small-sample bias in the coefficients (Banerjee et al. 1986). This, to some extent, is borne out when we look at the results from the Johansen procedure, since the estimated coefficients are very different between the two methods – particularly for the interest rate terms. These go from a plausible (semi-) elasticity of approximately 0.2 to the implausible 2.32. However, it should be noted that in estimating the maximum likelihood procedure, we could not set the vector autogressive (VAR) lag to be long enough to ensure white noise errors because of lack of degrees of freedom. Therefore, these results must be interpreted cautiously. We still believe that cointegration between the variables exists, supported by the informal evidence of the correlogram, but inference on the estimated coefficients remains subject to a degree of uncertainty.

Overall, therefore, we reject the hypothesis of non-cointegration for all countries, and this forms the basis for our ECMs in the next section. However, before we examine these, we further explore the problems experienced with the scale variable in all four data sets.

The scale variable elasticities are very low. Exactly what values we should accept are unknown, but Laidler (1977) argues that elasticities in excess of unity would not be out of place for the US, France and Germany, and approximately 0.5–0.75 should apply to the UK.[6]

We believe our estimates are low because of the proxy we have had to use for the scale variable. GDP/GNP figures, as far as we are aware, are not available monthly for this period. To overcome this, industrial production statistics are used (see table 7.1). Although regressions (on annual averages) between the two series give the relatively high correlations of

Table 7.2 Cointegrating vectors

(a) United Kingdom

Sample: 1928(2)–1936(12)

Dependent variable LM3

$LM3 = 5.2 - 0.91\Delta LP - 0.07R + 0.03LIBA + 0.2BDC$

BDC dummy variable to capture more from Gold Standard to managed exchange rates in September 1931 (=1 from 1931(9) onwards)

$R^2 = 0.91$, $\bar{R}^2 = 0.90$, SER = 0.04, 1931 (9) $T = 108$

DF = −4.21, ADF = −3.0, CRDW = 0.53

Johansen results:
$LM3 = C + 2.5\ LIBA + 0.4\ BDC - 0.02R - 1.10\ \Delta LP$

Test of number of cointegrating vectors (critical values in parentheses):

$r = 0$	135.9	(53.35)
$r \leqslant 1$	74.0	(35.07)
$r \leqslant 2$	44.85	(20.17)
$r \leqslant 3$	21.07	(9.09)

(b) United States

Sample: 1928(2)–1935(12)

Dependent variable LM3

$LM3 = 4.92 - 0.81\Delta LP - 0.05R - 0.03D333 + 0.12D2910 + 0.11LIP$

D333 dummy variable for new operating systems of the Fed (=1 from 1933(3) onwards)

D2910 dummy variable for Wall Street Crash effects (=1 between 1929(11) and 1932(6)

$R^2 = 0.92$, $\bar{R}^2 = 0.91$, SER = 0.02, $T = 94$

DF = −3.02, ADF = −2.94, CRDW = 0.39

Johansen results:
$LM3 = C + 0.09\ LIP - 1.27\Delta LP - 0.03R$

Test of number of cointegrating vectors (critical values in parentheses):

$r = 0$	89.47	(35.07)
$r \leqslant 1$	47.25	(20.17)
$r \leqslant 2$	20.32	(9.09)

(c) France

Sample: 1928(1)–1936(7)

Dependent variable LM3

LM3 = 5.32 – 1.08ΔLP – 0.09R – 0.44GOLD + 0.12LIP

GOLD dummy variable capturing gold/asset buildup between 1925 and 1930

R^2 = 0.88, $\bar{R}^2$ = 0.87, SER = 0.05, T = 103

DF = –5.34, ADF = –3.33, CRDW = 0.29

Johansen results:
LM3 = 0.13LIP – 0.04R – 0.56ΔLP – 0.49GOLD + C

Test of number of cointegrating vectors (critical values in parentheses):

$r = 0$	135.5	(53.35)
$r \leqslant 1$	77.55	(35.07)
$r \leqslant 2$	37.53	(20.17)
$r \leqslant 3$	18.85	(9.09)

(d) Germany

Sample: 1928(1)–1935(12)

Dependent variable LM3

LM3 = 5.3 – 1.16ΔLP – 0.2R – 0.2R + 0.03LIP

R^2 = 0.68, $\bar{R}^2$ = 0.67, SER = 0.06, T = 96

DF = –3.25, ADF = –3.25, CRDW = 0.29

Johansen results:
LM3 = –0.92ΔLP + 0.23LIP – 2.32R + C

Test of number of cointegrating vectors (critical values in parentheses):

$r = 0$	68.39	(35.07)
$r \leqslant 1$	23.34	(20.17)
$r \leqslant 2$	13.24	(9.09)

Critical values (5 per cent) (see Johansen and Juselius 1990 for details):

m	critical values
1	9.09
2	20.17
3	35.07
4	53.35
5	75.33

SER standard error of the regression
T sample size

0.75 for the UK to 0.95 for Germany (see Slow 1990), this may neglect the scale shift effect between the series. Using the Chow-Lin (1971) method of interpolation, the volumes of bank cleanings as proxies are avenues for further work.[7]

Another variable which perhaps has not been given enough emphasis at this stage is expectations; for example, expected inflation rates have been proxied in the past (Laidler 1977; Cuthbertson 1985). We propose to examine this question further by using Kalman filter techniques, as well as other forms of general ARIMA models (Cuthbertson 1988; Cuthbertson and Taylor 1986; Harvey and Todd 1983; Harvey 1981a). It should be noted however that, so long as the difference between expected and actual inflation rates defines a stationary series, our cointegration results are robust to assuming that expected rather than actual inflation should enter the specification.

We now proceed to analysis of the second-stage regressions, and specifically the ECMs underlying the cointegrating vectors above.

3 SECOND-STAGE RESULTS

The second stage of the Engle-Granger procedure is, again, quite straightforward. We place the residuals from the cointegrating regression (the error correction term) lagged one period into a general dynamic model of the form.

$$\Delta y_t = \sum_{i=1}^{m} \alpha \Delta y_{t-i} + \sum_{j=0}^{n} \beta_i \Delta X_{t-i} + \Gamma(\mathrm{RES})_{t-1} + c + u_t, \quad t = 1, \ldots, T \tag{7.1}$$

where the symbols have the following meanings:

y	real money balances
X	other explanatory variables
RES	residuals from the cointegrating regression
c	constant
u	IID errors
Δ	lag operator (i.e. $\Delta Q_t = Q_t - Q_{t-1}$)

This general model is simplified by imposing statistically significant restrictions. These models are outlined in tables 7.3a–d.[8]

Before analysing the results, we must point out a difficulty of the above approach. The bias arguments of Banerjee et al. (1986) apply in this case also.[9] However, this must be traded off against the simplicity of model (7.1). Simultaneous estimation of the α and β parameters along with the actual components of the long-run model (as performed in e.g. Cuthbertson and Slow 1989) means that we need to use non-linear estimation techniques.

3.1 United Kingdom

The results for the UK are given in table 7.3a. The first point to note is the correct signs on the variables in the parsimonious regression and the plausibility of the magnitudes of these estimates. The ECM term is significant at the 5 per cent level, and has the correct (negative) sign. This implies stability for the model and a correction time of approximately seven months. The term SDCONS is a smoothed measure of the long-run consol rate (the restriction that the three variables have the same sign is passed LR(3) = 1.74) and it has the correct negative sign and plausible semi-elasticity (see Hall et al. 1989).

Of particular importance is the insignificance of the risk proxy. This need not imply a negligible role for risk over the period in question, just that its effect is being picked up elsewhere. This implies a need to look at incorporation of risk terms (e.g. by using autogressive conditional heteroscedasticity (ARCH) models: see Engle 1982; Engle et al. 1987; Engle and Bollerslev 1986).

Statistically the model performs very well, passing the various autocorrelation tests (Bj, LM, FLM, *h*, CRDW). We can also reject ARCH effects in the errors (ARCH, F) heterosckedasticity (WHI) and dynamic misspecification (RESET), and we cannot reject good out-of-sample forecasting (HF). The standard error of the regression is 1.6 per cent.

We assess in-sample parameter stability by means of Chow tests. These are generally passed, but there are two failures. The first, in August 1931, corresponds to the period immediately prior to the UK coming off the Gold Standard, an event largely caused by France withdrawing large gold reserves and other assets deposited in London (see Jack 1932). The other, in December 1931, is harder to rationalise.

The final point of interest concerns the lack of short-run rate of interest in the dynamic equation. The effects of interest rates are captured by the SDCONS terms. This may signal a divorce between short and long rates, the latter perhaps being modelled as a measure of credibility of the government. This is still conjecture, but James (1984) provides evidence that this may have occurred in Germany.

3.2 United States

The results for the US are given in table 7.3b. Again, the second-stage model performs well, both economically and statistically. All the short-run parameters in the parsimonious model have the correct sign and are generally significant. The model is stable (Γ negative) and the adjustment lag is about seven months. The insignificance of the risk term is again present, and the change in interest rates seems to have little effect.

Statistically, very similar results apply here as for the UK. All the tests applied to the model are passed; the only point of instability appears to be during 1934, but even this is fairly borderline.

Consequently, the US equation is also a good representation of the data over this period. The lack of a short-run interest rate effect is perhaps a little worrying; however, for arguments concerning this see Hall et al. (1989).

3.3 France

The French results (table 7.3c) follow similar lines to those for the UK and the US. First, notice the short-run smoothed interest rate effect (LR test of equality of coefficients = 2.00). The size of this (short-run) semi-elasticity is plausible. Again, the change in inflation is important, perhaps due to agents, behaviour being influenced by the problems of 1924–6 and the 'Poincaré miracle' which followed (for an interesting examination see Sargent 1987). The risk term is again insignificant. The ECM has the correct negative sign, but the coefficient has fallen in value. The adjustment period is again less than one year. The change in dummy variable is important, reflecting the desire of the French to build up gold stocks, bringing them back to France when the European banking crisis (1931) deepened (Jack 1931).

The statistical performance is good, with all tests being passed; however, the model does show some parameter instability in 1934. This may have been caused by the withdrawal of international liquidity, an overvalued franc and a deepening recession at that time (Kindleberger 1984).

3.4 Germany

Statistically, this model (table 7.3d) fails the first-order ARCH test. In other words, large conditional error variances tend to follow each other. However, the consistency of point estimates is unaffected, and we can also use heteroscedastic consistent standard errors (see White 1980).

Table 7.3 Second-stage results
(a) United Kingdom

Sample: 1928(5)–1936(12)

Dependent variable ΔLM3

$$\Delta LM3_t = \underset{(4.25)}{0.36\ \Delta LM3_{t-1}} + \underset{(2.62)}{0.2\ \Delta LM3_{t-6}} + \underset{(1.04)}{0.00004\ MOVSD_t} - \underset{(1.42)}{0.26\ \Delta\Delta LP_t}$$

$$- \underset{(3.45)}{0.003\ SDCONS_t} - \underset{(3.06)}{0.13\ RES_{t-1}}$$

t ratios are in parentheses

SDCONS = ⅓ ($\Delta CONS_t + \Delta CONS_{t-1} + \Delta CONS_{t-12}$)
CONS consol (2½%) rate of interest

SER = 1.6%, DW = 1.96, T = 104, h = 0.37
Bj(1) = 0.08, Bj(4) = 1.53, Bj(6) = 4.21, Bj(9) = 6.69, Bj(12) = 8.52
RESET(2) = 0.31
LM(1) = 0.68, LM(4) = 0.89, LM(6) = 1.02, LM(9) = 2.72, LM(12) = 4.08
FLM(1) = 0.80, FLM(4) = 0.32, FLM(6) = 0.24, FLM(9) = 0.46, FLM(12) = 0.52
ARCH(1) = 1.36, ARCH(4) = 1.43, ARCH(6) = 1.5, ARCH(9) = 1.77, ARCH(12) = 2.04
F(1) = 2.0, F(4) = 0.51, F(6) = 0.5, F(9) = 0.34, F(12) = 0.25
HF(12) = 7.7, WHI = 0.68(1.75) (critical value)

Selected Chow tests from 1928(5) to dates given:

Date	Chow	CV
1931(6)	1.88	4.17
1931(7)	0.12	4.17
1931(8)	5.75	4.17F
1931(9)	0.18	4.17
1931(12)	3.43	1.99F
1933(12)	1.10	1.99
1934(12)	1.01	1.99
1935(12)	1.10	1.91
1936(12)	0.74	1.91

(b) United States

Sample: 1928(4)–1935(12)

Dependent variable $\Delta LM3$

$$\Delta LM3_t = \underset{(1.57)}{0.13\ \Delta LM3_{t-12}} + \underset{(0.96)}{0.0001\ MOVSD_t} + \underset{(1.03)}{0.002\ \Delta R_t} - \underset{(6.32)}{0.65\ \Delta\Delta LP_t}$$

$$- \underset{(3.84)}{0.05\ \Delta D333_t} - \underset{(2.83)}{0.02\ \Delta D2910_t} - \underset{(2.50)}{0.16\ RES_{t-1}}$$

t ratios are in parentheses

ΔD333 dummy: see table 7.2b
ΔD2910 dummy: see table 7.2b

SER = 1.1%, DW = 1.91, $T = 93$, $h = 0.47$
Bj(1) = 0.38, Bj(4) = 1.01, Bj(6) = 2.20, Bj(9) = 4.44, Bj(12) = 10.18
RESET(2) = 1.26
LM(1) = 0.23, LM(4) = 0.45, LM(6) =6.09, LM(9) = 6.72, LM(12) = 6.80
FLM(1) = 0.21, FLM(4) = 0.10, FLM(6) = 0.91, FLM(9) = 0.62, FLM(12) = 0.49
ARCH(1) = 2.4, ARCH(4) = 4.0, ARCH(6) = 4.08, ARCH(9) = 4.24, ARCH(12) = 4.32
F(1) = 2.41, F(4) = 0.90, F(6) = 0.57, F(9) = 0.39, F(12) = 0.32
HF(12) = 6.972, WHI = 0.91(1.75)

Selected Chow tests from 1928(4) to dates given:

Date	Chow	CV
1932(6)	2.25	2.34
1932(12)	0.35	2.34
1933(2)	1.88	4.17
1933(3)	≈ 0	4.17
1933(4)	≈ 0	4.17
1933(12)	2.10	2.25
1934(12)	2.08	1.99F
1935(12)	0.98	1.99

(c) France

Sample: 1928(4)–1936(7)

Dependent variable ΔLM3

$$\Delta LM3_t = \underset{(3.42)}{0.03\, \Delta R_t} + \underset{(1.60)}{0.06\, \Delta GOLD_t} + \underset{(0.71)}{0.004\, MOVSD_t} - \underset{(4.64)}{0.63\, \Delta\Delta LP_t} - \underset{(2.43)}{0.1\, RES_{t-1}}$$

t ratios are in parentheses

SER = 3%, DW = 1.91, T = 100, h = 0.61
Bj(1) = 0.29, Bj(4) = 0.72, Bj(6) = 1.94, Bj(9) = 3.07, Bj(12) = 9.2
RESET(2) = 0.74
LM(1) = 2.64, LM(4) = 3.52, LM(6) = 3.78, LM(9) = 4.14, LM(12) = 8.8
FLM(1) = 2.44, FLM(4) = 1.11, FLM(6) = 0.52, FLM(9) = 0.47, FLM(12) = 0.77
ARCH(1) = 1.33, ARCH(4) = 1.72, ARCH(6) = 1.82, ARCH(9) = 1.83, ARCH(12) = 2.06
F(1) = 1.27, F(4) = 0.41, F(6) = 0.25, F(9) = 0.24, F(12) = 0.17
HF(12) = 7.15, WHI = 0.85(1.75)

Selected Chow tests from 1929(6) to dates given:

Date	Chow	CV
1932(12)	0.88	1.93
1933(12)	0.59	1.93
1934(12)	2.98	1.79
1935(7)	1.99	2.20
1936(7)	0.89	1.69

(d) Germany

Sample: 1928(4)–1935(12)

Dependent variable ΔLM3

$$\Delta LM3_t = \underset{(3.70)}{-1.87\, \Delta R_t} + \underset{(2.76)}{1.39\, \Delta R_{t-1}} + \underset{(0.79)}{0.002\, MOVSD} - \underset{(5.21)}{0.57\, \Delta\Delta LP}$$

$$- \underset{(3.23)}{0.28\, \Delta LM3_{t-1}} + \underset{(3.49)}{0.29\, \Delta LM3_{t-12}} + \underset{(2.3)}{0.11\, RES_{t-1}}$$

t ratios are in parentheses

SER = 2.0%, DW = 2.03, T = 93, h = 0.29
Bj(1) = 4.56, Bj(4) = 5.22, Bj(6) = 5.59, Bj(9) = 7.07, Bj(12) = 15.4
RESET(2) = 0.27
LM(1) = 2.92, LM(4) = 4.38, LM(6) 4.9, LM(9) = 7.37, LM(12) = 8.19
FLM(1) = 2.44, FLM(4) = 1.11, FLM(6) = 0.52, FLM(9) = 0.47, FLM(12) = 0.77
ARCH(1) = 3.35, ARCH(4) = 5.67, ARCH(6) = 6.48, ARCH(9) = 8.10, ARCH(12) = 8.80
F(1) = 5.95, F(4) = 1.77, F(6) = 1.08, F(9) = 0.81, F(12) = 0.63
HF(12) = 6.17, WHI = 0.34(1.75)

Selected Chow tests from 1928(4) to dates given:

Date	Chow	CV
1931(6)	4.82	4.17F
1931(7)	5.36	4.17F
1931(8)	3.98	4.17
1931(9)	2.19	4.17
1931(12)	1.45	4.17
1932(6)	1.19	2.34
1932(12)	0.35	2.34
1933(1)	0.35	2.34
1933(2)	0.96	4.00
1933(12)	1.96	1.99
1934(12)	1.67	1.99
1935(12)	0.56	1.99

SER standard error of the regression
DW Durbin-Watson statistic: not valid in equations with lagged dependent variables
T sample size
h Durbin's h statistic for autocorrelation (first order). This version is distributed normally: critical value is 1.46
Bj(i) Box-Pierce portmanteau test for serial correlation in the residuals (see Box and Pierce 1970). Distributed asymptotically as $\chi^2(i)$ on H_0: no serial correlation in residuals
LM(i) Lagrange multiplier test for autocorrelation, asymptotically distributed as $\chi^2(i)$ on H_0: no serial correlation in residuals (Godfrey 1978)
FLM(i) F version of LM(i). Distributed as $F(i, T-k)$: better small-sample performance than LM(i) (see Kiviet 1983)
ARCH(i) Lagrange multiplier test for autogressive conditional heteroscedasticity in the residuals. Distributed as asymptotic $\chi^2(i)$ on H_0: no ARCH in residuals (see Engle 1982)
F(i) F version of ARCH(i) test
HF(12) Hendry forecast test for out-of-sample performance over twelve months. Distributed as asymptotic $\chi^2(12)$
WHI White test for heteroscedasticity in residuals (White 1980)
RESET(2) reset test for dynamic misspecification, i.e. excluding squared regressions from the model. Distributed as a t test: critical value 1.96 (Ramsay 1969)

Chow — Chow test for parameter instability. Distributed as $F(n_2, n_4)$, where n_2 is the number of degrees of freedom in the first sample period and n_l is the number of extra data points added. H_0: constant parameters between the two periods

Order	$\chi^2(i)$	F	
1	3.84	(1,120)	3.92
4	9.49	(4,120)	2.45
6	12.60	(6,120)	2.17
9	16.90	(9,120)	2.02
12	21.00	(12,120)	1.91

Despite this problem, the rest of the model fits quite well. The Box-Pierce autocorrelation test (see Harvey 1981b) implies failure, but the Lagrange multiplier (both χ^2 and F forms) implies acceptance of no residual serial correlation. All the other tests are passed, and the slight parameter instability in mid 1931 is consistent with the period of the German banking crisis (Jack 1932; James 1984).

In economic terms the equation is again well specified. The only insignificant variable is the risk term (as above). We cannot impose equality of the interest rate coefficients (LR = 5.1), but both variables are individually significant and of the correct sign. Although the effect may be a little large, it may be due to a loss of credibility in the German authorities and particularly their financing methods (James 1984). The change in inflation term has a plausible elasticity, although it may be a little small given previous German inflationary behaviour. The model is again stable with an adjustment lag of under a year.

To summarize this section: it seems that the second stage of the Engle and Granger (1987) approach has validity when applied to our monthly data set. The estimated models are, broadly speaking, statistically well determined and economically sensible.

4 CONCLUSIONS

The main conclusion of this chapter is that the Engle-Granger two-step model can be applied to monthly interwar data. We examined the long-run properties of the data using the analysis of cointegration, both the OLS form (Granger-Engle) and the maximum likelihood approach of Johansen. The estimated coefficients for inflation and interest rates are broadly in line with other studies and seem to be quite close across techniques (i.e. OLS versus ML).

The residuals from the cointegrating regressions are incorporated into an ECM. The results are promising. For the UK, the US and France, all the statistical tests are passed; for Germany, only one test (ARCH (1)) is failed. Moreover, the estimated coefficients are generally theoretically plausible, and provide a good link to later studies (see Laidler 1977; Cuthbertson 1985; Slow et al. 1990).

This should not, however, be seen as the final word on the matter. Much remains to be done on the question of an adequate scale variable; on better incorporation of expectations; on better analysis of risk; and on analysis of other forms of model. The last could include such hypotheses as buffer stock money, which may coincide with our finding that people 'rushed to liquidity' in the early 1930s (Slow et al. 1990) and may corroborate our findings of an increase in money demand about twelve months after stock-market failures.[10] There is much more to be done on this period with this data set; we hope this chapter has whetted the appetite.

Notes

The authors are grateful to many people for helpful discussions and comments particularly Keith Cuthbertson, David Gowland, Steven Hall, Mervyn Lewis, Mark Taylor, Paul Turner and the participants of a Money Study Group Workshop and the Leeds University Cliometrics Workshop. We are also grateful to Sandra Branney for computing help. None of these is of course responsible for any errors which remain. The authors also acknowledge the support of the ESRC under grant R000231534.

1 They actually converge at rate $O(T^{-1})$ rather than $O(T^{-1/2})$ as standard estimates do.
2 Results are available from the authors which relax this assumption, but the poor performance of this variable is unchanged whichever definition is used.
3 The DF and ADF tests used here follow the same form as those for the individual series, but are based on the residuals of the cointegrating regression rather than the individual series themselves.
4 Since this paper was written the question of non-uniqueness has been examined more closely (see Hendry and Mizon (1991)). However, that work is beyond the scope of this paper.
5 And this has little effect on the estimates for the second-stage dynamic model.
6 The latter being lower to reflect greater financial sophistication at that time in the UK (see Laidler 1977).
7 We are very grateful to Mervyn Lewis for bringing this to our notice as a possibility. Paul Turner has also provided useful insights on this point and on the Chow-Lin method.
8 The results reported are OLS estimates, but we have also used instrumental variables (IV) to assess the effect of (possible) right hand side endogenous variables. The estimated coefficients under the IV estimators are extremely similar to those of OLS and are consequently not reported here.
9 And will be reflected in bias in (at least) the Γ coefficient in (7.1).

10 A phenomenon discovered too by Hall et al. (1989) after the UK stock price falls of 1973–4

References

Banerjee, A., Dolado, J. J., Hendry, D. F., and Smith G. W. (1986) 'Exploring equilibrium relationships in econometrics through state models: some Monte Carlo evidence', *Oxford Bulletin of Economics and Statistics*, 48, 253–78.

Bhargava, A. (1980) 'Testing for random walk residuals', London Business School, working paper.

Box, G. E. P. and Pierce, D. A. (1970) 'Distribution of residual autocorrelations in autogressive integrated moving average time series models', *Journal of the American Statistical Association*, 65, 1509–26.

Chow, G. and Lin, A. (1971) 'Best linear unbiased interpretation, distribution and extrapolation of time series by related series', *Review of Economics and Statistics*, 53, 372–5.

Cuthbertson, K. (1985) *The Supply and Demand for Money*, Oxford: Basil Blackwell.

Cuthbertson, K. (1988) 'Expectations, learning and the Kalman filter', *The Manchester School*, 56, 223–46.

Cuthbertson, K. and Slow, J. S. (1989) 'Bank borrowing and liquid asset decisions of UK industrial and commercial companies', Newcastle University, mimeo.

Cuthbertson, K. and Taylor, M. P. (1986) 'Monetary anticipation and the demand for money in the UK: testing rationality in the shock-absorber hypothesis', *Journal of Applied Econometrics*, 7, 355–65.

Cuthbertson, K. and Taylor, M. P. (1987) 'Monetary anticipations and the demand for money: some evidence for the UK', *Weltwirtschafthiches Archiv*, 123 (3), 509–21.

Dickey, D. and Fuller, W. (1979) 'Distribution of the estimation for autogressive time series with a unit root', *Journal of the American Statistical Association*, 74, 427–31.

Dickey, D. and Fuller, W. (1981) 'The likelihood ratio statistic for autoregressive time series with a unit root', *Econometrica*, 169, 1057–72.

Engle, R. F. (1982) 'Autoregressive conditional heteroskedasticity with estimates of the variance of UK inflation', *Econometrica*, 50, 251–276.

Engle, R. and Bollerslev, T. (1986) 'Modelling the persistence of conditional variances', *Econometric Reviews*, 5, 1–50.

Engle, R. and Granger C. (1987) 'Cointegration and error correction: representation, estimation, and testing, *Econometrica*, 55, 251–76.

Engle, R., Lilien, D. and Robbins, R. (1987) 'Estimating time varying risk premia in the term structure: the ARCH-M model', *Econometrica*, 55 (2), pp. 391–407.

Friedman, M and Schwartz, A. J. (1982) *Monetary Trends in the United States and the United Kingdom*, Chicago: University of Chicago Press.

Fuller, W. (1976) *Introduction to Statistical Time Series*, New York: Wiley.

Godfrey, L. (1978) 'Testing for higher order serial correlation when the regressions include lagged dependent variables', *Econometrica*, 46, 1303–10.

Granger, C. (1986) 'Developments in the study of cointegrated economic variables', *Oxford Bulletin of Economics and Statistics*, 48, 213–28.

Granger, C. and Engle R. (1985) 'Cointegration and error correction: representation, estimation and testing', UCSD, discussion paper.

Granger, C. and Weiss, A. (1983) 'Time series analysis of error correcting models', in S. Karlin, T. Amemiya and L. Goodman (eds), *Studies in Econometrics, Time Series and Multivariate Statistics*, New York: Academic Press.

Hall, S. G. (1986) 'Applications of the Granger and Engle two-step estimation procedure to UK aggregate usage data', *Oxford Bulletin of Economics and Statistics*, 48, 229–40.

Hall, S. G., (1989) 'Maximum likelihood estimation of cointegrating vectors', *Oxford Bulletin of Economics and Statistics*, 51, 213–18.

Hall, S. G., Henry, S. G. B. and Wilcox, J. (1989) 'The long-run determination of the UK monetary aggregates', Bank of England, discussion paper 41.

Harvey, A. (1981a) *Time Series Models*, Oxford: Philip Allan.

Harvey, A. (1981b) *The Econometric Analysis of Time Series*, Oxford: Philip Allan.

Harvey, A. and Todd, P. (1983) 'Forecasting economic time series with structural and Box-Jenkins models', *Journal of Business and Economic Statistics*, 1, 299–315.

Hendry, D. (1986) 'Econometric modelling with cointegrated variables: an overview', *Oxford Bulletin of Economics and Statistics*, 48, 201–12.

Hendry, D. and Mizon G. (1991) "Evaluating dynamic econometric models by encompassing the VAR", in Models, Methods and Applications, Essays in Honor of Rex Bergstrom, (eds) P. C. B. Phillips and V. B. Hall.

Jack, D.T. (1932) *The Crises of 1931*, London: King.

James, H. (1984) 'The causes of the German banking crisis of 1931', *Economic History Review*, 37 (1), 68–87.

Johansen, S. (1988) 'Statistical analysis of cointegration vectors', *Journal of Economic Dynamics and Control*, 12 (2/3), 231–54.

Johansen, S. and Juselius, K. (1990) 'Maximum likelihood estimation and inference on cointegration – with applications to the demand for money', *Oxford Bulletin of Economics and Statistics*, 52, 169–210.

Kindleberger, C. (1984) *A Financial History of Western Europe*, London: Allen and Unwin.

Kiviet, J. (1983) 'On the rigour of some misspecification tests for modelling dynamic relationships', University of Amsterdam, report AE11/81.

Laidler, D. (1977) *The Demand for Money*, 2nd edn, New York: Harper and Row.

Park, J. and Phillips, P. (1986) 'Statistical inference in regressions with integrated processes: part 1', York University, discussion paper 811.

Perman, R. (1989) 'Cointegration: an introduction to the literature', University of Strathclyde, discussion paper 89/7.

Phillips, P. and Durlauf, S. (1986) 'Multiple time series regression with integrated processes', *Review of Economic Studies*, 53 (4), 473–96.

Ramsay, J. (1969) 'Tests for specification errors in classical linear least – squares regression analysis', *Journal of the Royal Statistical Society, Series B*, 31, 350–71.

Said, E. and Dickey, D. (1984) 'Testing for unit roots in autogressive moving average models of unknown order', *Biometrika*, 71, 599–607.

Sargan, J. D. and Bhargava, A. (1983) 'Testing residuals from least squares regression for being generated by the Gaussian random walk', *Econometrica*, 51, 153–74.

Sargent, T. (1987) *Rational Expectations and Inflation*, New York: Harper and Row.

Slow, J. S. (1990) 'Money demand in the inter-war period: some (very) preliminary results', Strathclude University, mimeo.

Slow, J.S., Foreman-Peck, J. and Hughes Hallett, A. J. (1990) 'Comparisons of money demand 1928–35 and 1968–86: what lessons can we learn for the 1990s?', paper presented to European Research Conference, University of Nottingham.

Stock, J. (1985) 'Asymptotic properties of a least squares estimator of cointegrating vectors', Harvard University, mimeo.

Stock, J. (1987) 'Asymptotic properties of least squares estimates of cointegration vectors', *Econometrica*, 55, 1035–56.

Taylor, M. P. (1990) 'Modelling the demand for UK broad money, 1871–1913', International Monetary Fund, Washington DC, mimeo, forthcoming, Review of Economics and Statistics.

White, H. (1980) 'A heteroskedasticity – consistent covariance matrix estimator and a direct test for heteroskedasticity', *Econometrica*, 48, 817–838.

8 Money Demand in High-Inflation Countries: A South American Perspective

Kate Phylaktis and Mark P. Taylor

1 INTRODUCTION

The number of academic research papers which are still widely referred to more than 30 years after they were first published – let alone the number which still inspire fresh research after such a period – is very small indeed. Cagan's 1956 paper on the demand for money during hyperinflation is one that has withstood such a test of time. It is widely acknowledged as one of the classic contributions to monetary economics in the postwar period, embodying a rare combination of analytical rigour and simplicity.

Although Cagan applies his model to a number of extremely severe inflations, the object of the present chapter is to examine what light the Cagan model can shed on the less severe inflationary episodes of two Latin American countries – Bolivia and Peru – during the period 1975–87. Although neither of the countries examined has experienced hyperinflation according to the strict definition of Cagan (1956) – i.e. a *monthly* rate of inflation in excess of 50 per cent – they have each experienced very high rates of inflation over sustained periods.[1] We investigate whether the Cagan model can be fruitfully applied to those countries during the period of analysis; if this is the case, then the very simplicity of the Cagan model suggests that it will be a powerful tool of analysis in understanding the salient features of the monetary experience of these countries.

Following Taylor (1990) we apply a test of the Cagan model which is not contingent on any particular assumption concerning expectations formation except that agents' errors in forecasting inflation are stationary. We also examine the hypothesis that the monetary authorities expanded the money supply in such a way as to maximize the revenue arising from a 'tax' on money balances which is the result of the ensuing inflation; this is also done subject only to very weak assumptions concerning expectations formation.

Table 8.1 Inflation and money creation in Bolivia and Peru, 1975–87

Country	Average monthly inflation rate (%) π	Average monthly increase in money supply (%) $\dot{m}$	$\pi/\dot{m}$
Bolivia	8.08	7.83	1.03
Peru	4.71	4.40	1.07

We then go on, however, to examine the rational expectations hypothesis in the context of the Cagan model.

2 INFLATION AND THE MONETARY EXPERIENCE OF BOLIVIA AND PERU

This chapter is concerned with the behaviour of money and prices in Bolivia and Peru over the period 1975–87. Prior to this period, Bolivia experienced an annual rate of inflation of some 41 per cent over the period 1950–69, while Peru experienced a more moderate rate of around 8.5 per cent over the same period (Vogel 1974). The historical development of inflation during the period 1975–87 is also different for the two countries. In Bolivia the average *monthly* rate of inflation during this period was around 8 per cent (table 8.1), implying an annual rate of about 152 per cent. Over the period 1982–5, however, the inflation rate was much more severe, reaching a monthly rate in excess of 100 per cent in February 1985 (figure 8.1). In fact, during the first half of 1985 Bolivia experienced an annual inflation rate of more than 10,000 per cent.

The acceleration of Bolivian inflation in 1982 was primarily the result of the monetization of the budget deficit following the sudden reduction in foreign credit by the international banking community. During the period 1975–80, government expenditure became increasingly financed by foreign borrowing. As the level of international debt built up, international lenders started to lose confidence in the government's ability to honour its liabilities and reduced or halted loans to Bolivia. At the same time, the budget deficit was reaching enormous proportions and was some 30 per cent of GDP at a time when explicit tax revenue amounted to less than 5 per cent of GDP. In general, the economy was going through a serious economic and financial crisis with widespread shortages, negative real growth rates, a large underground economy, dwindling international reserves and mounting internal and external payments arrears.

Between November 1982 and February 1985, six attempts were made to

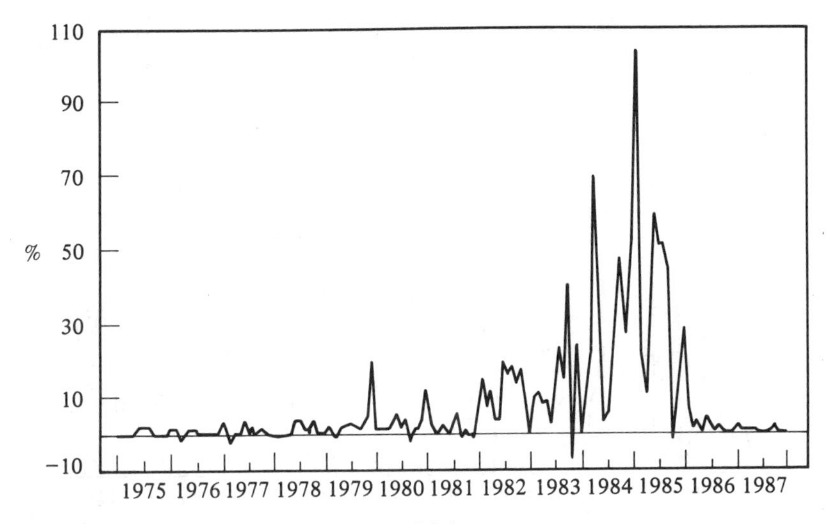

Figure 8.1 Bolivian inflation (monthly)

introduce stabilization programmes. Each one, however, was overthrown by political unrest, emanating from either public or governmental political opposition. In 1985, Paz Estenssoro resumed his fourth term of office since 1952, and embarked in August of the same year on Bolivia's most radical reorientation of economic policy in more than 30 years. The seriousness of the economic crisis finally convinced the major political factions to agree to a major overhaul of economic policies. The objectives of the New Economic Policy were to reduce inflation to single-digit level, to restore external balance, and to lay the basis for sustained growth. The policy entailed a dismantling of controls on prices, interest rates, international capital flows and exchange rates; the imposition of strict controls over public finances aimed at sharply reducing the budget deficit; and the adoption of several structural and institutional measures, such as a process of rationalization of state enterprises and of reducing the size of the public sector (see IMF 1987).

The stabilization programme had the desired effect. Prices in fact dropped by 2 per cent in October 1985. For the next three months the rate of inflation rose; thereafter, until the end of our sample period, December 1987, the average monthly rate was less than 1.5 per cent. Other countries in Latin America implemented stabilization programmes at about the same time (the Austral Plan in Argentina, the Cruzeiro Plan in Brazil). The programme in Bolivia, however, did not include price controls. On the contrary, the stabilization plan dismantled previously existing controls, and proceeded to liberalize markets.[2] At the same time, the plan did not include a currency reform, an important feature of similar plans which marked the

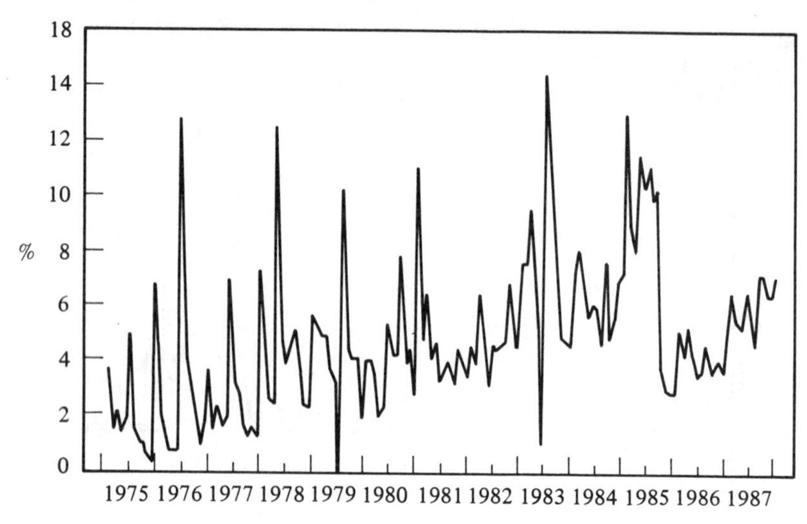

Figure 8.2 Peruvian inflation (monthly)

end of several European hyperinflations in the 1920s (Sargent 1982).

Unlike Bolivia, Peru has not implemented a drastic stabilization programme in an attempt to stabilize its soaring price level (see figure 8.2). In 1975 the average monthly inflation rate was about 2 per cent, while in 1987 it rose to about 8 per cent. There were times, however, when the montly rate of inflation was as high as 14 per cent, giving an annual rate of some 380 per cent.

The steady acceleration of Peruvian inflation over the period 1975–87 reflected the monetization of the government budget deficit following the general reluctane by the international banks to lend to Latin America in the early 1980s. Peru, since the early 1970s, resorted to foreign borrowing to finance its ambitious development plans, the result of which was a massive increase in its external debt. By 1974, Peru was the fourth largest borrower in the Eurodollar market (see Thorp 1987a: 368). The budget deficit, which was only 1 per cent of GDP in 1979, grew to 12 per cent in 1983. As the IMF (1984) states:

> The major cause of the internal and external imbalances experienced by Peru during the past two years has been the maintenance of a public sector deficit at a level averaging 9% of GDP. Public financial requirements of this magnitude led to an unsustainably high level of net foreign financing, a serious crowding out of the private sector in financial markets, and the maintenance of inflationary pressures.

During the period 1980–5, several unsuccessful attempts were made to correct the balance of payments deficit and the growing level of inflation.

These measures were imposed by the IMF and the international financial community. In April 1985, following a massive electoral swing away from the right, with the left taking a significant percentage of the vote, Peru made another attempt to stabilize the economy by freezing all prices and wages. No measures were taken with regard to the fiscal deficit. As figure 8.2 reveals, there was a sudden drop in inflation which was, however, short-lived.[3]

3 THE CAGAN MODEL

In the context of explaining the demand for money during several European hyperinflations in the interwar period, Cagan (1956) postulates a portfolio balance schedule of the following form:

$$(m - p)_t = \alpha \Delta p^e_{t+1} \tag{8.1}$$

where m_t is the natural logarithm of the money stock at time t, p_t is the natural logarithm of the price level, Δ is the first-difference operator and superscript e denotes agents' subjective expectation at time t.[4] Note that, regardless of the method used to form expectations, the actual rate of inflation at time $t + 1$ must be equal to the expected rate plus a forecasting error, η_{t+1} say:

$$\Delta p_{t+1} = \Delta p^e_{t+1} + \eta_{t+1} \tag{8.2}$$

The only restriction we shall place on the expectations formation mechanism is that the forecast error η_{t+1} be stationary in the sense of having a constant mean and finite variance. Substituting (8.2) into (8.1) we have

$$(m - p)_t = \alpha \Delta p_{t+1} + \epsilon_{t+1} \tag{8.3}$$

where $\epsilon_{t+1} = -\alpha\eta_{t+1}$. Now suppose that, under conditions of very high and accelerating inflation such as were experienced in Bolivia and Peru during much of the period of investigation, real money balances and inflation are non-stationary processes, with percentage changes which do, however, approximate to stationarity. Thus assume that $(m - p)_t$ and Δp_t are first-difference stationary or, in the terminology of Engle and Granger (1987), integrated of order one, I(1). Subtracting $\alpha \Delta p_t$ from both sides of (8.3) we have

$$(m - p)_t - \alpha \Delta p_t = \alpha \Delta^2 p_{t+1} + \epsilon_{t+1} \tag{8.4}$$

Since, by assumption, $\alpha \Delta^2 p_{t+1}$ and $\epsilon_{t+1} (= -\alpha\eta_{t+1})$ are stationary, (8.4) implies that the linear combination $[(m - p)_t - \alpha \Delta p_t]$ must also be stationary, even though $(m - p)_t$ and Δp_t are individually non-stationary. In the terminology of Engle and Granger (1987), real money balances and inflation are cointegrated with a cointegrating parameter just equal to the parameter of interest in the Cagan model (i.e. the semi-elasticity of real money demand with respect to expected inflation).[5]

As Stock (1987) has demonstrated, an extremely efficient (super-consistent) estimator of α can be obtained by choosing $\hat{\alpha}$ (the estimate) which minimizes the sample variance of this linear combination. Intuitively, this is because for values of $\hat{\alpha} \neq \alpha$, the linear combination

$$z_t = (m - p)_t - \alpha \Delta p_t \tag{8.5}$$

will itself be non-stationary and therefore have theoretically infinite variance. Only for $\hat{\alpha} = \alpha$ will the theoretical variance of z_t be finite. This, of course, suggests estimating (8.5) by ordinary least squares. In the empirical work reported below, we apply a maximum likelihood technique for estimating α due to Johansen (1988). Although there is no strong evidence to suggest that the small-sample performance of the Johansen method is superior to the least squares method, this technique had the added advantage of allowing tests of linear restrictions on the cointegrating parameters to be easily constructed.

The main results of this section are thus simple but powerful. If our conjecture concerning the time series properties of real money balances and inflation is correct, then an estimate of the main parameter of interest in the Cagan model of money demand can be obtained as the cointegrating parameter between current real money balances and current inflation. Moreover, this estimate will be highly efficient and non-specific with respect to the method used to form expectations.[6] A failure to find cointegration between real money balances and inflation would constitute a rejection of the Cagan model, regardless of the method used by agents to form expectations of future inflation, subject only to the maintained hypothesis of stationary forecasting errors.

4 TESTING THE CAGAN MODEL ON THE SOUTH AMERICAN DATA

Table 8.2 lists the results of tests for one or more unit roots in the real money balance and inflation rate series for Bolivia for the period 1975(2)–1987(12) and for Peru for the period 1975(2)–1987(11). Following the suggestion of Dickey and Pantula (1987), we tested sequentially for two, one and zero unit roots, using the augmented Dickey-Fuller (ADF) test (Fuller 1976). On the basis of these test statistics, our conjecture that real money balances and inflation are each I(1) variables during this period, for each of the countries under examination, appears to be borne out.

Table 8.2 Unit root tests using augmented Dickey-Fuller statistic

Country	Statistic	$\Delta^2(m-p)_t$	$\Delta(m-p)_t$	$(m-p)_t$	$\Delta^3 p_t$	$\Delta^2 p_t$	Δp_t
Bolivia	ADF	−13.64	−6.19	−0.78	−12.35	−9.16	−1.74
Peru	ADF	−20.09	−10.78	−1.67	−12.68	−7.74	−2.42

The null hypothesis is that the series in question contains a unit root in its univariate autoregressive representation. ADF is the regression 't-ratio' for the autoregressive coefficients to sum to unity. A constant and seasonal dummies were included in the auxiliary regressions. The rejection region, for a nominal test size of 5 per cent is $\{ADF \in \mathbb{R} | ADF < -2.89\}$ (Fuller 1976). Sample periods are 1975(2)–1987(12) for Bolivia and 1975(2)–1987(11) for Peru.

Table 8.3 Cointegration tests and estimates

	Johansen Statistics		
Country	$H_0: r \leq 1$	$H_0: r = 0$	$\hat{\alpha}$
Bolivia	4.33	58.04	−7.627
Peru	3.01	97.78	−19.730

If r denotes the number of significant cointegrating vectors, then the Johansen statistics test the hypothesis of at most one and zero cointegrating vectors respectively. A constant and seasonal dummies were included in the vector autoregressions. The 5 per cent critical value for $H_0: r \leq 1$ is 9.094 and for $H_0: r = 0$ is 20.168 (Johansen 1989), with rejection of the null hypothesis indicated for large values. Sample periods: Bolivia, 1975(2)–1987(12); Peru, 1975(2)–1987(11).

The results reported in table 8.3 reveal strong evidence of cointegration of current inflation and real money balances for both countries.[7] Applying the likelihood ratio test for cointegration due to Johansen (1988), the hypothesis of at most one cointegrating vector ($H_0: r \leq 1$) is in no case rejected, whilst the hypothesis of zero cointegrating vectors ($H_0: r = 0$) is strongly rejected in every case. This constitutes evidence in favour of the Cagan model as applied to these Latin American countries, subject only to the caveat that agents' forecasting errors are I(0).

Table 8.3 also lists point estimates of α; the estimated coefficients are in every case correctly signed and of a plausible magnitude.

It is well known that generating inflation through a constant increase in the money supply can be viewed as a means of raising revenue for the authorities – an 'inflation tax'. Cagan (1956) shows that, in the context of the hyperinflation model (8.1), the percentage rate of increase in prices and money which maximizes the revenue from the inflation tax, which results from money creation by the authorities, is just equal to $-(100/\alpha)$ per cent. Table 8.4 lists estimates of this rate derived from our estimates of α reported in table 8.3, together with the actual average monthly rate of inflation which

Table 8.4 Rate of inflation which maximizes inflation tax revenue

Country	$-100\hat{\alpha}^{-1}$	Average monthly inflation rate π	Likelihood ratio test $H_0: -100\hat{\alpha}^{-1} = \pi$
Bolivia	13.11	8.08	2.04 (0.15)
Peru	5.07	4.71	0.39 (0.53)

The likelihood ratio statistics are constructed as in Johansen (1988). They are central chi-square variates with one degree of freedom under the null hypothesis. Numbers in parentheses denote marginal significance levels. Sample periods: Bolivia, 1975(2)–1987(12); Peru, 1975(2)–1987(11).

prevailed and a likelihood ratio test statistic for the hypothesis that $-100/\alpha$ is in fact equal to the average inflation rate.

In the case of Peru, the unrestricted estimate of $-100/\alpha$ is numerically close to the average monthly inflation rate. More formally, the hypothesis that the authorities expanded the money supply, on average, in such a way as to maximize the inflation tax revenue cannot be rejected at the 5 per cent level.

For Bolivia, the average monthly rate of inflationπ over the period was approximately 8 per cent, while the point estimate of α suggests that the optimal rate, in terms of maximizing the inflation tax revenue, would have been in the region of 13 per cent. However, the hypothesis $H_0: \alpha = -100\pi^{-1}$ can only be rejected at significance levels in excess of 15 per cent.

5 TESTING THE RATIONAL EXPECTATIONS HYPOTHESES

5.1 Test procedure

According to the rational expectations hypothesis, agents' expectation of next period's inflation rate should be the true mathematical expectation conditional on information $\mathbf{I}_t$ at time t:

$$\Delta p^e_{t+1} = E(\Delta p_{t+1} \mid \mathbf{I}_t) \tag{8.6}$$

Substituting (8.6) into (8.1):

$$(m - p)_t = \alpha E(\Delta p_{t+1} \mid \mathbf{I}_t) \tag{8.7}$$

Equation (8.7) is the Cagan model under rational expectations (CMRE). It implies that current real money balances can be viewed as an optimal prediction of a multiple α of next period's inflation rate. Equation (8.7) thus suggests the following 'efficiency' test of the CMRE. The realization of Δp_{t+1} must be equal to its expected value plus a rational expectations forecast error, η_{t+1} say:

$$\Delta p_{t+1} = E(\Delta p_{t+1} \mid \mathbf{I}_t) + \eta_{t+1} \tag{8.8}$$

Substituting (8.8) into (8.7) and rearranging:

$$\alpha \Delta^2 p_{t+1} - e_t = \alpha \eta_{t+1} \tag{8.9}$$

where

$$e_t = (m - p)_t - \alpha \Delta p_t$$

By the preceding analysis, the variables entering the left hand side of (8.9) are stationary. Now consider an information set consisting of only current and lagged values of $\Delta^2 p_t$ and e_t:

$$\mathbf{H}_t = \{\Delta^2 p_t, \Delta^2 p_{t-1}, \ldots, e_t, e_{t-1}, \ldots\}$$

Projecting both sides of (8.9) on to $\mathbf{H}_t$ we have, by the properties of rational expectations forecasting errors (Shiller 1978),

$$E(\alpha \Delta^2 p_{t+1} - e_t \mid \mathbf{H}_t) = 0 \tag{8.10}$$

The orthogonality condition (8.10) thus implies that a test of the CMRE can be obtained by testing for zero coefficients in a least squares projection of $(\alpha \Delta^2 p_{t+1} - e_t)$ on to elements of $\mathbf{H}_t$. The parameter α can be estimated by cointegration analysis and, because of the super-consistency of such an estimate, treated as known in testing (8.10).

Although such a test may seem rather simple and weak, it can in fact be shown to be equivalent to testing a set of cross-equation rational expectations restrictions on the vector autoregressive representation of $(\Delta^2 p_t, e_t)'$ (see Taylor 1990).[8]

5.2 Empirical results

Table 8.5 lists results of regression-based tests of the CMRE of the kind suggested by (8.10). Specifically, two tests were carried out. First, $(\hat{\alpha} \Delta^2 p_{t+1} - e_t)$ was regressed on to the information set

$$\{\Delta^2 p_{t-i}, e_{t-i}\}_{i=0}^{4} \subset \mathbf{H}_t$$

with $\hat{\alpha}$ set equal to the unrestricted estimate of α reported in table 8.3. The second test was essentially the same except that $\hat{\alpha}$ was replaced with $-100\pi^{-1}$, where π is the relevant average monthly inflation rate over the

Table 8.5 Tests of the hyperinflation model under rational expectations

Country	$\alpha = \hat{\alpha}$	$\alpha = -100\pi^{-1}$
Bolivia	14.43	14.77
	(0.00)	(0.00)
Peru	0.91	0.89
	(0.51)	(0.53)

Test statistics are distributed as F under the null hypothesis. Numbers in parentheses denote marginal significance levels. Sample periods: Bolivia, 1975(2)–1987(12); Peru, 1975(2)–1987(11).

period, i.e. assuming inflation tax revenue maximization.

For Peru, the CMRE cannot be rejected at any standard significance level, using either the restricted or the unrestricted estimate of α. For Bolivia, however, the rational expectations restrictions are very easily rejected in both cases.

6 SUMMARY AND CONCLUSION

During the period 1975–87, Bolivia and Peru each experienced high and persistent rates of inflation which appear *prima facie*, to be closely related to the growth in the money supply. Although inflation in these countries during this period has not been *consistently* high enough to qualify as hyperinflation according to Cagan's (1956) strict definition, our main aim in this chapter was to see if the inflationary experience of these countries could in fact be adequately characterized by Cagan's model of money demand during hyperinflation.

We began by demonstrating that, under only very weak assumptions concerning expectations formation (the stationarity of forecasting errors), the Cagan model of money demand requires cointegration between real money balances and current inflation. Testing for cointegration between these variables thus constitutes a simple but unrestrictive test of the model. In addition, if cointegration is not rejected, a highly efficient estimate of the major parameter of interest in the model – the semi-elasticity of real money demand with respect to expected inflation – is obtained as the cointegrating parameter.

Applying this technique to data for Bolivia and Peru for the period 1971–87, our results were supportive of the Cagan model in that cointegration of real money balances and current inflation could in no case be rejected.

For both Bolivia and Peru, the estimate of the semi-elasticity with respect to expected inflation was of plausible sign and magnitude, and we could not reject, at standard levels of significance, the hypothesis that the authorities, on average, expanded the money supply in such a way as to maximize the inflation tax revenue.

We then used these first-stage estimates to test the stronger assumption of rational expectations in the context of the Cagan model. Here, the results differed significantly between the two countries: the hyperinflation model under rational expectations was rejected for Bolivia but could only be rejected at significance levels in excess of 50 per cent for Peru.

Overall, the research reported in this chapter is supportive both of the Cagan model and of the hypothesis of inflation tax revenue-maximizing behaviour on the part of the authorities in both countries. The most puzzling finding relates to the fact that the rational expectations restrictions are rejected for Bolivia but not for Peru. This provides an avenue for future research.[9]

Notes

The views represented in this paper are those of the authors and are not necessarily those of the International Monetary Fund.

1 The precise definition of hyperinflation has been the subject of some discussion in the literature (see e.g. Spechler 1984; Capie 1986), and Cagan himself admits that his definition is 'purely arbitrary' (Cagan 1956: 25).

2 For a discussion of the Bolivian stabilization programme see Helpman and Leiderman (1988).

3 For a discussion of this stabilization programme see Thorp (1987b).

4 For expositional purposes, we ignore the constant term in the portfolio balance schedule; a constant was included in our empirical work.

5 Under the *additional* assumption of rational expectations, this implication of the hyperinflation model is a particular case of a general result for present value models discussed by Campbell and Shiller (1987). A main purpose of the present analysis, however, is to derive a test of the hyperinflation model which is non-specific with respect to expectations formation. The importance of considering alternative forms of expectations formation in the context of testing present value models is demonstrated by Chow (1989).

6 Taylor (1990) investigates the plausibility of the assumption of stationary forecasting errors (when the variable being forecast is I(1)) for a range of alternative assumptions concerning expectations formation.

7 In choosing the lag length for the vector autoregressions for the implementation of the Johansen procedure, the most parsimonious parameterization was chosen which was consistent with insignificant exclusion restrictions on the next highest lag and white noise residuals. In both cases, a first-order VAR with seasonal dummies and an intercept term was chosen.

8 Hansen and Sargent (1981) term such cross-equation restrictions the 'hallmark' of dynamic rational expectations models.

9 One possibility is to adapt the analysis to test for other expectations formation mechanisms such as adaptive expectations (see e.g. Chow 1989).

References

Campbell, J. Y. and Shiller, R. J. (1987) 'Cointegration and tests of present value models', *Journal of Political Economy*, 95, 1062–88.

Cagan, P. (1956) 'The monetary dynamics of hyperinflation', in M. Friedman (ed.), *Studies in the Quantity Theory of Money*, Chicago: University of Chicago Press.

Capie, F. (1986) 'Conditions in which very rapid inflation has appeared', in Carnegie-Rochester Conference Series on Public Policy, vol. 24, Amsterdam: North-Holland 115–68.

Chow, G. C. (1989) 'Rational versus adaptive expectations in present value models', *Review of Economics and Statistics*, 71, 376–83.

Dickey, D. A and Pantula, S. G. (1987) 'Determining the order of differencing in autoregressive processes', *Journal of Business and Economic Statistics*, 5, 455–61.

Engle, R. F. and Granger, C. W. J. (1987) 'Cointegration and error correction: representation, estimation and testing', *Econometrica*, 55, 251–77.

Fuller, W. A. (1976) *Introduction to Statistical Time Series*, New York: Wiley.

Hansen, L. P. and Sargent, T. J. (1981) 'Linear rational expectations models for dynamically interrelated variables', in R. E. Lucas and T. J. Sargent (eds), *Rational Expectations and Econometric Practice*, Minneapolis: University of Minnesota Press.

Helpman, E. and Leiderman, L. (1988) 'Stabilization in high inflation countries: analytical foundations and recent experience', Carnegie-Rochester Conference Series on Public Policy, vol. 18, Amsterdam: North-Holland.

IMF (1984) *Report on the Economy of Peru*, Washington DC.

IMF (1987) *IMF Survey*, 26 January 1987, Washington DC.

Johansen, S. (1988) 'Statistical analysis of cointegration vectors', *Journal of Economic Dynamics and Control*, 12, 231–54.

Johansen, S. (1989) 'Estimation and hypothesis testing of cointegration vectors in Gaussian vector authoregressive models', Institute of Mathematical Statistics, Cop(e.d,)n, mimeo; *Econometrica*, forthcoming.

Sargent, T. J. (1982) 'The ends of four big inflations', in R. Hall (ed.), *Inflation*, Chicago: University of Chicago Press.

Shiller, R. J. (1978) 'Rational expectations and the dynamic structure of macroeconomic models', *Journal of Monetary Economics*, 4, 1–44.

Spechler, M. C. (1984) 'Ending big inflations: lessons from comparative European economic history', *Economic Quarterly*, 9, 17–35.

Stock, J. H. (1987) 'Asymptotic properties of a least squares estimator of cointegration vectors', *Econometrica*, 55, 1035–56.

Taylor, M. P. (1990) 'The hyperinflation model of money demand revisited', Centre for Economic Policy Research, discussion paper, forthcoming *Journal of Money, Credit and Banking*.

Thorp, R. (1987a) 'Trends and cycles in the Peruvian economy', *Journal of Development Economics*, 27, 355–74.

Thorp, R. (1987b) 'Peruvian adjustment policies, 1978–1985: the effects of prolonged crisis', in R. Thorp and L. Whitehead (eds), *Latin American Debt and the Adjustment Crisis*, London: Macmillan.

Vogel, R. (1974) 'The dynamics of inflation in Latin America, 1950–1969', *American Economic Review*, 64, 102–14.

Part III
Money and Financial Markets

9 Some 'News' on Covered Interest Arbitrage

Mark P. Taylor and Patricia Fraser

1 INTRODUCTION

The covered interest parity (CIP) theorem states that the nominal interest rate differential between two assets, identical in every respect except currency of denomination, should be zero once allowance is made for cover in the forward foreign exchange market. The CIP relationship appears to have a long history in financial economics. One of the earliest statements is due to Keynes (1923: ch. 3):

> Forward quotations for the purchase of the currency of the dearer money market tend to be cheaper than spot quotations by a percentage per month equal to the excess of the interest which can be earned in a month in the dearer market over what can be earned in the cheaper.

There now exists a large literature on empirical tests of CIP (for surveys see e.g. Officer and Willett 1970; MacDonald and Taylor 1990a). This sustained interest in CIP can be seen to be due to a number of factors. First, in so far as profitable deviations from covered interest rate parity represent riskless arbitrage opportunities, the existence of such deviations is indicative of market inefficiency. Tests of CIP thus form part of an ongoing research programme into the efficiency of international financial markets (for surveys see Levich 1979, 1985; MacDonald and Taylor 1989). Second, CIP provides an important link between spot and forward rates so that, for example, tests of the forward rate as an optimal spot rate predictor can be viewed as tests of *uncovered* interest rate parity, conditional on the maintained hypothesis of CIP (Boothe and Longworth 1986; MacDonald and Taylor 1989b). Similarly, CIP can be seen as linking the term structure of interest rates to the term structure of forward exchange permiums (Hakkio 1981; MacDonald and Taylor 1990b).

A number of studies exist which report deviations from CIP. More recently, therefore, the focus of empirical work has turned to attempts to rationalize deviations from CIP in terms of optimizing behaviour. This approach views deviations from CIP as a response to real world frictions such as transaction costs (Frenkel and Levich 1975, 1977), capital controls (Dooley and Isard 1980) and capital market imperfections (Otari and Tiwari 1981). Such frictions create a neutral band around the theoretical parity condition within which it would be unprofitable to engage in arbitrage activities. A feature of such studies, however, is that the empirical models are developed using published data, often averages of some kind, which can introduce imperfections into the data and in doing so may bias results (e.g. see Agmon and Bronfeld 1975). Taylor (1989: 382) argues that, as a true deviation from CIP

> represents a profitable arbitrage opportunity at a particular point in time to a market trader, . . . it is important to have data on the appropriate exchange rates and interest rates recorded *at the same instant in time and at which a trader could have dealt.*

Hence an unbiased test of covered interest parity should be conducted using data that market traders actually faced at particular points in time, i.e. contemporaneous trading data. This is the approach used by Taylor (1987, 1989). In the present chapter, we use high-frequency contemporaneous trading data to test for deviations from CIP around the release of important economic figures.

2 PREVIOUS EMPIRICAL WORK ON COVERED INTEREST PARITY

The CIP condition is often expressed as

$$\frac{F}{S} = \frac{1 + i^*}{1 + i} \tag{9.1}$$

where i and i^* are the domestic and foreign interest rates on similar assets of a certain maturity, S is the spot exchange rate (foreign price of domestic currency) and F is the forward exchange rate of same maturity as the interest rates.

If (9.1) does not hold then there will be a riskless profit opportunity available to arbitragers by borrowing one of the currencies, selling it spot for the other currency, which is then lent, and finally buying back the original currency in the forward market. Such arbitrage will tend to alter exchange and interest rates until (9.1) holds. Moreover, in a fully efficient market, (9.1) should hold even in the absence of any covered arbitrage transactions. Say, for example, (9.1) did not hold because cheap domestic money was available from a particular lender, i.e.

$$i < (S/F)(1 + i^*) - 1$$

It would seem that such a lender must be irrational, ill-informed or both, since either a higher rate could have been extracted (demand should be perfectly elastic so long as (9.1) fails to hold) or else a rate equivalent to

$$(S/F)(1 + i^*) - 1$$

could have been earned by selling the domestic currency spot, lending the foreign currency and effecting forward cover.

The literature on empirical tests of CIP in well-developed financial markets is abundant and a number of deviations from CIP have been reported. Officer and Willett (1970) argue that it may be unrealistic to assume that arbitrageurs focus narrowly on the covered interest differential. They suggest that, as covered arbitrage is essentially an interbank activity, it may be prudent to assume that arbitrageurs' information sets do, in fact, include a wider set of variables. If, for example, traders are expecting central bank intervention in an attempt to keep currencies within certain trading limits, then the rate of return from an expected central bank intervention may be greater than the expected rate of return from covered interest arbitrage on longer-term maturities. Market prices can therefore deviate from the parity condition by widening the available information set without necessarily relaxing the efficiency constraint. Officer and Willett also point out that as those engaged in arbitrage are predominantly banking institutions, they may be increasingly unlikely to sacrifice spot liquid assets for a return far into the future. This suggests that liquid assets may in fact yield some form of covenience return, implying that deviations may in fact increase with the length of maturity. The findings of Taylor (1989) support the above arguments. He argues that, in practice, agents engage in a wide range of activities, and dealers in covered interest arbitrage work within limits laid down by management reagarding the creditworthiness of other banks and the size of liabilities which it is considered prudent to have outstanding with each named bank. Such credit limits can therefore operate as an implicit liquidity constraint, as well as leading to a concentration of arbitrage activity in the shorter-term maturities where credit limits will be tied up for shorter periods.

The Officer and Willett survey concludes by suggesting that deviations from covered interest parity need not imply disequilibrium or market imperfections if viewed within a generalized portfolio approach to international capital movements. Such an approach implies that there may be rewards from empirical research directed towards explaining deviations from parity in terms of optimizing behaviour.

Aliber (1973), for instance, explains the apparent deviations from covered interest parity when assets are denominated in different currencies as reflecting political risk, arising out of differing tax tariff structures or capital controls and the expected change in these parameters. Aliber tests this hypothesis by comparing the interest rate differential on sterling–dollar and mark–dollar assets in Paris and London with the corresponding exchange rate differentials. The author concludes that arbitrageurs carry political risk; thus deviations from parity may represent risk premiums imposed by arbitrageurs as a price for carrying such risk.

Dooley and Isard (1980) explore Aliber's (1973) notion further by constructing a model of portfolio behaviour to study the effects of German capital controls (in force between 1970 and 1974) and their relationship with deviations from covered interest parity. Dooley and Isard's (1980: 370) findings suggest that the

> interest rate differential due to political risk, given the prospect of future capital controls, depends essentially on the gross stocks of debt outstanding against different governments and the distribution of world wealth among residents of different political jurisdictions.

The riskiness of capital controls is also explored by Otari and Tiwari (1981), who examine the extent to which capital controls influence deviations from covered interest parity in Japan for the period 1978–81. The authors conclude that capital controls do indeed create distortions in foreign exchange markets.

Similarly, Frankel and MacArthur (1987) and Frankel (1989) follow Aliber (1977) by viewing the covered interest differential as a political premium. This allows the *real* interest differential to be decomposed into a political premium (the covered interest differential), an exchange risk premium (the difference between the forward rate and the expected futureuspot rate) and the expected real depreciation. They are then able to explain deviations from real interest rate parity as due to political factors or currency factors. Frankel and MacArthur (1987) show, for a sample of 24 countries, that currency factors dominate strongly political factors in explaining real interest rate differentials. Similar findings are reported by Frankel (1989).

Frenkel and Levich (1975) provide a procedure for estimating frictions to short-run capital mobility by including in the concept of transaction costs such risk factors as capital controls and political risk as well as brokerage fees. They suggest that the introduction of such costs into the foreign exchange market will create a neutral band around the interest rate parity line. Thus, if assets are not denominated in the currency of the same political jurisdiction, this neutral band will reflect transaction costs. Frenkel and Levich (1975) estimate such costs indirectly by the study of triangular arbitrage. The authors conclude that allowance for such costs accounts for most of the apparent deviations from covered interest parity during the period of the study, January 1962 to November 1967. In a subsequent study, Frenkel and Levich (1977) suggest that the degree of turbulence may be an important factor in an analysis of covered interest parity. Their evidence suggesting that while transaction costs played a similar quantitative role in accounting for deviations from covered interest parity during the period of the tranquil peg 1962–9 and the managed float 1973–5, the importance of such costs was reduced during the turbulent peg 1968–9. Thus classification of data periods according to degree of turbulence may be more sensitive to tests of efficiency than other criteria, e.g. whether a fixed or floating exchange rate regime is in force.

While the Frenkel and Levich (1975) analysis attempts to construct a rationale for deviations from covered interest parity, the results from such empirical studies are brought into question by the quality of the data used (McCormick 1979). Thus Agmon and Bronfeld (1975) and Taylor (1987, 1989) are largely concerned that the observed, apparently unexploited profit opportunities for arbitrage may have resulted from the use of inappropriate data. Frenkel and Levich (1977: 1224) note that differentials may reflect measurement error as the data used in the study are based on the averaging procedure (averaging of bid–offer spreads), and they attempt to correct for the introduction of bias by using 95 per cent of the measured deviations from triangular arbitrage in their calculations. Agmon and Bronfeld (1975) attempt to remedy this problem by the use of trading data recorded on the Reuters telex, which are based on the Eurocurrency market in London, the quotation being 11 a.m. prices. However, the authors admit that the specification problem is not fully overcome as Reuters data are not actual trading data. Taylor (1987), using high-frequency (ten-minute) actual trading data contemporaneously sampled for 11, 12 and 13 November 1985, overwhelmingly confirmed the covered interest parity condition – finding only one tiny deviation. Similarly, in a subsequent study, Taylor (1989), using contemporaneous high-frequency data constructed from Bank of England dealers' pads for five historical periods during which markets were known to exhibit turbulence and one relatively calm (control) period, reports qualified support for the covered interest parity theorem (qualified in the sense that the author found a few persistent deviations in longer maturities).

The above tests of covered interest parity rely on computing actual deviations from CIP and relating them to a particular type of optimal behaviour. Another method which has been used for testing the validity of covered interest parity is that of regression-based tests. A typical estimating equation is

$$f_t - s_t = \alpha + - \beta(i - i^*)_t + u_t \tag{9.2}$$

where f_t is the logarithm of the forward rate at a time t and s_t is the logarithm of the spot rate (domestic price of foreign currency). Equation (9.2) is an approximation to (9.1), and suggests testing the hypothesis $H_0{:}\alpha = 0,\ \beta = 1$.

Taylor (1987) notes however that even when this hypothesis is not rejected, the fitted residuals themselves may represent unexploited arbitrage opportunities. He argues that regression-based tests are only able to determine *on average* over a particular period whether covered interest parity held. For regression-based tests to imply the absence of unexploited arbitrage opportunities would require $\alpha = 0$, $\beta = 1$ and $R^2 = 1$, i.e. that the regression line be a perfect fit.

Thus, while regression-based tests may validate the use of covered interest parity as axioms in models of exchange rate determination, they have little to say about market efficiency. Tests of (9.2) have been carried out by Branson (1969) who, using Treasury bill rates, cannot reject $\alpha = 0, \beta = 1$ for US–UK during the period July 1962 to December 1964, but rejects the null hypothesis for Canada–US for the same period. Other studies (e.g. Marston 1976; Cosander and Laing 1981; Fratianni and Wakeman 1982) use Eurodeposit rates when testing (9.2) and generally find that, in a substantial number of cases, deviations from covered interest parity occur. Turnovsky and Ball (1983), testing covered interest parity for Australia over the period September 1974 to December 1981, estimate

$$f_t - s_t = \beta_0 + \sum_{i=1}^{n} \beta_i (i^{A} - i^{US})_{t-i} + u_t \tag{9.3}$$

where i^{A} is the Australian interest rate on commercial bills of three-month maturities and i^{US} is the eurodollar three-month deposit rate. The estimating equation takes this form as the Australian forward rate was continually set by the Reserve Bank during the period under consideration, rather than market determined. The authors hypothesize that the margin set was consistent with attaining covered interest parity over a period. Thus they test

$$H_0{:}\ \beta = 0, \sum_{i=1}^{n} \beta_i = 1$$

Using overlapping monthly data and specifying a moving average structure for the error term (third-order moving average process), the F statistic suggests that the joint restrictions cannot be rejected at the 5 per cent level of significance. Using quarterly average data for the same period, the authors also estimate (9.3) with a fourth-order autoregressive process. They find that they cannot reject the restrictions at the 5 per cent level of significance, and thus confirm that the results from the alternative data set, i.e. covered interest parity, held on average throughout the period under consideration.

Roley (1987), however, when examining the responses of Japanese financial markets to US money announcements for subperiods between October 1977 and May 1985, rejects the null hypothesis of covered interest parity at the 5 per cent level for all subperiods, although the magnitude of the deviations from parity decline from 1984. The author suggests that restrictions on capital mobility in Japan are the most likely cause of the deviations from parity, and the observed post-1984 reduction in the value of such deviations due to a liberalization of restrictions on Japanese forward exchange transactions implemented in April 1984.

3 DATA

The data were recorded in the Bank of England dealing rooms on dates between 7 August 1987 and 1 September 1987. Brokers' rates were recorded for the US dollar to UK sterling and the US dollar to German mark spot exchange rates; the forward exchange rates for dollar–sterling and dollar–mark for maturities of one, two, three, six and twelve months; and Eurodeposit interest rates for sterling, mark and dollar for maturities of one, two, three, six and twelve months. Brokers' rates were used as they represent the highest-bid, lowest-offer prices available in the market at a point in time. The decision to use Eurodeposit rates arose from the consideration that since they

> can be comparable in terms of issuer, credit risk, maturity and all other respects except currency of denomination, they offer a proper test of [CIP]. (Levich 1985)

Under such conditions deviations from parity, should they occur, are less likely to be a result of an unobservable risk premium.

Observations were recorded every five minutes, before and after the release of a range of UK and US economic figures. Information on market expectations immediately prior to the release of the figures was collected from the *Financial Times*. Dates, information and market expectations are listed in table 9.1.

4 EMPIRICAL RESULTS

In order to provide an accurate test of whether arbitrage opportunities were generated around the news releases, it is important to use the actual formulas used by market traders. Equation (9.1) is clearly an approximation in this respect, since it does not make allowance for the bid–offer spread, for example. The approach adopted in this chapter, as in Taylor (1987), is to use

Table 9.1 Release of economic indicators, 7 August to 1 September 1987

Date	*Economic indicator*[a]	*Financial Times* comments
7 August	US unemployment figures	In line with expectations (8 August, p. 12, col. 1)
	US non-farm employment figures	Better than expected (8 August, p. 12, col. 1)
11 August	US trade figures	In line with expectations (12 August, p. 1, col. 7)
13 August	UK industrial production unemployment, and vacancy figures	In line with expectations (14 August, p. 21, col. 1)
14 August	US trade figures	Deficit a great deal larger than expected (15 August, p. 12, col. 1)
17 August	UK retail sales figures	Stronger than expected (18 August, p. 21, col. 1)
20 August	UK money supply figures	A great deal worse than expected (largest monthly increase on record) (21 August, p. 1, col. 3)
21 August	US GNP quarterly figures	Lower than expected (22 August, p. 12, col. 1)
	US consumer price index	Lower than expected (22 August, p. 12, col. 1)
24 August	US personal income and personal expenditure	In line with expectations (25 August, p. 23, col. 1)
25 August	US durable goods orders	Less than expected (26 August, p. 25, col. 1)
1 September	UK consumer credit figures	A great deal larger than expected (2 September, p. 1, col. 8)

[a] UK figures are released at 11.30 a.m. and US figures at 1.30 p.m. (local time).

accurate formulas to calculate whether or not profitable arbitrage was possible at each data point. What is at issue is not whether CIP holds on average or whether profitable opportunities are statistically significant, but whether covered arbitrage is *ever* profitable.

We now establish some notation. Let the superscripts B and O denote bid and offer. Then $i_{\pounds}^{B}$ will be the (annualized) interest rate available in the market for placements of Eurosterling deposits for, say, D days. Similarly $i_{\pounds}^{O}$ will be the rate at which Eurosterling can be borrowed for D days, with the D-day dollar rates $i_{\$}^{B}$ and $i_{\$}^{O}$ defined similarly. We denote the spot bid and offer dollar–sterling rates (dollars per pound) as $S_{\pounds}^{B}$ and $S_{\pounds}^{O}$ (so $S_{\pounds}^{B}$ is the spot market bid for sterling) and the corresponding D-day forward rates as $F_{\pounds}^{B}$ and $F_{\pounds}^{O}$.

The percentage return, in sterling, to an arbitrage from sterling to dollars (i.e. borrow sterling, lend dollars), is

$$R_1 = 100\left[\frac{S_{\pounds}^{B}}{F_{\pounds}^{O}}\left(1 + i_{\$}^{B}\frac{D}{360}\right) - \left(1 + i_{\pounds}^{0}\frac{D}{365}\right)\right] \tag{9.4}$$

while the percentage return, in dollars, to arbitraging in the opposite direction is

$$R_2 = 100\left[\frac{F_{\pounds}^{B}}{S_{\pounds}^{O}}\left(1 + i_{\pounds}^{B}\frac{D}{365}\right) - \left(1 + i_{\$}^{0}\frac{D}{360}\right)\right] \tag{9.5}$$

The percentage period returns to arbitraging in the four other possible directions are defined as follows:

Borrow marks, lend dollars:

$$R_3 = 100\left[\frac{F_{DM}^{B}}{S_{DM}^{O}}\left(1 + i_{\$}^{B}\frac{D}{360}\right)\left(1 + i_{DM}^{0}\frac{D}{360}\right)\right] \tag{9.6}$$

Borrow dollars, lend marks

$$R_4 = 100\left[\frac{S_{DM}^{B}}{F_{DM}^{O}}\left(1 + i_{DM}^{B}\frac{D}{360}\right) - \left(1 + i_{\$}^{0}\frac{D}{360}\right)\right] \tag{9.7}$$

Borrow marks, lend sterling:

$$R_5 = 100\left[\frac{F_{\$}^{B}F_{DM}^{B}}{S_{DM}^{O}S_{\pounds}^{O}}\left(1 + i_{\pounds}^{B}\frac{D}{365}\right) - \left(1 + i_{DM}^{0}\frac{D}{360}\right)\right] \tag{9.8}$$

Borrow sterling, lend marks:

$$R_6 = 100\left[\frac{S_{DM}^{B}S_{\pounds}^{B}}{F_{\$}^{O}F_{DM}^{O}}\left(1 + i_{DM}^{B}\frac{D}{360}\right) - \left(1 + i_{\pounds}^{0}\frac{D}{365}\right)\right] \tag{9.9}$$

R_1 and R_6 are percentage period returns denominated in sterling; R_2 and R_4 are demoniated in dollars; and R_3 and R_5 are denominated in marks. If any of these quantities is positive at some data point, then a profitable arbitrage opportunity is indicated.

Relations (9.4)–(9.9) were calculated for maturities of one, two, three, six and twelve months over twelve different periods – a total of 6330 opportunities – for arbitrage between UK sterling and US dollar, UK sterling and German mark, and US dollar and German mark exchange rates. The results for two periods – 7 August and 21 August – are shown in tables 9.2–9.6. Positive values, indicating profitable arbitrage opportunities, are marked with an asterisk.

The results appear remarkably consistent. Only 21 potentially profitable arbitrage opportunities arose from a possible 6330. Of these, eight rose in twelve-month maturities on 7 August 1987 between 12.30 and 12.45 p.m., prior to the introduction of the US employment figures for the month of July 1987. Four of these eight opportunities occur for US dollar to German mark arbitrage, where between $2800 and $3000 could have been realized by arbitraging $1 million into marks at the twelve months' maturity (table 9.2). Similarly, between £2400 and £2800 could have been risklessly realized by arbitraging £1 million at the same time and for the same maturity, but from UK sterling into German marks (table 9.3).

One very small arbitrage opportunity arose at 10.50 a.m. in one-month maturities, on 17 August 1987 in UK sterling to US dollar arbitrage, prior to the release of the UK retail sales figures for the month of July (table 9.4). It is certain, however, that brokerage fees, once accounted for would more than cancel the £142 that could have been realized from arbitraging £1 million.[1]

A further twelve apparently profitable arbitrage opportunities occur between 12.30 and 2 p.m. on 21 August 1987 around the time of the release of the US second-quarter GNP figures and the US CPI. Of these twelve, seven ocur for UK sterling to US dollar arbitrage in six-month maturities, where only between £47 and £110 (gross of brokerage fees) could have been realized by an arbitrage of £1 million (table 9.5). Similarly, the other five arbitrage opportunities, arising in UK sterling to German mark arbitrage with six-month maturities, could only have realized beetween £139 and £262 (gross) by arbitrage £1 million (table 9.6). These transactions would have been unprofitable when transaction costs were accounted for.

In all other cases no profitable opportunities arose even though the news released was quite significant. For example, on Thursday 20 August 1987 at 11.30 a.m. the UK money supply figures for June were released, the news being far worse than that expected. There had been a record surge in bank lending the previous month (rising £4.9 billion), leading to fears that inflationary pressures in the economy were building up. Although there was a strongly bearish tone in the sterling market (*Financial Times*, 21 August 1987, p. 23, col. 1d), after the release of the figures no deviations from covered interest parity were observed. Similarly, on 11 August 1987 UK trade figures were released, showing a deficit of £768 million in June compared with a £1.13 billion gap in May; while this in line with expectations, the

Table 9.2 Arbitrage opportunities $ to DM, 7 August 1987

	Maturity (months)				
Time	1	2	3	6	12
12.30	−0.0415	−0.0373	−0.0301	−0.0378	0.2957*
12.35	−0.0414	−0.0372	−0.0299	−0.0375	0.2965*
12.40	−0.0680	−0.0638	−0.0565	−0.0473	0.2759*
12.45	−0.0521	−0.0480	−0.0407	−0.0316	0.2911*
12.50	−0.0417	−0.0584	−0.0564	−0.0634	−0.0961
12.55	−0.0310	−0.0477	−0.0456	−0.0524	−0.0847
13.00	−0.0577	−0.0747	−0.0728	−0.0803	−0.1142
13.05	−0.0310	−0.0477	−0.0143	−0.0524	−0.0847
13.10	−0.0310	−0.0477	−0.0144	−0.0525	−0.0851
13.15	−0.0577	−0.0745	−0.0413	−0.0797	−0.1129
13.20	−0.0577	−0.0747	−0.0416	−0.0803	−0.1142
13.25	−0.0577	−0.0747	−0.0416	−0.0803	−0.1142
13.30	−0.0578	−0.0748	−0.0418	−0.0807	−0.1151
13.35	−0.0579	−0.0750	−0.0421	−0.0815	−0.1170
13.40	−0.0579	−0.0750	−0.0420	−0.0813	−0.1164
13.45	−0.0579	−0.0749	−0.0420	−0.0811	−0.1161
13.50	−0.2606	−0.2796	−0.2486	−0.2936	−0.3419
13.55	−0.0312	−0.0482	−0.0152	−0.0541	−0.0886
14.00	−0.0579	−0.0750	−0.0420	−0.0813	−0.1164
14.05	−0.0579	−0.0749	−0.0420	−0.0811	−0.1161
14.10	−0.0579	−0.0750	−0.0421	−0.0815	−0.1170
14.15	−0.0312	−0.0481	−0.0151	−0.0538	−0.0881
14.20	−0.0312	−0.0483	−0.0152	−0.0542	−0.0888
14.25	−0.0580	−0.0752	−0.0423	−0.0819	−0.1179
14.30	−0.0580	−0.0753	−0.0425	−0.0823	−0.1189

* Denotes a profitable arbitrage opportunity.

immediate reaction to the figures was confused by chaotic conditions on the London International Financial Futures Exchange (LIFFE). An incorrect price for a long-gilt future contract had been fed into LIFFE's electronic system – confusing traders and leading to a dramatic temporary fall in the contract which unsettled other markets (*Financial Times*, 12 August 1987, p. 1, col. 7 and 8). Arbitrageurs would, however, have seemed to handle such confusion efficientyly as no unexploited arbitrage opportunities arose, for the currencies and maturities considered in this study, between 10.15 a.m. and 12.30 p.m. on that day.

Table 9.3 Arbitrage opportunities £ to DM, 7 August 1987

	Maturity (months)				
Time	1	2	3	6	12
12.30	−0.0625	−0.0400	−0.0529	−0.0304	0.2795*
12.35	−0.0817	−0.0594	−0.0725	−0.0005	0.2587*
12.40	−0.1083	−0.0861	−0.0992	−0.0006	0.2376*
12.45	−0.0796	−0.0573	−0.0704	−0.0003	0.2667*
12.50	−0.0691	−0.0678	−0.0863	−0.0006	−0.1298
12.55	−0.0713	−0.0700	−0.0885	−0.0007	−0.1324
13.00	−0.0981	−0.0971	−0.1159	−0.0009	−0.1626
13.05	−0.0713	−0.0700	−0.0885	−0.0007	−0.1324
13.10	−0.0713	−0.0701	−0.0886	−0.0007	−0.1328
13.15	−0.0980	−0.0969	−0.1156	−0.0009	−0.1613
13.20	−0.0981	−0.0971	−0.1158	−0.0009	−0.1623
13.25	−0.0980	−0.0970	−0.1157	−0.0009	−0.1618
13.30	−0.0980	−0.0968	−0.1154	−0.0009	−0.1611
13.35	−0.0981	−0.0970	−0.1158	−0.0009	−0.1630
13.40	−0.0980	−0.0968	−0.1155	−0.0009	−0.1616
13.45	−0.0979	−0.0966	−0.1152	−0.0009	−0.1604
13.50	−0.2818	−0.2827	−0.3035	−0.0029	−0.3698
13.55	−0.0712	−0.0698	−0.0882	−0.0007	−0.1323
14.00	−0.0659	−0.0644	−0.0827	−0.0007	−0.1619
14.05	−0.0980	−0.0969	−0.1156	−0.0011	−0.1979
14.10	−0.0979	−0.0967	−0.1154	−0.0011	−0.1972
14.15	−0.0712	−0.0698	−0.0882	−0.0008	−0.1681
14.20	−0.0815	−0.0698	−0.0883	−0.0008	−0.1684
14.25	−0.0890	−0.0775	−0.0960	−0.0009	−0.1771
14.30	−0.0762	−0.0646	−0.0881	−0.0007	−0.1637

* Denotes a profitable arbitrage opportunity.

5 CONCLUSION

In this chapter, we have tested the efficiency of foreign exchange and international capital markets by carrying out an analysis of covered interest arbitrage using high-frequency, high-quality data sampled around the release of economic figures during the period 7 August to 1 September 1987. We considered 6330 data points and made explicit allowance for institutional detail such as the bid–offer spread, contemporaneously sampled data and the exact formulas as used by market participants. The empirical work revealed support for covered interest arbitrage when institutional detail was considered, and thus supports the data imperfection argument for explaining

Table 9.4 Arbitrage opportunities £ to $, 7 August 1987

Time	Maturity (months) 1	2	3	6	12
10.30	−0.0626	−0.2048	−0.0979	−0.1382	−0.3184
10.35	−0.0307	−0.1726	−0.0655	−0.1050	−0.2837
10.40	−0.0307	−0.1726	−0.0655	−0.1050	−0.2837
10.45	−0.0627	−0.2049	−0.0980	−0.1384	−0.3187
10.50	0.0142*	−0.1272	−0.0196	−0.0577	−0.2335
10.55	−0.0626	−0.2047	−0.0978	−0.1380	−0.3179
11.00	−0.0627	−0.2049	−0.0981	−0.1386	−0.3191
11.05	−0.0627	−0.2049	−0.0980	−0.1384	−0.3187
11.10	−0.0627	−0.2049	−0.0980	−0.1384	−0.3187
11.15	−0.0306	−0.1725	−0.0652	−0.1046	−0.2829
11.20	−0.0306	−0.1725	−0.0652	−0.1046	−0.2829
11.25	−0.0306	−0.1725	−0.0652	−0.0738	−0.2829
11.30	−0.0627	−0.2050	−0.0982	−0.1080	−0.3195
11.35	−0.0627	−0.2050	−0.0982	−0.1080	−0.3195
11.40	−0.0307	−0.1726	−0.0655	−0.0743	−0.2839
11.45	−0.0307	−0.1791	−0.0590	−0.0203	−0.1623
11.50	−0.0627	−0.2115	−0.0917	−0.0540	−0.1981
12.00	−0.0435	−0.1920	−0.0720	−0.0336	−0.1763
12.10	−0.0627	−0.2115	−0.0916	−0.0539	−0.1978

*Denotes a profitable arbitrage opportunity.

persistent deviations from covered interest parity. This implies that tests of market efficiency should pay meticulous attention to institutional detail and use prices that market traders were likely to face at particular points in time. Failure to do this may result in market inefficiency being undetected, thus affecting the allocative efficiency of the international economy.

The implications for allocative efficiency drawn from this study are as follows. As foreign exchange markets are efficient during periods of turbulence in ensuring that the term structure of exchange rates and the term structure of interest rates are effectively linked, the arbitrage mechanism, in its role of allocating scarce resources, is also efficient. There was however an implication, rather than hard evidence, that the imposition of restrictions on trading may have the effect of concentrating covered arbitrage activities in the shorter-term maturities. This would further imply that there may be a negative relationship between restrictions on trading activity and the usefulness of financial instruments at longer time horizons.

The consideration that covered interest arbitrage is essentially an interbank activity, and that international capital movements may follow a generalized portfolio balance approach, would further underline a preference of

Table 9.5 Arbitrage opportunities £ to $, 21 August 1987

	Maturity (months)				
Time	1	2	3	6	12
12.30	−0.0627	−0.2006	−0.0593	0.0043*	−0.0992
12.35	−0.0626	−0.2005	−0.0592	0.0045*	−0.0988
12.40	−0.0627	−0.2006	−0.0593	0.0043*	−0.0992
12.45	−0.0627	−0.2007	−0.0595	0.0038*	−0.1001
12.50	−0.0628	−0.2009	−0.0598	−0.0277	−0.1014
12.55	−0.0503	−0.1883	−0.0598	−0.0275	−0.0940
13.00	−0.0503	−0.2008	−0.0598	−0.0275	−0.1010
13.05	−0.0628	−0.2009	−0.0599	−0.0278	−0.1016
13.10	−0.0317	−0.1696	−0.0282	0.0047*	−0.0673
13.15	−0.0628	−0.2008	−0.0598	−0.0275	−0.1010
13.20	−0.0631	−0.2017	−0.0611	−0.0304	−0.1065
13.25	−0.0632	−0.2018	−0.0613	−0.0309	−0.1074
13.30	−0.1254	−0.2650	−0.1255	−0.0980	−0.1798
13.15	−0.0636	−0.2029	−0.0632	−0.0348	−0.1146
13.40	−0.0633	−0.2022	−0.0776	−0.0321	−0.1096
13.45	−0.0448	−0.1836	−0.0590	−0.0132	−0.0901
13.50	−0.0632	−0.2018	−0.0771	−0.0309	−0.1074
13.55	−0.0322	−0.1706	−0.0456	0.0015*	−0.0734
14.00	−0.0322	−0.1707	−0.0458	0.0010*	−0.0743
14.05	−0.0632	−0.2020	−0.0773	−0.0314	−0.1083
14.10	−0.0508	−0.1894	−0.0773	−0.0314	−0.1013
14.15	−0.0633	−0.2021	−0.0775	−0.0319	−0.1022
14.20	−0.0633	−0.2022	−0.0778	−0.0324	−0.1101
14.25	−0.0635	−0.2025	−0.0782	−0.0333	−0.1119

*Denotes a profitable arbitrage opportunity.

institutions to trade at the shorter end of the market. If market activity is influenced by the particular arrangement of exchange rates and interest rates, and if we assume that satisfaction gained from a riskless return decreases with the length of maturity considered, then the return from an expected event may be greater than a sure return six or twelve months' hence. A typical example would be when a currency reached particular trading limits thought to trigger central bank intervention. In such circumstances the operative effectiveness of longer-term financial instruments would be likely to bear the cost.

There is, however, overwhelming evidence to support the hypothesis that exchange rates will respond quickly to nominal monetary shocks. For example, a tightening of monetary policy, leading to an increase in nominal interest rates, will be reflected immediately on foreign exchange markets by

Table 9.6 Arbitrage opportunities £ to DM, 21 August 1987

	Maturity (months)				
Time	1	2	3	6	12
12.30	−0.0873	−0.2293	−0.0841	0.0262*	−0.9057
12.35	−0.0873	−0.2293	−0.0841	0.0262*	−0.9056
12.40	−0.1148	−0.2572	−0.1123	−0.0029	−0.9358
12.45	−0.0984	−0.2407	−0.0957	0.0139*	−0.9189
12.50	−0.0985	−0.2409	−0.0961	−0.0176	−0.9201
12.55	−0.1191	−0.2560	−0.1241	−0.0697	−0.9850
13.00	−0.1024	−0.2573	−0.1125	−0.0341	−0.9913
13.05	−0.0995	−0.2418	−0.0969	−0.0183	−0.9752
13.10	−0.0673	−0.2093	−0.0641	0.0157*	−0.9400
13.15	−0.1148	−0.2571	−0.1122	−0.0335	−0.9907
13.20	−0.0876	−0.2301	−0.0854	−0.0074	−0.9660
13.25	−0.0987	−0.2414	−0.0969	−0.0195	−0.9790
13.30	−0.2322	−0.3759	−0.2325	−0.1583	−0.1243
13.35	−0.1706	−0.3144	−0.1710	−0.0968	−0.0620
13.40	−0.1151	−0.2578	−0.1134	−0.0361	−0.9970
13.45	−0.0964	−0.2387	−0.0939	−0.0154	−0.9761
13.50	−0.1148	−0.2571	−0.1123	−0.0338	−0.9938
13.55	−0.0673	−0.2093	−0.0641	0.0156*	−0.9427
14.00	−0.0839	−0.2260	−0.0810	−0.0018	−0.9611
14.05	−0.1147	−0.2570	−0.1121	−0.0332	−0.9936
14.10	−0.1190	−0.2557	−0.1236	−0.0688	−0.9872
14.15	−0.0872	−0.2293	−0.0842	−0.0050	−0.9579
14.20	−0.1148	−0.2570	−0.1122	−0.0335	−0.9947
14.25	−0.1147	−0.2570	−0.1122	−0.0334	−0.9954

*Denotes a profitable arbitrage opportunity.

the currency overshooting its long-run value. Subsequent movements in exchange rates then depend on the extent to which speculative agents are efficient and the effiency of commodity arbitrage.

Notes

The views expressed in this chapter are those of the authors and are not necessarily those of the Bank of England or of the International Monetary Fund.

1 While brokerage fees can be specifically accounted for in calculations by adding *b* per cent to the offer price and subtracting *b*per cent from the bid price (e.g. see Taylor), the estimation of costs in particular transactions has become more difficult to compute as brokerage houses have, since January 1986, offered volume discounts on brokerage charges.

References

Agmon, T. and Bronfeld, S. (1975) 'The international mobility of short-term arbitrage capital', *Journal of Business Finance and Accounting*, 2, 269–79.

Aliber, R. (1973) 'The interest-rate parity theorem: a reinterpretation', *Journal of Political Economy*, 81, 1451–9.

Boothe, P. and Longworth, D. (1986) 'Foreign exchange market efficiency tests: implications of recent empirical findings', *Journal of International Money and Finance*, 5, 135–52.

Branson, W. J. (1969) 'The minimum covered interest differential needed for international arbitrage activity', *Journal of Political Economy*, 77, 1028–35.

Cosander, P. A. and Laing, B. R. (1981) 'Interest rate parity tests: Switzerland and some major Western countries', *Journal of Banking and Finance*, 5, 187–200.

Dooley, M. P. and Isard, P. (1980) 'Capital controls, political risk and deviations from interest-rate parity', *Journal of Political Economy*, 88(2), 370–83.

Frankel, J. A. (1989) 'International financial integration, relations among interest rates and exchange rates, and monetary indicators', paper given at a Colloquium on International Financial Integration and the Conduct of US Monetary Policy, Federal Reserve Bank, New York.

Frankel, J. A. and MacArthur, A. T. (1987) 'Political vs. currency premia in international interest differentials: a study of forward rates for 24 countries', paper given at International Seminar on Macroeconomics, Maison des Sciences de l'Homme and National Bureau of Economic Research, Bank of France, Chateau de Ragny, Burgundy.

Fratianni, M. and Wakeman, L. M. (1982) 'The law of one price in the Eurocurrency market', *Journal of International Money and Finance*, 1, 307–23.

Frenkel, J. A. and Levich, R. M. (1975) 'Covered interest arbitrage: unexploited profits?', *Journal of Political Economy*, 83, 325–38.

Frenkel, J. A. and Levich, R. M. (1977) 'Transaction costs and interest arbitrage: tranquil versus turbulent periods', *Journal of Political Economy*, 85(6), 1209–25.

Hakkio, C. S. (1981) 'A re-examination of purchasing power parity: a multi-country and multi-period study', *Journal of International Economics*, 17, 265–77.

Keynes, J. M. (1923) *A Tract on Monetary Reform*, London and Basingstoke: Macmillan.

Levich, R. M. (1979) 'On the efficiency of markets for foreign exchange', in R. Dornbusch and J. Frenkel (eds), *International Economic Policy Theory and Evidence*, Johns Hopkins University Press, 246–67.

Levich, R. M. (1985) 'Empirical studies of exchange rates: pricen behaviour, exchange rate determination and market efficiency', in R. W. Jones and P. B. Kenen (eds), *Handbook of International Economics*, 11, Amsterdam: North-Holland.

McCormick, F. (1979) 'Covered interest arbitrage: unexploited profits? Comment', *Journal of Political Economy*, 87, 171–86.

MacDonald, R. and Taylor, M. P. (1989) 'Economic analysis of foreign exchange markets: an expository survey', in R. MacDonald and M. P. Taylor (eds), *Exchange Rates and Open Economy Macroeconomics*, Oxford: Basil Blackwell.

MacDonald, R. and Taylor, M. P. (1990a) 'International parity conditions', in A. S. Courakis and M. P. Taylor (eds), *Private Behaviour and Government Policy in Interdependent Economies*, Oxford: Oxford University Press.

MacDonald, R. and Taylor, M. P. (1990b) 'The term structure of forward foreign exchange premiums: the interwar experience', *The Manchester School*, forthcoming.

Marston, R. C. (1976) 'Interest arbitrage in the Eurocurrency markets', *European Economic Review, 7, 1*–13.

Officer, L. H. and Willett, T. D. (1970) 'The covered arbitrage schedule: a critical survey of recent developments', *Journal of Money, Credit and Banking*', 2, 247–57.

Otari, I. and Tiwari, S. (1981) 'Capital controls and interest rate parity: the Japanese experience, 1978–81', *International Monetary Fund Staff Papers*, 28, pp. 793–815.

Roley, V. V. (1987) 'US money announcements and covered interest parity: the case of Japan', *Journal of International Money and Finance*, 6, 57–70.

Taylor, M. P. (1987) 'Covered interest parity: a high-frequency, high-quality data study', *Economica*, 54, 429–38.

Taylor, M. P. (1989) 'Covered interest arbitrage and market turbulence: an empirical analysis', *Economic Journal*, 99, 376–91.

Turnovsky, S. J. and Ball, K. (1983) 'Covered Interest Parity and speculative efficiency: some empirical evidence for Australia', *Economic Record*, 15, 271–80.

10 Monitoring Bank Risk: A Market-Based Approach

Stephen Hall and David Miles

1 INTRODUCTION

Banks in most developed countries are subject to various forms of supervision designed to monitor and control risks of insolvency and illiquidity. The type of supervision has differed significantly across countries, although the agreement reached by the governors of the G10 central banks at Basle in July 1988 will result in convergence in the measurement and regulation of bank capital, perhaps the key form of banking supervision.

Three major economic questions arise from the practice of banking regulation. First, what is the rationale for forms of regulation - such as limits on gearing, rules for portfolio diversification and requirements for reporting of balance sheet information at frequent intervals - which are *specific* to deposit-taking financial intermediaries? Put another way, what is the objective of bank regulators? Second, given the objective of bank regulation, how is it best achieved? Third, what are the effects of various types of regulation?

Most academic analysis of bank regulation has focused on the first and third of these questions. To regulators it is obvious that the aim of regulation is to maintain the safeness and soundness of the banking system, but to economists it is less clear that there is a form of market failure in the markets for bank deposits and bank credit which would justify rules which apply to banks but not to, say, a car company. Nor is it clear that the general equilibrium consequences of measures designed to reduce risks at the firm level are such as to improve the soundness of the system. Much academic work has focused on these two issues (for recent reviews see Marquand 1987; Chant 1987; Goodhart 1987; Miles 1989).

What is often argued is that information problems and externalities, whilst not unique to the financial sector, are sufficiently more serious there to warrant special supervision. Many of the information problems arise from the difficulty which individual customers of a financial institution may have in evaluating the risk involved in a transaction. This can give rise to incentives for financial intermediaries to take more risks than customers would choose. It has long been argued that such information problems also create an environment in which bank runs may occur (but for a counter-view see Kaufman 1987).

The externalities argument starts from the observation that financial institutions are heavily interlinked. The failure of one institution will have repercussions for other institutions. Whilst this is no less true for non-financial institutions, a common argument is that such interdependencies are particularly important in financial markets and that the default of one institution - even if it did not *directly* affect a large part of the financial system - might, by undermining confidence, come to trigger a system-wide problem. This contagious undermining of confidence is really dependent upon the existence of information problems, and so the externalities and information problems are rather hard to isolate. There is much academic debate about both the scale and importance of these, supposedly unusual, features of financial markets and about the appropriate response to them.

But for good reasons or bad, the significance of forms of market failure has appeared sufficient for governments over much of the world to construct special regulatory systems for financial intermediaries. This takes us on to the second of the three questions outlined above: the appropriate form of banking regulation. This subject has received rather less attention from theorists than either the rationale for, or the effects of, regulation. In practice the systems of banking regulation in force in most countries have one thing in common: they are all designed to monitor and control the default risks of individual banks. In particular there has been great attention paid to the adequacy of financial institutions' own capital funds in reducing default probabilities to acceptably low levels. If information asymmetries, giving rise to market failures at the micro level and perhaps systemic concerns at the macro level, are the justification for bank regulation, this attention to measuring and monitoring default risk does not look misplaced.

In short, any form of banking regulation will involve an assessment of the default risks of financial institutions. The aim of this chapter is to propose some techniques for measuring these risks and to assess whether market data, in particular market prices, provide useful information on default risks. The issue of whether market prices reveal much about the true risks of bankruptcy is important in its own right; those who advocate a free and unregulated market in the provision of banking services rely upon the market to provide the right incentives to bank managers. If the market fails to monitor bank it is hard to see how these incentives can be the right ones.

In section 2 we discuss the current methods used to assess and control default risk. In section 3 we propose a technique for measuring the market's perception of risk using data on the market valuation of companies. Section 4 reports some results for the measurement of risks of UK clearing banks. But it is hard to gauge the accuracy of market perceptions of default risk without some test as to whether banks which *ex post* did become insolvent would have been registered as problem banks. In section 5 we use data on failed American banks, and on a control group of solvent US banks, to assess this issue.

2 TRADITIONAL APPROACHES TO MEASURING DEFAULT RISKS

Defaults occur when net losses on a bank's balance sheets exceed the capital available to absorb those losses. It is for this reason that a great deal of effort by regulators has gone into measuring the risks of losses on intermediaries' portfolios. Estimating the risk of losses on banks' assets and liabilities is, however, difficult. There are three particularly hard problems to face in analysing the risk on portfolios:

(a) For banks, the number of different classes of assets and liabilities is large and is changing.
(b) Many balance sheet items do not have market prices, so analysis of the volatility of the value of such items is especially hard.
(c) The variability of asset returns is likely to change, often dramatically, over time.

The first problem is particularly tough. Suppose we can aggregate assets and liabilities held by an institution into J classes. Let the prices of the assets and liabilities be denoted by P_j ($j = 1, 2 \ldots, J$). The value of capital can be written as

$$K = \sum_{j=1}^{J} P_j X_j$$

where X_j is the amount of the jth asset or liability held; X_j is negative for liabilities and positive for assets. The variance of the value of the portfolio – the variance of the capital – is then

$$\sum_{j=1}^{J} \sigma_{p_j}^2 X_j^2 + \sum_{\substack{j=1 \\ j \neq k}}^{J} \sum_{k=1}^{J} \sigma_{p_j p_k} X_j X_k$$

where $\sigma_{p_j}^2$ is the variance of the price of the jth asset or liability, and $\sigma_{p_j p_k}$ is the covariance of prices between the jth and kth items on the balance sheet.

If there are as few as 10 classes of asset and liability, there are 55 variances and covariances to calculate (10 variances; 45 covariances). The number of variances and covariances, $J(J+1)/2$, goes up roughly in line with the square of J.

Because of the scale of the problem the empirical analysis of the variance of the value of capital, which under certain assumptions is a highly informative measure of volatility,[1] has usually proceeded by focusing on the individual variances of a small class of broadly defined balance sheet items. Covariances are often ignored. A ranking of the variability of asset prices is then produced from which a set of weights is defined to calculate minimum acceptable levels of capital. But usually the most important item on banks' balance sheets are bank loans, which do not generally have a market price. Consequently, it is almost impossible to directly measure the volatility of the value of these assets. As a result, regulators have tended to lump all loans together for capital adequacy purposes and have assigned what is essentially an arbitrary weight to assets in this class.

One way around the three problems associated with measuring volatility noted above is to use the market's valuation of an institution's balance sheet to infer its expectations of the volatility of the value of the underlying portfolio of assets and liabilities. Several US studies, for example, use the price of the stock of regulated banks to measure the value of the insurance provided by federal deposit guarantees, which in turn is related to their risk of default (see Marcus and Shaked 1984; Ronn and Verma 1986; Pennachi 1987). But the measurement of the changing volatilities of the value of bank assets is not the primary concern of these papers. In contrast, our aim is to devise techniques to measure these time dependent volatilities using stock market prices.

3 MEASURING RISK USING STOCK PRICES

Suppose that the market values an institution efficiently.[2] If we denote an institution's share price at time t as Q_t, this implies

$$Q_t = \sum_{j=1}^{J} P_{jt} X_{jt} / N \tag{10.1}$$

where N is the number of shares (assumed constant) and $\Sigma P_j X_j$ is the market value of the assets (+) and liabilities (−), as above. Since for most banks there will be items on the balance sheet which do not have market prices, there will not usually be a means of testing the validity of (10.1). Assuming the validity of (10.1) will, however, allow us to implicitly value balance sheet items for which secondary market prices do not exist.

If (10.1) holds, and one can model how the market assesses the expected value of a financial intermediary, one can use the variability in actual market valuations around their expected values to estimate the market's perceptions of the volatility of the institution's underlying portfolio. To implement the technique requires some theory about how share prices are determined.

The most widely used theory of how equilibrium prices of assets evolve is the capital asset pricing model (CAPM), originally developed almost 30 years ago (Sharpe 1964; Lintner 1965; Markowitz 1952). According to this theory the return on an asset, in our case a share of the financial institution, depends on the safe rate of interest and the expected or perceived risk of the asset. In periods when no dividends are paid, the return on a share in an institution is just the capital gain. Thus we can write

$$\frac{E\,(Q_t - Q_{t-1})}{Q_{t-1}} = R_{st} + rp_t \tag{10.2}$$

where R_s is the safe rate of return over one period (e.g. a Treasury bill yield), measured at the beginning of the period; rp_t is the risk premium at time t; and E is the conditional expectations operator. Expectations are formed at the end of $t-1$ when it is assumed R_{st} is known. We will initially draw no distinction between true mathematical expectations and the market's expectations. Thus, implicit in our definition of market efficiency is the assumption of rational expectations.

The risk premium can be expressed as the price of risk multiplied by the perceived amount of risk for which compensation is required. The price of risk, denoted λ_t, is dependent on the preferences of shareholders. Under the CAPM the only type of risk for which compensation is required is non-diversifiable risk. The CAPM has the implication that this measure of risk, which is *not* the same as risk from a regulatory perspective, is that part of the conditional variability in the institution's share price which is correlated with the return on an efficiently diversified market portfolio (the non-diversifiable risk). Denoting the expected non-diversifiable risk as $E(ND)_t$, we therefore have

$$rp_t = \lambda_t E\,(ND)_t$$

If, on the whole, the market gets it right, the actual return on the institution's shares between $t-1$ and t will equal the expected return, given by (10.2), plus some random mistake which is on average zero. Denoting this mistake e_t, we now have

$$\frac{Q_t - Q_{t-1}}{Q_{t-1}} = R_{st} + \lambda_t E\,(ND)_t + e_t \tag{10.3}$$

The value of capital at time t is, by (10.1), $Q_t N$. So at the end of period $t-1$, when Q_{t-1} can be observed, the expected value of capital at time

t can be derived by rearranging (10.2) to give

$$E(Q_tN) = Q_{t-1}N\,[1 + R_{st} + \lambda_t E(ND_t)] \qquad (10.4)$$

The variability of Q_tN about its expected, or average, value depends on e_t, since by (10.3) we have

$$Q_tN = Q_{t-1}N\,[1 + R_{st} + \lambda_t E(ND_t) + e_t] \qquad (10.5)$$

thus

$$Q_tN - E(Q_tN) = Q_{t-1}Ne_t \qquad (10.6)$$

Equation (10.6) is the one-step-ahead forecast error on the institution's value made by the market on the assumption that the CAPM is used to predict prices. By assumption the CAPM is the true model of share prices, so (10.6) is the rational expectations forecast error.

Now we can immediately write down the conditional variance, as measured at $t-1$, of the value of capital at time t (i.e. $E[(Q_tN - E(Q_tN)]^2)$. This is

$$(Q_{t-1}N)^2\sigma^2_{e_t}$$

where $\sigma^2_{e_t}$ is the variance of e at time t. This is a variability measure relevant to a regulator. It is the variability in the market value of the capital funds around the market's expected value. *If* the assumption of market efficiency is valid, this simple measure will be equal to the sums of variances and covariances of individual balance sheet items. This is because the conditional variance of the financial institution's portfolio can be expressed in terms of the conditional variability and covariability of individual assets and liabilities or, more directly, in terms of the conditional variance of the value of the total portfolio. Assuming stock market efficiency, we can estimate the conditional variance of the value of the total portfolio by estimating the differences between the expected value of the market valuation and the actual market value over time. Market efficiency implies that actual stock market valuations equal the value of the underlying portfolio. The conditional variance of market valuations around their expected values (i.e. $(Q_{t-1}N)^2\sigma^2_{e_t}$) is therefore equal to the conditional variance of the underlying portfolio. If a measure of $\sigma^2_{e_t}$ can be derived, and if e_t is approximately normally distributed, a natural measure of the adequacy of capital then suggests itself:

$$Q_{t-1}N/\sqrt{[(Q_{t-1}N)^2\sigma^2_{e_t}]} = 1/\sigma_{e_t}$$

This expression[3] shows the number of standard deviations that the value of capital represents at time $t-1$. So if $1/\sigma_{e_t}$ were around 3, the probability of bankruptcy by end t would be around 1 in 1000.

We now outline a method for estimating σ_{e_t}. Under the CAPM, one can rewrite (10.2) as

$$\frac{E(Q_t - Q_{t-1})}{Q_{t-1}} = R_{st} + \beta_t E(R_{mt} - R_{st}) \tag{10.7}$$

where R_{mt} is the return on an efficient market portfolio, and β_t is the expected conditional covariance between the returns on the institution's share and that of the market portfolio divided by the expected conditional variance of the return on the market portfolio ($\sigma^2_{R_{mt}}$). β_t is the beta usually defined in the theory of finance. The CAPM predicts that the expected return on the market portfolio depends on its risk. This risk is its variance since, by definition, no variability on the return from the efficient market portfolio is diversifiable. So the costly, or non-diversifiable, risk of the market portfolio is just its variance. Thus

$$E(R_{mt}) = R_{st} + \lambda_t E(\sigma^2_{R_{mt}}) \tag{10.8}$$

where

$$\lambda_t = \frac{E(R_{mt} - R_{st})}{E(\sigma^2_{R_{mt}})}$$

$\sigma^2_{R_{mt}}$ is the variance of the returns on the market portfolio. λ_t is the price of risk, the required excess in the return on the market portfolio over the risk-free rate divided by the amount of risk.

If expectations are on average correct but are subject to a random error v_t, we can write (10.8) as

$$R_{mt} = R_{st} + \lambda_t E(\sigma^2_{R_{mt}}) + v_t \tag{10.9}$$

and so

$$E(\sigma^2_{R_{mt}}) = E(v_t^2)$$

Adding the random noise term e_t to (10.7) and recalling the definition of β_t gives

$$\frac{Q_t - Q_{t-1}}{Q_{t-1}} = R_{st} + \frac{E\left[\operatorname{cov}\left(\frac{Q_t - Q_{t-1}}{Q_{t-1}}, R_{mt}\right)\right] E(R_{mt} - R_{st})}{E(v_t^2)} + e_t$$

From (10.9), $E(R_{mt} - R_{st}) = \lambda_t E(v_t^2)$, and we also know that

$$E\left[\operatorname{cov}\left(\frac{Q_t - Q_{t-1}}{Q_{t-1}}, R_{mt}\right)\right] = E(v_t e_t)$$

Putting all this together we have the following two-equation system:

$$R_{mt} = R_{st} + \lambda_t E(v_t^2) + v_t \tag{10.10}$$

$$\frac{Q_t - Q_{t-1}}{Q_{t-1}} = R_{st} + \lambda_t E(v_t e_t) + e_t \tag{10.11}$$

To estimate the unknown parameters we need to specify a process whereby expectations of variances and covariances are formed. There is now a large literature on the estimation of time-varying conditional moments. In particular, the work stemming from Engle's seminal 1982 paper on ARCH specifications has explored the use of time series models of conditional moments in modelling risk in asset markets (see Bollerslev 1985, 1986; Engle and Bollerslev 1986; Engle et al. 1987; Hall et al. 1989). We use the generalization of the auto regressive conditional heteroscedasticity (ARCH) formulation of conditional moments suggested by Bollerslev (1986). This GARCH specification of the conditional moments of (10.10) is

$$E(v_t^2) = \alpha_1 E_{-1}(v_{t-1}^2) + \alpha_2 v_{t-1}^2 \tag{10.12}$$

$$E(e_t^2) = \alpha_1 E_{-1}(e_{t-1}^2) + \alpha_2 e_{t-1}^2 \tag{10.13}$$

$$E(e_t v_t) = \alpha_1 E_{-1}(e_{t-1} v_{t-1}) + \alpha_2 (e_{t-1} v_{t-1}) \tag{10.14}$$

Since the conditional moments of e_t and v_t influence the conditional means of asset returns (10.10) and (10.11), the model represented by (10.10)–(10.14) constitutes a GARCH-in-mean specification of returns.

Inspection of (10.12)–(10.14) reveals that the expected variance or covariance at time t depends on the complete history of past residuals, with declining weights placed on past squares and cross-products of errors. The equations have a natural interpretation in terms of Bayesian updating. At the end of each period the variance forecast is updated in the light of the *ex post* variability of the asset return within that period. The weight attached to the news is α_2. If no weight is attached to news, α_2 is zero and the expected conditional variance is a constant. Clearly for (10.12) to make sense we require $\alpha_1, \alpha_2 \geq 0$.

In (10.12)–(10.14) we restricted the coefficients on past expected values (α_1) and the latest realizations (α_2) to be common for the variances and covariances of different assets. That is, we assume that the market attaches the same relative weights to past random forecast errors (v_{t-j} and e_{t-j}, $j = 1, 2, \ldots$) in forming expectations of current conditional variances and covariances across all assets. This restrictive assumption will make the (highly non-linear) estimation of the model far simpler; it is, in any case, plausible that individuals would adopt similar forecasting rules for what are similar forecasting problems.

The model comprising (10.10)–(10.14) has only three unknown parameters: α_1, α_2 and λ_t. But it will not be possible to esitmate the model unless some restrictions are placed upon the time series properties of the price of risk (λ_t). We make the extreme assumption that the price of risk is not time varying. This is restrictive. We believe, however, that over the relatively short period used for estimation the variability in the price of risk is likely to be small relative to the changes both in the perceived risk of holding shares and in the safe rate of interest. The price of risk is a deep parameter in the sense that it depends upon the preferences of individual shareholders; a usual assumption in economics is that parameters of utility functions are unchanging. Changes in the distribution of wealth allied with variability in attitudes to risk across individuals would, of course, be sufficient to cause variability in the market price of risk.

Using data on the share prices of individual banks and on the returns from holding a diversified portfolio, it is possible to identify the unknown parameters (λ, α_1, α_2) of the system. Engle et al. (1987) show how to simultaneously estimate all the unknown parameters of the system by maximum likelihood methods. We follow that procedure and describe the results from applying it to share price data on UK and US banks in the next sections.

Once parameters have been estimated it is possible to construct a time series for the conditional variance of each bank's market value. We showed above that if the random elements in the value of a company (e_t) are normally distributed, and if the market is efficient at valuing companies, then the inverse of the square root of this time-varying conditional variance shows the number of standard deviations that the value of capital represents through time; from this the market perception of the probability of default can be inferred. We will use the constructed values of $E(e_t^2)$ from our estimated versions of (10.13) to derive these default probabilities. We report these measure of default risk in the next sections.

4 RESULTS FOR UK BANKS

Monthly data on the share prices of Barclays, Midland, National Westminster and Lloyds over the period 1975(6)–1987(9) were used to define one-month rates of return. Adjustments were made for ex-dividend days using reported per-share dividend payments. We used the (value weighted) FT 500 index to construct a proxy for the return on the market index (R_{mt}). The one-month Treasury bill rate was used for the safe rate (R_{st}).

Table 10.1 shows the parameter values from the maximum likelihood estimation of the three-parameter model. The table also shows test statistics

Table 10.1 Parameters and test statistics for UK banks, 1975(6)–1987(9)

$\hat{\lambda}$	$\hat{\alpha}_1$	$\hat{\alpha}_2$	log-likelihood
2.287	0.89	0.20	−86.503
(3.74)	(134.1)	(11.9)	

t statistics in parenthesis

	L_1	L_2	L_3	L_4
Market returns	1.48	3.47	4.95	17.45
Midland	2.01	5.79	6.03	7.44
Barclays	2.75	4.22	5.48	8.78
NatWest	22.21	6.78	8.23	11.88
Lloyds	10.46	0.35	2.89	8.15

L_1 Bera and Jarque test statistic for normality of errors: $\sim\chi^2_2$ under null
L_2 Box-Pierce test for first-order serial correlation of errors: $\sim\chi^2_1$ under null
L_3 Box-Pierce test for up to fourth-order serial correlation of errors: $\sim\chi^2_4$ under null
L_4 Box-Pierce test for up to eight-order serial correlation of errors: $\sim\chi^2_8$ under null

for various forms of misspecification.

The three parameters are highly significant and each has the expected sign. The coefficient on news ($\hat{\alpha}_2$) is far enough from zero to strongly reject the hypothesis of constant variances and covariances. The relatively high value of $\hat{\alpha}_1$ implies that a significant weight is given to past residuals even beyond twelve periods. The mean lag in the conditional variance-covariance equation is ten months. This gives a fairly smooth path for risk measures. The estimated price of risk is plausible; the value of just over two is close to the average of several US studies (see, in particular, Merton 1980 and references therein).

For each of the four banks there is some evidence of negative first-order serial correlation in residuals. There are no signs of higher-order correlation for the banks and no indication of error correlation at any order for the market returns. There is some evidence of non-normality in the distribution of residuals. This is not surprising given the finding of Engle and Bollerslev that estimation of the GARCH specification often produces residuals apparently from distributions with fat tails. (See Bollerslev 1985 and Engle and Bollerslev 1986, where results are reported from the estimation of single-equation GARCH models assuming that residuals follow Student's *t* distribution. In a multi-equation system, maximum likelihood estimation of a GARCH-in-mean process with errors following Student's *t* distribution is more difficult.)

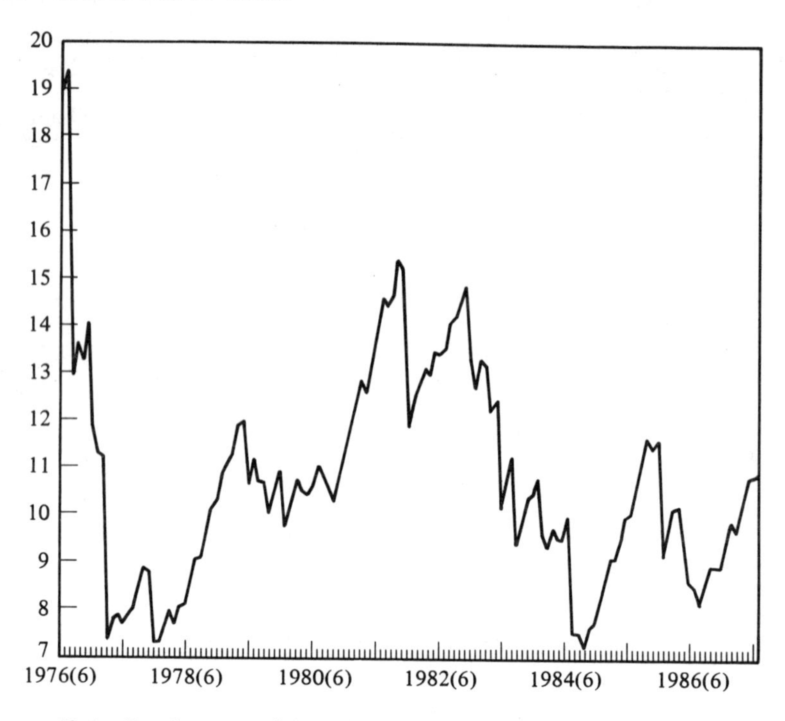

Figure 10.1 Bankruptcy risk: Midland Bank

Figures 10.1–10.4 show time series for each bank of $1/\surd[E(\sigma^2_{e_t})] = 1/\surd[E(e^2_t)]$. These measures are generated using (10.13) with the parameters of the expectation formation mechanisms for variances and covariances reported in table 10.1. As we noted above, these measures show the number of standard deviations that the value of capital represents for each bank at each period. Alternatively, the measures show the number of standard deviations away from its expected value that the value of the bank's portfolio would need to be to result in insolvency. This is a natural measure of bankruptcy risk.

The figures reveal that our measure of the market's perception of the one-period-ahead chances of insolvency are minute. Even allowing for the possibility that residuals come from a distribution with fatter tails than a normal distribution, the probability of being seven standard deviations below the expected return is infinitesimal. But probabilities of insolvency over periods further than one month into the future will increase significantly and could be calculated using the GARCH equations to dynamically forecast $E(e^2_{t+j})$ for $j > 1$. Given the size of $\hat{\alpha}_1$ and $\hat{\alpha}_2$ and the fact that the probability of insolvency over, say, a five-year horizon depends on the chances of perhaps only one of 60 monthly residuals being very strongly

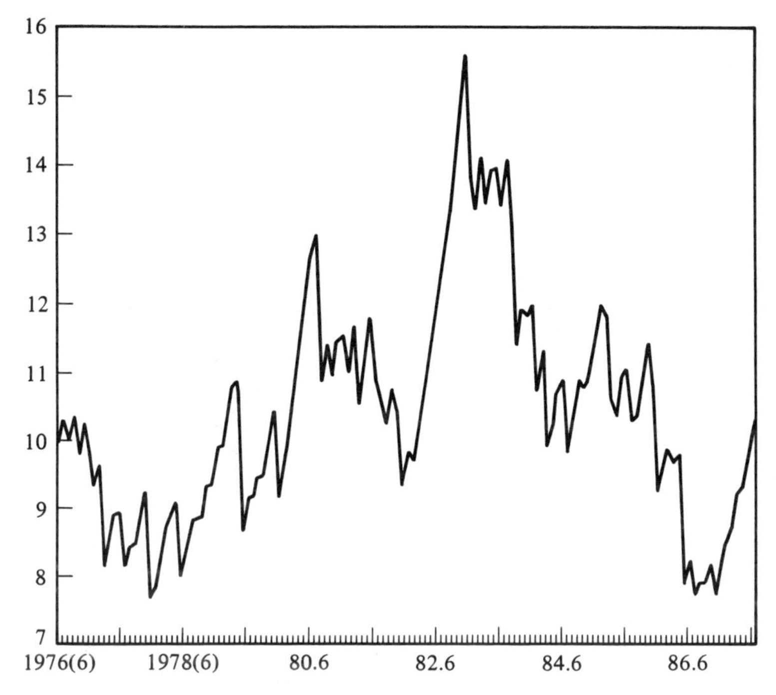

Figure 10.2 Bankruptcy risk: Barclays Bank

negative, the odds of bankruptcy can quickly become significant.

Figures 10.1–10.4 are best seen as indicative of trends in the market's perception of risk; they suggest that there has been significant variation in risk over the past decade. The periods around 1978 and mid 1986 would appear to have been relatively risky periods for banks.

5 RESULTS FOR US BANKS

Ultimately, the technique for measuring market perceptions of bank default risk is only of practical use to regulators if it gives an early warning that a particular institution is in danger. It is hard to judge this without having data on failed institutions, but so few banks in the UK fail that a test using UK data is not feasible.

There have, however, been spectacular bank failures in the US. Two of the largest US banks ever to fail were Continental Illinois in 1984, and First City BanCorporation of Texas (FCBT) in 1987. Using the procedure outlined above, we used returns data on these and on other US banks to construct measures of the market's perceptions of default risks. For each

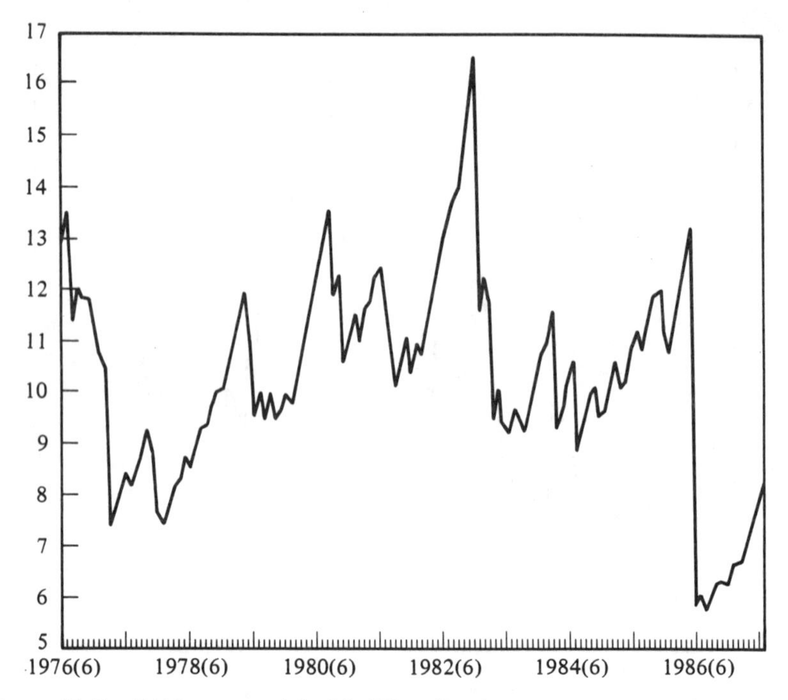

Figure 10.3 Bankruptcy risk: NatWest Bank

month from the mid 1970s, risk measures were constructed using share price data that were then available. We plot four figures, showing the index of risk $1/\surd[E(e_t^2)]$ for the two failed banks and for two control banks. We chose J.P. Morgan Bank and Bankers' Trust – large US banks that remained solvent throughout the 1980s – as our controls.

The measures of the market's perception of risk were constructed using the parameters from a model of US bank share prices identical in structure to that described for UK banks. Three parameters are estimated: λ, α_1 and α_2. We used monthly data on asset returns over the period 1977(1)–1987(9). Standard and Poor's all share index was used to construct an *ex post* return on the market portfolio. The one-month US Treasury bill rate was used as a safe rate. We used an index of the prices of all financial institutions to construct the returns on a portfolio of financial company shares. The resulting two-equation system of asset return is of the form given by (10.10) and (10.11), with (10.11) giving the return on the portfolio of financial shares. Table 10.2 shows the resulting parameters and the test statistics for various types of misspecification.

The results suggest that time variation in conditional moments is significant ($\hat{\alpha}_2 > 0$). There are no obvious signs of misspecification, and the

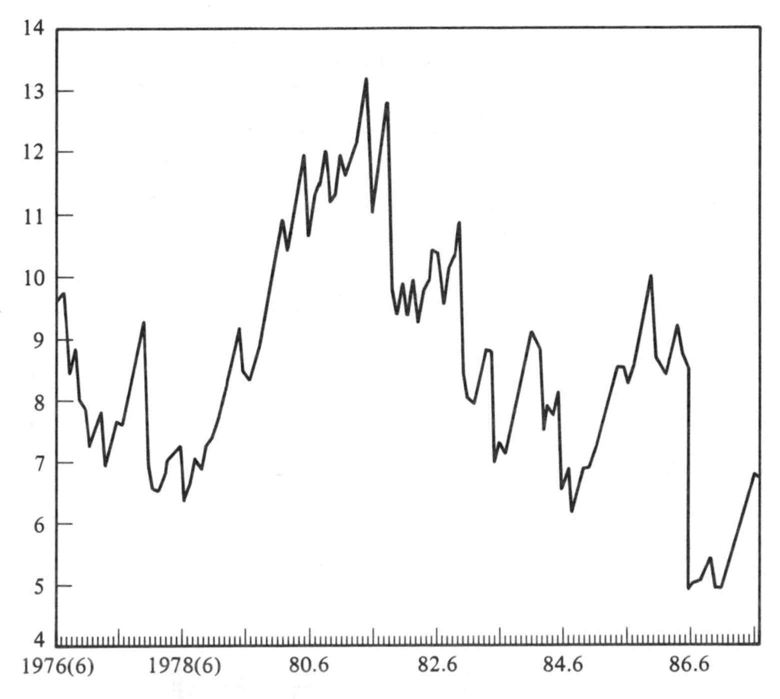

Figure 10.4 Bankruptcy risk: Lloyds Bank

Table 10.2 Parameters and test statistics for UK banks, 1977(1)–1987(9)

$\hat{\lambda}$	$\hat{\alpha}_1$	$\hat{\alpha}_2$
3.50 (5.9)	0.937 (167.7)	0.092 (10.8)

t statistics in parenthesis

	L_1	L_2	L_3	L_4
Market index	0.303	0.09	1.53	16.79
All financial stocks	1.172	1.11	7.48	13.02

L_1 Bera and Jarque test statistic for normality of errors: $\sim\chi_2^2$ under null
L_2 Box-Pierce test for up to first-order serial correlation of errors: $\sim\chi_1^2$ under null
L_3 Box-Pierce test for up to fourth-order serial correlation of errors: $\sim\chi_4^2$ under null
L_4 Box-Pierce test for up to twelfth-order serial correlation of errors: $\sim\chi_{12}^2$ under null

Table 10.3 Misspecification tests for US banks

	L_1	L_2	L_3	L_4
FCBT	1.56	3.43	4.16	20.39
Continental Illinois	2.40	0.01	3.90	10.36

Test statistics are as in table 10.2.

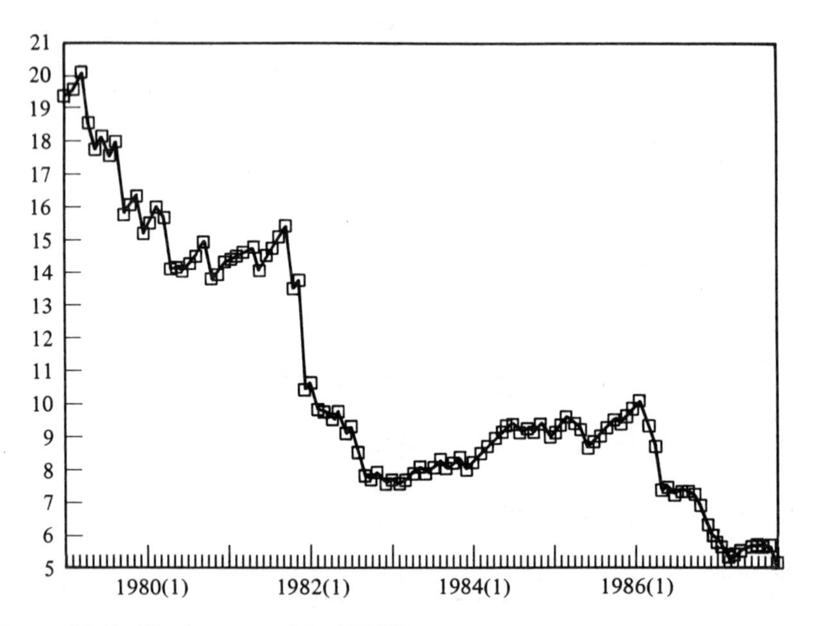

Figure 10.5 Bankruptcy risk: FCBT

parameter values are plausible. The coefficients were used to construct residuals for our four US banks. The residuals of the two banks which failed are of particular interest, as any signs of misspecification (particularly non-normality of residuals or serial correlation) would invalidate the measures of *ex ante* risk derived from them. Table 10.3 shows that misspecification tests reveal no signs of serial correlation or non-normality for either Continental Illinois or FCBT.

Figure 10.5 shows our constructed measure of risk for FCBT. The measure can be viewed as an index of market confidence: the higher the value, the greater the confidence in the solvency of the institution. The figure shows a fairly dramatic fall in the index of confidence over the 1980s. The FDIC (the US regulatory agency for banks) announced a rescue package for FCBT on 9 September 1987. Although FCBT was not taken over until

April 1988, when the FDIC injected $970 million, effectively the bank was declared insolvent in September of the previous year (this is the last monthly observation on the chart). It had been widely perceived that FCBT was in serious trouble long before this date. In *Business Week* of 8 june 1987, FCBT was singled out as one of the problem Texas banks. In the *Financial Times*, as long ago as January 1987, FCBT was again noted as a problem bank. More generally, reports of a crisis for Texan banks go back at least to 1983–4.

Our measure of risk does suggest rising perceptions of the chances of FCBT going under from the late 1970s. Figure 10.5 shows a steady decline in the index of confidence from 1979 until the early part of 1981. At the end of 1981, perceived risk appears to have risen rather dramatically. The situation worsened throughout 1982. The measure of risk was steady (indeed perceived chances of failure fell slightly) through the mid 1980s, but confidence fell sharply through 1986.

Thus our measure suggests that perceptions of FCBT default risk increased markedly in the early 1980s, failed to fall significantly in the 1983–5 period and rose further through 1986. But whether a bank supervisor using this measure would have spotted FCBT's problems earlier than otherwise is less clear. In fact between 1982 and 1986 the figure shows that the measure of default risk for FCBT was around the average of the market perceptions of risk of the four UK clearers. If the market was efficient at measuring risk, this suggests that in the mid 1980s FCBT was no more likely to go under than was Lloyds, Barclays, Midland or NatWest.

Figure 10.6 shows the risk measure for Continental Illinois. The failure of Continental Illinois came as much more of a shock than did the rescue of FCBT. In early May 1984 the FDIC put $4.5 billion into Continental Illinois; effectively the bank was declared insolvent at this date. Our measure shows a substantial increase in market perceptions of risk during the course of 1982 but a significant reduction in the probability of default during 1983. On the eve of default a regulator would not have seen anything in the figure to suggest imminent collapse. Indeed, compared with the UK clearing banks, market confidence in Continental Illinois appeared high on the eve of its collapse.

Figures 10.7 and 10.8 show the risk measures for the two sound US banks. Unlike with the failed US banks, the perceived default risks of J. P. Morgan and Bankers' Trust were relatively constant throughout the 1980s. Furthermore, the risk measures imply that default probabilities were consistently lower for the sound US banks than for the banks that *subsequently* failed and that the discrepancy in risk became more marked as the decade went on. The figures suggest that in the 1980s the market perceived the risks of bankruptcy of the two US banks *that went on to fail* to have been higher than for other large US banks which did not

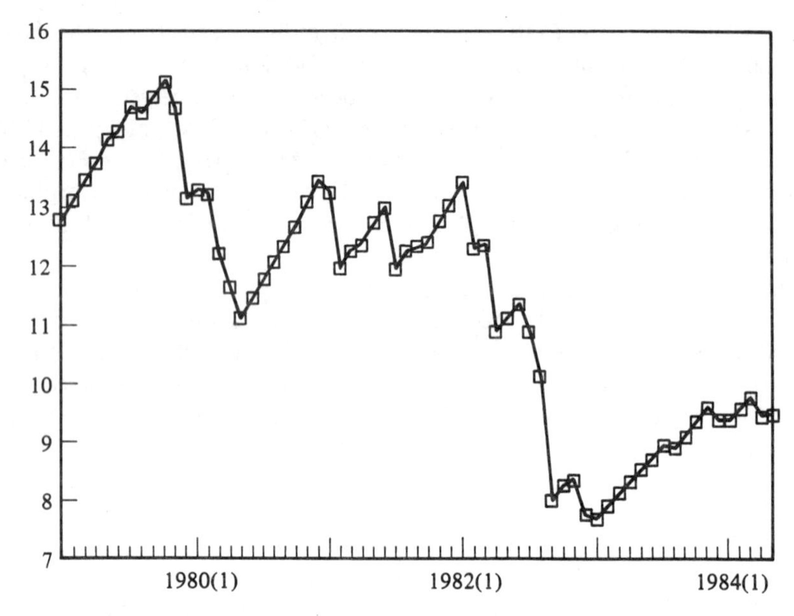

Figure 10.6 Bankruptcy risk: Continental Illinois

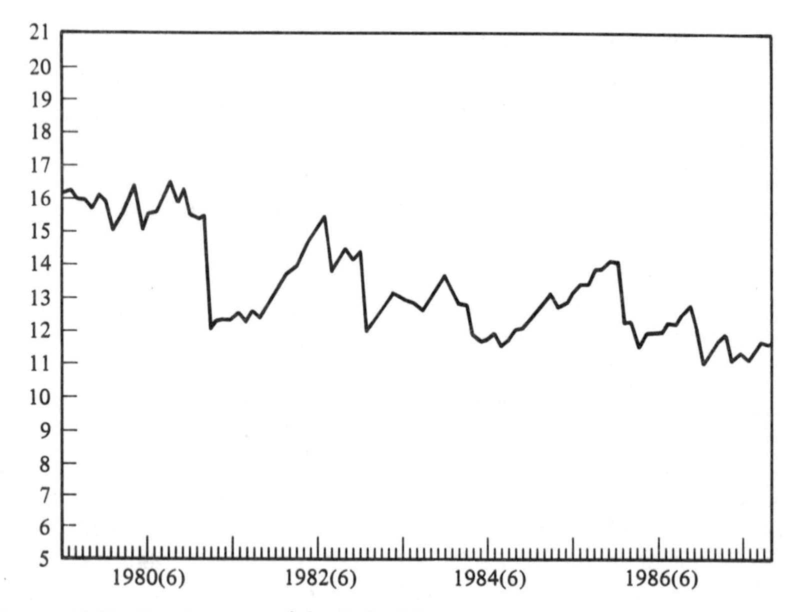

Figure 10.7 Bankruptcy risk: J. P. Morgan

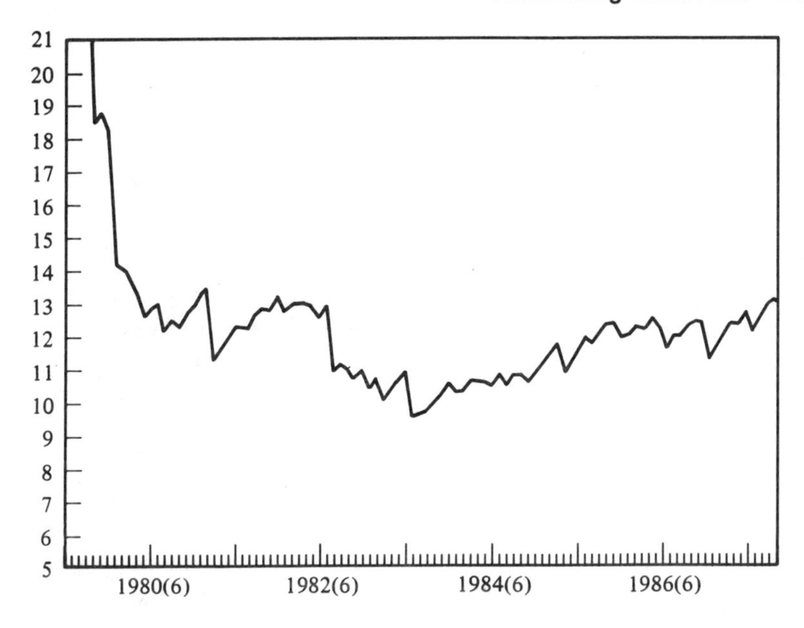

Figure 10.8 Bankruptcy risk: Bankers' Trust

subsequently fail, but not very different from the risks of failure of the major UK banks. Whilst this evidence clearly does not prove that the market is poor at evaluating default risk, it does not offer strong support for those who argue that the market can be left to provide appropriate incentives for bank management to avoid bankruptcy.

6 CONCLUSIONS

We have described a technique which uses stock market data to assess market perceptions of the default risks of banks. It should be noted that the technique is *not* invalidated by the perception that regulators are likely to bail out problem banks so long as bailouts only save depositors' monies and not equity holders' stakes. In practice, bailouts have never bailed out equity holders. Furthermore, the technique does not become invalid if the stock market is less than perfectly efficient (see Hall and Miles 1988: section 6 for a discussion of the robustness of the derived risk measure to stock market inefficiency). Our empirical results, however, throw up some puzzles and suggest that the market may find it hard to assess bankruptcy risk. But provided either that there is *some* information which stock market players have which is not available to regulators, or that some investors are better at analysing information than are regulators, then there should be some information of use to regulators in stock market prices. What this chapter provides is a technique for summarizing that information.

Notes

We are grateful to Mark Taylor for comments on a previous draft of this chapter. The usual disclaimer applies.

1 For example, if asset prices are normally distributed about their expected values.
2 This section follows closely the discussion in Hall and Miles (1988).
3 Strictly speaking the expression should also take account of the expected return over the period. This is not, in practice, significant over short periods since *expected* returns over short periods are small.

References

Bollerslev, T. (1985) 'A conditionally heteroskedastic time series model for security prices and rates of return data, University of California at San Diego, Department of Economics, discussion paper 85-32.

Bollerslev, T. (1986) 'Generalized autoregressive conditional heteroscedasticity', *Journal of Econometrics*, 31, 307-28.

Chant, J. (1987) 'Regulation of financial institutions - a functional analysis', Bank of Canada, technical paper 45.

Engle, R. (1982) 'Autoregressive conditional heteroskedasticity, with estimates of the variance of UK inflation', *Econometrica*, 50, 987-1008.

Engle, R. and Bollerslev, T. (1986) and 'Modelling the persistence of conditional variances', *Economic Reviews*, 5(1), 1-50.

Engle, R. Lilien, D. and Robbins, R. (1987) 'Estimating time varying risk premia in the term structure: the ARCH-M model', *Econometrica*, 55(2), 391-407.

Goodhart, C. (1987) 'Why do we need a central bank?', *Oxford Economic Papers*, 39, 75-89.

Hall, S. and Miles, D. (1988) 'Measuring the risk of financial institutions' portfolios: some suggestions for alternative techniques using stock prices', Bank of England, discussion paper 33.

Hall, S. G., Miles, D. K. and Taylor, M. P. (1989) 'Modelling asset prices with time-varying betas', *The Manchester School*, 57, 340-56.

Kaufman, G. (1987) 'The truth about bank runs', Federal Reserve Bank of Chicago, Staff memorandum SM-87-3.

Lintner, J. (1965) 'The valuation of risk assets and the selection of risky investments in stock portfolios and capital budgets', *Review of Economics and Statistics*, 47, 77-91.

Marcus, A. J. and Shaked. I. (1984) 'The valuation of F.D.I.C. deposit insurance using option pricing estimates', *Journal of Money, Credit and Banking*, 16, 446-60.

Markowitz, H. (1952) 'Portfolio selection', *Journal of Finance*, 7, 77-91.

Marquand, J. (1987) 'Financial market supervision: some conceptual issues', Bank for International Settlements, economic paper 19.

Merton, R. (1980) 'On estimating the expected return on the market', *Journal of Financial Economics*, 8, 323–61.

Miles, D. (1989) 'Some economic issues in the regulation of financial intermediaries', London School of Economics, Financial Markets Group, special paper 13.

Pennachi, R. (1987) 'A re-examination of the over (or under) pricing of deposit insurance', *Journal of Money, Credit and Banking*, 19, 340–60.

Ronn, E. I. and Verma, A. K. (1986) 'Pricing risk-adjusted deposit insurance: an option based model', *Journal of Finance*, 41, 871–95.

Sharpe, W. (1964) 'Capital asset prices: a theory of market equilibrium under conditions of risk', *Journal of Finance*, 19, 425–42.

11 A Model of Equity Volatility

Laurence S. Copeland and Richard C. Stapleton

1 INTRODUCTION

In this chapter we model the interest rate volatility of equities using techniques that have been applied previously to the analysis of bond volatility. The central idea is that as interest rates change, the discounted value of the cash flows received by equity holders changes. The degree of change depends upon the duration (Macaulay-Hicks average maturity) of the cash flows. Models of equity volatility are of interest in the light of recent studies of excess volatility (Shiller 1981; Grossman and Shiller 1981) and are important in the context of option valuation theory. We show that the principal factors influencing the interest rate volatility of equities are: the duration of the firm's cash flows; the degree to which cash flows covary with inflation and real interest rates; and the amount and nature of the debt in the firm's capital structure. Equities and their volatility are modelled as rather complex, partially indexed bonds.

The duration of a cash flow stream as a measure of interest rate volatility derives from the analysis of nominal bonds (see e.g. Bierwag et al. 1983 for a review). The most commonly used definition of duration is that of Macaulay (1938) and Hicks (1939). Although the same concept is applicable to the analysis of the interest rate sensitivity of stocks, some care has to be taken in applying the measure in a different context. A nominal bond is an instrument whose payoffs, once the bond is issued, are independent of the market interest rate. As a result, any fluctuations in interest rates result in changes in the value of the nominal bond. The longer its duration, the greater the percentage effect of any interest rate change. However, these well-recognized effects, which may accurately describe the behaviour of the nominal bond market, are much more complicated in the case of the equities market.

In the case of a stock, the cash payoff received by investors may be positively affected by the nominal interest rate. To the extent that it is affected, the connection between volatility and duration is weakened. A stock's payoff may have a long duration, but the sensitivity of its price to interest rate changes may be relatively low. This fact may help to explain empirical studies which have shown that the sensitivity of the stock market to interest rate changes is quite small.[1]

In this chapter we present a simple model of a firm's stock price in which the interest rate volatility of the stock depends upon the duration of the firm's cash flows, the degree to which the cash flows are indexed against changes in inflation and the real interest rate, and the firm's financing policy. We develop the model assuming initially that the firm generates a single cash flow with maturity t. Later, the results are generalized using the duration or average maturity of the cash flow stream.

The main reasons why stocks cannot be treated in a similar manner to nominal bonds are as follows:

(a) The cash flows of corporations are at least to some extent indexed against inflation. If interest rates rise owing to an increase in expected inflation, the effect on equity values will be partially offset by an increase in expected profit. Although we know that equities are by no means a perfect hedge against inflation, they are clearly a better hedge than nominal bonds (Fama and Schwert 1977).

(b) The way the firm is financed will affect the sensitivity of its equity cash flow and stock price to interest rate changes. If it holds many forward contracts allowing it to borrow at a fixed rate, its stock will be less adversely or even favourably affected by a rise in interest rates, relative to a firm which chooses to rely entirely on floating rate finance.

(c) It is very easy to change the maturity of a dividend payment. If the firm has a cash flow which matures in year t but chooses to pay it out in year $t + n$, it has changed the duration of the payments on the stock. However, if it places the cash on deposit for the intervening n years, there will be no resulting change in the volatility of its stock price. Any increase in interest rates will have the effect of increasing the final dividend as well as increasing the rate at which it is discounted. Hence the maturity or duration of the dividend stream may be a misleading indicator of equity volatility.

(d) Some firms (banks, for example) have earnings which are positively related to interest rates. As interest rates rise, their earnings rise, and this offsets to some extent the increase in the discount rate. For this reason, we would expect financial firms to be partially hedged against interest rate changes. The price of cash flows of a given maturity will be less volatile than those of other firms for this reason.

(e) Equities may be partially hedged against interest rate increases to the extent that higher interest rates are reflected in higher project rates of

Return, and in turn in higher growth rates of the dividend stream. This relationship depends upon the root cause of the interest rate increase. We have already discussed, in (a) above, the case of interest rate changes caused by change in expected inflation. If on the other hand the increase in interest rates reflects a rise in real interest rates caused by an increase in the real productivity of capital in the economy, the increase may be accompanied by an offsetting increase in the expected real growth rate of dividends. The volatility of stock prices could therefore be quite low even with respect to real interest rate changes.

For these five reasons, the connection between the maturity of a dividend and the volatility of its value with respect to interest rates is a tenuous one. The strength of the link depends upon the dividend and financing policy of the firm, and the extent to which the firm's cash flows are indexed to inflation or interest rates because of the nature of its business. Simply applying to the stock market the duration model used for estimating the volatility of nominal bonds could be completely misleading.

The plan of this chapter is as follows. We start by assuming that the firm generates a single cash flow at time t. With this simplification, we analyse volatility in the case where nominal interest rates change and the cash payoff is partially indexed against inflation. Volatility is seen to depend on the degree of indexation and the extent to which changes in the nominal rate reflect changes in the expected inflation rate. In the following section, we allow for indexation of cash flows to the real interest rate. We then derive volatility in the case where changes in the nominal rate of interest reflect in part changes in the real rate.

The analysis is then extended to cover the effect of the firm's financial policy. Leverage affects volatility in two opposing directions. Variable (or floating) rate debt increases the volatility of the firm's equity price, whereas fixed rate bonds provide shareholders with protection against increases in interest rates. The net effect depends upon the proportion of fixed and variable rate finance. In the final section of the chapter, we generalize our results to the case of multiperiod cash flows using the duration concept. The volatility of a stock depends upon the duration of its cash flows and upon the duration of its fixed rate liabilities.

2 VOLATILITY WHEN STOCKS ARE INDEX LINKED TO INFLATION

We model a stock as a partially indexed bond. As inflation increases, the dividends paid tend to increase. However, the investor is only partially compensated for the drop in purchasing power. In practice, equity investors may be fully compensated for inflation, but only after a delay of several years. In effect, this is the same as partial but incomplete adjustment. We assume that the dividend received from the firm at time t is

$$d_t = x_t e^{\alpha i t} \tag{11.1}$$

where d_t is the dividend at t, x_t is the cash flow at t before adjustment for inflation, α is the degree of indexation of the cash flow to inflation and i is the inflation rate.

For simplicity, we assume that the cash flow is non-stochastic. Also, the inflation rate is conditionally non-stochastic viewed from time 0. Note that we may regard x_t as the certainty equivalent cash flow before the inflation adjustment is applied. Also, we do not explicitly model the impact of personal and corporate taxes.[2]

If r is the continuously compounded nominal rate of interest, we define the real rate of interest R by the relationship

$$r = R + i \tag{11.2}$$

For simplicity, we assume a flat term structure of interest rates, with parallel shifts in both the nominal and the real term structures. Under these assumptions, and given that d_t is non-stochastic, the value of the stock at time 0 is simply

$$S = d_t e^{-rt} \tag{11.3}$$

Using (11.1) and (11.2), this can be written as

$$S = x_t e^{-[R+(1-\alpha)i]t} \tag{11.4}$$

The volatility of the stock price is defined as

$$\sigma_S = [\mathrm{var}(\ln S)]^{1/2} \tag{11.5}$$

For small changes in interest rates, it can be shown (see e.g. Ross 1989; Copeland and Stapleton 1990) that, if σ_r denotes interest rate volatility:

$$\sigma_s = \left| \frac{\mathrm{d} \ln S}{\mathrm{d}r} \right| \sigma_r \tag{11.6}$$

Hence volatility is directly related to the derivative dln S/dr, otherwise known as the elasticity of the stock price with respect to interest rates. In the literature on bond volatility, this elasticity is closely associated with the concept of duration. The Macaulay-Hicks duration of bonds is defined as

$$D = \left[\sum_{t=1}^{m} tB(t) \right] \Big/ B \tag{11.7}$$

where $B(t)$ is the present value of any cash flows (principal or coupon payments) made on the bond at time t, and B is the value of the bond. In the case of a multiperiod bond,

$$\frac{\mathrm{d}\ln B}{\mathrm{d}r} = -D \tag{11.8}$$

where D is defined in (11.7).

Differentiating (11.4) with respect to the nominal rate r, we have

$$\frac{\mathrm{d}\ln S}{\mathrm{d}r} = -t\left[\frac{\mathrm{d}R}{\mathrm{d}r} + (1-\alpha)\frac{\mathrm{d}i}{\mathrm{d}r}\right] \tag{11.9}$$

Using (11.2), we have

$$\frac{\mathrm{d}R}{\mathrm{d}r} + \frac{\mathrm{d}i}{\mathrm{d}r} = 1 \tag{11.10}$$

Hence, defining the *marginal* response of the real rate to a change in the nominal rate as

$$(1-\beta) \equiv \frac{\mathrm{d}R}{\mathrm{d}r} \tag{11.11}$$

we can write

$$\frac{\mathrm{d}\ln S}{\mathrm{d}r} = -t(1-\alpha\beta) \tag{11.12}$$

and, substituting in (11.6) and then (11.5),

$$\sigma_S = |t(1-\alpha\beta)|\sigma_r \tag{11.13}$$

From (11.13), note that volatility is higher the higher is the proportion of any nominal interest rate change that represents a change in real rates, i.e. the lower is β. This is because the dividend in (11.1) does not respond to an increase in the real rate. It is, however, partially indexed against changes in i, the inflation rate. Notice that, according to (11.13), the higher is the degree of indexation α, the lower is the volatility. To the extent that interest rates change because of higher expected inflation, they are partially offset by increases in the dividend payable at time t. The product $\alpha\beta$ is the effective degree of indexation of the stock against changes in nominal interest rates. The factor α is the indexation of the firm's cash flows against inflation, while β measures the extent to which nominal interest rate changes represent changes in inflation.[3]

3 VOLATILITY WHEN STOCKS ARE INDEXED TO CHANGES IN THE REAL RATE

In the introduction, we discussed two reasons why the earnings of firms may be related to changes in interest rates, even though the changes may not be associated with changes in inflation expectations. An increase in real rates may be good for equities if the cause of the increase is an increase in the real productivity of capital. This is a reason to expect equities in general to be partially indexed against those changes in interest rates that in turn represent changes in the real rate of interest. However, we also gave a specific reason why some firms may be positively affected by increases in interest rates. Firms in the financial sector, in particular banks, may benefit from higher interest rates if margins on financial services are positively related to interest rates.

In order to capture this effect, we assume that the dividend of the firm at time t is

$$d_t = x_t e^{\gamma R t} e^{\alpha i t} \tag{11.14}$$

where γ is the degree of indexation of the cash flow to changes in the real rate of interest.

The stock value in this case is

$$S = d_t e^{-rt} \tag{11.15}$$

which, using (11.14) and (11.2), can be written

$$S = x_t e^{-[R(1-\gamma)+i(1-\alpha)]t} \tag{11.16}$$

Differentiating (11.16) with respect to r, and using the definition of β in (11.11), we have

$$\frac{\mathrm{d}\ln S}{\mathrm{d}r} = -t[(1-\gamma)(1-\beta) + (1-\alpha)\beta] \tag{11.17}$$

and hence the stock volatility is

$$\sigma_S = |t(1-\theta)|\sigma_r \tag{11.18}$$

where

$$\theta \equiv \gamma(1-\beta) + \alpha\beta$$

θ is a composite indexation parameter, showing the degree to which the cash flow is protected from changes in the nominal rate of interest. It is a weighted average of the indexation of the dividend against inflation, α, and the indexation against real rate changes, γ. The factors β and $(1-\beta)$ represent the marginal weights on expected inflation and real rate changes in a small rise in the nominal rate of interest.

4 THE EFFECT OF CAPITAL STRUCTURE

In the model of stock price outlined in sections 2 and 3, we have assumed a 100 per cent dividend payout policy. The firm generates a cash flow at time t which, after adjustment for inflation and real growth, is paid out as a dividend at time t. We now consider the effects of financing policy on the volatility of the firm's stock price. This is a fundamental issue. If the firm is unable to raise debt finance, then any volatility (with respect to interest rates) inherent in the firm's business must be borne by the shareholders and will be reflected in the volatility of the stock price. However, a firm can usually manage to offset a part of this volatility by judicious use of debt. Alternatively, by its financing policy it can also increase the volatility of the stock beyond the volatility of its underlying operating cash flow. Financing policy weakens the link between the maturity and volatility of the firm's cash flow and the volatility of its stock price.

In the traditional analysis of the effect of leverage on the value of the firm, no distinction is made between fixed rate and variable rate debt. However, in the context of interest rate volatility, the distinction is crucial. If the firm's borrowing carries a variable (i.e. floating) rate, the value of this debt will be immune to interest rate changes, so that the whole of the volatility of the firm's assets falls on the equity and will be reflected in the firm's stock price. If, on the other hand, the firm issues fixed rate debt, the value of these securities will fluctuate with interest rates, offsetting to some extent the volatility of the firm's asset value. The volatility of its equity will be correspondingly lower.

4.1 Variable rate debt

Variable (i.e. floating) rate debt has two distinct effects on the relationship between the maturity of a firm's cash flow and its volatility.[4] First, if the firm has variable rate debt outstanding, this will affect the relative volatility of its stock value. Basically, if the firm's existing debt is floating rate, the equity stockholders bear the full impact of any change in interest rates. However, the equity base is smaller than in an all-equity firm, other things being equal. Hence, the relative volatility of the stock is positively related to the proportion of variable rate debt finance.

Let the current value of the variable rate debt be denoted by B. If the debt has maturity t and pays no interest between the current period and t, the dividend at t will be

$$d_t = x_t e^{\gamma R t} e^{\alpha i t} - B e^{rt} \tag{11.19}$$

The first term in (11.19) is the gross-of-interest cash flow from (11.14). The second term is the interest and principal repayment on the variable rate debt. It follows from (11.19) that the stock price of the levered firm is

$$S = x_t e^{-[R(1-\gamma)+i(1-\alpha)]t} - B \tag{11.20}$$

Differentiating (11.20),

$$\frac{\mathrm{d} \ln S}{\mathrm{d}r} = \{ -t(1-\theta) x_t e^{-[R(1-\gamma)+i(1-\alpha)]t} \} / S \tag{11.21}$$

and hence the stock volatility is

$$\sigma_S = \left| \frac{t(1-\theta)}{1-L} \right| \sigma_r \tag{11.22}$$

where $L = 1 - S/V$ is the leverage of the firm, θ is (as before) the degree of indexation of the firm's cash flow to interest rate changes, V is the total value of the debt and equity of the firm, and S is the value of its stock.

It is interesting to note that the effect of variable rate debt on volatility is similar to the effect of leverage on the business risk of the firm. The volatility is simply levered up by the proportion of debt in the capital structure. In a sense, the message from (11.22) is that the benefits of the firm's cash flow indexation may be offset by leverage. Even though the firm's cash flows are partially insulated from the effects of interest rate increases, the volatility of the stock may exceed t, the cash flow maturity, because of the leverage effect. Hence the effect of variable rate debt is to leave the stockholders with the total volatility of the firm's assets, thereby increasing the relative volatility of the equity price.

There is a secondary aspect to variable rate debt, however. Suppose that the firm decides to pay out its period t cash flow in the form of a dividend at time $t-1$ instead of time t. It brings forward its dividend by arranging a variable rate loan at time $t-1$, which is subsequently repaid out of its cash flow. The effect of this change in dividend policy financed by future variable rate finance is neutral. It has no effect at all on the volatility of the stock price at time 0. If interest rates rise, the dividend that can be paid at time $t-1$ is smaller, but the stockholder can reinvest it himself at a higher rate from time $t-1$ to t. He is in exactly the same position as he would have been if the firm had not made the dividend policy change.

This example illustrates an important point. If firms can use variable rate borrowing or lending to shift the *timing* of dividend payments, the volatility of the stock will be related to the maturity of the underlying cash flow rather than the resulting dividends. This might explain why some empirical estimates of equity duration are so high relative to observed volatility. It also suggests that previous attempts to model the duration of equities in terms of the dividend capitalization model may be somewhat misleading (e.g. Boquist et al. 1975).

4.2 Fixed rate debt and forward interest rate contracts

We have seen that the effect of floating rate debt is to leave the stockholders of the firm bearing the full weight of interest rate changes and hence to increase the volatility of its stock price. The effect of fixed rate debt is in the opposite direction. If the firm has long-term fixed rate bonds in its capital structure, there is an offsetting benefit to stockholders when interest rates rise. An increase in interest rates causes a reduction in bond values. Part of the risk of interest rate changes is therefore borne by the bondholders.

A long-term fixed rate loan may be viewed as a portfolio of forward interest rate contracts. A bond is a spot contract for one period, plus a series of forward contracts to borrow money in the future at a fixed rate. This suggests that the volatility of the stock of a firm will depend not only on the amount of fixed rate debt it has in place, but also on the number of forward interest rate contracts it holds. In this section, we focus explicitly on the impact of fixed rate bonds on volatility. A similar analysis could be applied to the effect of forward interest rate contracts. In order to proceed, suppose the firm has debt which pays a fixed interest rate r_n. If B_n is the nominal value of the debt, and if the firm has no variable rate debt, its dividend at time t is

$$d_t = x_t e^{\gamma R t} e^{\alpha i t} - B_n e^{r_n t} \tag{11.23}$$

and the price of the stock is therefore

$$S = x_t e^{-[R(1-\gamma)+i(1-\alpha)]t} - B_n e^{-(r-r_n)t} \tag{11.24}$$

Differentiating (11.24), we have

$$\frac{d \ln S}{dr} = \{-t(1-\theta)x_t e^{-[R(1-\gamma)+i(1-\alpha)]t} + tB_n e^{-(r-r_n)t}\}/S \tag{11.25}$$

Substituting for S from (11.24) and using the definition of leverage, we find the volatility is

$$\sigma_S = \left| \frac{t(1-\theta) - tL}{1-L} \right| \sigma_r \tag{11.26}$$

where t is the maturity of the cash flow, θ is the extent to which it adjusts to inflation, and L is the leverage of the firm.

From (11.26) we can see that the effect of fixed rate bonds on the volatility of the stock depends on the degree of indexation of the firm's cash flows. For example, if the firm's cash flows are completely unprotected from interest rate movements, either because interest rate changes are expected to be predominantly real or because the nature of the firm's business is such that its cash flows respond neither to inflation nor to real rate changes, then $\sigma_S = t\sigma_r$ in (11.26), regardless of the amount of debt in the capital structure. Essentially, in this case both the cash flows and the debt payments of the firm are fixed, and the result is that the stock has a volatility equal to the duration of its net cash flows, so that in this respect it behaves exactly like a nominal bond. At the other extreme, when the firm is fully indexed against interest rate fluctuations, $\theta = 1$, and the volatility of its stock would be zero if it had issued no bonds. However, the addition of bonds with value LV makes the volatility

$$\sigma_S = \left| \frac{tL}{1 - L} \right| \sigma_r \tag{11.27}$$

However, in this case the impact of an increase in interest rates on the stock price is *positive*. If interest rates increase, the value of the debt falls, to the advantage of the shareholders.

Firms are often recommended to use fixed rate debt and forward rate interest contracts to reduce their cash flow volatility. From (11.26) we can see that, where cash flows are only partially indexed against interest rates, the firm could choose the proportion of fixed rate debt L so as to reduce volatility to zero. This would be achieved by setting $L = 1 - \theta$, which is the capital structure of a fully hedged firm, for which the sensitivity of the equity price to interest rate fluctuations is zero, regardless of its cash flow maturity. In general, however, we would not expect firms to be completely hedged in this way, so their volatilities will depend on the degree of inherent indexation θ in their cash flows and on the volume of fixed rate bonds in their capital structure.

4.3 Fixed and variable rate debt

We have seen in previous sections that the effects of fixed and variable rate debt on the relationship between volatility and maturity are opposite in sign. Variable rate debt increases equity volatility, whereas fixed rate debt reduces it. The net effect will depend on the proportion of fixed and variable rate debt. We now proceed to analyse the general case where the firm has both fixed and variable rate debt.

Let B be the total value of the fixed and variable rate bonds in the firm's capital structure. If f is the proportion of B represented by fixed rate bonds, the dividend at time t is

$$d_t = x_t e^{\gamma Rt} e^{\alpha it} - B_n e^{r_n t} - B(1-f)e^{rt} \tag{11.28}$$

In (11.28), $B_n = fB$ is the value of the fixed rate bonds. $B(1-f)$ is the value of the variable rate debt. The second term is the interest and principal repayment on the fixed rate debt. The final term represents the variable rate debt repayments. The price of the stock is

$$S = x_t e^{-[R(1-\gamma)+i(1-\alpha)]t} - B_n e^{-(r-r_n)t} - B(1-f) \tag{11.29}$$

Differentiating (11.29), we then have

$$\frac{d \ln S}{dr} = \{-t(1-\theta)x_t e^{-[R(1-\gamma)+i(1-\alpha)]t} + tB_n e^{-(r-r_n)t}\}/S \tag{11.30}$$

The volatility is

$$\sigma_S = \left| \frac{t(1-\theta)V - tB_n e^{-(r-r_n)t}}{S} \right| \sigma_r \tag{11.31}$$

which can be expressed as

$$\sigma_S = \left| \frac{t(1-\theta) - tLf}{1-L} \right| \sigma_r \tag{11.32}$$

since the value of the fixed rate debt is

$$LVf = B_n e^{-(r-r_n)t} \tag{11.33}$$

The first term in (11.32) is the total volatility of the firm's earnings. This is the volatility that the stock would have if it were unleveraged. The second term is the volatility absorbed by the firm's bondholders. To the extent that the firm finances itself with fixed rate bonds, the asset volatility is offset by this liability volatility which acts in the opposite direction. The denominator shows how the net volatility is leveraged by the proportion of debt in the capital structure.

In figure 11.1 we illustrate the effect of leverage on volatility. The volatility of the unleveraged firm depends upon the maturity t and the extent of indexation of the cash flow θ. The change in volatility as leverage increases depends on the proportion of fixed rate finance. If this proportion f is greater than the degree to which cash flows are unindexed, then the addition of debt reduces volatility. However, if f is small, the net effect of leverage can be to increase volatility, as illustrated by the top curve in figure 11.1.

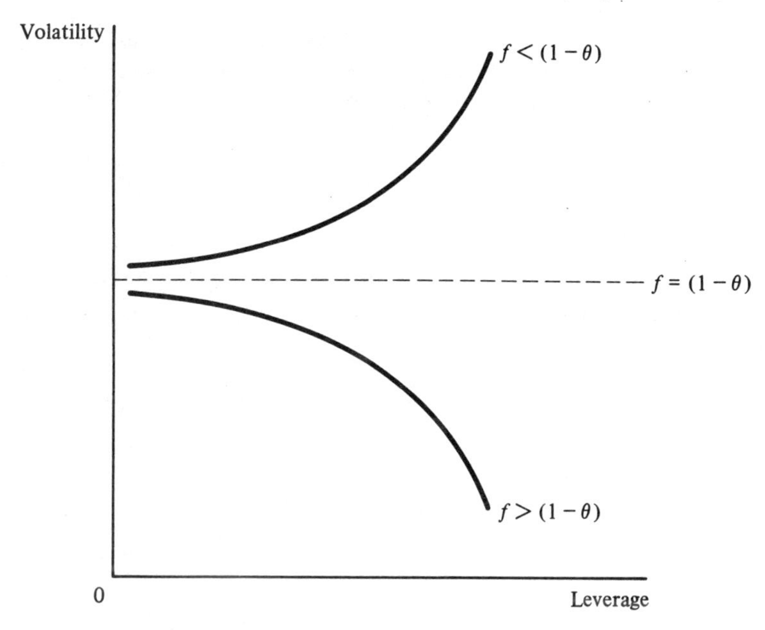

Figure 11.1 Volatility and leverage

5 DURATION AND THE VOLATILITY OF EQUITIES

So far in this chapter we have assumed that the firm has only a single cash flow, occurring at time t. This assumption was made for illustrative purposes only, and the analysis is easily extended to cover the more realistic case where there are multiple cash flows arising at different points in time. Generalizing from the case of a single cash flow to a cash flow stream is analogous to moving from analysing a discount bond to a coupon bond. An equity can be viewed as a partially indexed coupon bond, where the indexation is to the nominal interest rate.

In previous work on equity volatility by Boquist et al. (1975), the dividend stream of the firm is assumed to grow at a constant rate. However this assumption, which comes from the constant-growth dividend-discount model, is not necessary in order to derive simple measures of stock volatility. Instead, in the multiperiod case we will assume the following:

(a) The degree to which a cash flow is indexed to changes in the real rate of interest and to inflation is the same for each cash flow in the stream.
(b) Each dividend in the stream of dividends depends upon a base value which we denote x_t, in a manner similar to that described above.
(c) The firm finances itself with zero-coupon bonds which mature at t.

These comprise both fixed rate bonds with an interest rate r_n, which is the same for each bond maturity, and variable rate bonds. The proportion of the total bond value represented by fixed rate bonds is again denoted by f.

Given these assumptions, the dividend at t is

$$d_t = x_t e^{\gamma R t} e^{\alpha i t} - B_{nt} e^{r_n t} - B_{vt} e^{rt} \tag{11.34}$$

where B_{nt} is the fixed rate debt repayable at t and B_{vt} is the variable rate debt repayable at t, and the price of the stock is the discounted sum of the dividends:

$$S = \sum_t \{x_t e^{-[R(1-\gamma)+i(1-\alpha)]t} - B_{nt} e^{-(r-r_n)t}\} - B(1-f) \tag{11.35}$$

Differentiating (11.35), we have

$$\frac{\mathrm{d} \ln S}{\mathrm{d} r} = \left[\sum_t \{ -t(1-\theta) x_t e^{-[R(1-\gamma)+i(1-\alpha)]t} + tB_{nt} e^{-(r-r_n)t} \} \right] \Big/ S \tag{11.36}$$

and hence volatility is

$$\sigma_S = \left| \frac{\sum_t t(1-\theta) V_t}{V(1-L)} - \frac{\sum_t tB_{nt} e^{-(r-r_n)t}}{V(1-L)} \right| \sigma_r \tag{11.37}$$

where

$$V_t = x_t e^{-[R(1-\gamma)+i(1-\alpha)]t} \tag{11.38}$$

is the value of the period t cash flow. Hence we can write

$$\sigma_S = \left| \frac{\sum_t t(1-\theta) V_t}{V(1-L)} - \frac{\sum_t tB_{nt} e^{-(r-r_n)t}}{LVf} \frac{Lf}{1-L} \right| \sigma_r \tag{11.39}$$

and

$$\sigma_S = \left| \frac{[D_A(1-\theta) - D_L Lf]}{1-L} \right| \sigma_r \tag{11.40}$$

where D_A is the duration of the assets of the firm and D_L is the duration of its fixed rate liabilities.

Equation (11.40) is very similar in structure to the earlier expressions for equity volatility, with the duration of the firm's assets (that is, of its cash inflows) and the duration of its fixed rate liabilities substituted for maturity t. As in the case of a bond, the duration is defined as the average maturity of the cash flows, where the weights are the present values of the cash flows. The definitions of D_A and D_L are therefore

$$D_A = \left[\sum_t t x_t e^{-rt} \right] \Big/ V \tag{11.41}$$

$$D_L = \left[\sum_t t B_{nt} e^{-(r-r_n)t} \right] \Big/ LVf \tag{11.42}$$

Our previous results regarding the effect of leverage are unchanged as long as the durations of the assets and fixed rate liabilities are equal. However, if the durations differ, an increase in leverage which has no effect on the duration of the debt (that is, a scale increase in the debt) will increase or decrease volatility according to whether

$$fD_L > (1 - \theta) D_A \quad \text{or} \quad fD_L < (1 - \theta) D_A$$

If the duration of the fixed rate liabilities is relatively high compared with the term $D_A(1 - \theta)$, the indexation-adjusted duration of the assets, an increase in leverage will tend to reduce stock volatility. In this case, the increased leverage provides a degree of protection against interest rate changes that offsets the effect of levering up the asset volatility.

6 SUMMARY AND CONCLUSIONS

Stock prices are affected by interest rates. However, empirical work appears to indicate that the implied duration of equities is far lower than any reasonable estimate of the average maturity of aggregate dividends or cash flows. We have put forward a number of possible explanations of this phenomenon in the preceding sections. The volatility of a stock with respect to interest rates depends upon:

(a) The weighted average maturity of its cash flows (rather than its dividends)
(b) The degree to which its cash flows are indexed to inflation
(c) The degree to which its cash flows adjust to changes in the real rate of interest
(d) The extent to which changes in nominal interest rates represent changes in inflation expectations, as opposed to real rates of interest
(e) The leverage and dividend policy of the firm
(f) The degree to which the firm uses variable (floating) rate debt and fixed rate bonds in its capital structure.

An equity is really similar to a partially indexed bond. It is partially hedged because the volatility of its fixed rate liabilities to some extent offsets the volatility of its cash flows. It is partially indexed because its cash flows do react to some extent and with a delay to changes in inflation and possibly to changes in the real rate of interest. The degree to which equities are hedged against interest rate changes depends upon the firm's use of fixed rate debt as well as its holdings of forward rate contracts. In contrast to the usual analysis of the effect of leverage in discussions of the Modigliani-Miller hypothesis, the effect of fixed rate debt here is to reduce the volatility of the firm's equity. However, the effect of variable rate debt is to lever up the volatility inherent in the firm's assets and to increase the equity volatility. The net effect depends upon the proportion of fixed rate debt in the firm's total borrowing.

Notes

The first author is happy to acknowledge the generous support of the Leverhulme Foundation.

1 See, for example, Leibowitz (1986), who finds that volatility is small in comparison with a reasonable estimate of the duration of the dividend stream.

2 Under uncertainty, the volatility of stock prices depends upon changes in expectations of profits as well as changes in interest rates. For an analysis of the combined effect, see Copeland and Stapleton (1990). The effect of taxes is implicitly included in the degree to which the stock is indexed to inflation. For a discussion of the effect of variable rate debt, see section 4.1.

3 Some studies have suggested that $1 - \beta$, the proportion of any change in the nominal rate that is represented by a change in the real rate, is negative. For long periods in the 1970s, when inflation was high, the real interest rate was actually negative. Subsequently, when inflation fell in the 1980s, *ex post* real interest rates were high. This casual observation is confirmed by, among others, Fried and Howitt (1983). If $\beta > 1$, the importance of the indexation parameter α is enhanced.

4 In this analysis, we have not dealt explicitly with the existence of corporate taxes. But if we define the cash flow of the unlevered firm x_t as the after-tax cash flow, one reason why cash flows are not perfectly indexed to inflation may well be the tax effect. Fiscal drag, associated with the non-indexation of depreciation provisions and inventory valuation, provides one reason for the indexation parameter α being less than one. However, the tax relief afforded on interest payments works in the opposite direction. Variable rate debt has the advantage of reducing corporate tax payments in times of high interest rates. To this extent, the volatility of the equity with respect to interest rate changes is reduced. The analysis of stock volatility with tax deductibility of interest payments is complex, and we do not deal with it here.

References

Bierwag, G. O., Kaufman, G. G. and Toevs, A. (eds) (1983) *Innovations in Bond Portfolio Management: Duration Analysis and Immunization*, Greenwich, CT: JAI Press.

Boquist, J. A., Racette, G. A. and Schlarbaum, G. (1975) 'Duration and risk assessment of bonds and common stocks', *Journal of Finance*, December, 1360–5.

Copeland, L. S. and Stapleton, R. C. (1990) 'Information, interest rates and the volatility of asset prices in an arbitrage-free economy', presented at Money Study Group, London School of Economics, May.

Fama, E. F. and Schwert, W. (1977) 'Asset returns and inflation', *Journal of Financial Economics*, 4, November, 115–46.

Fried, J. and Howitt, P. (1983) 'The effects of inflation on real interest rates', *American Economic Review*, 73(5), 968–80.

Grossman, S. F. and Shiller, R. J. (1981) 'The determinants of the variability of stock market prices', *American Economic Review*, 71(2), 222–7.

Hicks, J. R. (1939) *Value and Capital*, Oxford: Clarendon Press.

Leibowitz, M. L. (1986) 'Total portfolio duration: a new perspective on asset allocation', *Financial Analysts Journal*, September/October, pp. 18–29.

Macaulay, F. R. (1938) *Some Theoretical Problems Suggested by the Movements of Interest Rates, Bonds Yields and Stock Prices in the US Since 1856*, New York: National Bureau of Economic Research.

Ross, S. A. (1989) 'Information and volatility: the no-arbitrage approach to timing and resolution of uncertainty', *Journal of Finance*, 44, 1–17.

Shiller, R. J. (1981) 'Do stock prices move too much to be justified by subsequent changes in dividends?', *American Economic Review*, 71, 421–36.

12 The Decision to Disclose Research and Development Expenditure in the Presence of a Takeover Threat

Jane M. Black and Ian Tonks

1 INTRODUCTION

The purpose of this chapter is to analyse why firms might choose to disclose information about the value of an input into its production process. We will examine the conditions under which the managers of the firm will choose to release the information publicly, and the conditions under which, given no public release, some investors will pay to observe imprecise information, which then in a rational expectations equilibrium is imperfectly reflected in prices. We focus on R & D expenditure as the production input because this issue is currently the subject of a great deal of debate in the UK following the decision to introduce SSAP 13, which will require large firms to publicly disclose R & D expenditure.[1] The problem is set up in a world of asymmetric information, where managers of the firm know the values of their production inputs but investors in the firm cannot costlessly observe this information unless managers choose to tell them. On the other hand, investors may be prepared to exert time and effort or pay investment analysts to collect information about the production inputs – though we might imagine that this would be a costly activity, and will involve the commitment of real resources.

Gonedes (1980) argues that in general it is not possible to ascertain the effect of public disclosure rules, since they will depend on the setting under consideration. Diamond (1985) examines the optimal release of information by firms, in terms of the effects of public disclosure or private information acquisition on the expected utility of traders. He shows that there are two benefits from public disclosure. First, since it seems reasonable to assume that the cost to the firm of releasing information is likely to be substantially lower than the total cost of different individuals collecting the same information, there is a cost saving by public announcements. Second, if different individuals collect different signals, the heterogeneity of beliefs may result in more speculative activity in the firm's share price. The firm can reduce this speculative activity by homogenizing beliefs through making public announcements.

In this chapter we modify the Diamond framework in two ways. First, instead of differential information collected by individuals, we assume that if individuals collect information then they all collect the same piece of information, so that there are no information aggregation issues. In addition, the information collected by individuals is taken to be imprecise, in the sense that it is not perfectly correlated with the underlying unknown parameter. On the other hand we assume that a public announcement is the actual value of the unknown parameter. We extend the Diamond paper by contrasting the value of imprecise information with the value of a perfect public announcement. It may well be the case that a firm deliberately lies about its level of R & D, so that the firm's announcement is a biased statement of the true R & D expenditure. However, over time the market will incorporate this bias into its expectations; we note Verrecchia's (1983) result that if managers have discretion over what to disclose, and they only disclose favourable information, the market comes to expect this in a true rational expectations equilibrium.

Second, it is well known (Hirshleifer 1971; Hakansson et al. 1983; Trueman 1984) that unless certain conditions are met, the public disclosure of information will not improve economic welfare. In Diamond's model, therefore, economic welfare would be improved if the firm did not commit resources to the release of information, though in this case there would be private incentives for individuals to collect the information. Again welfare would be improved if all individuals could be constrained from gathering this information. We provide a different criterion for judging welfare: we appeal to the idea that the managers of a firm are reluctant to see its share price be too volatile, since a low share price will increase the probability of a successful takeover bid, which would result in a change in the current management. Thus managers are motivated in their decision whether to release public information by their desire to minimize the variance of their share price.

We can identify another group of outsiders who would be interested in acquiring information about a firm's R & D policy: rival firms, who could use this information to obtain a strategic advantage (Brander and Spencer 1983). However, in this chapter we ignore the product market interactions; we suppose that the firm has decided upon the optimal first-best level of R & D activity to maximize the value of shareholder wealth, but must then decide whether to release this information to the public, given that they want to minimize the volatility of the share price. This is an application of Hirshleifer's separation theorem, which says that investment decisions are separable from financing decisions.

2 THE MODEL

The model we construct to examine this issue is a two-period rational expectations equilibrium adapted from Black and Tonks (1990a). We assume that managers adopt an information disclosure policy to minimize the variability of a firm's share price, in order to minimize the probability of a successful hostile takeover. To demonstrate how the public release or private collection of information may alter the variability of stock prices we consider the following simplified economy. There are two assets: a risky asset which has an outcome y at the terminal date, and a safe asset which can be borrowed or lent and pays a rate of return r per unit period. The outcome to the risky asset is random because it depends upon the success of the project which is financed by the research and development expenditure. A high R & D budget results in a distribution function for the random outcome that stochastically dominates a distribution generated by a lower level of R & D expenditure.

There are three periods and three relevant dates. Before $t = 1$, the firm makes its R & D decision. At $t = 1$, investors make their initial purchases of the two assets. Before the retrade date, but after the initial purchase, either perfect information is publicly released by the firm, or imprecise information can be collected about the likely values of y by individual traders. At $t = 2$, there is an opportunity for retrade. The terminal date is at $t = 3$, when the firm pays its realized outcome to its shareholders.

Managers of the firm make two decisions simultaneously. Before date $t = 1$, they decide how much R & D to undertake in order to maximize the value of shareholder wealth. This results in the first-best level of R & D. They must also decide on their optimal information disclosure policy in order to minimize the probability of takeover. We do not model the takeover process explicitly but assume that the probability of takeover increases as the firm's share price falls. So managers try to reduce the variability of the share price by minimizing a weighted average of the variance of each period's share price. It turns out that it is important that their disclosure policy is announced prior to the initial trading at $t = 1$, since the behaviour of investors at $t = 1$ will depend on whether they expect the firm to make a public disclosure or not.

It is assumed that there is a large number of investors of each of three types. First there are noise or liquidity investors, whose demands are assumed to be random and independent of price. Then there are two types of rational investors. One set is labelled informed traders, who take on the role of investment analysts, busily researching the information about the unknown R & D decision of the firm; they all acquire the same (imprecise) piece of information, prior to the retrade date, about the firm's R & D level. The other set is called uninformed traders, who base their portfolio allocation decisions on their own prior beliefs and on what they can infer from equilibrium prices. Both sets of traders have the same prior beliefs at $t = 1$, and both sets are risk-averse with constant absolute risk aversion preferences, represented by an exponential utility function, with a common level of risk tolerance b. Each group of traders chooses its portfolios at $t = 1$ and $t = 2$ to maximize the utility of terminal wealth W_3. The proportion of traders who are actively gathering information is assumed to be λ. If information is costly, λ is an endogenous variable. However, we shall treat it here as a parameter of the model, since our concern is to see how asset price variability is affected by changing λ and not to derive λ explicitly.

The supply of the risky asset to the rational traders depends upon the demands of the liquidity investors, which we assume to be normally distributed. The supply to the rational traders, net of these noise demands, is given by x_1, where x_1 is $N(Ex_1, v_{x_1})$ at time $t = 1$, and by x_2, where x_2 is $N(Ex_2, v_{x_2})$ at time $t = 2$.

The outcome from holding a unit of the risky asset y, paid out at $t = 3$, is assumed to be generated by the following process:

$$\tilde{y} = I + \tilde{\epsilon} \tag{12.1}$$

where

$$I = u + \theta$$

I is the first-best amount of R & D expenditure undertaken by the firm, which is unknown to investors, since it depends on the random profitable opportunities perceived by the managers of the firm. However, u is the amount of R & D expected by investors, so that θ is the forecast error or deviation of the actual from the expected R & D expenditure. Having undertaken a quantity of I expenditure, the subsequent returns from this investment are random owing to the disturbance term $\epsilon \sim N(0, v_\epsilon)$. Before $t = 1$ the value of θ is unknown to traders, but prior beliefs are $\theta \sim N(0, v_\theta)$, and $\text{cov}(\epsilon, \theta) = 0$. So the unconditional distribution of y is $N(u, v)$, where $v = v_\theta + v_\epsilon$. The value of θ, and hence the level of actual R & D, can be announced by the firm to all traders after the initial trading date, but before the retrade date, so that $\lambda = 1$ and all traders are informed.

Alternatively, suppose there are pieces of information that become available to the informed traders after the initial trading date. Informed traders are those traders who are willing to pay a cost c to observe these pieces of information. These pieces of information are random variables which give information about the unknown forecast error θ. More specifically, an informed trader observes an imprecise signal $\bar{z}$ where $\bar{z} \sim N(\theta, v_m)$, which is a sufficient statistic for the series of signals. From Bayes's rule, the conditional posterior distribution of y given $\bar{z}$ is $N(u + \theta^*, v_1)$, where

$$\theta^* = \frac{\bar{z} v_\theta}{v_\theta + v_m}, \quad v_1 = v_\epsilon + v_{\theta^*}, \quad v_{\theta^*} = \frac{v_\theta v_m}{v_\theta + v_m}$$

Note further than the unconditional distribution of $\bar{z}$ is $N(0, v_\theta + v_m)$ and the distribution of θ^* is $N(0, q)$, where $q = v_\theta^2/(v_\theta + v_m)$.

At time $t = 1$, traders allocate their initial wealth W_1 between the risk-free and the risky assets, selecting n_1 and m_1 respectively, subject to the budget constraint

$$n_1 + p_1 m_1 = W_1$$

At $t = 2$ they choose n_2 and m_2, subject to the constraint

$$n_2 + p_2 m_2 = n_1(1 + r) + p_2 m_1$$

Terminal wealth when y is received is given by

$$W_3 = (1 + r) n_2 + y m_2$$

p_1 and p_2 are market clearing prices for the risky asset at the two trading dates, and it is assumed that all trades take place at equilibrium prices. We will write p_1^λ and p_2^λ to denote these equilibrium prices in the event of private information collection when there is no public disclosure of R & D by the firm, so that these prices reflect the imprecise information held by the proportion λ of informed traders. We will not include the λ superscript when the firm has publicly disclosed R & D.

To derive the distribution of equilibrium prices at $t = 1$, it is first necessary to derive the distribution of prices at the retrade date.

3 THE RETRADE EQUILIBRIUM

Given the assumption of an exponential utility function, the demand function for the risky asset of each of the informed traders after he or she has observed the value of θ^* at the retrade date is given by

$$m_2^I = \frac{u + \theta^* - (1 + r) p_2^\lambda}{b v_1} \tag{12.2a}$$

That of each of the uninformed traders is given by

$$m_2^{\mathrm{U}} = \frac{E(y|p_2^\lambda) - (1+r)p_2^\lambda}{b\,\mathrm{var}\,(y|p_2^\lambda)} \tag{12.3}$$

Market equilibrium is given by

$$\lambda m_2^{\mathrm{I}} + (1-\lambda)\,m_2^{\mathrm{U}} = x_2 \tag{12.4}$$

Extending Grossman and Stiglitz (1980) to the case of imprecise information, we may derive a rational expectations solution for the distribution of p_2^λ when there is a proportion λ of informed traders who all observe θ^*. We can write the retrade price function as

$$(1+r)\,\tilde{p}_2^\lambda = u + \frac{c_2}{c_1}\tilde{w} - \frac{Ex_2}{c_1} \tag{12.5a}$$

where

$$\tilde{w} = \theta^* - \frac{bv_1}{\lambda}(\tilde{x}_2 - Ex_2)$$

$$c_1 = \frac{\lambda}{bv_1} + \frac{(1-\lambda)}{b\mathrm{var}\,(y|p_2^\lambda)}$$

$$c_2 = \frac{\lambda}{bv_1} + \frac{(1-\lambda)}{b\mathrm{var}\,(y|p_2^\lambda)}\frac{q}{v_w}$$

$$v_w = q + \frac{b^2 v_1^2}{\lambda^2} v_{x_2}$$

$$E(y|p_2^\lambda) = u + \frac{q}{v_w}(w - Ew)$$

$$\mathrm{var}\,(y|p_2^\lambda) = v - \frac{q^2}{v_w}$$

On the other hand, if there was a public announcement θ then this has the same effect as if everyone is informed. So $\lambda = 1$, and we can write the retrade demands as

$$m_2 = \frac{u + \theta - (1+r)p_2}{bv_\epsilon} \tag{12.2b}$$

The retrade price function becomes

$$(1+r)\,\tilde{p}_2 = u + \tilde{\omega} - \frac{Ex_2}{c_1} = u + \theta - bv_\epsilon \tilde{x}_2 \tag{12.5b}$$

where

$$\tilde{\omega} = \theta - bv_{\epsilon}(\tilde{x}_2 - Ex_2)$$

$$c_1 = c_2 = \frac{1}{bv_{\epsilon}}$$

$$v_{\omega} = v_{\theta} + b^2 v_{\epsilon}^2 v_{x_2}$$

We now state as a series of propositions the effect on the variance of retrade prices of disclosing information about R & D expenditure. Proofs are to be found in the appendix.

Proposition 1 **A sufficient condition for the public disclosure of R & D information to minimize the conditional retrade price variance is $(1 - vb^2 v_{x_2}) > 0$**

Proposition 1 states that the conditional variance of retrade prices will be minimized by the firm disclosing its R & D information. By conditional variance we mean the variance of retrade prices conditional upon either public or private information being released. If public information is released then the retrade price function is given by (12.5b). If private information is collected by a proportion λ of the population, the retrade price function is stated in (12.5a).

The retrade price function, conditional on the information has a variance because the behaviour of the noise traders is random. This variance is dependent on whether public information is disclosed or whether informed traders gather imprecise information, which is then imperfectly reflected in retrade prices according to (12.5a). Lemma 2 (see appendix) shows that if $(1 - vb^2 v_{x_2}) > 0$, starting from $\lambda = 0$, the effect of more informed traders will be to increase conditional retrade price variance. This surprising result is concerned with the informativeness of the price system in (12.5a). If very few people are informed, the uninformed can infer little from equilibrium prices about the underlying unknown parameter, and prices are stable. As the percentage of informed increases, the price system becomes more informative, and the remaining uninformed react to any unanticipated changes in price by resubmitting their demands; hence an initial price rise will result in further rises, and conversely for a price fall. Lemma 1 shows that there will be a maximum value to this variance for a value of λ lying between zero and unity, since as the percentage of the population who are informed increases, the economy runs out of uninformed traders who are reacting to the equilibrium prices, and consequently prices stabilize. Lemmas 1 and 2 together mean that there cannot be an internal value of λ which minimizes the conditional variance. Lemma 3 shows that the conditional variance of imprecise information θ^* is always greater than that of perfect information θ, so that we have the result of proposition 1 that the firm can minimize conditional variance at the retrade equilibrium by disclosing θ.

Proposition 2a **If $[1 - b^2 v_{x_2} (2v_1 + q)] < 0$, the unconditional retrade price variance with no disclosure and $\lambda = 1$ is less than the unconditional variance with no disclosure and $\lambda = 0$.**

Proposition 2a is concerned with the unconditional retrade price variance of imprecise information, which is the expected variance before the information has been incorporated into prices by the informed traders. Provided the condition in proposition 2a is satisfied, the retrade variance when all are informed is less than that with no one informed. This result occurs because of the stabilizing influence of information on retrade demands. We know from (12.2a) and (12.3) that retrade demands depend on the variance of the underlying random return. Information reduces this variance and hence retrade demands are more elastic, which means that retrade prices are less responsive to random noise trader demands. However, if the condition in proposition 2a is violated, which will occur when traders are not very risk-averse (b is low) or when the noise traders' demands are predictable (v_{x_2} is low), the retrade demands in (12.2a) are more sensitive to the variability in θ. The direct effect of the expected value of θ on demands will destabilize retrade prices.

Proposition 2b **If $[1 - b^2 v_{x_2} (2v_\epsilon + v_\theta)] < 0$, the unconditional retrade price variance with public disclosure and the unconditional retrade price variance with no disclosure but $\lambda = 1$ are both less than the unconditional retrade price variance with $\lambda = 0$.**

Proposition 2b extends proposition 2a to include public disclosure, and states that provided the condition is satisfied then unconditional retrade price variance with public disclosure is less than retrade price variance with imprecise information and no one informed. Further, the condition in proposition 2b implies the condition in proposition 2a and hence proposition 2a also holds.

Proposition 2c **If $[1 - b^2 v_{x_2}(2v_\epsilon + v_{\theta^*})] < 0$, the unconditional retrade price variance with public disclosure is less than the unconditional variance with no disclosure and $\lambda = 1$, which in turn is less than the unconditional variance with no disclosure and $\lambda = 0$.**

Provided the condition in proposition 2c is satisfied, the firm can ensure that the unconditional price variance following a public announcement is less than having everyone collect information or having no one collect information. In the next proposition we consider the value of a public announcement when only a proportion of the population of investors collects information, i.e. $0 < \lambda < 1$.

Proposition 3 **A sufficient condition for the disclosure of information to minimize retrade price variance is $(q - 3vb^2v_{x_2}) < 0$.**

Even allowing for private information collection by a proportion of investors, if the condition is satisfied it is sufficient to ensure that public disclosure will minimize retrade price variance.

The purpose of propositions 1–3 is to show the conditions under which the disclosure of R & D information will reduce the variance of retrade prices. Interestingly, if these conditions are not satisfied then this implies that in order to minimize retrade price variance the firm should not disclose. Whether or not disclosure results in excessive price volatility depends upon the informativeness of the price system. The implication from all of these propositions is that when the variance of the noise traders' demands is low, the public disclosure of information, or private information collection, may destabilize stock prices. Hence if we observe companies with a low level of noise activity in their equity turnover, we would expect these companies to be less likely to divulge information about production inputs.

4 THE INITIAL EQUILIBRIUM

We must now solve the initial portfolio allocation of the traders. Consider first the portfolio decision of the informed at the beginning of the period. Substituting their optimal demands m_2^{I} back into the expected utility function at the retrade date, we obtain the following indirect expected utility function:

$$EV_2^{\mathrm{I}} = -\exp\left\{ -b(1+r)\left[(1+r)(W_1 - p_1^{\lambda}m_1) + p_2^{\lambda}m_1\right] - \frac{[u + \theta^* - (1+r)p_2^{\lambda}]^2}{2v_1} \right\} \tag{12.6}$$

To find the informed traders' initial expected utility function EU_1^{I} it is necessary to integrate (12.6) over the retrade price, conditional on the information, and then integrate over the information. The necessary integration can be performed as in Black and Tonks (1990b). Differentiating EU_1^{I} with respect to m_1, and setting equal to zero, enables us to write the initial optimum demands of the informed for the risky asset as

$$m_1^{\mathrm{I}} = \frac{u - (1+r)^2 p_1^{\lambda} - \dfrac{bEx_2}{A}\left(v - \dfrac{c_2}{c_1}q\right)^2}{bv - \dfrac{b}{A}\left(v - \dfrac{c_2}{c}q\right)^2} \tag{12.7a}$$

where

$$A = v_1 + \mathrm{var}(p_2^{\lambda}|\theta^*) + \left(\frac{c_2}{c_1} - 1\right)^2 q$$

Equation (12.7a) shows the initial optimum demands for the risky asset by the informed traders, who know they will observe some information in the future. Theorem 1 of Black and Tonks (1990a) shows that these demands are the same as the demands by the uninformed. This is useful because the symmetry between the initial demands of the informed and the uninformed means that the initial price distribution can be written as

$$(1+r)^2 \tilde{p}_1^{\lambda} = u - \frac{bEx_2}{A}\left(v - \frac{c_2}{c_1}q\right)^2 - b\tilde{x}_1\left[v - \frac{1}{A}\left(v - \frac{c_2}{c_1}q\right)^2\right] \tag{12.8a}$$

and hence the variance of the initial price distribution is given by

$$\mathrm{var}[(1+r)^2 p_1^{\lambda}] = b^2\left[v - \frac{1}{A}\left(v - \frac{c_2}{c_1}q\right)^2\right]^2 v_{x_1} \tag{12.9a}$$

We can also calculate the initial demands by investors who know that public information will be released. In this case the demands in (12.7a) reduce to

$$m_1 = \frac{u - (1+r)^2 p_1 - \dfrac{bEx_2}{A_1} v_\epsilon^2}{bv - \dfrac{b}{A_1} v_\epsilon^2} \tag{12.7b}$$

where

$$A_1 = v_\epsilon(1 + b^2 v_\epsilon v_{x_1})$$

The initial price distribution is

$$(1+r)^2 \tilde{p}_1 = u - \frac{bv_\epsilon Ex_2}{1 + b^2 v_\epsilon v_{x_2}} - b\left[v_\theta + \frac{b^2 v_\epsilon^2 v_{x_2}}{1 + b^2 v_\epsilon v_{x_2}}\right]\tilde{x}_1 \tag{12.8b}$$

and hence the variance of the initial price distribution is given by

$$\mathrm{var}[(1+r)^2 p_1] = b^2\left[v_\theta + \frac{b^2 v_\epsilon^2 v_{x_2}}{1 + b^2 v_\epsilon v_{x_2}}\right]^2 v_{x_1} \tag{12.9b}$$

Comparing the variances in (12.9a) and (12.9b), we are able to state the following proposition.

Proposition 4 **(i) The variance of initial prices is minimized with no public disclosure. (ii) Further, the variance of zero-informed initial prices is less than the variance of all-informed prices.**

We obtain the result that in order to minimize initial price variance the firm should commit itself to not announcing the R & D expenditure. This is a very strong result and can be explained as follows. By announcing R & D expenditure, investors know that future prices will be highly correlated with the subsequent revealed information. The advantage of not having public disclosure is that next period's prices and the underlying performance of the firm are uncorrelated, so that by holding shares in the firm the investor is holding a portfolio of two independent random variables, which is good for price stabilization in the initial period. By not announcing, the firm can induce investors to speculate in the shares in the firm; the standard Friedman argument about speculation is that it is stabilizing, and hence the initial price variance is kept low.

5 CONCLUSIONS

The purpose of this chapter has been to investigate the effect on asset price volatility of a firm releasing information about the level of R & D expenditure undertaken by the firm. The firm knows that in the event of non-disclosure, investment analysts and other stock market participants will gather information which in a rational expectations equilibrium will be reflected in the firm's stock price. We have argued that a firm will choose its disclosure policy in order to minimize the variance of its stock price, on the basis that this policy will minimize the probability of a takeover threat, although we have not modelled this takeover process explicitly. We have identified the conditions under which a firm will choose to disclose its R & D information. It transpires that under certain conditions the firm can ensure more stable prices by not disclosing. This is certainly the case with respect to the initial price variance, but may also occur with the retrade price variance; that is, the revelation of information may so disturb retrade prices that the management of the firm would prefer to not allow information to be revealed.

We note that these results appear counter-intuitive, and we would guess that these are not the effects that the advocates of the new SSAP 13 had in mind when the changes to the accounting standard were proposed. Of course we have only identified the conditions under which the release of R & D information may be destabilizing, without saying whether these conditions are likely to hold in practice. One parameter in particular which determines whether retrade prices are more or less volatile (propositions 1–3) is the variance of the noise traders' demands. When a stock has a low noise trader variance, the release of information is more likely to destabilize prices. A testable proposition, therefore, is that we should observe that stocks with high noise trader variance have a high level of public disclosure.

In this chapter we assumed that the level of R&D undertaken by the firm was the first-best level. In future work we intend to go on to examine the effect of disclosure on the outlay of R & D in the first place, since it is likely that proponents of the change in SSAP 13 would argue that disclosure will have a positive effect on R & D activity. In particular we wish to ask what the effect of forced disclosure of R & D in line with SSAP 13 will have on the level of R&D undertaken, given that the firm wishes to minimize its share price volatility.

Appendix

Proof of proposition 1

From (12.5a), define the conditional variance of retrade prices given the imperfect information θ^* as

$$\mathrm{var}[(1+r)p_2^{\lambda}|\theta^*] = \left(\frac{c_2}{c_1}\right)^2 \frac{b^2 v_1^2}{\lambda^2} v_{x_2} = \mathrm{var}(p_2^{\lambda}|\theta^*) \tag{12.10}$$

Let

$$\Omega \equiv \frac{c_2}{c_1^{\lambda}} = \frac{\lambda q + (q + v_1) b^2 v_1 v_{x_2}}{\lambda^2 q + \lambda q b^2 v_1 v_{x_2} + b^2 v_1^2 v_{x_2}} \tag{12.11}$$

Lemma 1 The derivative $\mathrm{d}\Omega/\mathrm{d}\lambda = 0$ has no more than one solution in the range $0 \leq \lambda \leq 1$.

Proof At a turning point,

$$\frac{\mathrm{d}\,\mathrm{var}(p_2^{\lambda}|\theta^*)}{\mathrm{d}\lambda} = 2b^2 v_1^2 v_{x_2} \Omega \frac{\mathrm{d}\Omega}{\mathrm{d}\lambda} = 0$$

where

$$\frac{d\Omega}{d\lambda} = [-\lambda^2 q^2 - 2\lambda b^2 v q v_1 v_{x_2} + q b^2 v_1^2 v_{x_2}(1 - v b^2 v_{x_2})]/ \\ (\text{denom } (12.11))^2 = 0 \quad (12.12)$$

$d\Omega/d\lambda = 0$ is a quadratic function in λ, and only has one solution in the range $0 \leq \lambda \leq 1$. ||

Lemma 2 The turning point will be a maximum if $\text{var}(p_2^\lambda | \theta]^*)|_{\lambda=0} > \text{var}(p_2^\lambda | \theta^*)|_{\lambda=1}$ and $(d\Omega/d\lambda)|_{\lambda=0} > 0$.

Proof From (12.12),

$$\frac{d\Omega}{d\lambda}\Big|_{\lambda=0} = \frac{q}{b^2 v_1^2 v_{x_2}}(1 - v b^2 v_{x_2}) \quad (12.13)$$

Hence $\text{var}(p_2^\lambda | \theta^*)$ initially increases as λ increases if $(1 - v b^2 v_{x_2}) > 0$, and if from (12.11), when $\lambda = 0$, $\Omega = v/v_1$ so from (12.10)

$$\text{var}(p_2^\lambda | \theta^*) = b^2 v^2 v_{x_2}$$

and when $\lambda = 1, \Omega = 1$, so

$$\text{var}(p_2^\lambda | \theta^*) = b^2 v_1^2 v_{x_2}$$

So

$$\text{var}(p_2^\lambda | \theta^*)|_{\lambda=0} > \text{var}(p_2^\lambda | \theta^*)|_{\lambda=1} \quad \|$$

Lemma 3

$$\text{var}(p_2^\lambda | \theta^*)|_{\lambda=1} > \text{var}(p_2 | \theta)$$

Proof From (12.5b), following a public announcement the conditional variance of the prices is

$$\text{var}(p_2 | \theta) = b^2 v_\epsilon^2 v_{x_2}$$

which is less than the conditional variance given θ^* at $\lambda = 1$, since $v_\epsilon < v_1$.||

Lemmas 1 and 2 showed that a sufficient condition for $\text{var}(p_2^\lambda | \theta^*)|_{\lambda=1}$ to be minimized is $(1 - v b^2 v_{x_2}) > 0$. Lemma 3 showed that the conditional variance given θ^* at $\lambda = 1$ is always greater than the conditional variance given θ. Hence provided $(1 - v b^2 v_{x_2}) > 0$, a public announcement will minimize the variance of retrade prices. QED

Proof of proposition 2a
From (12.5a), define the unconditional variance of prices as

$$\operatorname{var}[(1+r)p_2^\lambda] = \left(\frac{c_2}{c_1}\right)^2 v_w = \Omega^2[q\lambda^2 + b^2 v_1^2 v_{x_2}] \equiv \operatorname{var}(p_2^\lambda) \qquad (12.14)$$

So if $\lambda = 0$,

$$\operatorname{var}(p_2^\lambda)\,|_{\lambda=0} = b^2 v^2 v_{x_2}$$

So if $\lambda = 1$,

$$\operatorname{var}(p_2^\lambda)\,|_{\lambda=1} = q + b^2 v_1^2 v_{x_2}$$

So $\operatorname{var}(p_2^\lambda)\,|_{\lambda=1} < \operatorname{var}(p_2^\lambda)\,|_{\lambda=0}$ when $[1 - b^2 v_{x_2}(q + 2v_1)] < 0$. QED

Proof of proposition 2b

$$\operatorname{var}(p_2) < \operatorname{var}(p_2^\lambda)\,|_{\lambda=0}$$

$$\text{iff} \quad v_\theta + b^2 v_\epsilon^2 v_{x_2} < b^2 v^2 v_{x_2}$$

i.e.

$$\text{iff} \quad [1 - b^2 v_{x_2}(2v_\epsilon + v_\theta) < 0$$

But $[1 - b^2 v_{x_2}(2v_\epsilon + v_\theta)] < 0$ implies $[1 - b^2 v_{x_2}(q + 2v_1)] < 0$. QED

Proof of proposition 2c
From (12.5b), the conditional variance of prices with the public announcement is

$$\operatorname{var}(p_2) = v_\theta + b^2 v_\epsilon^2 v_{x_2}$$

So

$$\operatorname{var}(p_2) < \operatorname{var}(p_2^\lambda)\,|_{\lambda=1}$$

$$\text{iff} \quad (v_\theta - q) + b^2 v_{x_2}(v_\epsilon^2 - v_1^2) < 0$$

i.e.

$$\text{iff} \quad 1 - b^2 v_{x_2}(2v_\epsilon + v_{\theta^*}) < 0$$

But $[1 - b^2 v_{x_2}(2v_\epsilon + v_{\theta^*})] < 0$ implies $[1 - b^2 v_{x_2}(2v_\epsilon + v_\theta)] < 0$. QED

Proof of proposition 3
From (12.14),

$$\frac{\mathrm{d}\ \mathrm{var}\,[\,(1+r)p_2^\lambda]}{\mathrm{d}\lambda} = 2\Omega\left(\frac{c_2}{c_1}q + (q\lambda^2 + b^2v_1^2v_{x_2})\frac{\mathrm{d}\Omega}{\mathrm{d}\lambda}\right)$$

where $\mathrm{d}\Omega/\mathrm{d}\lambda$ is given by (12.12). There will be turning points when $\mathrm{d}\ \mathrm{var}(p_2^\lambda)/\mathrm{d}\lambda = 0$, i.e. when

$$\lambda q\,(\lambda q + vb^2v_1v_{x_2})\,[\lambda^2q + \lambda qb^2v_1v_{x_2} + b^2v_1^2v_{x_2}] + (\lambda^2q + b^2v_1^2v_{x_2})\,[-\lambda^2q^2 + qb^2v_1v_{x_2}\,(v_1(1 - vb^2v_{x_2}) - 2\lambda v)\,] = 0$$

which can be rearranged as a cubic expression in λ:

$$\varphi(\lambda) = qv_1\,(1-\lambda)\lambda^2 - vb^2v_1v_{x_2}\lambda + b^2v_1^2v_{x_2}\,(1 - vb^2v_{x_2}) = 0 \quad (12.15)$$

We now show in lemma 4 that under certain conditions φ is positive at $\lambda = 0$ and negative at $\lambda = 1$, implying that there must be at least one turning point for $\mathrm{var}(p_2^\lambda)$ in the interval $0 < \lambda < 1$. In lemma 5, we state the conditions under which there is not more than one turning point, implying that $\mathrm{var}(p_2^\lambda)$ is minimized at $\lambda = 1$. In lemma 6 we show that, even if the condition in lemma 4 is violated, there is still a condition that will ensure $\mathrm{var}(p_2^\lambda)$ is minimized at $\lambda = 1$.

Lemma 4 If $(1 - vb^2v_{x_2}) > 0$, $\mathrm{var}(p_2^\lambda)$ has a maximum in the range $0 < \lambda < 1$.

Proof From (12.14) and (12.12),

$$\frac{\mathrm{d}\ \mathrm{var}\,(p_2^\lambda)}{\mathrm{d}\lambda}\Big|_{\lambda=0} = \frac{2qv}{v_1} \quad (12.16)$$

So if $(1 - b^2v_1v_{x_2}) > 0$ then $\mathrm{var}(p_2^\lambda)$ is rising at $\lambda = 0$.

$$\frac{\mathrm{d}\ \mathrm{var}\,(p_2^\lambda)}{\mathrm{d}\lambda}\Big|_{\lambda=1} = -\frac{2qb^2v_1^2v_{x_2}\,(1 + b^2v_1v_{x_2})}{q + vb^2v_1v_{x_2}} < 0 \quad (12.17)$$

So $\mathrm{var}(p_2^\lambda)$ is falling at $\lambda = 1$. ||

Lemma 5 If $q < 3vb^2v_{x_2}$, $\varphi(\lambda) = 0$ has only one solution in the range $0 < \lambda < 1$.

Proof It is sufficient to show that $\mathrm{d}\varphi/\mathrm{d}\lambda$ is always negative. From (12.15),

$$d\varphi/d\lambda = qv_1(2 - 3\lambda)\lambda - vb^2v_1v_{x_2}$$

The function $d\varphi/d\lambda$ will itself achieve a maximum value at $\lambda = 1/3$. But at $\lambda = 1/3$, $d\varphi/d\lambda < 0$, if $q < 3vb^2v_{x_2}$. So provided the condition is satisfied, $\varphi(\lambda)$ will always be falling over the interval $0 < \lambda < 1$, and can only have one solution to $\varphi(\lambda) = 0$ over this interval. ||

Lemma 6 If $(1 - vb^2v_{x_2}) < 0$, then $\varphi(\lambda) = 0$ has no solutions in the range $0 < \lambda < 1$, if $q < 3vb^2v_{x_2}$.

Proof If $(1 - vb^2v_{x_2}) > 0$, then from (12.16) $\varphi(0) < 0$. From (12.17) $\varphi(1) < 0$, so we need to find the conditions under which $d\varphi/d\lambda < 0$. From lemma 5, $d\varphi/d\lambda < 0$ if $q < 3vb^2v_{x_2}$. ||

Hence if the conditions in lemmas 4 and 5 or in lemma 6 are satisfied, the variance of retrade prices is minimized at $\lambda = 1$. Further, from proposition 2c these conditions will ensure that the public disclosure of information will minimize retrade variance. QED

Proof of proposition 4

We can write two special cases of (12.9a) when $\lambda = 0$ and $\lambda = 1$:

$$\text{var}\,[\,(1 + r)^2p_1^\lambda|\lambda = 0] = \left[\frac{b^3v^2v_{x_2}}{1 + b^2vv_{x_2}}\right]^2 v_{x_1} \tag{12.18}$$

$$\text{var}\,[\,(1 + r)^2p_1^\lambda|\lambda = 1] = b^2\left[q + \frac{b^2v_1^2v_{x_2}}{1 + b^2v_1v_{x_2}}\right]^2 v_{x_1} \tag{12.19}$$

Part (i) From (12.9b) and (12.19),

$$\text{var}\,[\,(1 + r)^2p_1] > \text{var}\,[\,(1 + r)^2p_1^\lambda|\lambda = 1]$$

$$\text{iff} \quad v_\theta + \frac{b^2v_\epsilon^2v_{x_2}}{1 + b^2v_\epsilon v_{x_2}} > q + \frac{b^2v_1^2v_{x_2}}{1 + b^2v_1v_{x_2}}$$

and we have $v_1 = v_\epsilon + v_{\theta*}$ and $v_\theta = q + v_{\theta*}$, so

$$\text{iff} \quad v_{\theta*}\left\{1 - \frac{b^2v_{x_2}\,[2v_\epsilon + v_{\theta*} + b^2v_\epsilon v_{x_2}(v_\epsilon + v_{\theta*})\,]}{(1 + b^2v_\epsilon v_{x_2})\,(1 + b^2v_1v_{x_2})}\right\} > 0$$

but the LHS reduces to $v_{\theta*}/(1 + b^2v_\epsilon v_{x_2})\,(1 + b^2v_1v_{x_2}) > 0$. QED

Part (ii) From (12.18) and (12.19),

$$\text{var}\,[\,(1 + r)^2p_1|\lambda = 1] > \text{var}\,[\,(1 + r)^2p_1|\lambda = 0]$$

$$\text{iff} \quad q + \frac{b^2 v_1^2 v_{x_2}}{1 + b^2 v_1 v_{x_2}} > \frac{b^2 v^2 v_{x_2}}{1 + b^2 v v_{x_2}}$$

i.e.

$$\text{iff} \quad \frac{v_1 (1 + b^2 v_1 v_{x_2}) + q (1 + b^2 v_1 v_{x_2}) - v_1 (1 + b^2 v_1 v_{x_2} + b^2 q v_{x_2})}{(1 + b^2 v_1 v_{x_2}) (1 + b^2 v v_{x_2})} > 0$$

which is always satisfied. QED

Notes

This Chapter was presented at the ESRC New Technologies and the Firm Initiative, Brunel University, 24–5 May 1990, and represents research undertaken on the ESRC project 'Stock market valuation of research and development'.

1 Statement of Standard Accounting Practices 13 (SSAP 13) relates to the treatment of R&D expenditure in the audited published accounts.

References

Black, J. M. and Tonks, I. (1990a) 'Asset price volatility under asymmetric information', *Economic Journal*, Conference Supplement, 100, 67–77.

Black, J. M. and Tonks, I. (1990b) 'Portfolio allocation and equilibrium prices when institutional investors can gain inside information', Exeter University Centre for Research in Accounting and Finance, discussion paper 9004.

Brander, J. and Spencer, B. (1983) 'Strategic commitment with R & D: the symmetric case', *Bell Journal of Economics*, 14, 225–35.

Diamond, D. (1985) 'On the optimal release of information by firms', *Journal of Finance*, 40, 1071–94.

Gonedes, N. J. (1980) 'Public disclosure rules, private information-production decisions, and capital market equilibrium', *Journal of Accounting Research*, 18, 441–76.

Grossman, S. J. and Stiglitz, J. E. (1980) 'The impossibility of informationally efficient markets', *American Economic Review*, 70, 393–408.

Hakansson, N. H., Kunkel, J. G. and Ohlson,J. A. (1983) 'Sufficient and necessary conditions for information to have social value in pure exchange', *Journal of Finance*, 37, 1169–81.

Hirshleifer, J. (1971) 'The private and social value of information and the reward to inventive activity', *American Economic Review*, 61, 561–74.

Trueman, B. (1984) 'Optimality of the disclosure of private information in a production–exchange economy', *Journal of Finance*, 38, 913–24.

Verrecchia, R. E. (1983) 'Discretionary disclosure', *Journal of Accounting and Economics*, 5, 179–194.

13 Persistence in UK Stock Market Returns: Aggregated and Disaggregated Perspectives

Ronald MacDonald and David Power

1 INTRODUCTION

Persistence in stock market returns is an extremely topical and important issue in the current finance literature. A number of researchers have demonstrated, using US data, that stock returns are predictable for both short and long horizons (see, *inter alia*, Fama and French 1988; Lo and Mackinley 1988; Poterba and Summers 1988). For example, Fama and French (1988) report that 24–45 per cent of the variation in three- to five-year stock returns is predictable from past returns. Such findings seem to conflict with the results in the earlier empirical literature summarized by Fama (1970), which confirmed the belief of many researchers that share prices follow a random walk.[1] The type of persistence that researchers have recently reported is generally of the mean-reverting variety, whereby negative autocorrelations are commonly found for long horizons. The picture is unfortunately complicated by the fact that positive autocorrelations are sometimes reported for short horizons.

The first objective of the chapter is to undertake two types of persistence test for a UK database. We examine monthly share return data from the London Share Price Database (LSPD) for the period 1966–88 at both an aggregated and a disaggregated level. This analysis should help to determine the extent of persistence in UK share returns and whether the degree of persistence differs according to the level of aggregation. There are good reasons for believing that aggregation may affect the outcome. For example, arbitrageurs should be more skilled at correcting mispricing arising from trading in individual securities than at taking positions in the entire market to offset persistent under- or overvaluation.

A second objective is to test a trading rule which seeks to exploit any mean-reverting tendencies in share returns. Such a strategy was first examined in the UK by Jones et al. (1976) and in the USA by Beaver and Landsman (1981). In a comprehensive examination of US data, De Bondt and Thaler (1985, 1987) established that systematic price reversals seem to exist for 'winner' and 'loser' company portfolios which are not apparently explained by changes in size or risk. Their results indicate that portfolios formed on the basis of extreme past returns tend to experience a reversal of fortune. Shares of winner (loser) companies which have performed outstandingly well (poorly) in the past tend to have more average returns in the future.

There has been remarkable consistency between De Bondt and Thaler's findings and the results of other US investigations of the same phenomena, including studies by Howe (1986) and West (1988). More recent evidence from Lehmann (1990) and Zarowin (1989a, 1990) documents mean reversion in share returns over shorter time horizons.

The remainder of this chapter is organized as follows. Section 2 outlines the methodology and examines the results, using UK data, of two tests of persistence in share returns: the variance ratio test and the rescaled range test. Section 3 investigates whether the winner–loser effect exists for shares traded on the London Stock Exchange. The methodology is outlined and the results discussed against a background of findings from the US. Section 4 offers some preliminary conclusions.

2 PERSISTENCE TESTS AND RESULTS

2.1 Variance ratio test

In this section we briefly outline the test statistics used to measure persistence. The first test which we consider is the variance ratio test originally proposed by Cochrane (1988). This test may be explained in the following way. We define the continuously compounded return (exclusive of dividend payments) X_t as

$$X_t = \ln P_t - \ln P_{t-1} \tag{13.1}$$

where P denotes the stock price. Assuming that returns may be modelled as a Wold process, we have

$$X_t = c(L)\epsilon_t \tag{13.2}$$

where $c(L) = 1 + c_1 L + c_2 L^2 + c_3 L^3 + \ldots$ is an infinite polynomial in the lag operator and ϵ_t is a white noise process with variance σ^2. It is useful to put some structure on this representation by modelling the log of the stock price as

$$p_t = z_t + v_t \tag{13.3}$$

where $p_t = \ln P_t$; v_t is a covariance stationary process, which has the interpretation of a cyclical component; and z_t is a random walk process described by the infinite sum of the moving average components,

$$z_t = z_{t-1} + c(1)\epsilon_t, \quad c(1) = 1 + c_1 + c_2 + \ldots \tag{13.4}$$

Hence z_t is given the interpretation of the permanent component. In this part of the chapter we are interested in discerning how important this random walk, or permanent component, actually is in the determination of stock prices. Recently it has become fashionable to test for random walks in a variety of economic series, from GNP (see, for example, Stock and Watson 1986) through to exchange rates (see, for example, Corbae and Ouliaris 1986) using the Dickey-Fuller or modified Dickey-Fuller unit root tests. But it is now widely accepted (see, for example, Cochrane 1988) that such tests have extremely low power in this regard. Since a series with a unit root is equivalent to a series composed of a unit root and a stationary component, such tests do not give an indication of how important the random walk component is to the behaviour of the series. In order to capture the importance of the random walk component we assume that 2π times the spectral density function of X_t at frequency zero is well defined and may be written as

$$S(0) = \gamma_0 + 2\sum_{j=1}^{\infty} \gamma_i \tag{13.5}$$

where γ_i is the covariance at lag i of X. The spectral procedure can therefore be thought of as estimation of the term

$$s(0) = S(0)/\gamma_0 = 1 + 2\sum_{i=1}^{\infty} \rho_i \tag{13.6}$$

where ρ_i represents the autocorrelation coefficient at lag i of the first difference of the stock price X_t. It is easily demonstrated that the $c(1)$ term from our permanent/transitory model is described by

$$c(1) = [s(0)]^{1/2} [\gamma_0/\sigma^2]^{1/2} \tag{13.7}$$

and so

$$s(0) = \mathrm{var}(z_t - z_{t-1})/\gamma_0 \tag{13.8}$$

Hence $s(0)$ may be interpreted as the ratio of the variance of the change in the permanent component of the stock price to the variance of the actual change. If a series is a pure random walk, this variance ratio should be one. Alternatively, if the variance of the numerator is zero, the series is stationary. It is worth noting the usefulness of this procedure as a way of determining the importance of the random walk component. First, the measure is a *long-run* measure because it utilizes *all* of the autocorrelations of X_t and not just those close to lags zero (which would be the traditional way of determining randomness). This may be potentially important, as we shall see below, because the pattern of long autocorrelations may have an important bearing on whether X_t is mean-reverting or not. Second, and in contrast to standard unit root tests, the statistic (13.8) can shed light on the *extent* to which the series deviates from the extremes of random walk or stationary behaviour. For example, values of $s(0)$ less than 1 indicate that a majority of autocorrelations of returns must be negative, which in turn is indicative of mean reversion; it implies that an increase in the level of the current stock price will be reversed by decreases in the future. In contrast, evidence against mean reversion would be reflected in a value of $s(0)$ above unity; a current increase in the value of the stock price will be reinforced in the future by further positive increases.

2.2 Rescaled range test

In addition to estimating the variance ratio (13.8) we also estimate an alternative measure of persistence, the rescaled range statistic. This measure, first proposed by Hurst (1951) and subsequently developed and refined by Mandelbrot (1972, 1975) has its origins in the field of hydrology, where it was developed to study river flow and dam overflow. Mandelbrot (1972, 1975) has demonstrated that this is a more powerful test of long-term persistence, such as non-periodic cycles, than an alternative measure such as autocorrelation or spectral analysis. To detect such persistence Mandelbrot suggests using the range over standard deviation statistic Q, also called the rescaled range.

The rescaled range statistic is the range of partial sums of deviations of a time series from its mean, rescaled by some measure of standard deviation. To construct this statistic, consider a sample of returns $X_1, X_2, \ldots, X_n$ and let $\bar{X}_n$ denote the sample mean $(1/n)\Sigma_j X_j$. Then

$$Q_n = \frac{1}{\hat{\sigma}_n(k)}\left[\max_{1 \leq S \leq n} \sum_{j=1}^{k} (X_j - \bar{X}_n) - \max_{1 \leq S \leq n} \sum_{j=1}^{k} (X_j - \bar{X}_n)\right] \qquad (13.9)$$

In his original work, Mandelbrot suggested using the sample standard deviation estimator for the scaling factor, $\hat{\sigma}_n$. However, Lo (1988) has demonstrated that this statistic may be significantly biased when X_t exhibits short-run dependence. Given the mounting evidence to indicate that stock returns do exhibit short-run dependence in the form of heteroscedasticity or autocorrelation, it is important to account for this dependence. One way of accommodating a broad class of short-term dependence, under the null hypothesis, would be to use (13.6), estimated with an appropriate lag truncation, for the scaling factor:

$$\hat{\sigma}_n^2 = \hat{\sigma}_x^2 + 2\sum_{j=1}^{k} \omega_j(k)\,\hat{\gamma}_j, \quad \omega_j(k) \equiv 1 - \frac{j}{k+1}, \quad k < n \tag{13.10}$$

where $\hat{\sigma}_x^2$ and $\hat{\gamma}_j$ are the sample variance and autocovariance estimators of X_t, and the weighting scheme is that proposed by Newey and West (1987). Phillips (1987) demonstrates under what conditions $\hat{\sigma}_n^2$ will be consistent. These conditions are sufficiently general to allow the errors, the ϵs, in (13.2) to be heterogeneous (in other words, a wide variety of heteroscedastic processes) and have a degree of dependence, whilst still permitting some law of large numbers and the (functional) central limit theorem to obtain. Lo (1988) demonstrates that the statistic $V = \hat{Q}/\sqrt{n}$ converges to a well-defined random variable under the null hypothesis of short-term dependence; it converges weakly to the range of a Brownian bridge under general forms of weak dependence.

One particularly appealing feature of the statistic (13.9) constructed using (13.10) is that since it incorporates a moment condition it allows for strong mixing (or short-term dependence) and heterogeneously distributed errors. It therefore enables a researcher to identify whether the results of a study like that of Poterba and Summers (1988) do in fact indicate substantial long-term dependence or whether such tests simply detect short-term dependence. Lo (1988) has demonstrated for US data that the latter is indeed the case. The distinction is important because strongly dependent processes behave in a very different manner from weakly dependent processes: their spectral densities at frequency zero are either unbounded or zero; their partial sums do not converge in distribution at the same rate as weakly dependent series; and graphically their behaviour exhibits cyclical patterns of all kinds, some of which are indistinguishable from trends.

2.3 Persistence Results

All data are from the LSPD and consist of two types of continuously compounded return series. The first data set consists of monthly returns of various aggregate indices over the period May 1962 to December 1987. The second group consists of monthly returns of 40 individual firms for the period January 1968 to December 1987. The returns in this second set have been chosen at random to ensure that all of the main industrial classifications are represented. The former set of returns is exclusive of dividend payments, whilst the latter includes dividends.[2]

In table 13.1 we present some descriptive statistics for the aggregate

Table 13.1 Descriptive statistics for a selection of UK stock returns, monthly 1962(5)–1987(12)

	SD	*AC*1	*AC*2	*AC*3	*AC*4	*PP*(NT)	*PP*(T)
CAP	0.08	0.124	−0.092	0.061	0.006	−16.55	−15.27
CON	0.06	0.094	−0.036	0.115	0.050	−15.79	−15.95
FIV	0.06	0.111	−0.073	0.117	0.048	−15.90	−15.95
FIN	0.07	0.139	−0.083	0.075	−0.005	−15.99	−15.11
ALL	0.06	0.119	−0.078	0.117	0.028	−15.92	−15.44
CCO	0.09	0.201	−0.052	0.026	−0.051	−15.46	−13.92
MOT	0.08	0.175	0.063	0.076	−0.037	−14.05	−14.74
BRD	0.06	0.029	−0.035	0.028	0.088	−16.91	−17.05
LEI	0.08	0.109	−0.006	0.138	0.023	−15.12	−15.71
CHE	0.06	0.068	−0.078	0.079	0.017	−17.22	−16.28
SHI	0.07	0.063	−0.025	0.035	0.038	−17.91	−16.37
BAN	0.08	0.052	−0.054	0.057	0.005	−17.01	−16.56
INS	0.08	0.037	−0.117	0.104	0.057	−17.57	−17.04

SD denotes standard deviation. *AC*1 through *AC*4 denote, respectively, autocorrelations 1 to 4. *PP* denotes a Dickey-Fuller *t* ratio adjusted for non-LID errors as suggested by Phillips and Perron (1988); the letters NT in parentheses after *PP* indicate that a linear time trend was not included in the regression, while T denotes that such a trend was included. The 5 per cent critical value for the *PP* statistic is −2.88. The mnemonics of the industrial classifications indices have the following interpretation:

CAP capital group
CON consumer group
FIV FT 500 share index
FIN financial group
ALL FT all share index
CCO contracting, construction group
MOT motor group
BRD brewers and distillers group
LEI leisure group
CHE chemicals group
SHI shipping and transport group
BAN banking group
INS insurance group

indices.[3] The monthly standard deviation of the aggregate indices averages around 7 per cent. Also reported in this table are the first four autocorrelations. On the basis of this evidence it is clear that there is very little autocorrelation in the series. For our sample size the standard error of the reported autocorrelations will be approximately 0.06. Some (three in total) of these autocorrelations are occasionally greater than twice this magnitude, but not by very much. Furthermore, there is little evidence of mean reversion in the data in that the preponderance of estimated autocorrelations are positive.

In the final columns of the table we present Dickey-Fuller statistics, modified along the lines suggested by Phillips and Perron (1988), which facilitate testing the null hypothesis that our returns series each contain a unit root. All of these statistics are strongly significant, allowing us to reject the null hypothesis that all the series contain a unit root in favour of the alternative hypothesis that they are stationary. Working back from this result, we strongly suspect that an equivalent test on the underlying price series would not allow rejection of the null; unfortunately, these data were not available to us. But, as we have indicated, such tests are not very interesting since they do not tell us the magnitude of the random walk component in stock prices or (if it exists) the degree of stationarity of returns.

In order to implement (13.6), the variance ratio statistic, the lag length has to be truncated. Here we use a standard estimator, namely

$$\hat{s}(0) = 1 + 2\sum_{j=1}^{k} \omega_j \rho_j \tag{13.11}$$

where the weights are those suggested by Newey and West (1987): $\omega_j^k = [1 - j(k+1)^{-1}]$. In table 13.2 we present our estimates of (13.11) for the aggregate indicates using a number of different values of k. The first thing to note about these results is the generally hump-shaped pattern for our estimates of $s(0)$. For example, in the case of the capital goods sector grouping the ratio initially rises above one, but by the end of the first year has returned to a unitary value and thereafter continually falls through to lag 60. Such behaviour indicates initial positive autocorrelation in returns which is more than fully offset at longer lags (i.e. beyond a year) by negative autocorrelation, revealing that there is considerable evidence to indicate mean reversion for periods beyond a year. Indeed from our earlier interpretation of the variance ratio we find that, on average, the permanent component of returns is 60 per cent of the variance of actual returns. This in turn suggests that a substantial component (40 per cent) of the variance of actual returns is composed of a transitory element; it would therefore seem that an important element of stock returns, and hence prices, can be predicted. Clearly, such findings are of considerable interest from an economic perspective; but are they significant from a statistical perspective?

The standard errors below the variance ratios indicate that in all cases the ratios differ significantly from zero at conventional significance levels. However, for variance ratios down to 12 lags, in no case can we reject the hypothesis that the ratio differs significantly from unity. At lag 60 there are three ratios which do differ significantly from unity (this represents 23 per cent of the total) but overall these results are similar to those down to a year. In the majority of cases, therefore, we cannot reject, from a statistical perspective, the hypothesis that stock returns are stationary.

Table 13.2 Variance ratios, estimated using $s(0)$, for a selection of UK stock returns, monthly 1962(5)–1987(12)

	Lag length							
	2	4	8	12	24	36	48	60
CAP	1.098	1.135	1.053	1.020	0.832	0.643	0.520	0.513
	(0.12)	(0.16)	(0.20)	(0.24)	(0.27)	(0.25)	(0.23)	(0.26)
CON	1.094	1.212	1.202	1.832	1.051	0.900	0.784	0.791
	(0.12)	(0.18)	(0.23)	(0.28)	(0.34)	(0.35)	(0.35)	(0.39)
FIV	1.094	1.199	1.165	1.140	0.977	0.803	0.671	0.674
	(0.12)	(0.17)	(0.23)	(0.27)	(0.31)	(0.32)	(0.30)	(0.34)
FIN	1.119	1.169	1.109	1.103	0.932	0.820	0.719	0.691
	(0.13)	(0.17)	(0.22)	(0.26)	(0.30)	(0.32)	(0.33)	(0.35)
ALL	1.100	1.196	1.151	1.129	0.949	0.776	0.651	0.650
	(0.12)	(0.17)	(0.22)	(0.26)	(0.31)	(0.31)	(0.29)	(0.33)
CCO	1.229	1.257	1.114	1.128	0.793	0.601	0.475	0.424*
	(0.14)	(0.18)	(0.22)	(0.26)	(0.25)	(0.23)	(0.21)	(0.21)
MOT	1.272	1.399	1.466	1.538	1.561	1.324	1.066	0.953
	(0.14)	(0.20)	(0.28)	(0.35)	(0.50)	(0.52)	(0.48)	(0.48)
BRD	1.009	1.056	1.058	1.064	0.977	0.817	0.690	0.633
	(0.11)	(0.15)	(0.21)	(0.25)	(0.32)	(0.32)	(0.31)	(0.32)
LEI	1.133	1.279	1.295	1.306	1.106	0.873	0.716	0.677
	(0.13)	(0.18)	(0.25)	(0.30)	(0.35)	(0.34)	(0.32)	(0.34)
CHE	1.035	1.081	1.009	0.962	0.824	0.671	0.583	0.578
	(0.12)	(0.15)	(0.20)	(0.22)	(0.27)	(0.26)	(0.26)	(0.29)
SHI	1.070	1.118	0.961	0.892	0.758	0.627	0.536	0.485*
	(0.12)	(0.16)	(0.19)	(0.21)	(0.24)	(0.25)	(0.24)	(0.24)
BAN	1.025	1.058	0.988	1.004	0.864	0.675	0.538	0.498*
	(0.12)	(0.15)	(0.19)	(0.23)	(0.28)	(0.26)	(0.24)	(0.25)
INS	0.959	1.012	0.980	0.934	0.809	0.761	0.691	0.690
	(0.10)	(0.15)	(0.19)	(0.21)	(0.26)	(0.29)	(0.31)	(0.35)

Numbers in parentheses are asymptotic standard errors calculated using the formula $s(0)/\sqrt{[3T/4(k+1)]}$.

In table 13.3 we repeat the above exercise for our individual company returns. Such disaggregated data are of interest for two reasons. First, they should help to illuminate any firm-specific factors at work which tend to get washed out of the aggregate indices because of diversification. Second, as Poterba and Summers (1988) have noted, investors should find it easier to arbitrage any mispricing rapidly away at the individual firm level, compared with the aggregate level; the transitory component is expected to be of a lesser order of magnitude for individual returns. Although there is a wide variety of behaviour exhibited at the firm level, some form of mean reversion is displayed in the vast majority of cases (either continuous mean reversion or mean reversion after a movement of the ratio above one). On the basis of the reported standard errors, most of the ratios in question are statistically different from zero, and eleven ratios (28 per cent of the total) are significantly different from one after 60 months, a proportion which is slightly larger than that for the aggregate series. Interestingly, the ratios that are significantly different from one are fairly evenly spread across the different industrial groupings.

In table 13.4 for the aggregate data we report our estimates of the rescaled range statistic, computed with both the sample standard deviation and the moment estimator described above, which is robust to short-term dependence.[4] Hence we have to two sets of hypotheses: the first consists of the null of no temporal dependence against the alternative of long-term persistence, and the second consists of the null of short-term dependence against the alternative of long-term dependence. It is interesting to note that, irrespective of the degree of temporal dependence captured in the null, none of the statistics is significant. This result is repeated in table 13.5 for the disaggregated indices. Such findings indicate that monthly UK stock returns do not contain long-term memory.

3 TESTING THE WINNER–LOSER EFFECT

The mean reversion which we found in the results from the tests described in the previous section has been attributed by De Bondt and Thaler to an initial overreaction by investors which subsequently corrects itself. In support of the overreaction hypothesis, De Bondt and Thaler quote Keynes's belief in the tendency of investors to weight 'the facts of the existing situation' disproportionately in the formation of long-term expectations, assuming that 'the existing state of affairs will continue indefinitely, except in so far as we have specific reason to expect a change' (Keynes 1936: 148, 152). They also cite research from the area of cognitive psychology which suggests that individuals tend to overweight current information and disregard prior data in violation of Bayes's rule (Kahneman and Tversky 1973). This argument may be illustrated by a simple example. Consider a company which until this year has had earnings similar to the industry average but suddenly reports a large jump in profits. The overreaction hypothesis argues that there will be an exaggerated response by investors to the increase in earnings when they extrapolate into the future on the basis of the higher current profits and, in consequence, bid up share price (De Bondt and Thaler 1990). Since future reported profits turn out to be less than expected, investors recognize their mistake and the share price falls.

The winner–loser effect is therefore readily explained with the help of such

Table 13.3 Variance ratios for a selection of disaggregated UK stock returns, 1968(1)–1987(12)

Company	Grouping	Lag 2	4	8	12	24	36	48	60
Aaronson Bros	CAP	1.07	1.08	1.06	1.08	1.03	0.92	0.72	0.58
		(0.14)	(0.18)	(0.24)	(0.29)	(0.38)	(0.42)	(0.37)	(0.34)
Alliance Trust	FIN	0.98	0.98	0.90	0.93	0.78	0.64	0.65	0.66
		(0.13)	(0.16)	(0.20)	(0.25)	(0.28)	(0.29)	(0.37)	(0.38)
Anchor Chemical	O	0.88	0.84	0.84	0.92	1.01	1.05	1.20	1.26
		(0.11)	(0.14)	(0.19)	(0.25)	(0.38)	(0.48)	(0.63)	(0.73)
Aquascutum	CD	0.79	0.78	0.73	0.70	0.80	0.82	0.77	0.70
		(0.10)	(0.13)	(0.16)	(0.19)	(0.29)	(0.36)	(0.40)	(0.41)
Bass	CND	0.92	0.91	0.86	0.86	0.83	0.78	0.64	.54
		(0.12)	(0.15)	(0.19)	(0.22)	(0.31)	(0.35)	(0.34)	(0.32)
Berisford (S&W)	CND	0.97	0.98	0.96	0.98	0.81	0.08	0.44	0.36*
		(0.12)	(0.16)	(0.21)	(0.26)	(0.30)	(0.26)	(0.23)	(0.21)
Bestwood PLC	O	1.05	1.15	1.21	1.30	1.38	1.15	0.79	0.59
		(0.14)	(0.19)	(0.27)	(0.35)	(0.52)	(0.52)	(0.41)	(0.34)
Braithwaite Group	CAP	1.02	1.06	1.15	1.15	0.97	0.63	0.28	0.16*
		(0.13)	(0.18)	(0.26)	(0.31)	(0.36)	(0.28)	(0.15)	(0.09)
BSG	CD	1.13	1.23	1.40	1.62	1.86	1.67	1.30	0.94
		(0.15)	(0.21)	(0.31)	(0.44)	(0.69)	(0.75)	(0.68)	(0.54)
Coalite group	O	0.98	0.92	0.84	0.71	0.61	0.69	0.73	0.71
		(0.13)	(0.15)	(0.18)	(0.19)	(0.22)	(0.32)	(0.38)	(0.41)
Corah PLC	CND	0.88	0.86	0.69	0.72	0.69	0.61	0.54	0.52
		(0.11)	(0.13)	(0.15)	(0.19)	(0.26)	(0.28)	(0.28)	(0.30)
Crystalate Group	CD	0.78	0.88	0.94	0.94	0.99	0.99	0.94	0.81
		(0.10)	(0.15)	(0.21)	(0.25)	(0.37)	(0.45)	(0.48)	(0.47)
Davy Group PLC	CAP	1.11	1.03	1.06	1.09	0.86	0.68	0.62	0.55
		(0.11)	(0.17)	(0.24)	(0.29)	(0.32)	(0.31)	(0.33)	(0.32)
Devenish	CND	1.02	1.03	1.17	1.26	1.19	1.00	0.89	0.84
		(0.13)	(0.17)	(0.26)	(0.34)	(0.44)	(0.45)	(0.47)	(0.49)
Equity and Law	FIN	0.95	0.98	0.96	1.00	0.89	0.93	1.03	1.09
		(0.12)	(0.16)	(0.21)	(0.27)	(0.33)	(0.42)	(0.54)	(0.64)
ERF Holdings	CD	0.83	0.82	0.91	0.98	1.23	1.26	1.06	0.83
		(0.11)	(0.14)	(0.20)	(0.26)	(0.46)	(0.37)	(0.55)	(0.48)
Fisher and Son	O	0.92	0.94	0.98	1.15	1.57	1.80	1.82	1.72
		(0.11)	(0.15)	(0.22)	(0.31)	(0.56)	(0.81)	(0.95)	(1.00)
Garthmore Am. Sec.	FIN	0.99	1.01	0.96	0.98	0.82	0.68	0.63	0.59
		(0.13)	(0.16)	(0.21)	(0.26)	(0.31)	(0.31)	(0.33)	(0.34)
Gaskell Boardloom	CD	0.97	0.91	0.91	1.00	0.86	0.70	0.52	0.38*
		(0.13)	(0.15)	(0.20)	(0.27)	(0.32)	(0.32)	(0.27)	(0.22)
General Accident	FIN	0.98	1.03	0.96	0.94	0.76	0.54	0.41	0.37*
		(0.12)	(0.17)	(0.22)	(0.28)	(0.28)	(0.40)	(0.21)	(0.22)
Glynwed	CAP	1.09	1.10	0.98	1.06	1.18	1.08	0.94	0.90
		(0.14)	(0.18)	(0.22)	(0.28)	(0.44)	(0.48)	(0.49)	(0.53)
Govett Strategic	FIN	1.01	1.02	0.93	0.92	0.73	0.61	0.65	0.63
		(0.13)	(0.17)	(0.21)	(0.25)	(0.27)	(0.28)	(0.34)	(0.36)

Table 13.3 *(cont.)*

Company	Grouping	Lag 2	4	8	12	24	36	48	60
Grampian Holdings	O	0.91	0.80	0.75	0.78	0.72	0.63	0.64	0.68
		(0.12)	(0.13)	(0.17)	(0.21)	(0.27)	(0.28)	(0.33)	(0.40)
Helene of London	CND	0.82	0.78	0.74	0.64	0.59	0.48	0.37	0.30*
		(0.11)	(0.13)	(0.17)	(0.18)	(0.22)	(0.22)	(0.19)	(0.18)
Kleinworth Charter	FIN	0.93	0.94	0.86	0.88	0.76	0.59	0.62	0.64
		(0.12)	(0.16)	(0.19)	(0.24)	(0.28)	(0.28)	(0.32)	(0.37)
Laing (John)	CAP	1.19	1.17	0.97	0.95	0.76	0.62	0.57	0.44*
		(0.15)	(0.20)	(0.22)	(0.25)	(0.28)	(0.28)	(0.29)	(0.26)
Laird Group	CAP	1.08	1.14	1.14	1.22	1.14	0.67	0.45	0.37*
		(0.14)	(0.18)	(0.26)	(0.33)	(0.43)	(0.30)	(0.23)	(0.21)
Macarthy Group	O	1.15	1.24	1.35	1.34	1.20	0.81	0.47	0.32
		(0.15)	(0.21)	(0.30)	(0.36)	(0.45)	(0.37)	(0.28)	(0.58)
Mansfield Brewery	CND	1.26	1.46	1.66	1.85	2.16	2.06	1.84	1.70
		(0.16)	(0.24)	(0.37)	(0.49)	(0.81)	(0.93)	(0.96)	(0.99)
Parker Knoll	CD	1.05	1.11	1.27	1.37	1.31	0.85	0.49	0.42*
		(0.14)	(0.18)	(0.28)	(0.37)	(0.49)	(0.38)	(0.28)	(0.24)
Royal Insurance	FIN	1.00	1.06	1.03	1.01	0.84	0.70	0.51	0.40*
		(0.13)	(0.17)	(0.23)	(0.27)	(0.32)	(0.32)	(0.27)	(0.23)
Scott and Robertson	O	0.95	0.99	1.08	1.21	1.29	0.97	0.62	0.59
		(0.12)	(0.17)	(0.24)	(0.33)	(0.48)	(0.44)	(0.32)	(0.22)
Slingsby PLC	CAP	0.83	0.79	0.78	0.79	0.82	0.78	0.72	0.63
		(0.11)	(0.13)	(0.17)	(0.21)	(0.31)	(0.36)	(0.38)	(0.37)
Stormgaurd	CND	0.99	0.91	0.71	0.68	0.59	0.59	0.58	0.56
		(0.13)	(0.15)	(0.16)	(0.18)	(0.22)	(0.28)	(0.30)	(0.33)
Thorn EMI	CD	1.12	1.15	1.16	1.12	0.89	0.71	0.50	0.36*
		(0.14)	(0.19)	(0.26)	(0.30)	(0.33)	(0.32)	(0.26)	(0.21)
T & N PLC	CAP	1.00	1.04	0.99	0.92	0.77	0.68	0.62	0.50
		(0.13)	(0.17)	(0.22)	(0.25)	(0.28)	(0.31)	(0.32)	(0.29)
Unilever	CND	1.28	1.38	1.11	1.07	0.85	0.63	0.57	0.57
		(0.16)	(0.23)	(0.25)	(0.28)	(0.32)	(0.28)	(0.29)	(0.33)
Wade Potteries	O	0.84	0.88	0.81	0.81	0.77	0.65	0.49	0.38*
		(0.11)	(0.15)	(0.18)	(0.27)	(0.28)	(0.29)	(0.26)	(0.23)
Witan Investment	FIN	0.99	1.04	0.98	0.98	0.84	0.71	0.77	0.81
		(0.13)	(0.17)	(0.22)	(0.27)	(0.31)	(0.32)	(0.40)	(0.47)
W. and D. Brewery	CND	1.14	1.40	1.40	1.48	1.46	1.21	0.91	0.78
		(0.15)	(0.21)	(0.31)	(0.40)	(0.55)	(0.54)	(0.48)	(0.45)

Of industrial classifications mnemonics not already defined in table 13.1, CD denotes consumer durables, CND denotes consumer non-durables and O denotes other.

Table 13.4 Rescaled range statistics, scaled using the sample standard deviation and the square root of the spectral density function at frequency zero, for a selection of UK stock returns, monthly 1962(5)–1987(12)

	V	$V(2)$	$V(4)$	$V(8)$	$V(12)$
CAP	1.56	1.49	1.47	1.52	1.55
CON	1.73	1.66	1.58	1.58	1.60
FIV	1.74	1.67	1.60	1.62	1.64
FIN	1.56	1.48	1.45	1.49	1.49
ALL	1.70	1.63	1.56	1.59	1.61
CCO	1.36	1.23	1.22	1.27	1.28
MOT	1.78	1.58	1.51	1.47	1.44
BRD	1.48	1.49	1.45	1.45	1.44
LEI	1.53	1.44	1.36	1.35	1.34
CHE	1.59	1.57	1.54	1.59	1.63
SHI	0.95	0.92	0.89	0.96	1.00
BAN	1.33	1.32	1.29	1.34	1.33
INS	1.52	1.56	1.52	1.54	1.58

The V statistic is computed as $\sqrt{(R_n/n)}$, where R_n is the rescaled range statistic defined in the text. Numbers in parentheses after V denote the lag depth used in the calculation of the spectral density function. The 95 per cent confidence interval for V is (0.809, 1.862) (see Lo 1988).

behavioural and cognitive theories. Whether the individual invests or conducts some other evaluation of future prospects, he forecasts the future on the basis of the present. The winner share, once stereotyped, is not easily reclassified in spite of adverse outcomes until some major event leads to a correction of the underlying beliefs in its prospects. The opposite occurs for the shares of those companies in the loser portfolio once they are categorized as non-excellent; improvements in the earnings of the shares of loser companies are likely to be regarded as aberrations in the results of an enterprise where management's mediocrity is well established.

The method for investigating the winner–loser effect is as follows. Monthly share return data were again obtained from the LSPD for 1959 to 1985. For each three-year period beginning in January 1959, excess returns were calculated for every share with at least 36 months of return data, according to the equation

$$AR_{it} = R_{it} - R_{mt} \tag{13.12}$$

where AR_{it} is the excess return on share i for month t, R_{it} is the actual month t return for share i, and R_{mt} is the return on the FT all share index for share i. These monthly excess returns are summed over a three-year period and cumulative Excess Returns estimated as

Table 13.5 Rescaled range statistics for a selection of disaggregated UK stock returns, 1968(1)–1987(12)

Company	Grouping	V	$V(2)$	$V(4)$	$V(8)$	$V(12)$
Aaronson Bros	CAP	1.30	1.26	1.26	1.27	1.25
Alliance Trust	FIN	1.38	1.40	1.40	1.46	1.43
Anchor Chemical	O	1.41	1.51	1.54	1.55	1.48
Aquascutum	CD	1.24	1.39	1.41	1.45	1.48
Bass	CND	1.26	1.32	1.33	1.36	1.37
Berisford (S&W)	CND	1.15	1.17	1.16	1.78	1.16
Bestwood PLC	O	1.24	1.21	1.16	1.13	1.08
Braithwaite Group	CAP	1.19	1.18	1.16	1.12	1.12
BSG	CD	1.23	1.16	1.11	1.04	0.97
Coalite group	O	1.29	1.31	1.36	1.42	1.54
Corah PLC	CND	1.12	1.20	1.27	1.36	1.33
Crystalate Group	CD	1.43	1.62	1.53	1.48	1.48
Davy Group PLC	CAP	0.97	0.92	0.96	0.94	0.93
Devenish	CND	1.37	1.36	1.35	1.27	1.22
Equity and Law	FIN	1.49	1.54	1.52	1.53	1.49
ERF Holdings	CD	0.92	1.01	1.01	0.96	0.93
Fisher and Son	O	1.54	1.60	1.59	1.56	1.44
Garthmore Am. Sec.	FIN	1.36	1.36	1.36	1.38	1.38
Gaskell Boardloom	CD	1.15	1.16	1.21	1.21	1.15
General Accident	FIN	1.26	1.17	1.24	1.28	1.30
Glynwed	CAP	1.44	1.38	1.37	1.45	1.39
Govett Strategic	FIN	1.46	1.45	1.45	1.52	1.53
Grampian Holdings	O	1.03	1.08	1.15	1.18	1.16
Helene of London	CND	0.84	0.93	0.95	0.98	1.01
Kleinworth Charter	FIN	1.46	1.52	1.51	1.57	1.56
Laing (John)	CAP	1.04	0.95	0.95	1.06	1.07
Laird Group	CAP	1.12	1.08	1.05	1.05	1.02
Macarthy Group	O	1.11	1.03	0.99	0.96	0.96
Mansfield Brewery	CND	1.97	1.76	1.64	1.53	1.45
Parker Knoll	CD	1.03	1.01	0.98	0.91	0.88
Royal Insurance	FIN	1.23	1.22	1.19	1.21	1.22
Scott and Robertson	O	1.04	1.07	1.05	1.00	0.95
Slingsby PLC	CAP	1.02	1.12	1.15	1.16	1.16
Stormgaurd	CND	0.78	0.79	0.82	0.93	0.95
Thorn EMI	CD	1.21	1.14	1.13	1.13	1.15
T & N PLC	CAP	1.25	1.26	1.23	1.26	1.31
Unilever	CND	1.45	1.28	1.24	1.38	1.41
Wade Potteries	O	0.94	1.02	0.99	1.04	1.04
Witan Investment	FIN	1.44	1.45	1.41	1.46	1.45
W. and D. Brewery	CND	1.49	1.39	1.32	1.26	1.23

$$CAR_{it} = \sum_{t=1}^{36} AR_{it} \tag{13.13}$$

The cumulative excess returns are then ranked from high to low and portfolios are formed. Firms in the top 5 per cent of this ranking have their shares assigned to a winner portfolio, while the shares for firms in the bottom 5 per cent are combined to form a loser portfolio. This process is repeated for every three-year portfolio formation period, with each successive iteration beginning on 1 January in 1959, 1962, 1965, 1968, 1971, 1974, 1977 and 1980.

The cumulative excess returns for these winner and loser portfolio are then calculated over a three-year portfolio test period (CAR_W and CAR_L). If security returns are missing for any month subsequent to portfolio formation, then that share is dropped from the portfolio and the *CAR* is the average over the remaining available excess returns.[5]

Using the *CAR*s from the eight different test periods, average *CAR*s are estimated for both portfolios (ACR_W and ACR_L). The overreaction hypothesis predicts that average cumulative excess returns from purchasing the loser portfolio shares and selling short the shares in the winner portfolio will be positive, i.e.

$$ACR_L - ACR_W > 0$$

Figure 13.1 shows the average cumulative excess returns for both portfolios. As the overreaction hypothesis predicts, a strategy based on the short selling of shares which have outperformed the market in the portfolio formation period, and the purchase of shares which have previously underperformed the market, achieved excellent results on average. The average cumulative excess return for the eight test periods was a statistically significant 29.15 per cent ($t = 2.96$). This outcome compares with an average return difference of 24.5 per cent over three years for the portfolios in De Bondt and Thaler's US study. However, the favourable performance of the mean-reverting trading strategy is not uniform across all subperiods (see table 13.6). In six of the test periods the *CAR* was positive, while for 1971–3 and 1980–2 the mean portfolio returns arising from this contrarian strategy underperformed the market.

In common with De Bondt and Thaler (1985) and Zarowin (1989a) we find a January effect in which average excess returns for January are significantly different from the monthly excess returns for the rest of the sample. The average *CAR* in January was 3.09 per cent compared with a *CAR* of 0.62 per cent for the other months.

Although the portfolio strategy appears profitable, this conclusion may change once risk is taken into account.[6] However, the usual procedure for estimating risk using a market model based on prior periods returns is

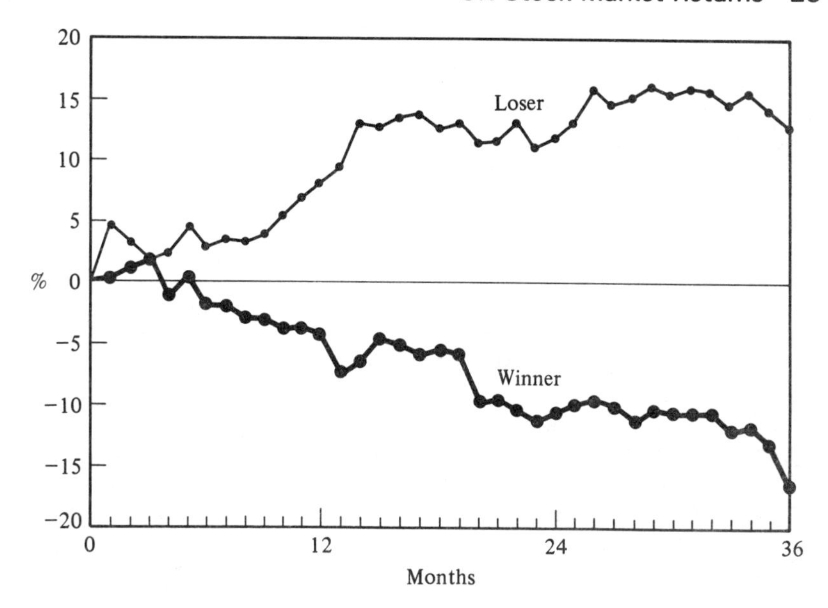

Figure 13.1 Average cumulative excess returns for winner and loser portfolios

inappropriate for this study. Chan (1988) and Ball and Kothari (1990) have documented evidence from US data of the non-stationarity of beta over the portfolio formation and test period. They argue that as the market value of loser portfolio shares diminishes over the test period, the financial gearing of these compánies rises, increasing the market risk. The opposite result occurs for the shares in the winner portfolio, with the reverse argument being applied.[7] Unless this change in risk is accounted for, the beta of the losers (winners) will tend to be underestimated (overestimated), yielding possibly spurious abnormal returns.

To overcome this problem we account for risk using the following equation which simultaneously estimates beta and abnormal returns:

$$R_{pt} - R_{ft} = \alpha_p + \beta_p \, (R_{mt} - R_{pt}) \tag{13.14}$$

where R_{ft} is an adjusted three-month Treasury bill rate, and α_p is the monthly abnormal return for portfolio p (p = W for winners and L for losers).

The results for a period cross-sectional time series regression, with a correction for autocorrelation using a Kalman filter maximum likelihood estimator, are shown in table 13.7. As expected, the average monthly abnormal return is mainly negative for the winner portfolio's shares and positive for the shares in the loser portfolio, implying a positive abnormal return for

Table 13.6 Cumulative and average excess returns for arbitrage portfolios

Portfolio formation year	Portfolio test year	No. of companies	Average monthly[a] excess returns *AR* (%)	Cumulative[b] excess returns *CAR* (%)
1959–61	1962–64	63	0.180 (0.41)	6.49
1962–64	1965–67	63	0.482 (1.05)	17.34
1965–67	1968–70	61	0.673 (0.96)	24.22
1968–70	1971–73	51	−0.145 (−0.20)	−5.23
1971–73	1974–76	45	1.687 (2.61)[c]	60.71
1974–76	1977–79	70	2.280 (2.73)[c]	82.1
1977–79	1980–82	97	−0.329 (0.068)	−11.86
1980–82	1983–85	87	1.650 (2.66)[c]	59.42
Average				29.15

t statistics are in parentheses
[a]The results are given for the arbitrage portfolio AR_L-AR_W.
[b]The results are given for the arbitrage portfolio CAR_L-CAR_W.
[c]Significant at the 5 per cent level.

De Bondt and Thaler's trading strategy. The notable exceptions are again 1971–3 and 1980–2. In the former case both portfolios yield positive abnormal returns; however, the winner shares outperformed their loser counterparts. In the latter case, both portfolios significantly underperformed when measured against the risk being borne and the return earned by the market. In this instance, the average monthly abnormal loss was greater for the loser shares.

4 CONCLUDING COMMENTS

In this chapter we have been concerned to examine the existence and extent of mean reversion in UK stock returns using both aggregate and disaggregate data. The chapter is essentially in two parts. In the first part, mean reversion is examined from a statistical perspective using variance ratio and rescaled range tests. The former test indicates that a number of returns indices contain an important transitory mean-reverting element, although a low

Table 13.7 Abnormal return and risk for Winner and Loser Portfolios

Portfolio test period	Winner α	Winner β	Loser α	Loser β
1962–64	0.0033 (2.02)[a]	0.6895 (13.55)[a]	0.0048 (1.71)	0.7777 (9.10)[a]
1965–67	−0.0030 (−1.43)	0.9210 (17.20)[a]	0.0041 (1.66)	0.6750 (9.75)[a]
1968–70	−0.0014 (−1.16)	0.7514 (14.76)[a]	0.0075 (1.74)	0.4857 (5.51)[a]
1971–73	0.0080 (2.47)[a]	1.0237 (16.05)[a]	0.0058 (1.38)	1.1671 (14.04)[a]
1974–76	−0.0181 (−4.49)[a]	0.5460 (15.41)[a]	−0.0022 (−0.64)	0.6456 (20.51)[a]
1977–79	0.0012 (0.58)[a]	0.8465 (20.34)[a]	0.0221 (6.23)[a]	0.9785 (12.33)[a]
1980–82	−0.0042 (−2.03)[a]	0.7030 (18.31)[a]	−0.0068 (−2.22)[a]	0.6549 (11.14)[a]
1983–85	−0.0051 (−2.42)[a]	0.8358 (18.41)[a]	0.0079 (2.31)[a]	1.0447 (12.38)[a]

t statistics are in parentheses.
[a]Significant at the 5 per cent level.

proportion of two ratios are statistically significant. The rescaled range tests indicates that for both the aggregate and the disaggregate data any dependence that does exist is of a short-term nature. In the second part of the paper, mean reversion is examined from the perspective of the winner–loser effect. Since the average cumulative excess return of operating a strategy of shorting winners and buying losers is a statistically significant 29.15 per cent, the evidence here strongly suggests the existence of mean reversion.

Our findings in the two parts of the chapter are therefore entirely complementary, since they both indicate mean reversion. Although the statistical significance of this result is much stronger for the winner–loser effect, this may simply reflect the different modelling strategy used to construct the portfolios and, in particular, the different sampling of the data. A further explanation for this finding may lie in the work of Zarowin (1989b, 1990). He argues that most of the impressive performance of the winner–loser effect can be explained by size differences amongst companies and by the abnormal return which is generally found in January. Once size and seasonality factors have been taken into account, mean reversion becomes insignificant. This is a topic we hope to pursue in future work.

Notes

We are grateful to Alasdair Lonie and Donald Sinclair for their helpful comments on an earlier draft of this chapter. The authors gratefully acknowledge financial support from E. S. R. L. grant number R000232727.

1 However, as Poterba and Summers (1988) and Fama and French (1988) have demonstrated, randomness of returns is neither necessary nor sufficient for stock market efficiency. For instance, predictability may be the result of time-varying equilibrium expected returns generated by rational pricing in an efficient market.
2 Since dividends are constant relative to price, we do not believe that this difference should not affect the comparability of the results.
3 To save space, the descriptive statistics for the individual company returns are not reported (in fact, these returns exhibit similiar properties to the aggregate data). These may be obtained from the authors on request.
4 The 95 per cent confidence interval for this latter statistic is (0.809, 1.862). See Lo (1988) for a complete table of significance levels.
5 It is not believed that such a strategy will produce a survivorship bias. Available evidence suggests that very few quoted companies become bankrupt: McElreath and Wiggins (1984) report that only sixteen companies were deleted from the New York Stock Exchange due to bankruptcy from 1970 to 1979. Unpublished work by Robert Semple reported that the average annual number of quoted companies going into liquidation in the UK was 2–3 per cent in the 1970s. A much more plausible explanation for the disappearance of companies is that they have merged with, or been taken over by, other firms. Since the majority of companies subject to takeover are characterized by low growth and poor profitability (Palepu 1986), most would be included in the loser portfolio. Such acquired companies may make a positive contribution to the new entity and by ignoring any post-merger return earned by these companies, we may be biasing our results against the overreaction hypothesis.
6 Other factors such as transaction costs which may also affect the profitability of the trading strategy are ignored in this chapter.
7 In this sample, the average change in market capitalization for the shares in the loser portfolio was −33.6 per cent, while the corresponding change for the portfolio of winner shares was 163.9 per cent. These results are less extreme than those of Chan (1988) where the average percentage changes in market value were −45 per cent for the losers and 365 per cent for the winners.

References

Ball, R. and Kothari, S. P. (1990) 'Non-stationary expected returns: implications for tests of market efficiency and serial correlations in returns', *Journal of Financial Economics*, 25, 51–74.

Beaver, W. and Landsman, W. (1981) 'Note on the behaviour of residual security returns for winner and loser portfolios', *Journal of Accounting and Economics*, 233–41.

Chan, K. C. (1988) 'On the contrarian investment strategy', *Journal of Business*, 61 (2), 147–64.

Cochrane, J. (1988) 'How big is the random walk in GNP?', *Journal of Political Economy*, 96, 893–920.

Corbae, D. and Ouliaris, S. (1986) 'Robust tests for unit root tests in foreign exchange markets', *Economics Letters*, 22, 375–80.

De Bondt, W. F. M. and Thaler, R. (1985) 'Does the stock market overreact?', *Journal of Finance*, 50 (3), 793–805.

De Bondt, W. F. W. and Thaler, R. (1987) 'Further evidence on overreaction and stock market seasonality', *Journal of Finance*, 42 (3), 557–81.

De Bondt, W. F. W. and Thaler, R. (1990) 'Do security analysts overreact?', *American Economic Review*, 80 (2), 52–7.

Fama, E. F. (1970) 'Efficient capital markets: a review of theory and empirical work', *Journal of Finance*, 25, 383–417.

Fama, E. F. and French, K. R. (1988) 'Permanent and temporary components of stock prices', *Journal of Political Economy*, 96, 246–76.

Howe, J. S. (1986) 'Evidence on stock market overreaction', *Financial Analysts Journal*, 42, 74–7.

Hurst, H. (1951) 'Long term storage capacity of reservoirs', *Transactions of the American Society of Civil Engineers*, 116, 770–99.

Jones, C. J. Tweedie, D. P. and Whittington, G. (1976) 'The R portfolio: a statistical investigation of a relative decline portfolio', *Journal of Business, Finance and Accounting*, 3, 71–92.

Kahneman, D. and Tversky, A. (1973) 'On the psychology of the prediction', *Psychological Review*, 80, 237–51.

Keynes, J. M. (1936) *The General Theory of Employment, Interest and Money*, London: Macmillan.

Lehmann, B. N. (1990) 'Fads, martingales, and market efficiency', *Quarterly Journal of Economics*, 105 (1), 718–51.

Lo, A. (1988) 'Long-term memory in stock market prices', MIT, mimeo.

Lo, A. and MacKinley, C. (1988) 'Stock prices do not follow random walks: evidence from a simple specification test', *Review of Financial Studies*, 1, 41–66.

McElreath, R. B. and Wiggins, C. D. (1984) 'Using the COMPUSTAT tapes in financial research: problems and solutions', *Financial Analysts Journal*, 40, 22–55.

Mandelbrot, B. (1972) 'Statistical methodology for non-periodic cycles: from the covariance to R/S analysis', *Annals of Economic and Social Measurement*, 1, 259–90.

Mandelbrot, B. (1975) 'Limit theorems on the self-normalized range for weakly and strongly dependent processes', *Wahrscheinlichkeitstheorie verw. Gebiete*, 31, 271–85.

Newey, W. and West, K. (1987) 'A simple positive definite, heteroscedasticity and autocorrelation consistent covariance matrix', *Econometrica*, 55, 703–83.

Palepu, K. (1986) 'Predicting turnover targets: a methodological and empirical analysis', *Journal of Accounting and Economics*, 8, 3–35.

Phillips, P. C. B. (1987) 'Time series regression with a unit root', *Econometrica*, 55, 277–301.

Phillips, P. C. B. and Perron, P. (1988) 'Testing for a unit root in time series regression', *Brometrika*, 75, 335–46.

Poterba, J. M. and Summers, L. H. (1988) 'Mean reversion in stock prices', *Journal of Financial Economics*, 88, 27–59.

Stock, J. H. and Watson, M. W. (1986) 'Does GNP have a unit root?', *Economics Letters*, 22, 147–51.

West, K. D. (1988) 'Bubbles, fads, and stock price volatility tests: partial evaluation', *Journal of Finance*, 42 (3), 639–56.

Zarowin, P. (1989a) 'Short-run market overreaction: size and seasonality effects', *Journal of Portfolio Management*, 15 (3), 26–9.

Zarowin, P. (1989b) 'Does the stock market overreact to corporate earnings information?', *Journal of Finance*, 43 (4), 1385–99.

Zarowin, P. (1990) 'Size, seaonality, and stock market overreaction', *Journal of Financial and Quantitative Analysis*, 25 (1), 113–25.

14 Global Capital Market Integration and the Current Account

M. J. Artis and T. Bayoumi

1 INTRODUCTION

Casual observation suggests that the global capital market has become progressively more integrated since the financial autarky of the decade immediately after World War II. In particular, during the most recent decade there has been a widespread reduction in official regulatory barriers to international capital movements; 'liberalization calendars' have been documented by Frankel (1989) and Cooper (1990) which give detailed support to this contention.

The intertemporal approach to balance of payments theory (Sachs, 1981; Frenkel and Razin, 1987) suggests that a process of increasing capital market integration, *ceteris paribus*, will make current account imbalance more likely. By removing liquidity constraints such a process of integration makes the intertemporal approach more fully applicable, reducing current account imbalance to the role of residual. There is a close analogy with the way in which, in the domestic economy, liberalized capital markets make the 'consumption-smoothing' paradigm of consumer behaviour more applicable and that of the liquidity-constrained consumer less so.

In an influential but controversial paper, Feldstein and Horioka (1980) capitalized on this insight by noting that, if the world capital market was integrated, there should be no correlation between national saving and national investment in an international cross-section. This expectation, it is easy to show, is in principle not well supported. Feldstein and Horioka should have stressed more clearly than they did that the existence of an integrated world capital market simply removes the *necessity* for a correlation between rates of investment and saving: in fact, although they conceded that a high correlation could simply reflect 'other common causes of the variation in both savings and investment' (ibid: p 319), they stressed that findings of a high correlation 'would however be strong evidence against the hypothesis of perfect world capital mobility and would place on the defenders of that hypothesis the burden of identifying such common causal factors' (ibid: p 319). In subsequent work, Tesar (1988) and Obstfeld (1986) have demonstrated that it is easy hypothetically to generate high correlations between savings and investment even in a world of high capital mobility, reinforcing the strength of Feldstein and Horioka's qualifying remark.

Feldstein and Horioka's own estimates were that national rates of saving and investment were in fact highly correlated across the OECD countries in their data set (which covered the period 1960–74), and similarly high correlations have been reported by numerous other investigators for alternative definitions of the variables in question, later time periods and other estimation techniques. The later estimates (see particularly Bayoumi, 1990; Feldstein and Baccheta, 1989) do, however, give the impression that the correlation is falling over time.

In what follows, we first explain in more detail the basis for the Feldstein-Horioka null hypothesis and draw attention to regimes under which their null that saving and investment are not correlated appears to be supported. These stand in contrast to the evidence hitherto generated from the post-World War II regime. In the next section, we review evidence drawn from the most recent release of OECD national accounts. This provides some support for the hypothesis that the correlation is falling over time, although it still remains relatively high. In the final section, we argue that the evidence reflects the interraction of two factors: a commitment, weakening over time, by governments to target the current account; and a trend towards a more closely integrated global capital market.

2 THE FELDSTEIN-HORIOKA 'NULL'

Elementary manipulation of the balance of payments identities shows that the current account of the balance of payments may be written as the balance of national saving and investment, or equivalently as the sum of the private and public sector's saving-investment balances.

Letting X and M represent exports and imports of goods and services and NPI net property income from overseas, the current account of the balance of payments (CAB) is defined:

$$CAB \equiv X - M + NPI \tag{14.1}$$

The GNP identity is

$$GNP \equiv GDP + NPI \tag{14.2}$$

Expanding the GDP as the sum of expenditure components with the usual mnemonics (14.3) and noting the definitions of private disposable income (as in 14.4), where T is tax payments and S_p is private sector saving, leads to equation 14.5:

$$GDP = C + I + G + X - M \tag{14.3}$$

$$GNP - T = C + S_p \tag{14.4}$$

$$CAB = (S_p - I) + (T - G) \tag{14.5}$$

If some investment is done by the private sector and some by government ($I = I_p + I_g$) and noting $S = S_p + S_g$, where $S_g = T - G$, equation (14.5) can be re-expressed as

$$CAB = (S_p - I_g) + (S_g - I_g) = S - I \tag{14.6}$$

Since the capital account is simply the inverse of the current account of the balance of payments, it follows that any restriction of the former implies a constraint upon the latter. When capital is immobile, the current account is forced to balance and national savings and investment will equally be obliged to balance. This is the basis for the Feldstein-Horioka test for financial integration. If lack of financial integration forces the current account to balance, then the coefficient β in a cross-sectional regression of the form $(I/Y)_i = \alpha + \beta(S/Y)_i + e_i$ should be unity; with financial integration a value of zero is predicted. As already suggested, this criterion can be criticized as conflating necessary and sufficient conditions. But whilst it is possible to construct models in which the expected value of β is close to unity even under the assumption of perfect capital mobility, theoretical possibility and empirical likelihood are logically distinct. Two pieces of evidence, in particular, suggest that the Feldstein-Horioka null can be taken seriously. Firstly, in cross-section correlations on classical gold standard data, Bayoumi (1990) found $\hat{\beta}$ to be insignificantly different from zero. Secondly, in cross-section correlations across the regions of the UK, Bayoumi and Rose (1989) showed that estimates of β were again not significantly different from zero. Representative equations from those two studies are shown in Table 14.1, alongside representative equations drawn from the original Feldstein-Horioka study. The juxaposition of these estimates could provoke the response (as in Feldstein-Horioka) that the estimates for the period since World War II are simply indicative of a low degree of financial integration; if this is not accepted, then a question is provoked. What can explain such high correlations in a world which causal empiricism suggests is in fact one in which capital is highly mobile? Before suggesting an answer to this question, we take the opportunity to introduce more recent evidence on the correlation.

Table 14.1 (OLS) Estimates of β in the regression $(I/Y)_i = \alpha + \beta(S/Y)_i$

Regression	β	(SE)
Gold standard[1]		
1880–1890	0.48	(0.50)
1891–1901	0.69	(0.48)
1902–1913	−0.10	(0.43)
1880–1913	0.29	(0.46)
UK regions[2]		
1971–1975	−0.99	(0.53)
1976–1980	0.54	(0.80)
1981–1985	0.03	(0.33)
Post-war[3]		
1960–1964	0.91	(0.06)
1965–1969	0.87	(0.10)
1970–1974	0.87	(0.09)
1960–1974	0.89	(0.07)

[1] Drawn from Bayoumi (1990); the sample includes Germany, Italy, the UK, Australia, Denmark, Norway and Sweden.
[2] Drawn from Bayoumi and Rose (1989); the sample covers the ten standard regions of the United Kingdom.
[3] Drawn from Feldstein and Horioka (1980); the sample covers sixteen OECD countries: Australia, Austria, Belgium, Canada, Denmark, Finland, Germany, Greece, Ireland, Italy, Japan, the Netherlands, New Zealand, the UK and the USA.

Notes: Standard errors shown in parentheses.

3 RECENT TRENDS IN THE SAVING-INVESTMENT CORRELATION

Table 14.2 summarizes the correlation evidence derived from the 1990 release of the OECD National Accounts data diskettes.

Three country-groupings are distinguished: the G–10 plus Switzerland (the group of most developed countries), the full group of 25 OECD countries and the six EMS core countries. Results are quoted for the whole period 1960–88 and for the separate subperiods 1960–66; 1967–73; 1974–80; 1981–88. The reason for concentrating on the most developed countries in the sample is that these are likely to demonstrate most obviously the effects of any trend towards greater financial integration and to be free of problems provoked by considerations of possible insolvency.

Table 14.2 OLS estimates of β in the regression $(I/Y)_i = \alpha + \beta\,(S/Y)_i$

	G-11		G-25		ERM6	
1960–66	0.98	(0.07)	0.70	(0.07)	0.67	(0.15)
1967–73	0.94	(0.05)	0.57	(0.11)	0.42	(0.30)
1974–80	0.92	(0.07)	0.53	(0.18)	0.56	(0.26)
1981–88	0.78	(0.12)	0.79	(0.12)	0.58	(0.33)
1960–88	0.85	(0.08)	0.76	(0.12)	0.55	(0.23)

G-11 is the Group of Ten countries plus Switzerland. G-25 is the 25 member states of the OECD. ERM6 is Germany, France, Italy, Belgium, Netherlands and Denmark. Investment is defined as gross fixed capital formation plus increase in stockbuilding and saving as GDP/GNP less private and government consumption. The data source is the 1990 OECD National Accounts diskettes.

The result for the G–11 are interesting in that they do in fact show a decline in the estimated value of β over the sample period. Indeed, while in early subsamples the value of $\hat{\beta}$ was not significantly different from unity, in the most recent data slice this can – by a whisker! – be rejected. The estimate however is still significantly different from zero. Pooling all the G–11 data and estimating a time varying coefficient model (results not reported in detail here) confirmed this conclusion: a downward trend in the value of $\hat{\beta}$ is significant but small and the value of $\hat{\beta}$ itself, though significantly below unity, is not predicted by this model to fall below 0.8 in the sample period. For the wider group of 25 OECD countries, the data reveals an opposing trend, with $\hat{\beta}$ rising over time and shown not to be significantly different from unity in the latest subperiod. This finding may reflect the inclusion of solvency constrained countries in the sample.[1]

The ERM results reported in Table 14.2 are of interest since they demonstrate a case in which $\hat{\beta}$ is not different from zero in the 1980s. This might be read as confirming that these countries are already substantially integrated, even without EMU, and despite the presence of exchange control barriers to the movement of certain categories of capital.

4 TARGETING THE CURRENT ACCOUNT

The identity (14.6) specifies the current account balance as the sum of private and public (government) sector savings-investment balances. Common cause variations in savings and investment of either kind (positively correlated shocks), or inversely correlated shocks to public and private balances, will suffice to induce a high correlation between total savings and investment.

The likelihood that common cause variations in savings and investment (presumably affecting principally the private sector) are the proximate explanation of the high postwar correlations seems to us diminished by the evidence that has been derived from other regimes (as shown in Table 14.1). If common cause variations did not produce high correlation for those regimes, why should they do so for the postwar world? Two alternative explanations suggest themselves.

The alternative regimes for which evidence is supplied in Table 14.1 have at least two features in common. Government intervention to target the balance of payments was absent and exchange rates were, or expected to be, stable. The post-war regime lacks both features. It is reasonable to think that flexible exchange rate regimes induce departures from full integration because of aversion to exchange rate risk. Thus, the fact that exchange rates are flexible may enforce a degree of financial autarky, *ceteris paribus*. We treat this as a residual explanation in what follows, preferring to concentrate on the alternative hypothesis of government intervention. How does this work? Is it rational? And, is there empirical evidence in favour of it?

At the level of the identity (14.6) it is easy to see that if government has a target for the current account, it can adjust its own savings-investment balance to offset changes in the private sector balance. It would be natural to think of fiscal policy in this connection. But the possibility for government intervention is not limited to this case. The government may also use other policy instruments to influence the private sector's balance in the light of its current account target and the factors determining its own saving-investment balance. The obvious case in point here is the use of monetary policy.

Is it rational to target the current account? The usual argument for government intervention proceeds by identifying an externality which intervention may help correct. In a world of limited capital mobility, such an externality is implied since, in essence, the supply of world savings to an individual economy is *ex hypothesi* limited in this case. Since in these conditions the current account has to be cleared by the exchange rate, the decisions of potential borrowers will have first order effects on other agents' welfare, and intervention by the government to stem the need for exchange rate changes seems understandable and justifiable. In financially integrated worlds, arguments for targeting the current account seem less compelling, though they can still be constructed (Summers, 1988). An important point here, however, concerns the feedback from government targeting to private sector decision making and vice versa. The fact that a government targets its current account will obviously affect private sector decision making; for example, it will make news about the current account relevant to decisions taken in the foreign exchange markets. There is also a feedback in the other direction. If private sector decision makers treat news about the current account as relevant in decisions about foreign currency exposure, then government may feel obliged to validate this apprehension (however unwarranted it may be in the first instance) by, in fact, treating the current account as a target in order to stabilize the exchange rate. There thus seems a possibility of a self-supporting vicious circle being maintained, from which it may be quite difficult to break away. The practice of current account targeting might easily outlive the conditions which rationally gave rise to its inception.

The prevalence of current account targeting, and evidence as to whether it has diminished in importance, may be examined by estimating policy reaction functions. In Artis and Bayoumi (1990) we examine monetary policy reaction functions and review the relationship between private and public sector financial (saving-investment) balances. A summary of the results of the former is given in Table 14.3.

The general form of the reaction function for which estimates are given in Table 14.3 is $\Delta r = \alpha + \beta\Delta y + \gamma\Delta p + \delta CA/Y$, where r is a rediscount rate administered by the monetary authorities, Δy is growth, Δp is inflation and CA/Y is the current account balance in ratio to GDP/GNP. If governments target the current account, the coefficient δ should be negative. In testing this equation, particular interest attaches to the question of whether behaviour changed in the 1980s (supporting the fall in the overall saving-investment correlation detected for this period). For this reason each regressor has two coefficients associated with it, one representing the value of the coefficient in the 1970s, the other the change in this value in the 1980s; their sum thus represents the value of the coefficient in the 1980s.

The coefficients relating to the current account in the 1970s in Table 14.3 have the expected sign and t ratios well above unity. Furthermore, all the regressions show a fall in the size of the current account coefficient between in 1970s and the 1980s.[2] This fall reduces the coefficient to near zero for the United States and the Federal Republic of Germany and halves the coefficient for Italy while leaving it relatively unchanged in the case of Japan. Turning to the domestic targets, in the 1970s inflation has a larger and more significant coefficient than growth in all the regressions, and is significant at conventional levels in three of the four.[3] The results for the 1980s show less uniformity, with growth becoming more important than inflation in the United States and Japan, but not in the Federal Republic of Germany or Italy.

Overall, these results appear to confirm that the current account was a significant policy target for monetary policy in the 1970s, but that its importance diminished somewhat in the 1980s. This behaviour appears to correspond to a reduction in the correlation between saving and investment among OECD countries. Since the major impact of monetary policy is probably on private sector saving and investment, rather than on the government balance, these data do not provide support for the hypothesis of

Table 14.3 Monetary Policy Reaction Functions: 1971(3)–1983(2)
Dependent variable is Δr (see text)

	United States		Japan		Germany		Italy	
Growth	21.9	(9.4)	0.0	(10.0)	2.7	(8.5)	6.3	(5.6)
DUM[1] × growth	27.1	(13.9)	18.4	(15.8)	−1.5	(12.1)	−10.8	(8.7)
Inflation	39.5	(10.5)	6.0	(6.7)	21.7	(14.4)	−23.4	(12.4)
DUM[1] × inflation	−17.9	(9.0)	−2.1	(13.0)	−13.2	(14.7)	−10.7	(11.1)
CA/Y	−26.5	(14.6)	−11.4	(8.7)	−12.6	(7.8)	−12.9	(8.8)
DUM[1] × CA/Y	30.7	(16.3)	1.5	(9.8)	9.0	(8.9)	6.5	(16.4)
DW	2.16		1.17		1.24		2.19	
R^2	0.42		0.13		0.09		0.18	
SE	0.59		0.63		0.56		1.19	

Standard errors are shown in parentheses.
[1]*DUM* is a dummy variable equal to zero in the 1970s and unity in the 1980s.
Source: Artis and Bayoumi (1990).

Table 14.4 Difference in Saving Investment Correlations Between the 1970s and 1980s[1].

$$Priv\,(S-I)/Y = \alpha + \beta\ Govt\,(S-I)/Y + \gamma(DUM^{*}Govt\,(S-I)/Y) - e_t$$
$$e_t = \rho e_{t-1} - \epsilon_t$$

	β	γ	ρ	R^2
United States	−1.17 (0.18)	0.28 (0.26)	0.83 (0.14)	0.83
Japan	−1.10 (0.29)	0.31 (0.37)	0.78 (0.17)	0.55
Germany Fed. Rep. of	0.88 (0.24)	0.69 (0.63)	0.53 (0.29)	0.51
France	−1.68 (0.34)	0.87 (0.48)	0.40 (0.31)	0.72
United Kingdom	0.59 (0.50)	−0.92 (0.44)	0.47 (0.24)	0.30
Canada	−0.43 (0.18)	−0.62 (0.18)	−0.01 (0.35)	0.92
Belgium	−1.17 (0.36)	0.20 (0.24)	0.87 (0.11)	0.61
Finland	−1.03 (0.32)	0.54 (0.89)	0.31 (0.27)	0.47
Norway	−0.24 (0.94)	0.39 (0.43)	0.62 (0.23)	0.03
Sweden	−0.84 (0.28)	0.40 (0.46)	0.41 (0.25)	0.56

[1]The estimation period is 1972–1986. Standard errors are indicated in parentheses. DUM is a variable equal to zero for the 1970s and unity for the 1980.

Source: Artis and Bayoumi (1990).

Summers (1988) that it is fiscal policy which has been used to target the current account; rather it appears that governments have sought to influence private sector behaviour in response to current account imbalances.

Direct testing of the Summers hypothesis was hampered by difficulties in defining appropriately the policy variables and by a lack of degrees of freedom. However, an examination of the contemporaneous relationship between private and public sector balances, again allowing for a possible change in the relationship in the 1980s, was instructive. The test equation and the main results are summarized in Table 14.4. These show that the value of β, the 'offset' coefficient in the 1970s is generally not significantly different from (minus) one, indicating that movements in public and private sector balances offset each other in this period. The generally positive value of γ (the change in the coefficient in the 1980s) shows that the offset coefficient fell in value in the later decade[4]; though rarely significant at conventional levels, the results imply a decline in the value of the offset coefficient in the 1980s in eight out of ten cases (which is significant at the 5 per cent level using a sign test).

CONCLUSIONS

In this note we have presented fresh evidence on the cross country correlations of savings and investment. These indicate some evidence of a decline in the 1980s, though they remain high. It is not easy to accept that this evidence should be taken as implying that the world capital market is far from integrated. Rather, it seems likely that government targeting of the current account helps account for the high correlation. Over time, it seems that this practice is diminishing whilst casual evidence suggests that capital market integration is growing. As a result, we might expect to see further declines in saving-investment correlations and more persistence in current account imbalances in the future.

Notes

M. J. Artis acknowledges financial support from the Ford and Alfred P. Sloan Foundations administered through the CEPR under its programme 'Macroeconomic Interactions and Policy Design in Interdependent Economics'. Yue Ma provided expert research assistance whilst Lucy O'Carroll assisted on a pilot for some of the work reported here. None of the above nor our respective institutions can be assumed to share the opinions expressed in the paper, which are our own.

1. Inspection of the corresponding scatter diagram shows that observations for Yugoslavia and Turkey have an 'outlier' effect on the estimates. Their exclusion lowers the recorded value of $\hat{\beta}$ throughout and permits rejection of the hypothesis that β is unity in any period.
2. Using a simple sign test, the probability of four coefficients all turning up negative is 6.25 per cent, close to conventional significance levels.
3. However, these results are not robust to the inclusion of lags.
4. The value of the offset coefficient in the 1980s is the *sum* of the β and γ estimates.

References

Artis, M. J. and Bayoumi, T. (1990) 'Saving, investment, financial integration and the balance of payments', *Staff Studies for the World Economic Outlook*.

Bayoumi, T. (1990) 'Savings-investment correlations: Immobile capital, government policy of endogenous behaviour?', *IMF Staff Papers*, 37, 360–387.

Bayoumi, T. and Rose, A. (1989) 'Domestic Saving and Intra-National Capital Flows, *mimeo*, International Monetary Fund.

Cooper, S. (1990) 'Internationally mobile savings', Bank of England Discussion Paper, (forthcoming).

Feldstein, M. and Horioka, C. (1980) 'Domestic saving and international capital flows', *Economic Journal*, 90, 314–29.

Feldstein, M. and Bacchelta, P. (1989) "National saving and international investment", NBER Working Paper No. 3164.

Frankel, J. (1989) 'Quantifying international capital mobility in the 1980s', in Berntheim, D. and Shoven, J. (eds), *Saving*, Chicago: University of Chicago Press.

Frenkel, J. and Razin, A. (1987) *Fiscal Policies and the World Economy* Cambridge, Mass: MIT Press.

Obstfeld, M. (1986) 'Capital mobility in the world economy: theory and measurement', *Carnegie-Rochester Conference Series on Public Policy*, vol 24, Amsterdam: North Holland, 55–104.

Sachs, J. (1981) 'The current account and macroeconomic adjustment in the 1970s', *Brookings Papers on Economic Activity*, 1.

Summers, L. (1988) 'Tax policy and international competitiveness', in Frankel, J. (ed.) *Aspects of Fiscal Policies*, Chicago: Chicago University Press.

Tesar, L. (1988) 'Savings, investment and international capital flows', University of Rochester, Working Paper No. 154.

15 Financial Disorder and the Theory of Crisis

E. P. Davis

1 INTRODUCTION

Recent financial problems such as the debt crisis and the equity market crash have refocused attention on the causes, nature and consequences of periods of financial disorder. What is the appropriate policy response, and how can such potential crises be avoided? Were the periods of instability unique events or can common features be discerned? This chapter attempts to cast light on these issues by analysing four periods of financial instability in the Euromarkets in relation to the economic theory of financial crisis (much of which has been developed as part of the analysis of the Great Depression). In the course of the study, the chapter also offers a literature survey of the theory of crisis and a comparative analysis of recent periods of disorder, in contrast to most extant analyses of financial crises which assess only one theory and/or event.

The Euromarkets are a particularly suitable vehicle for analysis, because intermediaries, borrowers and lenders have not historically been subject to restrictive regulations on entry, capitalization or lending practices. Thus a free and non-segmented market exists and financial market behaviour can be observed largely untrammelled by regulations and directions of domestic authorities. National markets are themselves becoming more like the Euromarkets as increased competition, innovation and deregulation proceed, implying a wider relevance to behaviour patterns observed in the Euromarkets.

The chapter is organized as follows. In section 2, paradigms of financial crisis are outlined and compared. In section 3, the events of the principal periods of disorder in the international capital markets in the 1970s and 1980s are outlined as they affected the principal Euromarkets (interbank, syndicated credits and Eurobonds).[1] The behaviour of key economic indicators as well as market prices and quantities surrounding these events is examined in more detail in section 4. These sections permit a qualitative evaluation in section 5 of the theories of crisis. Section 6 draws together these conclusions, indicating which aspects of the various theories are relevant under current conditions and suggesting implications of policy.

Before commencing, it is appropriate to clarify terms. 'Disorder' and 'instability' are used to describe a disturbance in fnancial markets which entails unanticipated changes in prices and quantities in credit or asset markets, which may disrupt the capacity of the financial system to allocate capital and lead to a potential for systemic risk. The term 'crises' is deliberately excluded from the title because the events discussed did not lead in themselves to macroeconomic depressions, widespread financial collapse and dysfunction of the payments mechanism, in contrast to prewar crises that did entail such results.[2]

2 THEORIES OF FINANCIAL CRISIS

2.1 The monetarist approach

Monetarists identify financial crises with banking panics, which may cause monetary contraction or may worsen the effects of prior monetary contraction on economic activity. For example, Friedman and Schwartz (1963) noted that of six major contractions in the US over 1867–1960, four were associated with major banking or monetary disturbances. Banking panics were held to arise out of public loss of confidence in banks' abilities to convert deposits into currency. This loss was often caused by failure of an important institution, which in turn may have been triggered by failure of the authorities to pursue a steady and predictable monetary policy. Given fractional reserves, attempts by the public to increase the fraction of its money holdings can only be met by a multiple contraction of deposits, unless there is a suspension of convertibility of deposits into currency or intervention of the authorities (e.g. open market operations). A panic may lead to widespread bank failures, unless the central bank acts to expand the money supply, as sound banks are forced into insolvency by falls in the value of their assets caused by a scramble for liquidity. Failures in turn affect economic activity via reductions in the money stock as the deposit–currency and deposit–reserve ratios fall. Of course the introduction of deposit insurance does much to alleviate the dangers of such a syndrome, as it removes the public's fear for its ability to convert deposits into currency.

Cagan (1965) noted that crises did not tend to cause economic downturns as they tended to follow peaks in activity, though the attendant monetary contraction could aggravate the downturn. In addition, some panics occurred without severe downturns and some severe downturns without panics, proving that panics were not necessary or sufficient for a severe contraction.

2.2 Debt and financial fragility

The monetary approach stresses only monetary factors and views real effects of crises as mainly being the acceleration of downturns caused by other forces. An alternative approach regards financial crises as an essential component of the turning point of the business cycle – a response to previous excesses which can operate through a variety of financial markets.

Fisher (1932) attributed the downturn in the business cycle to over-indebtedness and deflation. The upswing is caused by an exogenous event leading to improved opportunities for profitable investment (what Kindleberger 1978 called a displacement). This leads to increased fixed investment as well as speculation in asset markets for capital gain. The process is debt financed, mainly by bank loans, which increases deposits, the money supply and the price level. Velocity also increases, further fuelling the expansion. Rising prices reduce the real value of outstanding debt, offsetting the increase in nominal debt and encouraging further borrowing. This leads to a state of over-indebtedness, i.e. a degree of indebtedness which multiplies unduly the chances of being insolvent (or alternatively a state of indebtedness implying a negative present value of borrowers' net worth in a wide variety of states of nature).

When agents have insufficient liquid assets to meet liabilities, a crisis can be triggered. Debtors unable to pay debts and refinance positions can be forced by creditors to liquidate assets (distress selling). If this is widespread, and in the absence of lender-of-last-resort intervention by the monetary authorities, it triggers further crises and a deep depression; distress selling by the whole community leads to falling prices, with bank deposits declining as loans are withdrawn. Deflation increases the real value of outstanding debt. Creditors see the nominal value of collateral declining with prices, so they call loans; the real debt burden of debtors increases and they continue to liquidate. Each individual hopes to be better off by liquidating but the community is worse off owing to deflation. If nominal rates are sticky, real rates increase. Bank runs may be triggered as fears for their solvency increase, especially as falling prices reduce companies' net worth and profits and lead to bankruptcy. Output and employment fall until bankruptcy has eliminated over-indebtedness or reflationary monetary policy is adopted. The process then repeats itself.

Minsky (1982) elaborated Fisher's approach and introduced the concept of fragility to attempt to clarify the problem of over-indebtedness during an upswing. Fragility depends on: first, the mix of hedge, speculative and Ponzi finance; second, the liquidity of portfolios; and third, the extent to which ongoing investment is debt financed. Hedge financing occurs when a unit's cash flow commitments to debt servicing are such that cash receipts exceed cash payments over a long period; speculative financing entails cash flow payments over a short period that exceed cash flow receipts; and Ponzi finance occurs when a unit has interest portions of its cash payment commitments exceeding cash receipts. A Ponzi unit has to increase its debt to meet outstanding commitments. For speculative and Ponzi units a rise in the interest rate can entail negative net worth and insolvency.

How does the mechanism operate? In the unswing, the demand for new investment leads to an excess demand for finance, which increases interest rates, though this is partly offset by monetary financial innovations (giving an elastic money supply and velocity) which increase the supply of finance for further investment. Higher interest rates create fragility via an increase in debt finance, a shift from long- to short-term debt, a shift from hedge to speculative or Ponzi finance and a reduction in margins of safety for financial institutions. Further rises in interest rates[3] can cause a refinancing crisis with firms unable to roll over their debt, leading to Fisher's distress selling cycle unless the central bank intervenes.

Finally, Kindleberger (1978) stressed the importance of euphoria in the upturn, which leads banks to make insufficient provision for risk and also to a high degree of speculative activity among investors. Asset prices start off in close touch with reality but become progressively more excessive.

Besides the focus on lender-of-last-resort intervention, the policy implications of the financial fragility approach also include limitation of tax advantages to debt relative to equity.

2.3 Rational expectations

Some attempts have been made to model crises in a rational expectations manner. According to such models, manias (as stressed in financial fragility approaches) are viewed as rational speculative bubbles; a run (the key monetarist conduit) is a speculative attack on a price fixing scheme; and a panic is a run whose timing is imperfectly foreseen. However, as discussed below, those emphasizing the importance of uncertainty in crises would tend to dismiss such models.

Definitions of a rational bubble (Blanchard and Watson 1982) typically incorporate an assumed probability that the bubble will remain or crash.[4] While the bubble lasts, the average return must exceed the risk-free rate to compensate for the risk of a crash. This will be true *a fortiori* for risk-averse agents; indeed, as the probability of the crash may increase over time, the price will have to increase exponentially to compensate both for the increased probability of a fall and for the large risk in holding an asset. (This theory may be contrasted with Kindleberger's looser definition of euphoria, where asset prices progressively lose touch with the fundamentals in an irrational manner.)

Runs are also explicable in terms of rational expectations (Flood and Garber 1982) – a run being an event that terminates a price fixing scheme. An agent (e.g. a bank) may be ready to buy or sell an asset at a given fixed price (i.e. to fix the price of deposits in terms of government currency). The viability of the scheme depends on the agent holding a stock of the asset. If other agents see the price fixing as temporary and assume that prices will rise eventually (they will take a capital loss on their deposits) then they will draw down the stock (of reserves), backing the price fixing scheme. Alternatively put, they draw down the stock when the net worth of the institution is exhausted. If the stock is depleted rapidly, this is a run (leading to closure) although all depositors (having perfect foresight) are paid off without loss.[5] The theory can be extended by introducing calculated risks to show losses to depositors (panics), but only to the extent that a sudden event led directly and proportionately to real losses *exceeding the net worth* of the institution. (Compare the discussion of uncertainty in section 2.4.) A similar analysis can be applied to national foreign exchange reserves in a currency crisis.

2.4 Uncertainty

Economic uncertainty as opposed to risk was suggested by Knight (1921) to be central to economic activity. Meltzer (1982) pointed out its importance in understanding financial crises. Uncertainty pertains to future events such as financial crises and shifts of policy regime not susceptible to being reduced to objective probabilities, and also provides opportunities for profits in competitive markets. These aspects are discussed in turn below. Meltzer argues that events not susceptible to probability analysis are excluded from rational expectations models of decision making and optimal diversification of risks. Rational expectations models have not, in his view, provided a basis for reliable predictions concerning the behaviour of macroeconomic financial prices such as exchange rates; nor have they provided convincing explanations of financial crises.

There is no precise economic theory as to how decisions are made under uncertainty. It may be ignored if events are felt to have a sufficiently low probability and information is costly to obtain. Alternatively, subjective probabilities may be applied, together with a risk premium to cover unspecified adverse events. In each case people tend to watch others and do not deviate widely from the norm in terms of factors taken into account and weights given to them. When the crowd is wrong, there is the making of a financial crises, but there is no objective basis to prove before the event that the crowd will be wrong.[6]

In terms of opportunity for profit, uncertainty rooted in change was suggested by Knight to be its main source in competitive markets. If all probabilities were known and risks diversified, profits would be bid away. Profits are earnt by innovating and seeking opportunities where there is uneven information and uncertainty. These processes[7] increasingly characterize financial markets. Whether the process leads to crisis depends on the form of the destruction; if innovators take market share from inefficient firms and firms are adequately capitalized it may not, but it will if deteriorating balance sheet quality follows the innovation process or if financial intermediaries fail to understand the properties of financial innovations. Uncertainty is likely to be increased by this innovation process, and hence it may be greatest in unregulated markets like the Euromarkets where innovation is untrammelled by restrictions on product design. When uncertainty is reduced in one area and profits are competed away, innovation may recur, exposing the market to new uncertainties. (See also the discussion of innovation and risk in Bank for International Settlements (BIS) 1986.)

An increased level of uncertainty may lead to a loss of *confidence* in financial institutions (it is notable that confidence plays no role in a model with stationary probabilities). Confidence increases as innovators receive profits and their practices are emulated. Adverse surprises, given uncertainty and imperfect information, may trigger shifts in confidence and hence runs which affect markets *more than appears warranted* by their intrinsic significance because they lead to a rethinking of decision processes as well as to decisions themselves. This helps explain the wide variety of proximate causes of financial crises.

Policy recommendations based on the lessons of the uncertainty approach (Shafer 1986) include reduction of uncertainty by avoidance of unstable macroeconomic policy (and also microeconomic, for example sudden changes in the level of assistance to particular sectors such as agriculture) and firm prudential supervision to check the risky behaviour of financial institutions. The power of markets to check (via high costs of credit) any risky behaviour of financial institutions can be increased by more disclosure and limitation of depositor protection only to retail markets.

2.5 Credit rationing – and a partial synthesis

Paradigms of credit rationing (Guttentag and Herring 1984a) suggest financial crises are characterized by abrupt increases in rationing, both by price (i.e. higher risk premiums) and quantity (i.e. following Stiglitz and Weiss 1981, absolute limits on borrowing resulting from information asymmetries between borrower and a (profit-maximizing) lender and lack of control of the borrower by the lender). Such increases may follow previous periods when rationing has been loosened to an excessive extent. The incidence of (equilibrium) price or quantity rationing is held to depend on the borrower's capital position.

Extending the theories stressing uncertainty outlined above, a further distinction is made between on the one hand systematic market risks such as recession, and on the other financial crises – the latter being subject to much greater uncertainty as outlined above.[8] In the case of recession it is suggested that objective probabilities are known and subjective probabilities tend to the objective, because unfavourable outcomes are frequent enough to ensure that an over-optimistic intermediary is driven from the market (this does however assume a suitably long time horizon). But for financial crises and other uncertain events there is no such presumption; competition may drive prudent creditors from the market as they are undercut by those disregarding the likelihood of financial crisis for reasons of ignorance or competitive advantage.[9]

Various psychological factors underlying this pattern may be identified, notably a tendency to calculate probabilities by the ease with which past occurrences are brought to mind (which declines with time), as well as institutional factors such as the short periods over which loan officers are assessed, and the asymmetry of outcomes for managers and shareholders. These tendencies, which imply declining *subjective* probabilities of shocks during periods of calm, may lead to declining capital positions, the loosening of equilibrium price and the quantity rationing of credit, and hence to the increased *objective* vulnerability of creditors to shocks. Subjective and objective probabilities may thus drift further apart during a period of calm, until a shock leads to an abrupt increase in credit rationing which triggers a crisis, as lenders become aware of their imprudence.

Policy recommendations based on the Guttentag and Herring analysis are for direct control of bank capital ratios (i.e. prudential supervision) but with the proviso that additional mechanisms may be needed to prevent disaster myopia – in this context, insufficient risk weights. The onus may be both on the supervisors to remain vigilant and on the banks to evolve strategic planning structures to offset the tendencies outlined above towards short termism (Guttentag and Herring 1984b).

Five approaches to financial crises have been outlined. Although partly substitutes (particularly monetarist versus financial fragility and rational expectations versus uncertainty) these approaches are also to some extent complementary. Uncertainty and credit rationing may add to our understanding of how crises triggered by the earlier macroeconomic mechanisms come about. Even the main macro theories may illuminate each other: a monetary tightening could help trigger a collapse of a financially fragile economy. Finally, the credit rationing approaches make some attempt at general reconciliation. In the following sections some instances of financial disorder in the Euromarkets are examined and the realism of these mechanisms is assessed in the light of those events.

3 FINANCIAL DISORDER IN THE EUROMARKETS

This section offers a brief narrative of the events of the four main Euromarket crises of the past two decades, namely the Herstatt crisis of June 1974, the advent of the debt crisis in August 1982, the crisis in the FRN market of December 1986 and the equity market crash of October 1987, as material for their analysis in the light of theory.

3.1 The interbank crises of the mid 1970s

The international interbank market grew rapidly in the early 1970s; foreign currency interbank credits to European BIS reporting banks rose from $9 billion in 1970 to $21.8 billion in 1974 (see Johnston 1983). In this context, in 1974 losses by several banks were linked to rash foreign exchange dealing and inadequate appraisal of risks. After the generalized floating of exchange rates in March 1973, many commercial banks expanded their foreign exchange positions. For example, currency instability increased the demand for forward cover for non-bank firms. Since contracts could not always be matched in the forward markets, banks would often accommodate their customers by covering themselves by spot exchange transactions plus Eurocurrency borrowing. The oil price increase heightened the volatility of markets and disrupted patterns of capital flow. Several banks were caught by unexpected depreciation in some currencies together with a tightening of US monetary policy. One serious banking failure was at Bankhaus Herstatt in Cologne in June 1974. Foreign exchange losses also occurred at Franklin National Bank, Lloyds Bank in Lugano, the Bank of Belgium, and Westdeutsche Landesbank. Accounts emerged of unauthorized foreign exchange dealings by relatively junior staff, and of high-risk speculation as banks tried to recover their losses.

The Herstatt crisis raised questions about banks' international exposure and operations. Initially, confidence fell in the interbank market, and many banks began to assess their interbank lending in much more detail. They tended to discriminate sharply between the credit standings of different institutions, causing interbank interest rates to experience marked tiering. For a while, there was widespread concern for the stability of the international banking system.[10] Consequently, in September 1974, the central bank governors of the G10 and Switzerland expressed their commitment to the continued stability of the markets. This move did not guarantee automatic lender-of-last-resort intervention, but did indicate the willingness of central banks to intervene in a crisis. The absence of further banking failures also helped to stabilize the Eurocurrency market by early 1975.

3.2 The debt crisis

During the 1970s, many countries increased their demand for external finance, largely because of sharp increases in the price of oil relative to other commodities and manufactured goods. Meanwhile, the OPEC surpluses were invested through the banking system (though some banks built up holdings of Eurobonds financed by these deposits) and not in securities markets.[11] Partly as a result of these developments, the syndicated credit became the preferred means for international lending by banks. The syndicated credit enabled banks to cope with the demands made on the financial system during the 1970s, by mobilizing substantial quantities of funds with little complexity or delay. However, viewed in retrospect, the simplicity of syndicated credits may also have drawn into international lending a wider range of banks and borrowers than would have been ideal, while many loans were made at excessively fine spreads, i.e. there was a form of bull market and a slippage in credit standards. Thus by 1979 the following conditions were established; high levels of lending, low spreads, little consideration of the capital or ability to pay of borrowers, and a wide range of borrowers of varying credit quality obtaining loans (but a concentration of loans in Mexico, Brazil, Argentina and South Korea).

Alterations to US monetary policy in late 1979 (the shift to a system of trageting non-borrowed reserves) lifted dollar interest rates to unusually high levels and the dollar appreciated strongly. As debt servicing difficulties emerged, market confidence was increasingly undermined. Spreads rose for non-prime borrowers, maturities shortened and the number of credits fell. The debt crisis effectively began with the shock of Mexico's sudden suspension of external debt servicing in August 1982. Borrowing subsequently became more difficult for a number of heavily indebted countries, particularly in Latin America (i.e. quantity rationing applied strongly). However, central banks intervened to prevent a crisis in the interbank market by persuading creditor banks to roll over their claims on Mexican banks (Price 1985) and the Federal Reserve relaxed monetary policy, reducing interest rates sharply.

3.3 The crisis in the FRN market

The origins of the market in floating rate notes[12] lie in the 1960s, when banks used them as a means for raising short- or medium-term funds to support their international lending operations. However, a major spur was given by the debt crisis (outlined above) which led to a sharp decline in new lending as well as in inflows of funds to international banks. As a substitute for syndicated loans (in banks' asset portfolios and as a liability of companies and sovereigns), FRN issues grew particularly stronglyover 1981–5, while the fixed rate Eurobond market was relatively subdued. The main issuers of FRNs were governments and banks (companies preferred to issue in the fixed rate markets). Banks sought to issue subordinated and/or perpetual debt in order to increase their capital bases, but were also attempting to reduce the degree of maturity mismatch in their international lending. Banks also emerged as major investors in the FRN market, holding a large proportion of paper outstanding.

The FRN crisis began with sharp price falls in Deember 1986 in the perpetual sector, which have been blamed on investors' re-evaluation of the equity characteristics of these instruments; fears that the Cooke Committee capital convergence guidelines for international banks would deduct any holdings from capital; an excess supply of bonds given the size of the investor base; the underpricing of issues in relation to risk; and false expectations of liquidity given the size of the market. At the outset of the crisis, it was expected that the problem might be resolved by an issuing hiatus followed by adjustment of terms (Fisher 1988). But large underwriting exposures undermined the market. Rumours of heavy selling became self-fulfilling and prices went into free fall as market makers withdrew. Short selling worsened the situation.

A similar crisis hit the much larger dated sector a month later; yields soared and issuance became virtually impossible. Although the problems of the perpetual sector helped to trigger this, the problems of capital convergence, oversupply and illusion of liquidity were also present in the dated sector. As described by Meuhring (1987) the market had been subjected to relentless downward pressure on yields, which fell below LIBOR in 1986. This tended to exclude banks as investors (given that their ability to buy FRNs is premised on borrowing funds at LIBOR) although they held 80–90 per cent of extant bonds. Lead managers tried to compensate for low spreads with innovations which relied largely on risky interest rate plays, while trading also increased sharply in an attempt by investors to maintain profits - which helped further to compress spreads. Underwriters and investors assumed that risks in the market were limited due to the coupon reset mechanism and built up large positions, failing to note that profits were largely a function of the bull market conditions. (There was an illusion of safety in liquidity.) Last, it was assumed that an investor base existed beyond the banking sector. This was not the case, so short-term speculative demand was mistaken for genuine end buyers. After the crisis, more and more market makers withdrew and liquidity continued to decline. Both the perpetual and dated FRN markets have been largely moribund since then, except for some development of mortgage related issues.

3.4 The equity market crash

During 1987, participants in financial markets became increasingly concerned with the persistence of large current account imbalances between the US, Japan and Germany. The fear was that the imbalances would lead to investor reluctance to hold dollars, entailing downward pressure on the dollar, and higher US interest rates. In addition there was some increase in world inflation expectations, associated both with a strengthening in commodity prices and with the buildup of liquidity in countries such as the UK and Japan with appreciating currencies, the latter being partly a result of official intervention to stem the dollar's decline following the Louvre Accord. As a result of fears of inflation, monetary policy was tightened in several countries. Market concern was compounded by the limited macroeconomic policy coordination that had been achieved and associated policy discords between the US and some other countries in mid October.

A further notable feature prior to the crash was the widening yield gap between government bonds and equities in the US, Japan and the UK, which implied the need for a portfolio shift at some point to re-establish more normal differentials. The fall in equity prices may have represented such a portfolio shift.

A possible explanation of the strong rise in equity prices in 1987 may be couched in terms of a deviation from the fundamental determinants of value. The reasons for the overvaluation of equities are difficult to identify, but may have included falls in the number of shares outstanding owing to buybacks and management buyouts in the United States, and the merger wave in many countries. Falling interest rates, buoyant economic prospects and strong monetary and credit growth also fuelled share price growth. More generally, in the UK and the US but particularly in Japan, a speculative bubble may have occurred. The key underlying factor was the belief that overpriced shares would always find a buyer at current prices and that the level of liquidity would always be the same. Speculative bubbles throughout history have tended to deflate extremely rapidly, as did the 1987 bubble on 19 October.[13]

The equity market crash had sharp consequences for quantities and prices of credit in the international capital markets. International primary markets in both equities and bonds had also been experiencing bull market conditions, with rapid growth of issuance and intense competition among intermediaries. Corporations' debt–income and debt–equity ratios had been rising over the longer term despite the increase in share prices (Davis 1987). Leveraged buyouts and the plentiful availability of credit (including junk bonds) secured on inflated asset values left many individuals firms with extreme levels of gearing.

After the crash, sales of international equity came virtually to a halt, and new issues remained weak for a lengthy period. Several investment banks were left with large tranches of devaluing international equity after they had applied bought deal techniques to primary equity issues. There were fears of commercial banks cutting credit lines to such securities houses, with potential systemic consequences, until the Federal Reserve calmed the markets with its announcement that ample liquidity would be provided. There were also consequences in the international bond market, where issuance fell sharply, especially in the equity warrant sector, and there was marked tiering of yields to sovereign and corporate borrowers, with some of the latter finding themselves excluded from the markets. On the other hand, problems in the Eurobond sector, aggravated by the stock market turmoil, as well as a sharp increase in inflows to banks on deposit of funds withdrawn from the securities markets, left banks flush with funds. This, and the lack of alternative opportunities for income, probably contributed to strong competition among banks in the credit markets, which provided an alternative source of funds to many borrowers excluded from the securities markets.[14]

4 A COMPARATIVE EMPIRICAL ANALYSIS OF THE PERIODS OF INSTABILITY

This section focuses on developments in major economic indicators in the periods immediately surrounding the crises.

Table 15.1 to 15.4 examine potential longer-term precursors to financial crises. Table 15.1 illustrates the growth of debt outstanding prior to the crises. The table shows the rapid expansion of credit in the year prior to these crises; as the accounts above have illustrated (and as emphasized by theories of financial fragility), this was an integral part of the crises themselves.

Table 15.1 Growth of indebtedness (indices)

	Years before crisis				
Crisis and index	$t-4$	$t-3$	$t-2$	$t-1$	t
1974: growth of interbank market[a]	100	152	201	217	232
1982: growth of IDC debt[b]	100	124	152	180	200
1986: growth of FRN market[c]	100	109[e]	244[e]	398	502
1987: growth of US corporations' debt[d]	100	115	127	142	156

[a] Outstanding foreign currency interbank credits (reporting banks). Source: Bank of International Settlements (BIS) (1975).
[b] Evolution of non-OPEC IDCs' external indebtedness. Source: BIS (1983).
[c] Stock of FRNs outstanding. Source: BIS.
[d] US corporations' total liabilities. Source: US flow of funds.
[e] Estimated.

Table 15.2 Indicators of risk pricing prior to crises

Crisis and index	Years before crisis $t-5$	$t-4$	$t-3$	$t-2$	$t-1$	t
1974: interbank spreads[a]	n/a	n/a	2.4	1.3	2.2	3.1
1982: spreads on new IDC credits[b]	1.6	1.3	1.0	0.9	1.1	1.0
1986: spreads on FRNs for banks[c]	-	0.23	0.19	0.14	0.17	0.19
1987: spreads on corporate borrowing:[d]						
credits	0.6	0.6	0.7	0.4	0.4	0.3
bonds	0.8	0.63	0.02	0.09	0.29	0.99

[a] Eurodollar three-month rate less US Treasury bill rate.
[b] Average spread over LIBOR of syndicated credits of IDCs.
[c] Average spread over LIBOR in primary Eurodollar dated FRN market for US bank debt.
[d] OECD corporations; spread over LIBOR for US dollar credits; over US Treasury bonds for Eurodollar bonds.

What was the pattern of spreads prior to the periods of instability? Although data cannot be conclusive (spreads are determined by a variety of factors), table 15.2 offers tentative evidence that standards of risk appraisal were relaxed on each occasion. Interbank spreads in 1972–3 were below those in 1971; spreads on credits to IDCs and on bank FRNs (except in 1986 itself) declined before their respective crises. Corporate borrowing, at least on syndicated credits, was made on progressively more generous terms prior to 1987. Nor were these patterns only observable in the markets where the crises occurred; for example, as noted in section 3, interbank margins fell sharply in the 1970s prior to the debt crisis.

Table 15.3 illustrates patterns in banks' capitalization, an important concomitant of vulnerable situations, as highlighted by theories of credit rationing. Both UK and US banks' capitalization declined prior to the 1974 crisis. In 1982, UK banks' capitalization fell while that in the US remained low. In contrast for 1986 and 1987 – crises which had little impact on commercial banks – capitalization increased. The stronger capitalization of banks in recent years is partly a result of the development of prudential regulation and associated increases in capital ratios. Such regulation should in principle make banks more resilient to the type of crisis outlined in this chapter.

Table 15.4 shows shifts in regime prior to financial crises, the effects of which were acknowledged to be important at the time of the events (see section 3) and the effects of which on systemic vulnerability are highlighted by theories emphasizing uncertainty. The shift from fixed to floating exchange rates and the US switch to monetary targeting based on non-borrowed reserves both increased volatility in markets, though the latter was probably more important for its effect on the *level* of interest rates. The announcement

Table 15.3 Commercial banks' capital ratios

	Years before crisis				
Crisis	$t-4$	$t-3$	$t-2$	$t-1$	t
US banks[a]					
1974	6.58	6.4	6.1	5.77	5.71
1982	5.80	5.75	5.79	5.83	5.87
1986	5.87	6.00	6.14	6.2	6.19
1987	6.00	6.14	6.2	6.19	6.89
UK banks[b]					
1974	7.7	7.6	7.3	6.8	6.4
1982	8.0	7.7	7.4	6.9	6.9
1986	6.9	7.3	6.9	8.5	8.9
1987	7.3	6.9	8.5	8.9	8.5

[a] All insured commercial banks, ratios of capital plus reserves to assets.
[b] Major UK banks' capital–asset ratios (1974 primary book capital–asset ratios), estimated.

Sources: OECD (1987), Revell (1980), Llewellyn (1988)

Table 15.4 Shifts in regime prior to financial crises

Date	Event	Indicator	Statistics	Prior period	Following period
May 1971[a]	Shift fixed–floating exchange rates	$/DM exchange rate	Mean coefficient of variation	3.82 0.05	2.98 0.12
October 1979[b]	Change in US monetary policy	US Treasury bill rate	Mean coefficient of variation	8.29 0.16	12.32 0.17
December 1986[c]	Basle agreement on treatment of bank FRNs	US bank FRN discount margin	Mean coefficient of variation	4.75 0.23	24.58 0.31
November 1986[d]	Introduction of programme trading techniques	US share prices	Mean coefficient of variation	131.9 0.07	162.6 0.08

Observation periods:
[a] 1968(6)–1971(5); 1971(6)–1974(5)
[b] 1976(1)–1979(9); 1979(10)–1982(8)
[c] 1986(1)–1986(12); 1987(1)–1987(12)
[d] 1985(11)–1986(10); 1986(11)–1987(10)

Table 15.5 Share price[a] movements and financial crisis (percentage changes)

Crisis	12 months prior	1 month prior	1 month after	12 months after
1974 (June)	−14.3	0.0	−7.8	+2.9
1982 (August)	−15.4	0.0	+11.7	+48.1
1986 (December)	+20.0	+1.4	+6.4	−3.1
1987 (October)	+18.0	−12.1	−12.5	1.0

[a] US Standard and Poor's 500 share.

of new measures for banks' capital increased volatility in the FRN market. The case for a regime shift in equity markets in 1987 is less clear cut, but the data show that there were increases in volatility which coincided with the widespread introduction of market innovations such as portfolio insurance (as well as the bull market itself).

Table 15.5 and 15.6 examine some factors often held to be directly associated with financial crises. Thus table 15.5 shows share price movements before (and after) the crises as highlighted by the financial fragility approach. Each crises except 1986 was associated with a sharp downwards movement in share prices – most obviously the crash of 1987 which was centred on the equity market. These data suggest that share price weakness may, directly or indirectly, be associated with disorder in the Euromarkets. Whether it is a causal factor rather than an indicator of deteriorating economic conditions is of course less clear (though declines in equity prices tend to entail strong quantity rationing in new issue markets, thus aggravating funding problems for firms that are quantity rationed in credit markets).

Table 15.6 illustrates some other potential causal factors. First, real monetary growth was low or declining prior to the 1974, 1982 and 1987

Table 15.6 Developments in US monetary growth and GNP prior to financial crises

	US monetary growth (M1) (real, change on same quarter a year before), quarter					US GNP growth (real, change on same quarter a year before), quarter				
Crisis	$t-4$	$t-3$	$t-2$	$t-1$	t	$t-4$	$t-3$	$t-2$	$t-1$	t
1974(Q2)	2.8	−0.3	−2.4	−3.5	−5.0	5.4	4.1	3.1	0.1	0.2
1982(Q3)	3.2	−1.4	−1.0	−0.2	1.3	3.4	0.3	−2.7	−2.2	−3.3
1986(Q4)	8.5	8.7	10.0	11.1	14.3	3.8	4.0	3.4	2.5	2.3
1987(Q4)	14.3	12.0	7.2	3.8	−1.5	2.3	1.8	3.1	4.1	5.1

Table 15.7 Percentage changes in the flows of Euromarket lending during crises

Crisis	Change in gross flow[a] (%)	Quarter of crisis on previous year[b]	Following year[b] on quarter of crisis	Year beginning crisis on previous year
1974(Q2)	Credits	−8.6	−40.8	−38.0
	Fixed rate bonds	+15.2	+60.7	+43.8
	FRNs	-	-	-
	Interbank claims	−44.8	−57.8	−82.7
1982(Q3)	Credits	−25.7	−49.2	−50.0
	Fixed rate bonds	28.3	−17.2	+19.4
	FRNs	−43.7	+62.5	−16.4
	Interbank claims	+37.4	−75.5	−44.1
1986(Q4)	Credits	+78.1	+117.4	+214.4
	Fixed rate bonds	−7.1	−9.4	−5.3
	FRNs	−31.2	−68.0	−75.1
	Interbank claims	+120.4	−34.4	+66.1
1987(Q4)	Credits	+49.4	−3.5	+39.7
	Fixed rate bonds	−40.0	+101.1	+9.5
	FRNs	+23.5	+17.0	+30.2
	Interbank claims	−17.5	−45.0	−43.4

[a] Net flow for interbank claims.
[b] Quarterly averages.

crises, suggesting a degree of monetary restraint by the authorities (given the prevailing level of inflation) and concurring with the descriptions in section 3. The 1986 event is again the exception – monetary growth was consistently rapid over the preceding year – suggesting that the FRN crisis was a localized rather than a general macroeconomic phenomenon. As for the economic cycle, the data show that in 1974 and 1982, and to a lesser extent in 1986, there had been a sharp slowdown in economic activity prior to the crisis. In 1987, however, the opposite is true. The occurrence of crises at different phases of the cycle suggests strongly that they were not causal factors in relation to GNP; if anything the contrary (i.e. weakened economic activity may have created the conditions in which the crisis could occur).

Table 15.7 and 15.8 show quantity and price developments in the major Euromarkets at the times of the crises. As might be expected, table 15.7 shows that the markets directly concerned in the crisis were worst hit in each case: interbank claims fell by 45 per cent in the quarter of the crisis of 1974 compared with the previous year; credits by 26 per cent in 1982; FRNs by

31 per cent in 1986; and bonds by 40 per cent in 1987. It is also evident that in 1974, 1982 and 1986 the crises were prolonged in the market concerned; there was no rapid recovery. In contrast, the fixed rate bond market recovered strongly in the year after the crash.

The table also gives indications of effects in other markets. Did quantities decline, suggesting systemic dimensions, or increase in order to substitute for the worst hit market? Patterns for the earlier crises suggest some degree of contagion (though of course general economic conditions also affected issuance). In 1974 the credits market declined sharply along with interbank claims over all the subperiods analysed. In 1982 there was an initial increase in fixed rate bond issue and interbank claims in the quarter of the crisis; however, comparing the year beginning the crisis with the previous year, only the fixed rate bond market showed any increase (the beginning of the securitization process). The FRN crisis appeared to be more localized. Again, in 1987 activity in the credits market increased sharply while bond issuance plunged, and issuance of FRNs also recovered. Over the following year, there were increases in all but interbank claims.

These data suggest that in no case was contagion pervasive (though of course not all borrowers could freely substitute between markets). One can nonetheless distinguish between 1974/1982 on the one hand and 1986/1987 on the other in that a greater substitutability between instruments (i.e. a lesser degree of contagion) is apparent during the later crises, possibly because the markets were more developed; or, conversely, that systemic effects in the Euromarkets were more muted in these cases. Saunders (1985) also found little evidence of contagion between groups of banks in the interbank market in the crises of the early 1980s.

Table 15.8 shows in more detail the price responses associated with the crises, for example the sharp increase in LIBOR relative to US Treasury bills (illustrating stress in the interbank markets) in 1974. It is notable that secondary market yields on fixed rate bonds and (to a lesser extent) spreads on new syndicated credits also increased over this period, suggesting a degree of contagion between markets and concomitant price rationing of credit. The other crises are less clear cut in terms of price responses. During the debt crisis, average realized spreads on syndicated credits did not increase, suggesting the existence of quantity rationing of credit to account for the decline in lending shown in table 15.7. Fixed rate bond yields increased, suggesting concerns over default risk, but the increase in borrowing over the year of the crisis suggests there were still willing borrowers at these rates. Finally, although interbank claims declined sharply there was no strong increase in LIBOR compared with the US Treasury bill rate. As with syndicated credits, this may imply some quantity rationing.

For the 1986 crisis, there was little detectable effect in markets other than the FRN market. (Some slight upward pressure on spreads on credits is also

Table 15.8 Percentage changes in interest rate relationships during crises

Crisis	Month								
	$t-12$	$t-3$	$t-2$	$t-1$	t	$t+1$	$t+2$	$t+3$	$t+12$
1974 (June)									
Credits[a]	0.1	0.3	0.5	0.5	0.7	0.6	1.3	0.9	1.2
Fixed rate bonds[b]	1.8	1.8	1.9	2.0	2.2	3.0	3.1	3.6	1.2
FRNs[c]	-	-	-	-	-	-	-	-	-
Interbank[d]	1.6	1.2	2.3	3.3	3.9	5.7	4.8	4.0	0.9
US Treasury bills	7.2	8.0	8.2	8.4	8.2	7.8	8.7	8.4	5.2
1982 (August)									
Credits[a]	1.0	0.9	1.1	0.9	1.0	0.9	0.9	0.9	0.7
Fixed rate bonds[b]	−0.3	0.9	0.7	1.6	2.8	3.2	3.7	3.2	1.1
FRNs[c]	-	-	-	-	-	-	-	-	-
Interbank[d]	3.3	2.4	3.3	2.5	2.5	3.6	2.7	1.7	0.9
US Treasury bills	15.6	12.2	12.1	11.9	9.0	8.2	7.8	8.0	9.4
1986 (December)									
Credits[a]	0.3	0.3	0.4	0.3	0.6	0.3	0.6	0.6	0.3
Fixed rate bonds[b]	1.3	1.2	1.3	1.4	1.4	1.2	0.9	1.0	1.2
FRNs[c]	0.03	0.06	0.07	0.07	0.07	0.12	0.12	0.24	0.38
Interbank[d]	0.9	0.7	0.7	0.6	0.7	0.6	0.7	0.8	2.1
US Treasury bills	7.1	5.2	5.2	5.4	5.5	5.5	5.6	5.6	5.8
1987 (October)									
Credits[a]	0.4	0.7	0.2	0.3	0.3	0.4	0.3	0.4	0.3
Fixed rate bonds[b]	1.3	0.8	0.7	0.6	0.9	1.4	1.2	1.3	0.6
FRNs[c]	0.07	0.32	0.28	0.25	0.2	0.32	0.38	0.36	0.28
Interbank[d]	0.7	1.0	1.0	1.1	1.9	1.6	2.1	1.2	1.2
US Treasury bills	5.2	5.8	6.0	6.4	6.4	5.8	5.9	5.7	7.3

[a] Average spread over LIBOR (US dollar credits).
[b] Secondary market: private sector Eurodollar bonds minus US Treasuries.
[c] Secondary market: discounted margin over LIBOR (US banks' dollar FRNs).
[d] Three-month Eurodollar rate less US Treasury bill rate.

apparent.) In October 1987 the increase in yields on fixed rate bonds is marked. Pricing in the credits market appears unaffected, but LIBOR relative to US Treasury bill increased sharply from 1 to 1.9 per cent, perhaps reflecting perceptions of risks in interbank lending relative to domestic government paper. Finally, it is notable that the US Treasury bill rate itself fell sharply after the 1987 crisis, reflecting relaxation of monetary policy and the flight to quality by investors. A similar pattern is evident after the advent of the debt crisis.

5 THE THEORY OF CRISES VIEWED IN THE LIGHT OF EMPIRICAL EVIDENCE

This section assesses the applicability of the theories of financial crisis in the light of the four periods of instability in the Euromarkets outlined and illustrated in sections 3 and 4. The results are summarized in table 15.9. These suggest that while all of the theories have important contributions to make to the understanding of recent financial disorder, none is all-embracing and a form of synthesis would seem to be called for. Some attempt at this is made in the concluding section.

5.1 The monetarist approach

The acknowledged influence of monetary tightening on the crises of 1974, 1982 and 1987 and the fact that the 1974 and 1982 crises occurred after cyclical peaks (see table 15.6) lends at least partial credence to monetarist views of financial crisis. However, it is less clear that the crises caused a reduction in the money supply, thus aggravating the contraction. The nearest to this may have been in 1974, when the reduced supply of short-term inter-bank credit may have influenced the price of credit (syndicated credits) to final users. Although the debt crisis may have worsened the recession of the early 1980s, this was due to the effects on global demand of the reduced ability of IDCs to purchase imports rather than enhanced monetary contraction. Central bank intervention to loosen monetary conditions generally helped to prevent adverse macroeconomic changes. Bank panics were not a feature of most of the crises, though the insolvency of Herstatt in 1974 (and the accompanying collapse of Franklin National in the US domestic markets) had many of the features of a panic. The lack of panic may again be partly attributed to the role of central bank intervention, particularly in 1982 and 1987 when bankruptcy of some borrowers was feared. On these occasions, relaxations of monetary policy also helped to offset any tendency for monetary contraction. It was the initial absence of strong intervention in 1974 that led to the Herstatt crisis (while US intervention helped contain the effects of Franklin National), and necessitated the communiqué by the G10 governors in September 1974.

5.2 Financial fragility

Again, some but not all of the mechanisms highlighted by this approach seem validated by the evidence. There clearly was rapid accumulation of debt

Table 15.9 Summary of features of periods of instability

	Crisis			
Paradigm	1974	1982	1986	1987
Monetary				
Prior monetary tightening	yes	yes	no	yes
Occurred beyond cyclical peak	yes	yes	no	no
Banking panics	yes	no	no	no
Aggravated downturn	no	yes	no	no
Caused reduction in money supply	no	no	no	no
Financial fragility				
Prior displacement	(no)	yes	(no)	(no)
Accumulation of risky debt	yes	yes	yes	(yes)
Occurred at cyclical peak	no	no	no	no
Speculation	yes	yes	yes	yes
Distress selling in credit markets	no	no	(yes)	no
Deflation, increased real rates	no	no	no	no
Rational expectations				
Bubble in asset/security prices	no	no	yes	yes
Uncertainty				
Regime shift	yes	yes	yes	(yes)
Competitive innovation	no	yes	yes	yes
Evidence of crowd psychology (low risk premiums)	yes	yes	yes	yes
Credit rationing				
Declining risk premiums	yes	yes	yes	yes
Declining capital ratios	yes	yes	no	yes
Increased quantity rationing	yes	yes	(yes)	(yes)
Long-term quantity rationing	yes	yes	(no)	no
Increased price rationing	yes	yes	yes	yes
Concentration of risk	(yes)	yes	(yes)	(yes)
Intense competition between intermediaries	yes	yes	yes	yes
General				
International transmission	yes	yes	yes	yes
Intervention of authorities	(yes)	yes	no	yes
Contagion between markets	yes	yes	(yes)	yes

in each case (see table 15.1). The nature of the risk concerned differs of course: in 1974 and 1982, concerns were centred on default risk; in 1986, liquidity risk was perhaps crucial; in 1987, a mixture of both. Again, these accumulations were accompanied by speculation in 1986 and 1987. Speculative underwriting exposures were a particular problem during the crash. Foreign exchange speculation caused the 1974 crisis. The LDC debt crisis arguably also had a speculative side, banks always wishing to earn spreads while expecting to be able to exit at the next rollover date (despite the fact that borrowers needed new credits to cover their interest payment obligations). The same false expectations of liquidity of course helped to create the conditions for the equity market crash. The FRN market collapsed after speculators had become the main holders. Adopting Minsky's (1982) terminology, some of the episodes could at least partly be characterized as speculative or Ponzi financing.

On the other hand, the crises did not tend to occur at cyclical peaks and cause the following downturn; again, this may partly be due to the policy response (for example, the loosening of monetary policy in 1982 and 1987). This may also account for the absence of widespread distress selling and of deflation with concomitant increased real rates. Equally, wealth effects on consumption which were widely feared in 1987 turned out to be minor, as investors had not fully taken into account the previous rise in share prices.

The existence of a prior displacement triggering rapid growth in debt and of accompanying monetary innovation is debatable. The period of the debt crisis opened with the displacement of the oil shock, though its precise links to the crisis (the need for balance of payments financing) are less direct than in the theories of financial fragility. The relevant displacement for the other crises is less clear. Innovations with significant monetary effects have been a feature of the 1970s and 1980s (money market mutual funds in the US, high-interest cheque accounts in the UK). However, apart from the development of the interbank market itself, these were arguably less relevant to the crises than the more general types of financial innovation emphasized by theories noting the role of uncertainty.

5.3 Rational expectations

As noted above, several of the crises had features resembling speculative bubbles and runs. However, particularly in the case of bubbles it is less clear that the bubbles were rational in the sense that returns increased exponentially in order to encourage risk-averse individuals to remain in the market concerned. The bubbles (for example in 1987) are more reminiscent of irrational bubbles, where agents were prepared to remain in the market regardless of the pattern of excess returns, so long as they were not strongly negative.[15] A degree of irrationality may have been present, which expressed itself in the beliefs that the fundamentals had changed - and that the agent would always be able to exit first (the illusion of liquidity). Such hypotheses are of course difficult to test formally. The rational expectations theory of runs again seems somewhat too precise to characterize the respective crises, given that seemingly trivial causes led funds to be withdrawn (from lower-rated banks in the interbank market, and from the FRN and equity markets) and in each case many lenders/investors were left with disproportionately large losses.

5.4 Uncertainty

Most of the mechanisms outlined in section 2.4 had a role to play in these crises; for example, a shift of regime with unforeseen consequences, evidence of crowd psychology in lending, and competitive innovation.

In terms of a regime shift, the direct cause of the 1974 crisis was the shift from fixed to floating exchange rates, the dynamics of which were unforeseen by market participants. Similarly, the banks prior to the debt crisis did not foresee the possibility of a second oil shock, the deep recession and the new US monetary policy which drove up interest rates so sharply and increased their volatility. As noted, the evidence of a regime shift is weaker for the FRN market and the crash.

Crowd psychology, notably reduced risk premiums, was evident in each episode: lending on the interbank market in 1974 without careful assessment of credit risk and risky practices in foreign exchange markets; similar risky lending to IDCs, even when new loans were needed to pay interest on existing ones; launching of ever-greater volumes of FRNs at lower and lower spreads; and an equity market bubble and speculative debt finance dependent on high equity values. In each case lenders (or intermediaries) were comforted by the knowledge that others were making the same judgements; in each case they were proved wrong, and risk premiums proved too low in retrospect.

Innovation played a key part in the crises of the 1980s; in each case there was a flaw in the market's understanding of the innovation. In the case of the debt crisis the main innovation was the syndicated credit together with sovereign lending itself, as outlined. The securities market crashes of 1986 and 1987were even more fundamentally linked to innovation, which provided at least part of the driving force behind the move to crisis conditions. The FRN market, as noted, was characterized by a wide variety of innovations which attempted to compensate for declining spreads. Investors may have failed to understand liquidity risks in the market. The equity market crash has been linked to numerous innovations (programme trading, portfolio insurance) which gave rise to an illusion of liquidity.

5.5 Credit rationing

Like uncertainty, credit rationing has been a widely observed feature of recent financial crises. As shown in table 15.8, risk premiums (i.e. price rationing of credit) for classes of institution affected increased, and there is also some evidence of quantity rationing for lower-quality institutions: certain classes of banks in the interbank market after 1974; the most indebted IDCs since 1982; closure of the FRN for new issues in 1986 and partial closure of the equity warrant and straight Eurobond sector in 1987; and severe quantity rationing of bank credit for securities houses with equity exposures in 1987. However, banks in 1986 and corporations in 1987 did not find themselves excluded from credit altogether, but instead shifted to other, more expensive, markets. Again, such quantity rationing as there was only remained for a relatively short time. These may suggest a declining segmentation of the markets, which makes a credit crunch for a borrowing sector (i.e. closing of all sources of credit) less likely.

Guttentag and Herring (1984a) also highlighted declines in borrowers' and lenders' capital ratios together with concentration of risk - a somewhat more precise form of Minsky's (1982) fragility. Declining capital ratios for banks were certainly evident prior to the 1974 and 1982 crises, especially if risks are correctly weighted. Low capitalization exacerbated the crises when they did occur. Concentration of risk was also apparent, particularly in the IDC debt crisis. Again, in the equity market crash there were concerns over heavily indebted corporations (especially those involved in speculative takeover plays) as well as for investment banks that had taken on concentrated risks (large underwriting exposures). Intense competition between intermediaries was also present in each crisis - and helped to prompt risky behaviour.

5.6 General issues

We conclude with observations on issues common to several of the theories. For example, international transmission was a feature of each crisis (the crises were not confined to one national market). This is partly to be expected: the Euromarkets are an important conduit for international capital flows; they also involve commercial and investment banks from all the major countries, which if involved in similar business would all be hit in a systemic crisis. The effects of the debt crisis are an example of this. Transnational effects of financial crises are also, however, increasing owing to the growing integration of domestic and international markets, with the same borrowers, intermediaries and lenders active in each. This has reduced the insulation of domestic markets from shocks originating in international or other domestic markets, as the 1987 crash illustrated.

Intervention by the authorities was highlighted by most of the theories as the immediate solution to financial crises when they occur. These were not felt to be events that the market can sort out painlessly for itself. Decisive intervention (by the US Federal Reserve and other central banks) was particularly apparent in the equity market crash, but was also evident after the debt crisis and the 1974 debacle. Only the FRN crisis was felt sufficiently localized to blow itself out.

Lastly, in terms of contagion between markets, it was shown in section 4 that this was a particularly marked feature of the 1974 and 1982 crises. In the FRN crisis it was largely confined to the market itself (effects of the perpetual FRN market on the dated market). The crisis in the Eurobond markets in 1987 was itself a result of contagion from the equity markets, though contagion to other Euromarkets and to domestic government bond markets was more muted.

6 CONCLUSIONS

Subject to the limitations of the qualitative analytical approach adopted, this chapter offers several types of conclusion. First, it allows one to assess whether the crises were unique events or had common features. Second, it allows one to evaluate theories of financial crisis under current conditions - which factors should be highlighted and which discarded, and whether a synthesis is possible. This allows an assessment to be made of implications for the authorities and market participants.

The data and descriptions presented, informed by the theoretical summary, suggest that the crises studied were not unique events but had discernible common features. Perhaps the most important of these common features of financial instability in the Euromarkets over 1974–87 were the following:[16]

(a) They followed accumulation of debt and substantial speculation in assets which were often characterized by crowd-like behaviour among lenders, low risk premiums and concentration of risk.
(b) They followed a shift in regime which had unforeseeable or unforeseen consequences.
(c) Innovation was often an important concomitant, as were declining capital ratios of lenders and borrowers.
(d) They often followed a period of monetary tightening (necessitated by inflationary pressures) and/or recession.
(e) They were accompanied by sharp increases in price and quantity

rationing of credit, but this did not always prevent rationed borrowers from obtaining credit elsewhere.

(f) International transmission was strong and rapid.

(g) Contagion between markets was limited; in no case were all Euromarkets strongly affected.

(h) Decisive action by the authorities prevented the crises from having serious systemic and macroeconomic consequences.

Features (a)–(f) were also present during the Great Depression. Any synthesis would therefore emphasize the monetary and fragility precursors of financial crises, while stressing also the role of uncertainty in the conditions for crisis, the likelihood of credit rationing as a consequence of such crises, and the importance of intervention.

Put more precisely, a synthesis of the theory of financial crises applicable to conditions in contemporary financial markets, drawing on economic theory and recent experience in the Euromarkets, should offer predictions regarding the preconditions, causes, nature and consequences of financial crises. For example, a long period of relative calm conditions with intense competition between financial institutions,[17] increasing debt accumulation at increasingly low risk premiums (partly as a consequence of these), financial innovation and declining capital ratios may constitute the preconditions for a financial crisis. Supervisory pressure to maintain capitalization and prevent excessive risk taking may consequently help to prevent these conditions from arising. The crisis may be triggered by a tightening of monetary conditions and the unforeseen consequences of a shift in regime (including the unforeseen properties of financial innovations). It may be accompanied by a sizeable deviation of asset values from their fundamental determinants (a speculative bubble). The crisis may entail runs or panics, which eliminate such deviations in asset values, and a sharp increase in price and quantity rationing of credit. However, it may not lead to strong contagion between markets, further monetary contraction and economic recession, although prevention of these effects may require the authorities to intervene firmly and decisively.[18]

The analysis of this chapter has implications both for the authorities and for market participants in deregulated financial markets (drawn mainly from the recommendations of the theoretical paradigms). For supervisors, it is suggested that the common features of financial crises identified above could be of assistance in helping to assess when heightened vigilance and examination of financial institutions' balance sheets are required. Theory and experience suggest that such examinations could cover not only capitalization but also growth of debt, gearing of creditors, vulnerability to crises in other national or international markets, asset prices, concentration of risk, implications of innovations, intensity of competition, risk pricing, indirect exposures, strength of control mechanisms over borrowers, and potential liquidity of intermediaries' assets and liabilities in crisis situations. Given that supervisory regimes covering many of these aspects have been developed and refined recently (including enhanced international cooperation), the possibility of serious crisis may be judged to have been reduced. However, supervisors still need to be vigilant to ensure not only that the institutions they supervise are not becoming subject to disaster myopia but also that they are not becoming complacent themselves, accepting prevailing judgements of risk which may have become distorted by a period of calm and intense competition. A possible indicator of such myopia is declining risk premiums (table 15.2).[19] Finally, an equalization of the tax treatment of debt and equity may reduce tendencies to over-indebtedness.

For macroeconomic policy makers the relationship of crises to shifts of policy regime and turning points in the tightness of policy has several implications. First, there is a need for policy to seek to avoid conditions such as rapid inflation which may necessitate such sudden shifts or tightening of policy. Second, should such changes be required, there is a need for vigilance for financial stability. Third, although the lender-of-last-resort function should be retained, its use should be sparing and bank management (and their shareholders) who have made mistakes should always be sacrificed. Otherwise the existence of the lender of last resort may actually induce the development of the financial fragile conditions that its use is aimed to counteract.

For market participants, several of the same implications apply. They need to examine market conditions frequently in the light of the factors identified above, perhaps by use of strategic planning divisions, in order to assess the likelihood of crisis situations and the consequent appropriateness of their pricing of risk. How assured are their credit lines? How strong is their asset backing? Has their exposure to credit or liquidity risk been increasing? Depositors and investors also need to be aware of these potential risks – though, as noted above, this may require limitation of depositor protection and of moral hazard created by intervention. Private rating agencies may have an important role to play in monitoring firms' exposures as well as taking the longer and broader view recommended in this chapter.

Notes

The views expressed are those of the author and not necessarily those of the Bank of England. I am grateful to Mark Taylor for helpful comments on a previous draft; the usual disclaimer applies.

1 Certain other crises largely confined to domestic markets (Penn Central, US thrifts; the UK secondary banking crisis) are thus omitted from the main analysis.

2 In this the chapter follows Schwartz (1986) who described recent events as 'pseudo financial crises', although it disagrees with her conclusion that such pseudo crises are matters of little import.

3 See also Bernanke (1983), who suggests that the main transmission mechanism of bank failures was the ability of the financial sector to allocate funds.

4 Rational bubbles will follow if a long-run transversality condition fails, so a multiplicity of RE solutions is possible (MacDonald and Taylor 1989).

5 Here, the transversality condition is satisfied so there are no multiple RE solutions; the run is just a jump in the RE path.

6 Herding may be rationalized to some extent in finance if all (large) banks expect to be rescued in a systemic crisis, whereas one bank going alone in a different direction would be allowed to go bankrupt (Price 1985).

7 Which Shafer (1986) noted are similar to the 'creative destruction of innovation' of Schumpeter (1942).

8 For recessions, participants either know the mechanisms underlying investment returns or can infer objective probabilities from the frequency distribution of the returns.

9 An example may be predatory pricing to drive other firms from the market; see Davis (1988) for an analysis of such competitive behaviour and associated risks in the Eurobond market.

10 Lepetit (1982) notes: 'In the Herstatt affair, it seems the German authorities wanted to teach speculators, as well as banks dealing with speculators, a lesson. But the US clearing system nearly collapsed with Herstatt on 26 June 1974; the CHIPS computer was switched off, and it was necessary for the clearing US banks to barter checks during the whole night and afterwards to use the impossible device of conditional transfers.'

11 However, as noted by Bond and Briault (1983), it would be wrong to see banks as mere recyclers of funds. First, the correlation between IDC loans and OPEC deposits is highly imperfect. Second, banks evidently bid aggressively for deposits and also for loans, stimulated by such factors as: an increasing focus on balance sheet growth rather than only profitability; the shift from asset to liability management; the ability to cross-subsidize international business from profits made in oligopolistic domestic markets and from the insurance provided by banks to depositors via their capital; as well as misjudgement of the risks – notably of the potential correlation between sovereign risks when economic conditions deteriorated – and of the intensity of competition in the market, which kept spreads low.

12 Defined as medium-term securities carrying a floating rate of interest that is reset at regular intervals in relation to some predetermined market rate.

13 It is notable that the consensus at the time was that the price falls were not proportionate to the macroeconomic changes immediately preceding the crash (as rational expectations would predict) but were *greater than appeared* warranted, suggesting a rethinking of decision processes (as the uncertainty approach would predict).

14 For further details of the reactions of the Euromarkets to the crash, see Davis (1989).

15 For a discussion of rational and irrational bubbles in this context, see Artis and Taylor (1988).
16 Analysis of selected domestic crises over the same period (see Davis 1989) reveals many similar features.
17 We note that the theories outlined here offer few suggestions on the genesis and nature of this competition, and on structural developments in markets that may accompany it. Industrial aspects of crisis are probed in Davis (1990).
18 Not that such intervention is always required. Some crises are localized enough not to offer systemic risks, either because institutions involved are sufficiently robust or because the market concerned is relatively unimportant. Indeed, some would argue that minor crises may be salutary in leading intermediaries and the authorities to tighten up control and supervision.
19 Other possible indicators based on the industrial dynamics of financial markets are suggested in Davis (1990).

References

Artis, M. J. and Taylor, M. P. (1988) 'Policy coordination and exchange rate stabilization', evidence submitted to the UK Treasury and Civil Service Committee on International Monetary Coordination, House of Commons, HC paper 384, London: HMSO.

Bank for International Settlements (1975) *Forty Fifth Annual Report* Basle: BIS.

Bank for International Settlements (1983) 'The international interbank market: a descriptive study', BIS, economics paper 8.

Bank for International Settlements (1986) *Recent Innovations in International Banking* (the Cross Report), Basle: BIS.

Bernanke, B. S. (1983) 'Non-monetary effects of the financial crisis in the propagation of the Great Depression', *American Economic Review*, 73, 257–76.

Blanchard, O. J. and Watson, M. W. (1982) 'Bubbles, rational expectations and financial markets', in P. Wachtel (ed.), *Crises in the Economic and Financial Structure*, Salomon Bros Center Series on Financial Institutions and Markets, Lexington, MA: Lexington Books.

Bond, I. D. and Briault, C. B. (1983) 'Commercial banks and international debt; the experience of the 1970s', Bank of England, mimeo.

Cagan, P. (1965) *Determinants and Effects of Changes in the Stock of Money*, NBER Studies in Business Cycles vol 13, New York: Columbia University Press.

Davis, E. P. (1987) 'Rising sectoral debt–income ratios; a cause for concern?', BIS, economics paper 20.

Davis, E. P. (1988) 'Industrial structure and dynamics of financial markets; the primary Eurobond market', Bank of England, discussion paper 35.

Davis, E. P. (1989) 'Instability in the Euromarket and the economic theory of financial crisis', Bank of England, discussion paper 43.

Davis, E. P. (1990) 'An industrial approach to financial instability', Bank of England, discussion paper 50.

Fisher, F. G. (1988) *Eurobonds*, London: Euromoney Publications.

Fisher, I. (1932) *Booms and Depressions*, New York: Adelphi.

Flood, R. P. and Garber, P. M. (1982) 'Bubbles, rational expectations and gold monetization', in P. Wachtel (ed.), *Crises in the Economic and Financial Structure*, Salomon Bros Center Series on Financial Institutions and Markets, Lexington, MA: Lexington Books.

Friedman, M. and Schwartz, A. J. (1963) *A Monetary History of the United States 1867–1960*, Princeton, NJ: Princeton University Press.

Guttentag, J. and Herring, R. (1984a) 'Credit rationing and financial disorder', *Journal of Finance*, 39, 1359–82.

Guttentag, J. and Herring, R. (1984b) 'Strategic planning by international banks to cope with uncertainty', Brookings discussion papers in international economics 23.

Johnston, R. B. (1983) *The Economics of the Euromarket*, London and Basingstoke: Macmillan.

Kindleberger, O. P. (1978) *Manias, Panics and Crashes: a History of Financial Crises*, New York: Basic Books.

Knight, F. H. (1921) *Risk, Uncertainty and Profit*, Boston; no. 16 in series of reprints of scarce texts in economics, London School of Economics.

Lepetit, J. F. (1982) 'Comment on the lender of last resort', in O. P. Kindleberger and J.-P. Laffargue (eds), *Financial Crises: Theory, History and Policy*, Cambridge: Cambridge University Press.

Llewellyn, D. T. (1988) 'The strategic dilemma of world banking; implication of Basle capital convergence', paper presented at the Prince Bertil Lectures, Gotenburg.

MacDonald, R. and Taylor, M. P. (1989) 'Economic analysis of foreign exchange markets: an expository survey', in R. McDonald and M. P. Taylor (eds), *Exchange Rates and Open Economy Macroeconomics*, Oxford: Basil Blackwell.

Meltzer, A. H. (1982) 'Rational expectations, risk, uncertainty, and market responses', in P. Wachtel (ed.), *Crises in the Economic and Financial Structure*, Salomon Bros Center Series on Financial Institutions and Markets, Lexington, MA: Lexington Books.

Minsky, H. (1982) 'The financial instability hypothesis, capitalist processes and the behaviour of the economy', in O. P. Kindleberger and J.-P. Laffargue (eds), *Financial crises: Theory, History and Policy* Cambridge: Cambridge University Press.

Muehring, K. (1987) 'Turmoil in the FRN market', *Institutional Investor*, January, 79–82.

OECD (1987) *Bank Profitability*, Paris: OECD.

Price, L. D. D. (1985) 'Discussion of contagion effects in the interbank market', in R. Portes and A. Swaboda (eds), *Threats to International Financial Stability*, Cambridge: Cambridge University Press.

Revell, J. (1980) *Costs and Margins in Banking; an International Study*, Paris: OECD.

Saunders, A. (1985) 'Contagion effects in the interbank market', in R. Portes and A. Swoboda (eds), *Threats to International Financial Stability*, Cambridge: Cambridge University Press.

Schumpeter, J. A. (1942) *Capitalism, Socialism and Democracy*; republished London: Unwin, 1974.

Schwartz, A. J. (1986) 'Real and pseudo financial crises', in F. Capie and G. E. Wood (eds), *Financial Crises and the World Banking System*, London: MacMillan.

Shafer, J. R. (1986) 'Managing crises in the emerging financial landscape', *OECD Economic Studies*, 8, 56–77.

Stiglitz, J. E. and Weiss, A. (1981) 'Credit rationing in markets with imperfect information', *American Economic Review*, 71, 393–410.

Part IV
New Directions in Financial Markets Analysis

16 Neural Networks in Economics

Paul Ormerod, John C. Taylor and Ted Walker

1 INTRODUCTION

According to the Kuhnian model of scientific progress, most science takes place within a particular paradigm. It is when progress within the paradigm begins to slow and when it is increasingly unable to account for natural phenomena that a search for a new paradigm begins.

The current state-of-the-art approach to the econometric analysis of time series data appears to be a paradigm which is close to exhaustion. Founded in the work of Sargan at the LSE in the 1960s and developed by Hendry in the 1970s, the approach represented an important step forward and enhanced our ability to understand how the economy behaves. The benefits which it has brought are evident on a wide scale in the applied macroeconomic literature.

Neural networks represent a promising but as yet unproven methodology for extending the accuracy of forecasting economic time series. We describe below the approach which these systems take. They are quite different from most conventional computer-based methodologies. They operate on the basis of pattern recognition, and mimic the way in which the human brain is believed to function. A key feature of such networks is that they are learning systems. In other words, they are trained to recognize patterns in relating vectors of input information to vectors of output information.

2 HISTORY

Macroeconometric modelling in particular became strikingly more sophisticated through the new approaches to estimation which began to circulate amongst UK modellers in the mid 1970s. There were clear improvements in forecasting accuracy obtained during the 1970s, and the new techniques of estimation played an important part in this. Since then, however, there has been no general improvement in forecasting ability. Burns (1986) did establish that the longer-term (two-year) Treasury forecasts, adjusted for changes in the inherent noisiness of the economy, had improved in the early 1980s compared with the 1970s, but he could find no such improvements in short-term forecasts. Wallis (1989) extended Burns's methodology to other UK forecasts, but he could not report any clear example of improvements in forecasting accuracy.

Of course, as the work of Artis in particular has demonstrated, many more factors are involved in macro forecasting accuracy than the choice of estimation methodology. A further point to be considered, however, is the fact that the new methodology has proved disappointing in resolving theoretical disputes in economics. Practitioners in the mid and late 1970s, as one of the current authors can affirm, felt a real sense of excitement that the new estimation approach would enable real progress to be made in resolving theoretical arguments in macroeconomics. Some progress has been made, but radically different views as to how the economy operates still abound within the UK economics profession.

The longer-term (four- and five-year) forecasting of economic models has in any event been poor. Holden (1990) is one example of a study of such accuracy whose findings are typical of the rest. An important reason for this is that economic models are notorious for their inability to predict turning points in data out of the sample period. One possible source of this weakness is parameter instability, but it is more likely that a lack of non-linearities in macro models is the cause. It is unlikely that a structure as complex as a Western economy can be captured adequately by a linear system of equations. The assumption of linearity is not completely absurd, since low-order linear autoregressive schemes such as most existing macro models do forecast well for quite a lot of the time. Even so, macro models exhibit few non-linearities, which may well be an important reason for their weakness in identifying turning points on an *ex ante* basis.

More generally, macro models have been subjected to the Lucas critique. Advanced in 1976, this hypothesis claims that parameter values are not robust with respect to changes in policy regime. Ultimately, the validity or otherwise of this critique is an empirical one. Theoretically it is correct, but does it matter in practice? Hendry (1988) has proposed a method for testing whether an estimated relationship survives the Lucas critique in-sample, but the general failure of models in longer-term prediction provides *prima facie* evidence for its validity.

Asset price data are an area where the critiques of econometric modelling of time series data apply with particular force. In general, it has not proved possible to estimate relationships which can be used to generate profits *ex ante*. There are three main reasons for the failure of the current state-of-the-art modelling techniques in explaining and forecasting asset price movements. First, the fact that the basic methodology is statistical means that only a limited number of determinants of any given asset price can be analysed at the same time. But in these markets, a large number of factors will be in operation at any one time. Second, and even more important, the structural relationship between an asset price and its determinants changes over time. These changes can be abrupt. For example, one month a rise in interest rates will strengthen sterling, whilst the next month a rise will weaken sterling. This phenomenon of unstable structural parameters in asset price models is a special case of the Lucas critique of econometric models. The third reason is that many of the rules which drive asset prices are qualitative or fuzzy, requiring judgement, and hence by definition are not susceptible to purely quantitative analysis. Neural networks seem well suited to deal with these problems.

3 NEURAL NETWORKS

Neural computing is a new but rapidly expanding branch of computer science. To illustrate how new, figure 16.1 shows how the number of papers written on the subject of neural computing has risen per year (data taken from Wasserman and Oetzel (1990)). There has been a tremendous surge of interest in the past few years. The subject is not an entirely new one, however; the first work on mathematical modelling of neurons was done in the 1940s by McCulloch and Pitts (1943).

In the 1960s there was a certain amount of interest in assemblies of artificial neurons called perceptrons, but in 1969 Minsky and Papert demonstrated some inherent learning difficulties in the assemblies then under consideration. Interest in the area of research died for a while, but resumed in the mid 1980s when Rumelhart et al. (1985) showed that the difficulties could be overcome in more complex networks – and provided an algorithm which could perform that learning.

Neural computing is multidisciplinary, bringing together biologists, computer scientists, mathematicians, psychologists, electronic engineers and other researchers. A division exists between neural science, principally concerned with the biological aspects of neural nets, and neural computing, which tries to use some of the structures and mechanisms discovered by neural science in a computer context. These mechanisms are clearly tremendously powerful and are able to cope with problems which are quite intractable for the most sophisticated conventional computing techniques. Whereas brain cells can respond to stimuli relatively slowly, in milliseconds, electronic circuits switch in nanoseconds – a million times faster. Nevertheless, brains can perform complex pattern recognition operations much quicker than is possible using existing electronic devices. Since we take only

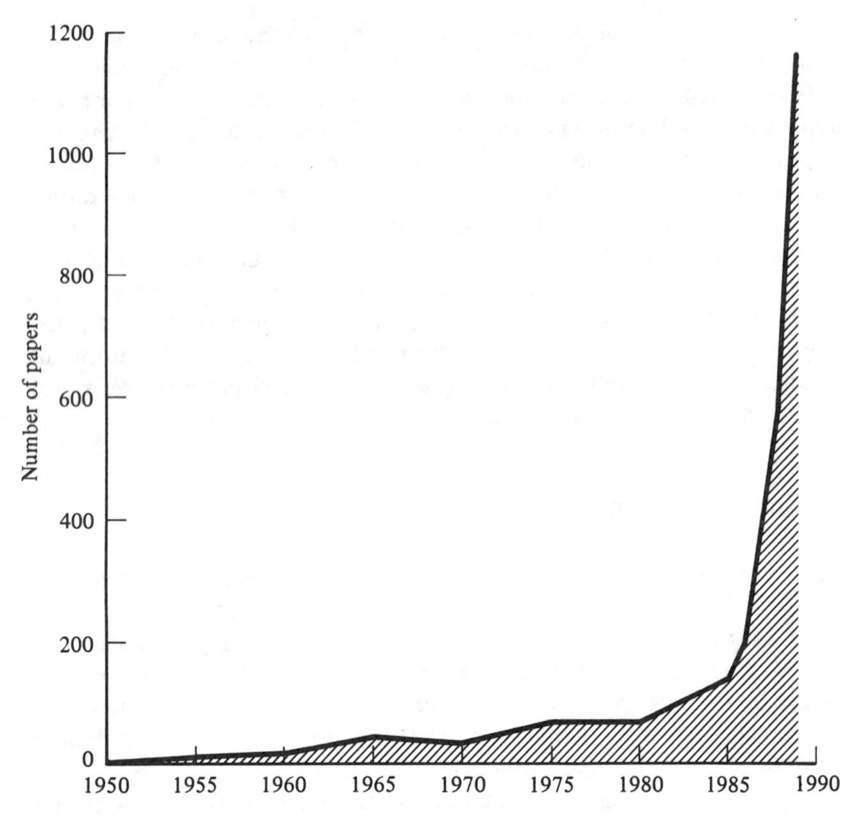

Figure 16.1 Growth in research in neural computing

a fraction of a second to identify a familiar face, for example, the slowness of biological cells as switches places an upper limit on the number of sequential operations which are performed during the recognition – of the order of 100 or less. Clearly it is the parallel organization of the brain that allows these tasks to be possible.

An artificial computer neuron is an analogue of a biological neuron, which models the salient features without attempting to represent faithfully the structure or internal mechanisms of a cell. For example, the current state of an artificial neuron is usually held as a number, but this corresponds to a firing frequency in a biological neuron. Cells are clearly very complex machines; only the most important features are copied to the computer analogue.

In a computer neural network, as in the brain, neurons can only perform useful functions by acting in concert. Many connections are established between neurons, typically by forming layers, each composed of many neurons,

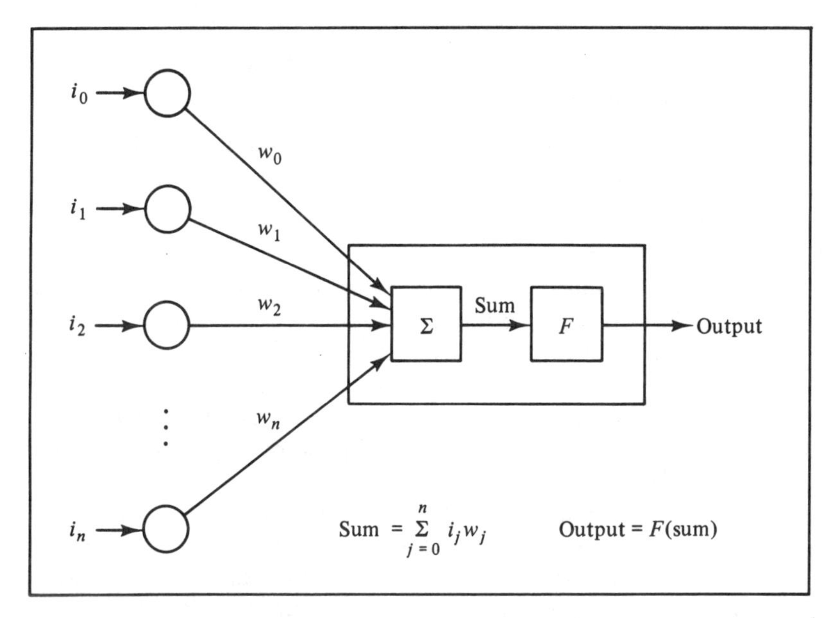

Figure 16.2 Artificial neuron

where the majority of connections are between adjacent layers. If every neuron in a particular layer is connected to every one in the next layer, the layers are said to be fully connected. Figure 16.2 shows the basic structure of an artificial neuron. The inputs are (typically many) connections either from other neurons or from some interface to the network from the outside world, that is the computing environment in which the net is constructed. Each input has an associated weight value corresponding to a synaptic connection strength. Inputs to a neuron from other neurons are therefore the current state (output) values of those neurons multiplied by the appropriate connection weights. Two operations take place in the neuron. First, all input values are added together; then this sum is operated on by an activation function (F in the figure) to obtain an output value. This activation function may take several forms. For some networks a simple threshold or step function is used, so that output from the neuron is zero unless the input total exceeds a critical value, when the output changes to a fixed positive value - typically one. Other networks use a continuous differentiable function such as the sigmoid function:

$$y = 1/[1 + \exp(-x)]$$

Many different connection schemes (architectures) are possible, for example self-connected layers and random interconnections. There is evidence that brain cells are organized in layers, and the majority of neural network models also consist of well-defined layers.

The principal advantages enjoyed by neural networks over conventional computational techniques are:

(a) They are able to perform complex pattern recognition tasks.
(b) They can self-adjust to map functional relationships between inputs and outputs.
(c) They are explicitly parallel.

Although the development of parallel computer hardware is at an early stage, moving neural network implementations on to such machines is a natural and relatively straightforward task. By contrast, there are considerable difficulties in recoding traditional sequential algorithms to take advantage of parallelism. Of course neural networks are not complete systems in themselves; they are generally embedded in the workings of a more conventional software environment.

The inputs and outputs of neural networks are patterns of values which may be binary or continuous. Networks may be constructed to learn in one of two ways. In supervised learning, training input patterns are associated with corresponding output (target) patterns. In unsupervised learning, no explicit information is provided to the network regarding the desired outputs; instead the network automatically finds associations and relationships between different groups of input patterns. Networks in this latter category are used in classification problems. Once trained, a network may be used to perform a recognition or classification task by presenting a new vector to the input layer and allowing the network to generate the corresponding output.

Most neural network models are composed of many neurons similar to the one shown in figure 16.2. The differences between the models are mainly concerned with the topology (the connectivity arrangement), the form in which inputs and targets are presented to the network, and the learn and recall mechanisms.

4 BACK PROPAGATION

The algorithm developed by Rumelhart et al. (1985) is called back propagation. This algorithm is applied to multiple-layer networks with at least one hidden layer; the layers are usually fully connected. Neurons in these layers employ a continuous activation function such as the sigmoid function shown above. The name refers to the training mechanism by which differences between the output values and the desired target values of the net are used to adjust the weights within the network. Forward propagation is the process by which input values are processed to produce an output. This takes place layer by layer, starting at the input. Each neuron in a layer computes its own

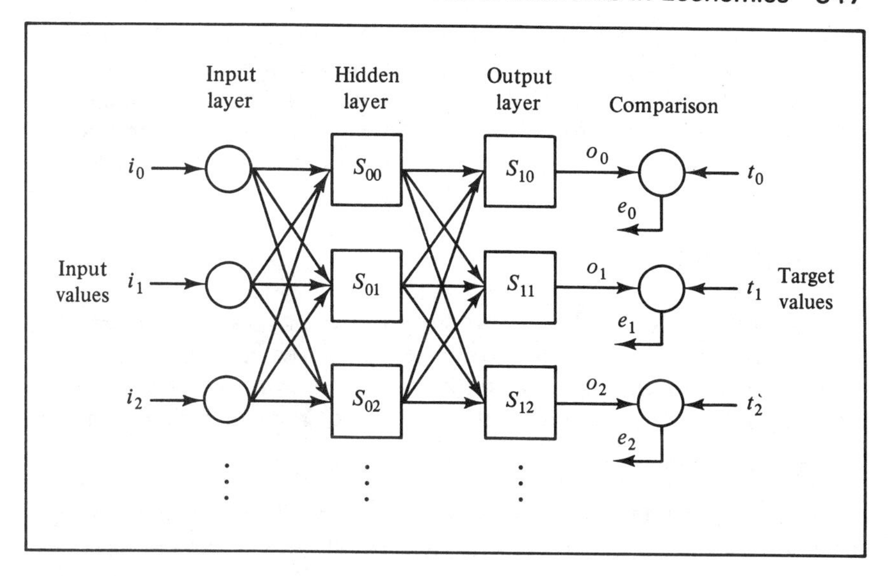

Figure 16.3 Two-layer back propagation network

output value from its input connections. These output values are then used as inputs to the next layer, so the values propagate forward through the net. Figure 16.3 shows a simple two-layer network. The purpose of the input layer is to distribute the input values to all neurons in the hidden layer; it does not perform any processing on the data. Outputs are compared with target values and the corresponding error values (e_0, e_1 etc.) are used to adjust the weights, first of all to the output layer, then moving backwards to the hidden layer(s). The main difficulty comes in adjusting weights to hidden layers, which have no explicit target values. This is overcome by defining an error signal for a hidden unit recursively in terms of those of the units to which it connects directly – each weighted by the appropriate link weight value.

Networks trained using back propagation are able, in principle, to map any arbitrary function between inputs and outputs. A network uses training examples to discover the implicit relationships between those inputs and the associated targets. To be successful, this mapping operation requires sufficient training examples. In addition, the training time can be very long; that is, the examples have to be presented to the network many times in the course of training.

Figure 16.3 illustrates a fully connected network. The topology of a network generally does not change as it is trained and used. However, sometimes there is dynamic pruning: links with very low weight values are excised since they have very little effect in transmitting values forward through the net. The knowledge contained in a trained network is distributed over the weight values; these weights are only accessed in the context of the local connectivity. Thus it can be difficult to determine precisely what knowledge is present; that is, there is no explicit representation of the functional relationships embodied in the net. This may be compared with a conventional modelling exercise where explicit parameter estimates are obtained.

5 FORECASTING

Initial results with neural networks suggest that they have the potential to handle non-linear data sets with parameter shifts in an impressive way. Jones et al. (1989) report how a fairly straightforward network was able to forecast accurately over long periods the data generated from the logistic function:

$$x(t+1) = kx(t)[1 - x(t)]$$

where k takes values such as to generate data which are deterministically chaotic. Econometrics has a very limited ability to model such data processes.

Neural networks may be employed in two categories of problem. In *functional representation* there are grounds for expecting that a functional relationship (possibly non-linear) exists between a set of explanatory variables and the dependent variable(s). Note that the neural network receives no special information about the relationship it is trying to map. It is, of course, possible and useful to make use of econometric insights for variable selection, weighting etc. One disadvantage of using neural networks is that the trained network does not have an explicit representation of the functional relationship learned. There are ways to try to elucidate this by, for example, perturbing inputs and looking for corresponding differences in the outputs. The implied functional relationship should then be viewed critically in econometric terms. Neural networks should not be regarded simply as magic black boxes.

There are some time series data (for example asset prices) which are noisy and very difficult to predict. An approach being developed by Thomson in France is *pattern matching* (Vergnes 1980). The technique is to match specific sections of time series corresponding to significant events - e.g. changes in trend - then monitor the series as it evolves, looking for recurrences of those patterns. The assumption is that future behaviour is likely to be similar to that which followed earlier occurrences of these characteristic patterns. Neural networks are very good at such pattern recognition operations. A second stage would be to examine the underlying assumed explanatory variables at the times of these pattern events to try to find associations.

Two problems arise when presenting econometric data to a network. First, the different explanatory variables may not be commensurate; they need to

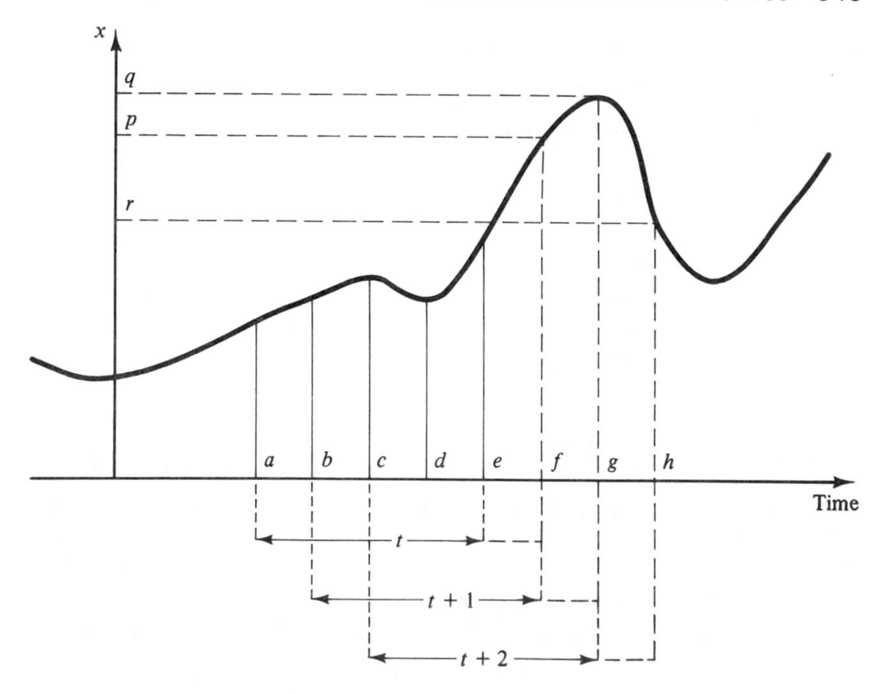

Figure 16.4 Moving window onto time series

be prescaled so that the values placed on the imput neurons of the net are of similar magnitude. Second, lagged data values must be presented as explicit extra inputs.

Figure 16.4 illustrates how a univariate time series can be presented to a neural net. The net is trained to predict one period ahead using a fixed number of data points. Thus, in this example, the first set of input data is the values at times (a, b, c, d, e), labelled t. The associated target value at the next sample point (at time f) is p. Next, the window is shifted by one time increment, so that a new input set ($t + 1$) consists of (b, c, d, e, f) and an associated target q (at time g). This process is repeated to extract many sets from the series. Here the series is assumed to depend only on prior values of the same variable (x), and with a maximum lag of five time increments. If appropriate, the most recent samples (at the end of the series) can be given extra weighting in the training process to try to accommodate any time variation in the underlying relationship itself. This can be accomplished by placing a more stringent tolerance test on more recent data.

Table 16.1 Percentage *ex post* prediction errors of real UK non-durable consumption

Year	Muellbauer and Murphy	Basic neural net
1982	0.31	−0.73
1983	0.78	−0.77
1984	0.66	0.07
1985	0.99	−0.69
1986	2.22	−2.86
1987	3.01	−5.02
1988	4.36	−8.18

6 CONSUMPTION FUNCTION

As an illustration of the potential of neural networks in the context of the UK economy, we constructed an extremely simple net to predict consumer expenditure in the UK. An enormous amount of effort has been devoted by econometricians to the consumption function, because of its empirical and theoretical importance. The work of Muellbauer and Murphy (1989) perhaps represents the state of the art on this topic. We built a rudimentary network using annual data 1957–71, enabling a direct comparison of out-of-sample forecast errors for 1982–8 (table 16.1).

Although the network does not perform as well in 1987 and 1988, its out-of-sample behaviour up to five years ahead compares favourably with the econometric model. Our research programme will investigate the improvements which can be made by applying more powerful networks to this data series.

7 MONEY DEMAND

An investigation of more direct relevance to financial markets was carried out by Ormerod and Walker (1990). An issue which arises frequently in the analysis of monetary growth is that the money series being examined may sometimes be endogenous and sometimes exogenous. Most published empirical analysis assumes implicitly or explicitly that a demand for money function can be identified even over data sets which include periods of monetary control.

Kohli (1989) proposes a general, consistent estimation method for regression equations with a left hand variable which is endogenous for some observations and exogenous for others. The method is applied to the estimation of a demand for money function for Switzerland over a time interval which includes intervals of monetary control, in other words when the supposition is that the quantity of money can best be viewed as exogenous.

Arguments can be put forward (for example, Cooley and Le Roy (1981)) that the existence of a monetary rule which the authorities follow does not in itself guarantee the exogeneity of money. The central bank, for example, might watch a number of economic factors in implementing its monetary policy, so that the quantity of money depends upon the reaction function of the bank.

Kohli argues that, first, Switzerland is the only industrialized country to target the monetary base M0 rather than broader aggregates such as M1, M2 or M3. Second, the Swiss authorities are known to be committed to monetary rules. For much of the past 30 years the Swiss have followed a regime of monetary control in which money has been exogenous. Kohli reports the results of a demand for money equation in which real M0 depends on the rate of three-month time deposits held at commercial banks, real GNP, lagged money and a dummy variable for periods when money was exogenous.

Results are reported by Kohli over the 1959–87 period using annual data, along with his data set. We reproduced these results to the third place of decimals using econometrics (differences in the degree of rounding of data can easily account for these very small differences). Because of the way in which data had to be transformed to accommodate it within our neural network, the first observation had to be discarded. Accordingly, we re-estimated Kohli's equation whenever relevant, beginning in 1960. The loss of the 1959 observation made very little difference to the econometric result.

A straightforward two-layer network was constructed by Ormerod and Walker over the 1960–87 period, relating real monetary growth to its lagged value, to real GNP and its lagged value, to real GNP and its lagged value, to the interest rate and its lagged value and to two regime dummy variables, which took the value zero and one respectively depending upon whether or not a monetary target regime was in operation.

The standard error of the econometric model estimated by Kohli over the 1960–87 period was 3.42 per cent. In comparison, a neural network was constructed using just over two hours' computing time on a Sun Sparcstation 1+ in which the calculated standard error was only 0.043 per cent - in other words, an almost perfect fit.

However, training the neural network over the period 1960–79 gave poor forecasts out of sample. The econometric model did very badly, and, although the neural network was better, both were poor by reasonable standards. Using the 1960–84 period to train and estimate the models, the neural network outperformed the econometric approach quite clearly. The dynamic forecast error in 1987 was −15.1 per cent for the econometric model and 4.9 per cent for the network.

A much more successful neural network was constructed by omitting the information on the type of policy regime which was being followed.

Table 16.2 Percentage *ex ante* dynamic prediction errors of Swiss real monetary base

Year	Econometric model (Kohli)	Neural network omitting information on policy regime
1980	−3.78	2.14
1981	−6.51	3.36
1982	4.71	4.34
1983	9.58	4.44
1984	11.80	3.29
1985	14.00	3.62
1986	20.70	0.88
1987	23.20	0.75

Table 16.2 shows the out-of-sample dynamic forecast errors for the network trained from 1960 to 1979, with the econometric model for comparison. Not only does the neural network perform much better, but the fact that it works better than a network trained using information on the type of policy regime suggests that even in Switzerland the monetary base might well be endogenous rather than exogenous.

8 SUMMARY

Overall, neural network technology seems to represent an area of research with great potential for improving the accuracy of economic forecasts in general, and of asset prices in particular. It is a particularly attractive methodology to investigate, given the exhaustion of the current paradigm in applied macroeconomics.

Note

The authors are grateful to the editor, Mark Taylor, for comments on a previous version of this chapter, although responsibility for remaining errors or omissions rests with them.

References

Burns, T. (1986) 'The interpretation and use of economic predictions', *Proceedings of the Royal Society, Series A*, 12, 103–25.

Cooley, T. F. and LeRoy, S. F. (1981) 'Identification and estimation of money demand', *American Economic Review*, 71, 825.44.

Hendry, D. F. (1988) 'Encompassing implications of feedback versus feedforward mechanisms in econometrics', *Oxford Economic Papers*, 40, 132.49.

Holden, K. (1990) in D. Greenaway (ed.), *Current Issues in Macroeconomics*, London: Croom Helm.

Jones, R. D., Lee, Y. C., Barnes, C. W., Flake, G. W., Lee, K., Lewis, P. S. and Qian, S. (1989) 'Function approximation and time series prediction with neural networks', Center for Nonlinear Studies, Los Alamos.

Kohli, U. (1989) 'Consistent estimation when the left hand variable is exogenous over part of the sample period', *Journal of Applied Econometrics*, 4, 283.92.

Lucas, R. E. Jr (1976) 'Econometric policy evaluation: a critique', in K. Brunner and A. H. Meltzer (eds), *The Phillips Curve and Labor Markets*, Carnegie-Rochester Conference Series on Public Policy, vol. 6, Amsterdam: North-Holland.

McCulloch, W. S. and Pitts, W. H. (1943) 'Neural modelling', *Bulletin of Mathematical Biophysics*, 5.

Minski, M. and Papert, S. (1969) *Perceptrons*, MIT Press.

Muellbauer, J. and Murphy, A. (1989) 'Why has UK personal savings collapsed?', Credit Suisse First Boston, London.

Ormerod, P. and Walker, T. (1990) 'Neural networks and the Swiss monetary base', Henley Centre, mimeo.

Rumelhart, D. E., Hinton, G. E. and Williams, R. J. (1985) ICS report 8506.

Vergnes, M. (1990) 'Neural Trader's assistant', Proceedings of Third European Seminar on Neural Computing.

Wallis, K. F. (1989) 'Macroeconomic forecasting: a survey', *Economic Journal*, 99, 28–61.

Wasserman, P. D. and Oetzel, R. M. (1990) *NeuralSource: the Bibliographic Guide to Artificial Neural Networks*, Van Nostrand Reinhold.

17 Epidemics of Opinion and Speculative Bubbles in Financial Markets

Alan Kirman

There is a widespread though far from universal belief, among those who study financial markets, that there are periods during which asset prices do not reflect underlying fundamentals. Prices, in this view, reflect what prevailing market opinion expects them to be – and this expectation may simply be an extrapolation of previous prices, not necessarily related to market fundamentals.

This chapter presents a simple theoretical explanation of how swings in market opinion may be generated and suggests how these swings may be transmitted into market prices. Changes in opinion occur as a result of stochastic interaction between individuals. The latter then try to assess what market opinion is and act accordingly. In this we follow Keynes (1936) when he says that, in financial markets, agents consider 'what average opinion expects average opinion to be'. This process gives rise to bubble-like phenomena in which prices rise or fall away from fundamental values for periods of unpredictable length.

The view that markets do, in fact, behave like this has been questioned. Indeed there is a long-standing debate in the economic literature as to whether the prices of financial assets are, or are not, determined by market fundamentals alone. In particular there is a discussion about the existence of excessive movement in these prices, which can be attributed to bubbles or fads. There are two basic questions involved. First, is there empirical evidence for such phenomena? We shall look at this briefly. Second, and this is our main concern here, if the answer is affirmative, are there reasonable theoretical models which generate them?

1 THE NATURE OF BUBBLES AND THE EMPIRICAL EVIDENCE FOR THEIR EXISTENCE

Before proceeding it is worth specifying what we have in mind when we speak of bubbles. One conventional reply, in the economic literature, is that any prolonged departure from a price justified by the underlying fundamentals, appropriately defined, constitutes a bubble. This definition is adopted, for example, by Froot and Obstfeld (1990). They describe as a bubble, a situation in which fundamentals remain constant and the asset price is also constant but above its true value.

This idea does not really coincide with the more intuitive notion of a bubble, indeed that conveyed by the word itself, which is that bubbles expand and burst. Our view is that if bubbles are present then they should give rise to dynamics which evolve, at least in part, independently of fundamentals and which involve surges and crashes.

When it was first suggested that asset prices do not reflect underlying fundamentals, it was claimed that this was precisely because they are excessively volatile, that is that they present just the picture we have described. This view is reflected in the early contributions of LeRoy and Porter (1981), Shiller (1981) and Blanchard and Watson (1982). Rational bubbles, it has been argued, could explain these characteristics. In the case of foreign exchange, which interests us particularly here, Meese and Rogoff (1983) found empirical evidence that exchange rates were too volatile to be explained by standard equilibrium models, and again this might be explained by the presence of bubbles. Had this remained the accepted point of view, one would need no further justification for constructing theoretical models with bubble-like features.

However, more recently the existence of rational bubbles has been questioned again, since it has been claimed by several authors that the econometric analysis on which the previously mentioned papers were based was faulty (for contributions to this debate, see Campbell and Shiller (1987); Flavin (1983); Kleidon (1986); Mankiw et al. (1985); Marsh and Merton (1986); West (1987), (1988). An attack on the existence of rational bubbles was made by Diba and Grossman (1988) who argued that stock prices are not more explosive than dividends. Hence bubbles can be ruled out since they would add an explosive component to stock prices. They conclude, using unit root tests, autocorrelation patterns and cointegration tests, that 'The analysis supports the conclusion that stock prices do not contain explosive rational bubbles.' Furthermore, Hamilton and Whiteman (1985) argue that evidence which apparently supports the existence of bubbles may be due to unobserved fundamentals.[1] All of this might seem to undermine the case for the sort of model that we build.

However, Evans (1989) shows convincingly that the standard tests, used by those authors who conclude that bubbles do not occur, fail to detect rational bubbles even in models in which they are present by construction, as indeed a theoretical result of Reichlin (1989) would lead us to expect. The debate as to whether bubbles can be, or have been, detected econometrically is thus still open. As Flood and Hodrick (1990) point out, there seems to be general agreement that simple models based on fundamentals perform poorly, but whether this is due to the presence of bubbles or to model misspecification[2] is an unresolved question. Thus the case for or against bubbles is not proven, at least from econometric examination of the price data.

However, there is a more direct reason for being interested in models with bubble-like dynamics. Consider the following simple observation. Whilst bubbles imply the existence of non-fundamentalist traders, it is also true that, if there are enough of the latter, bubbles must occur. Thus one only has to find direct evidence for the existence of such traders. In fact there is a substantial body of such evidence, based on studies of actual market behaviour, where it is found that many traders do behave as chartists or non-fundamentalists (see e.g. Goodhart (1988); Allen and Taylor (1989); and the references cited therein). Goodhart refers, for example, to the functioning of the foreign exchange market as a constant tug of war between chartists and fundamentalists. It is this view that is reflected in the theoretical model that we now present.

This model has two advantages. First, it provides a theoretical basis for characteristics of financial markets described by those who have made a close empirical study of the actual functioning of such markets. Second, it explicitly takes account of non-fundamentalist behaviour whose importance varies over time and has dynamics with the bubble-like characteristics described earlier. It can therefore be simulated in order to generate data which can then be used to evaluate the effectiveness of the econometric tests for bubbles, discussed above.[3]

2 A MODEL OF OPINION FORMATION AND TRANSMISSION

This model, based on that in Kirman (1990), explains the evolution of agents' opinions. There are two[4] prevalent views of the world, and each agent holds one of them. There are N agents and the state of the system is defined by the number k of agents holding view 1, i.e. $k \in (0, 1, \ldots, N)$.

The system evolves in the following way. Two individuals meet at random (one could think of drawing two balls from an urn containing balls of two different colours). The first is converted to the second's view with probability $1 - \delta$. Which is the first and which is the second is, of course, of no importance since with the same probability they could have been drawn in the other order. There is also a small probability ϵ that the first will change his own opinion independently. This may be thought of as due to either the arrival of exogenous news or the replacements of an existing trader by a new one who does not necessarily share the same view. The probability ϵ is technically necessary to prevent the process getting stuck at $k = 0$ or $k = N$, but we will allow ϵ to go to zero as N becomes large.

The dynamic evolution of the process is then given by

$$k \begin{cases} \nearrow k+1 & \text{with probability } P(k,k+1) = \left(1 - \frac{k}{n}\right)\left[\epsilon + (1-\delta)\frac{k}{N-1}\right] \\ \searrow k-1 & \text{with probability } P(k,k-1) = \frac{k}{n}\left[\epsilon + (1-\delta)\frac{N-k}{N-1}\right] \end{cases} \tag{17.1}$$

Clearly, with probability $1 - P(k, k+1) - P(k, k-1)$, k does not change. This simple Markov chain is related to several standard urn models (see Kirman (1990)). For an interesting class of more general cases see Arthur et al. (1985). What is of interest here, and was the subject of Arthur et al.'s paper, is the equilibrium distribution $\mu(k)$, $k = (0, 1, \ldots, N)$ of the Markov chain defined in (17.1). That is, we wish to know what proportion of the time the system will spend in each state. This is given by

$$\mu(k) = \sum_{l=0}^{N} \mu(l)P(l, k) \tag{17.2}$$

Using the detailed balance condition for our symmetric process,

$$\mu(k)P(k, l) = \mu(l)P(l, k) \tag{17.3}$$

We can write

$$\mu(k) = \frac{\frac{\mu(1)}{\mu(0)} \cdots \frac{\mu(k)}{\mu(k-1)}}{1 + \sum_{l=1}^{N} \frac{\mu(1)}{\mu(0)} \cdots \frac{\mu(l)}{\mu(l-1)}} \tag{17.4}$$

where

$$\frac{\mu(k+1)}{\mu(k)} = \frac{P(k, k+1)}{P(k+1, k)} = \frac{\left(1 - \frac{k}{N}\right)\left[\epsilon + (1+\delta)\frac{k}{N-1}\right]}{\frac{k+1}{N}\left[\epsilon + (1-\delta)\left(1 - \frac{k}{N-1}\right)\right]} \tag{17.5}$$

The precise form of $\mu(k)$ depends on the relative values of ϵ and δ. Since it is clear from our discussion that we are interested in the case where opinion

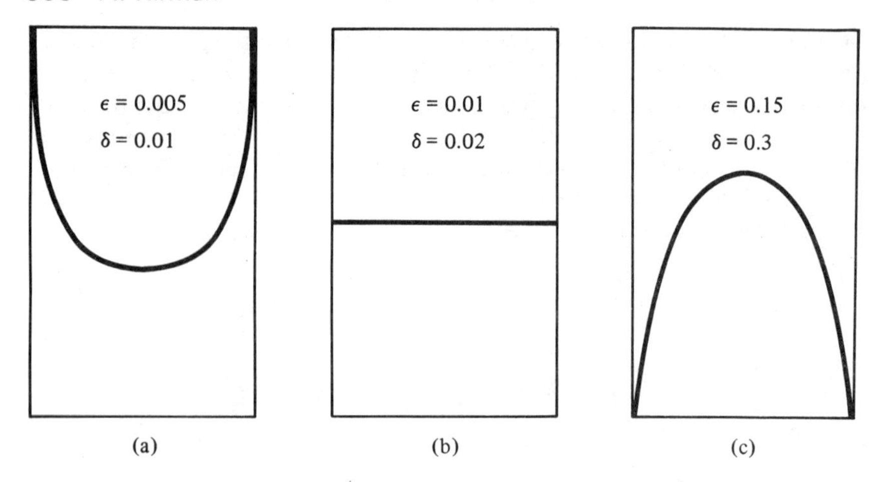

Figure 17.1 Equilibrium distributions for the model with state space $\{0, 1, . . ., N\}$ with three different values of ϵ and δ, and $n = 100$

is concentrated at one of the extremes, it is of interest to know for which values of the parameters ϵ and δ this will occur. In figure 17.1 we illustrate three cases. It is obviously figure 17.1(a) which corresponds to the situation we are describing. The uniform distribution (figure 17.1(b)) occurs when $\upsilon(k+1)/\mu(k) = 1$ for all k, that is when $P(k, k+1) = P(k+1, k)$ for all k. But this is easily calculated and requires that $\epsilon = (1-\delta)/(N-1)$.

If then $\epsilon < (1-\delta)/(N-1)$ we have the form of the distribution shown in figure 17.1(a). Two things are worth noting about the process. First, no specific assumption about the size of δ is necessary to obtain the distributional form of figure 17.1(a). Thus we need no assumption about how persuasive individuals are. All we need is that the probability of self-conversion be relatively small. Second, although persuasiveness is independent of the number in each group, the probability *a priori* that a meeting will result in an increase in the majority is higher than that of the minority increasing. This is important in what follows, since it implies that the majority opinion will tend to recruit the minority agents.

To see exactly how the process evolves when the number of agents becomes large, consider the asymptotic form of μ when N becomes large and ϵ becomes small. In this case we can approximate μ by a continuous distribution f on the unit interval, i.e. when $x = k/N \in [0, 1]$.

Thus let $N \to \infty$ and $\epsilon = \alpha/N$ and $\delta = 2\alpha/N$. Redefine μ as $\mu(k/N)$ and consider the continuous limit distribution f as $N \to \infty$. Then we have the following:

Proposition
f is the density of a symmetric beta distribution, i.e.
$f(x) = \text{const}\, x^{\alpha-1}(1-x)^{\alpha-1}$.[5]

For α less than 1, the distribution has the required form and the process will be such that the system is, in general, in one of the extreme states. To see the evolution of k in the finite case, we simulated the process.

The behaviour is illustrated for different values of ϵ and δ in figure 17.2. Clearly the smaller ϵ relative to δ the more time the system spends at the extremes.

Having developed a model to explain how shifts of opinion occur, let us now apply this to a simple model of foreign exchange and see to what extent it produces dynamics similar to those which characterize exchange rate movements.

3 A MODEL OF FOREIGN EXCHANGE

This model is taken from Frankel and Froot (1986). There are two views as to changes in the value of the exchange rate. On the one hand there are fundamentalists who believe that the value of the exchange rate at time t, S_t, will tend back to an equilibrium value $\bar{S}$. Thus their forecast of the change in the next period is denoted

$$\Delta^{\mathrm{f}} S_{t+1} = v(\bar{S} - S_t) \tag{17.6}$$

where v is a constant. Chartists, however, extrapolate in a simple linear way and forecast the change by

$$\Delta^{\mathrm{c}} S_{t-1} = S_t - S_{t-1} \tag{17.7}$$

In Frankel and Froot (1986) the market view of the change is a weighted combination of (17.6) and (17.7), where the weights are chosen by a portfolio manager to make the forecast rational. We assume, however, that the weights are determined by the proportions of the N agents who *act* as fundamentalists and chartists in the market. We consider two stages:

(a) Agents meet each other and modify their opinions. At time t the proportion of agents who hold fundamentalist views is given by $q_t = k_t/N$, where k_t evolves according to the Markov chain specified previously.
(b) Agents now try to assess what is the majority opinion. Each agent i observes q_t but with some noise. He receives a signal q_{it} given by $q_i = q_t + \epsilon_{it}$, where $\epsilon_{it} \sim N(0, \sigma_i^2)$. If agent i observes $q_{it} \geqq ½$ then he *acts* as a fundamentalist, whilst if he observes $q_{it} < ½$ then he *acts* as a chartist. The proportion of agents who act as fundamentalists w_t is then given by

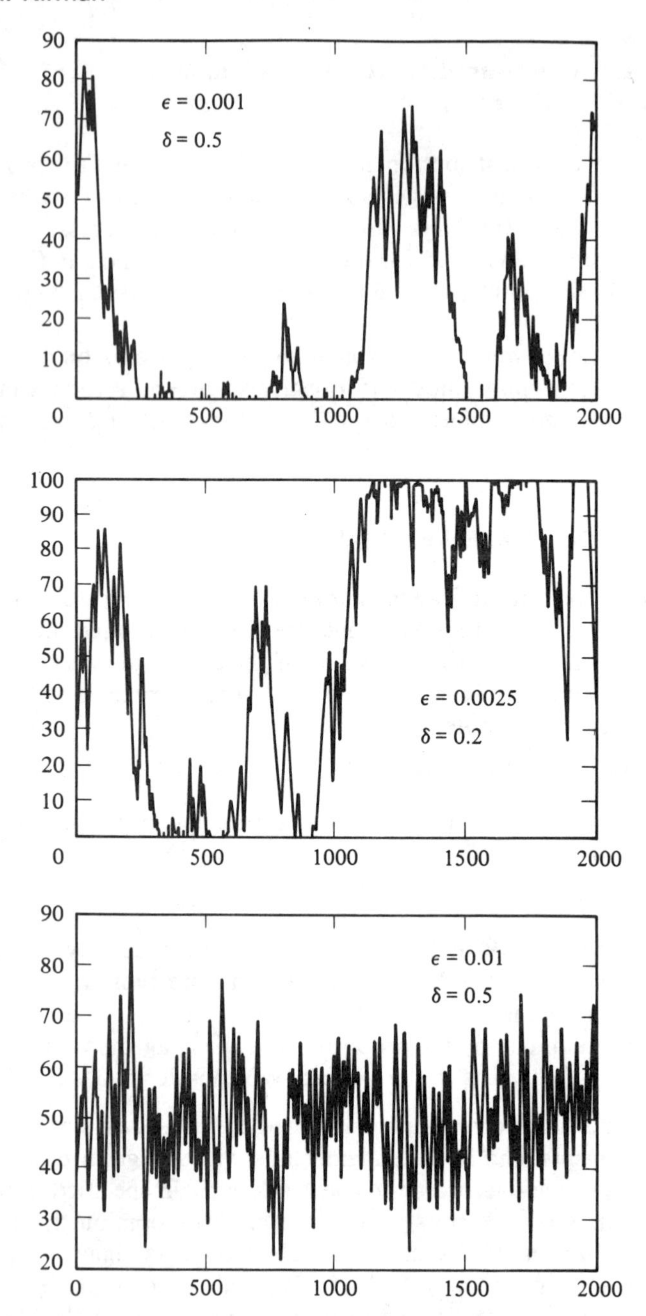

Figure 17.2 Simulations of the process governing the evolution of k: 100,000 iterations, of which every 50th is plotted

$$w_t = \frac{\#\{i | q_{it} \geqq ½\}}{N} \tag{17.8}$$

where # denotes 'the number of'.

Two observations are important here. First, it would be irrational, in general, for an agent who knows his opinion to be in the minority to act upon it. Second, if everybody *knows* that all the other agents are observing majority opinion and acting upon it, then optimal behaviour is to do so oneself. This common knowledge problem is inherent in Keynes's suggestion mentioned previously. What is an equilibrium depends, of course, on the agents' views of how the market works.

Once the proportion of agents who act as fundamentalists w_t has been determined, then the market view as to the forecast change in the exchange rate $\Delta^m S_{t+1}$ is given by

$$\Delta^m S_{t+1} = w_t \Delta^f S_{t+1} + (1 - w_t)\Delta^c S_{t+1} \tag{17.9}$$

The market exchange rate is then determined by the following equation:

$$S_t = c\Delta^m S_{t+1} + Z_t \tag{17.10}$$

where Z_t is, according to Frankel and Froot (1986), an index of fundamental variables.

There are several ways of justifying such a model on the basis of individual behaviour, and we give two variants.

3.1 Variant 1

Let E denote expectation and V variance and let the utility function of individual i be given by

$$U^i(W^i_{t+1}) = E(W^i_{t+1}) - \mu^i V(W^i_{t+1}) \tag{17.11}$$

where W^i_{t+1} is his wealth at time $t + 1$ and is given by

$$W^i_{t+1} = (S_{t+1} + x_{t+1})d^i_t + b^i_t(1 + r) \tag{17.12}$$

where d^i_t is the demand for foreign currency; x_{t+1} is the dividend, in domestic currency, paid on one unit of foreign currency; and b^i_t is the demand for a safe domestic asset which yields a certain interest rate r.

The exchange rate S_{t+1} and the dividend x_{t+1} at $t + 1$ are random variables. In particular, the variance of S_{t+1} is given by $V(S_{t+1}) = \sigma^2_S$. The mean and variance of x_t are given respectively by $E(x_{t+1}) = \delta$ and $V(x_{t+1}) = \sigma^2_x$.

The budget constraint at time τ is

$$W_t^i = S_t d_t^i + b_t^i \tag{17.13}$$

Substituting for b_t^i from (17.13) in (17.12) we have

$$W_{t+1}^i = (S_{t+1} - rS_t + x_{t+1})d_t^i + W_t^i(1 + r) = (\Delta S_{t+1} - rS_t + x_{t+1})d_t^i + W_t^i(1 + r) \tag{17.14}$$

Defining $\alpha = V(S_{t+1} + x_{t+1})$ and recalling that $V(W_{t+1}^i) = (d_t^{\,i})^2\alpha$, substituting in the utility function gives

$$U^i(W_{t+1}^i) = (\Delta^i S_{t+1} - rS_t + \delta)d_t^i + W_t^i(1 + r) - \mu^i\alpha(d_t^i)^2 \tag{17.15}$$

$\Delta^i S_{t+1}$ represents the expected change in exchange rate on which the ith agent acts, and in our model is given by his views of the market's expectation.

The demand for foreign currency is given by maximizing with respect to d_t^i, which gives

$$\delta U_i/\delta d_t^i = \Delta^i S_{t+1} - rS_t + \delta - d_t^i 2\alpha\mu^i = 0$$

and hence

$$d_t^i = a^i - b^i S_t + c^i \Delta^i S_{t+1}$$

where

$$a^i = \delta/2\mu^i\alpha,\ b^i = r/2\mu^i\alpha \text{ and } c^i = 1/2\mu i\alpha.$$

If X_t is the total supply of foreign exchange, and agents only differ in their parameters because they are either chartists or fundamentalists, we have equilibrium when

$$X_t = w_t[a^{\mathrm{f}} - b^{\mathrm{f}}S_t + c^{\mathrm{f}}(\Delta^{\mathrm{f}} s_{t+1}^{\mathrm{f}})] + (1 - w_t)[a^{\mathrm{c}} - b^{\mathrm{c}}S_t + c^{\mathrm{c}}(\Delta^{\mathrm{c}} S_{t+1}^{c})] \tag{17.16}$$

If, in addition, we assume $c^{\mathrm{f}} = c^{\mathrm{c}}$, since we only wish agents to differ in terms of their forecasts, then the model reduces to the Frankel and Froot form.

Since for every agent i we have $b_i/c_i = r$ then $c^{\mathrm{f}} = c^{\mathrm{i}}$ implies $b^{\mathrm{f}} = b^{\mathrm{c}}$; so, for $c = c^{\mathrm{f}}/[w_t b^{\mathrm{f}} + (1 - w_t)b^{\mathrm{c}}]$ we have $c = 1/r$.

If we now solve our simple model, we obtain

$$S_t = (1 + cw_t v - c + cw_t)^{-1}[(1 + cw_t v)\bar{S} - c(1 - w_t)S_{t-1}] \tag{17.17}$$

For the system to be stable the following condition must hold:

$$\left| \frac{c(1 - w_t)}{1 + cw_t v - c + cw_t} \right| \leqq 1 \tag{17.18}$$

If chartists dominate the market, that is $w_t \to 0$, then this condition becomes $|c/(1 - c) \leqq 1$, i.e. if c is greater than 1/2 or, in our example, r

is less than 2 then the system is explosive. However, given the underlying stochastic process generating w_t, such an explosive bubble must eventually collapse.

A problem of interpretation here is that if we require chartist periods not to be always unstable we would need r to be greater than 2. Yet an interest rate of this level would imply an unrealistically long period between price settings. However, by damping the extrapolations of the chartists this can be attenuated. It is not clear, of course, that one would not want chartist domination to be destabilizing.

A defect of the model in this case is that if ever $w_t = 1$ then the system will settle at $\bar{S}$ and never move again even if the chartists take over. To avoid this one needs to add noise to the X_t, the supply of foreign exchange, which amounts to adding noise to S_t.

3.2 Variant 2

Consider a modified version of the previous example in which x_{t+1}, the dividend, is now evaluated in foreign currency terms as would seem more natural. Then wealth in the next period W^i_{t+1} will be given by

$$W^i_{t+1} = (S_{t+1} + S_{t+1}x_{t+1})d^i_t + W^i_t(1 + r) - S_t d^i_t(1 + r) \qquad (17.19)$$

and by simple calculations we get

$$W^i_{t+1} = (1 + x_{t+1})\Delta S_{t+1}d^i_t - (r - x_{t+1})S_t d_t + W_t(1 + r) \qquad (17.20)$$

Assume that S_{t+1} and x_{t+1} are *independent*; then

$$E(W^i_{t+1}) = (\Delta^i S_{t+1})(1 + \delta)d^i_t + S_t(\delta - r)d^i_t + W^i_t(1 + r) \qquad (17.21)$$

and

$$V(W^i_{t+1}) = (d^i_t)^2 V(S_{t+1} + S_{t+1}x_{t+1}) \qquad (17.22)$$

Write

$$V(S_{t+1} + S_{t+1}x_{t+1}) = \beta$$

Demand is given by maximizing utility, and the first-order condition is

$$\Delta^i S_{t+1}(1 - \delta) + S_t(\delta - r) - 2\beta\mu^i d^i_t = 0 \qquad (17.23)$$

i.e.

$$d^i_t = b^i S_t + c^i \Delta^i S_{t+1}$$

where $b^i = (\delta - r)/2\beta\mu^i$ and $c^i = (1 + \delta)/2\beta\mu^i$. Reasoning as in the first example, we have $c = (1 + \delta)/(\delta - r)$, and the stability conditions are modified accordingly.

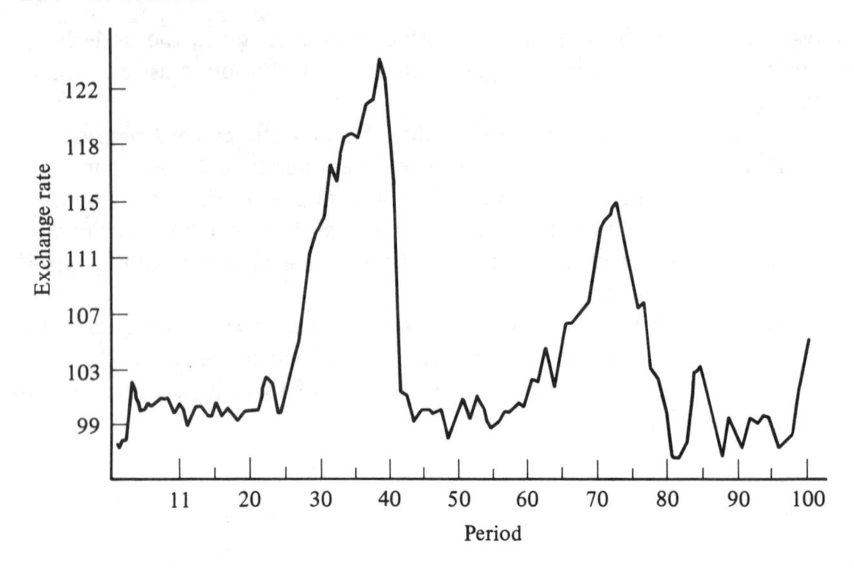

Figure 17.3 Simulated exchange rate for 100 periods with $\bar{S} = 100$

4 SIMULATIONS

We ran a number of simulations[6] and they exhibit some of the characteristics of foreign exchange markets. There are, as one would expect, periods in one regime when the exchange rate vacillates around the fundamental equilibrium value, interspersed with bubbles. An example is shown in figure 17.3. We have also considered examples in which agents' expectations were formed on the basis of earlier rather than current observations. Although analytically this complicates matters somewhat, it allows for symmetric bubbles (both rising and falling).

5 COMPARISON WITH OTHER THEORETICAL MODELS

It is worth briefly reviewing other models which have been constructed to illustrate the role of non-fundamentalist traders in generating bubble-like phenomena. These models show two basic features:

(a) They have at least two types of traders who differ in their forecasts, beliefs or tastes.
(b) They are capable of generating the sort of complicated non-stationary dynamics which, it is generally thought, characterize financial markets. The dynamics may reflect movement along an equilibrium path or

adjustment to equilibrium. The dynamics may be generated by either deterministic or stochastic behaviour.

Varian (1987) emphasizes the importance of different opinions. Day and Huang (1989) have a model with different types of agents who are more or less sophisticated. The underlying demand is highly non-linear and has a rather particular form which means that price adjustment can give rise even to chaotic behaviour. Frankel and Froot's (1986) model has two types of agents and the weights attached to their opinions vary in order to rationalize the evolution of the exchange rate. The presence of chartists generates bubbles. In a series of papers, DeLong et al. ((1988), (1989), (1990a), (1990b)) have models with noise traders (a term from Black 1986) who are systematically too optimistic in their expectations but who, in some circumstances, do better on average than their sophisticated counterparts. Thus their very presence may generate price histories which make their trading profitable, and the usual argument that mistaken individuals will be eliminated in the long run does not hold. DeLong et al. also allow the relative proportions of noise traders and sophisticated traders to vary according to their respective profitability. In effect, this corresponds to the evolution of opinions in the model presented in this chapter, since individuals are most likely to be converted to the majority opinion, and it is this which is reflected by market prices and is therefore the most profitable to follow.

Shiller (1990) gives evidence that, as in our model, investors are concerned with other investors' psychology. As he says: 'Whether or not "hot markets" are indeed fads, investors themselves think that there are fads in these markets, contrary to the assumptions of the rational expectations models in the literature.'

A final class of models is that developed by Föllmer (1974), in which agents have different characteristics but interact randomly and modify their own characteristics as a result of the interaction. This line of research using the Ising model has been neglected, but is clearly directly related to the problems discussed here.

6 CONCLUSION

There seems to be too much evidence that agents in financial markets act on non-fundamentals for this to be ignored. The model constructed here shows some features in addition to those found in other models in which non-fundamental traders play a role.

The model, when simulated, presents characteristics which are usually associated with the behaviour of financial markets. Periods of steady evolution are interspersed with bubbles and crashes, with noise around the turning point as there is a switch from one regime to another. Opinions are modified endogenously as a result of interaction between individual agents. These agents, however, take account of the majority opinion when trading, and if this is known to be their behaviour it is completely rational. Mistakes will be made at turning points when the majority is not clear, but these episodes will not last long enough either for learning or for profitable arbitrage to take place.

This double process - opinion formation, and the assessment of majority opinion and ensuing action - explains the schizophrenic attitude of foreign exchange traders reported by Goodhart (1988). Although they may claim that the dollar is overvalued they may still buy, perceiving the market trend to be upward in the short term.

The model presented here could be modified in several ways, but seems a step closer to realism than the standard efficient markets models in which non-fundamental traders have no role to play. As LeRoy (1989) says: 'Large discrepancies between price and fundamental value occur.' Our simple model provides one theoretical argument as to why this may be so.

Notes

I am indebted to Hans Föllmer, whose help was invaluable and with whom I am pursuing joint work on this problem, and to Luigi Brighi, Vincent Brousseau, Jim Mirrlees, Lucrezia Reichlin, Mark Taylor, Hal Varian and Michael Woodford for help, comments and suggestions. The usual disclaimer applies.

1 Indeed Garber (1990) argues that three famous historical episodes traditionally described as bubbles can, in fact, be attributed to underlying fundamentals.
2 Goldberg and Frydman (1990) suggest that different fundamentals may be relevant at different periods and find empirical support for this. Such an explanation would be consistent with the idea that agents change their view of the true economy over time and corresponds to a type of deterministic sunspots model.
3 Preliminary investigations show that, like Evans (1989), using standard tests we were unable to reject the unit root hypothesis for data generated by the model, even though no unit root was present.
4 This is for simplicity, but there could be an arbitrary number of opinions.
5 This proposition was proved by Hans Föllmer and the proof is given in Kirman (1990). As is explained there, this model is clearly related to Polya's urn model.
6 A noise term was added to S_2 for the reason explained previously, but its variance was kept sufficiently small so as not to interfere with the basic characteristics of the process.

References

Allen, H. and Taylor, M. P. (1989) 'Charts, noise and fundamentals: a study of the London foreign exchange market', Centre for Economic Policy Research, discussion paper 341.

Arthur, W. B. A., Ermoliev, Y. and Kamovski, Y. (1985) 'Strong laws for a class of path-dependent stochastic processes with applications', in: J. Arkin, L. Shiryaev and B. Wets (eds), *Proceedings of International Conference in Stochastic Optimisation*, New York: Springer.

Black, F. (1986) 'Noise', *Journal of Finance*, 41, 529–43.

Blanchard, O. J. and Watson, M. (1982) 'Bubbles, rational expectations, and financial markets', in P. Wach (ed.), *Crises in the Economic and Financial Structure*, Lexington, MA: Lexington Books.

Campbell, J. Y. and Shiller, R. J. (1987) 'Cointegration and tests of present value models', *Journal of Political Economy*, 95, 1062–88.

Day, R. and Huang, B. (1989) 'Bulls, bears, and market sheep', University of Southern California, working paper.

DeLong, J. B., Schleifer, A., Summers, L. H. and Waldmann, R. J. (1988) 'The survival of noise traders in financial markets', National Bureau of Economic Research, working paper 2715.

DeLong, J. B., Schleifer, A., Summers, L. H. and Waldmann, R. J. (1989) 'The size and incidence of the losses from noise trading', *Journal of Finance*, 44, 681–99.

DeLong, J. B., Schleifer, A., Summers, L. H. and Waldmann, R. J. (1990a) 'Noise trader risk in financial markets', *Journal of Political Economy*, forthcoming.

DeLong, J. B., Schleifer, A., Summers, L. H. and Waldmann, R. J. (1990b) 'Positive feedback investment strategies and destabilising rational speculation', *Journal of Finance*, 45, 379–96.

Diba, B. T. and Grossman, H. I. (1988) 'Explosive rational bubbles in stock prices?', *American Economic Review*, 78, 520–30.

Evans, G. (1989) 'Pitfalls in testing for explosive bubbles in asset prices', London School of Economics Financial Markets Group, discussion paper 65.

Flavin, M. A. (1983) 'Excess volatility in the financial markets: a reassessment of the empirical evidence', *Journal of Political Economy*, 91, 929–56.

Flood, R. P. and Hodrick, R. J. (1990) 'On testing for speculative bubbles', *Journal of Economic Perspectives*, 4 (2), 85–102.

Föllmer, H. (1974) 'Random economies with many interacting agents', *Journal of Mathematical Economics*, 1 (1), 51–62.

Frankel, J. A. and Froot, K. A. (1986) 'The dollar as an irrational speculative bubble: a tale of fundamentalists and chartists', *Marcus Wallenberg Papers on International Finance*, 1, 27–55.

Froot, K. and Obstfeld, M. (1990) 'Intrinsic bubbles: the case of stock prices', National Bureau of Economic Research, working paper 3091.

Garber, P. M. (1990) 'Famous first bubbles', *Journal of Economic Perspectives*, 4 (2), 35–54.

Goldberg, M. D. and Frydman, R. (1990) 'Is there a connection between exchange rate dynamics and macroeconomic fundamentals?', Economics Department, New York University, mimeo.

Goodhart, C. (1988) 'The foreign exchange market: a random walk with a dragging anchor', *Economica*, 55 (220), 437–60.

Hamilton, J. D. and Whiteman, C. H. (1985) 'The observable implications of self fulfilling expectations', *Journal of Monetary Economics*, 16, 353–74.

Keynes, J. M. (1936) *General Theory of Employment, Interest and Money*, London: Macmillan.

Kirman, A. (1990) 'On ants and markets', revised version, European University Institute, Florence, mimeo.

Kleidon, A. A. (1986) 'Variance bounds tests and stock price valuation models', *Journal of Political Economy*, 94, 953–1001.

LeRoy, S. F. (1989) 'Efficient capital markets and martingales', *Journal of Economic Literature*, 27 (4), 1583–621.

LeRoy, S. F. and Porter, R. D. (1981) 'The present value relation: tests based on implied variance bounds', *Econometrica*, 49 (3), 555–74.

Mankiw, N., Romer, G. D. and Shapiro, M. (1985) 'An unbiased re-examination of stock market volatility', *Journal of Finance*, 40, 677–87.

Marsh, T. and Merton, R. (1986) 'Dividend variation and variance bounds tests for the rationality of stock market prices', *American Economic Review*, 76, 483–98.

Meese, R. A. and Rogoff, K. (1983) 'Empirical exchange rate models of the seventies: do they fit out of sample?', *Journal of International Economics*, 14, 3–24.

Reichlin, L. (1989) 'Structural change and unit root econometrics', *Economics Letters*, 31, 231–3.

Shiller, R. J. (1981) 'Do stock markets move too much to be justified by subsequent changes in dividends?', *American Economic Review*, 7 (3), 421–36.

Shiller, R. J. (1990) 'Speculative prices and popular models', *Journal of Economic Perspectives*, 4 (2), 55–66.

Varian, H. (1987) 'Differences of opinion in financial markets', in *Financial Risk: Theory, Evidence and Implications*, Proceedings of the Eleventh Annual Economic Policy Conference of the Federal Reserve Bank of St Louis.

West, K. D. (1987) 'A specification test for speculative bubbles', *Quarterly Journal of Economics*, 102, 553–80.

West, K. D. (1988) 'Bubbles, fads, and stock price volatility tests: a partial evaluation', *Journal of Finance*, 43, 639–55.

Index